A History of Carp Fishing

A History of Carp Fishing

Kevin Clifford

Dedicated to my parents.

First published in Great Britain by Sandholme Publishing—1992

© Kevin Clifford—1992

All rights reserved. No part of this publication may be reproduced, stored in a retrieval system, or transmitted, in any form or by any means, electronic, mechanical, photocopying, recording, or otherwise, without the prior permission of the publishers.

Sandholme Publishing
Sandholme Grange
Newport
North Humberside
HU15 2QG

ISBN 1-874776-00-8

Designed and typeset by the publishers—Sandhome Publishing in association with The Palm Group.

Front cover photographs: Pete Thomas and Pat Russell with Redmire 20-pounders; Maurice Ingham with his 24lb. 12oz. Redmire carp caught in 1952; a priceless collection of carp fishing memorabilia—including Mk. IV rods and reels owned by Richard Walker, B.B., Albert Buckley and Bill Keal. The lower cased fish is Pete Frost's 25-pounder caught from Tiddenfoot Pit in 1960.
Back cover photographs: A recent painting by Maurice Ingham of his recollection of the moment when the Carp Catchers' Club was formed at Mapperley Reservoir; Dave Steuart with John Andrews' 20lb. 3oz. Cheshunt carp after refurbishment; Bob Richards outside his home with the 31lb. 4oz. record carp shortly after its capture; a cased 17lb. 2½oz. Cheshunt carp caught by John Andrews in 1915.

Contents

	Preface	*vii*
1	The Origins and Introduction of Carp into Britain	1
2	Some Early Notable Carp Fisheries	21
3	Croxby Pond and Otto Overbeck	35
4	Cheshunt Reservoir	45
5	Mapperley Reservoir	59
6	Dagenham Lake	81
7	Redmire Pool	95
8	Billing Aquadrome	121
9	The Peterborough Electricity Cut	135
10	Nothing New Under the Sun	147
11	A History of Carp Tackle	159
12	Wadhurst, Stoneham and Contemporary Times	163

Acknowledgements

"Evermore thanks, the exchequer of the poor", wrote Shakespeare. And yet that is all I can provide to the countless kindred spirits who readily strove to accommodate my pleas for help. But I am rich through knowing them, my poverty cast aside with a wealth of kindness. So many are good friends, yet others remain just passing acquaintances, drifting out of reach by the surreptitious traitor, time.

There is an argument that suggests I refrain from specifying individuals, for surely I will err and forget someone. And indeed I know this will be the case. To those I must ask them to forgive the fallibility of a mind I know is not what it once was. Notes on bits of paper are just as hard to find as faltering memories in darkened, unused corners of the brain. But my obligation is no less diminished through a moment's transgression.

There are so many that I must thank. My wife — I use the term advisedly, for she has often seen so little of me during this prolonged sabbatical that she must clearly doubt that I am a man of my word. My children, Beverley and Michael, for being patient with unfulfilled promises, yet giving me so many reasons to be happy. Len Arbery, Dick Kefford, Bob James, Maurice Ingham, Gerry Berth-Jones, John Nixon, Dr. Bruno Broughton, Harry Grief, Ron Grief, Mike Wilson, the late Don Leney, Fred J. Taylor, Shaun Russell, Chris Currie, Chris Wright, Bob Buteux, Chris Sandford, Fred Buller, Michael Leney, the late Richard Walker, Ken Sutton, Ron Barnett, James Bruce, the late Denys Watkins-Pitchford, Mike Winter, Eric Hodson, Bob Church, Muriel Norman, Fred Sykes, Peter Sharpe, Graham Daubney, Elliott Symak, Bud Jessop, A. Scott-Davies, Ron Groombridge, Alan Clarke, Alwyne Wheeler, Ken Watkins, Chris Ball, Pete Rogers, Eric Buckley, Ted Meakin, Kenneth Clower, Dave and Kay Steuart, Ted Duro, Alan Otter, Archie Braddock, Ray Longland, Dave Allen, Alan Hinde, the late Pat Russell, Neil Pope and the staff at Angling Times, Tim Paisley, Martyn Rust and Mrs Singer, Dave Goodrum, Tony Fordham, Trevor Housby, Cliff Hatton, the late Alec Lewis, Duncan Kay, Christopher Richards, Dave Moore, Peter Frost, Ken Drayton, Peter Chillingsworth, Keith Griffiths, Phil Shatford, Kevin Roberts, Pat Walker, Pete Thomas, Professor Eugene Balon, Roy Westwood, Brian Gull, Jeffrey Seddon, John Neville, Henni Hoefakker, Jan Eggers, C.M. Bungenberg de Jong, H.J.G. Bloemen, Mike Smith, all are deserving of my gratitude.

To all those I have mentioned, to those I have forgotten, and all true brothers of the angle, if I can repay you in a small way by entertaining you for a moment in time, I shall be happy that my toil has not been in vain.

Preface

*Wherever men have lived there is a story to be told,
and it depends chiefly on the story-teller or historian
whether it is interesting or not.*
  Thoreau (1860)

There have been so many people who have helped with the preparation of this book that without their generosity and assistance it quite simply would never have been completed. Even so it has taken, I am loathed to admit, eight years. It was born out of the desire to carry on from *Redmire Pool*, the book written by my good friend, Len Arbery, and myself in the early 1980's. So many people have told us that the parts of the book they enjoyed the most were those sections dealing with the period leading up to, and pertaining to, the Carp Catchers' Club. In truth, this was the part of *Redmire Pool* that I enjoyed researching and writing about. So, the labour of love began. A thousand telephone calls, sackfuls of letters, meetings, trips to distant parts, ferreting in newspaper libraries, adverts seeking help, faxes to foreign lands, months reading and re-reading old books and magazines, protracted attempts to squeeze a little better quality photograph from some ancient, faded negative, cross-checking disputed points, then days, weeks spent pounding the keyboard—oh, there were times when I was fed up with the whole affair. But it always drew me back, as a magnet draws a piece of steel. I was hooked, an addict. Like the obsessive carp angler all normal activities were denied, pressed aside in the urge to satisfy the craving. Perhaps now, as I write this, the malady nears its end. The race is almost run. Soon the book will be published, and I shall turn away, cured. Perhaps.

At the beginning it was to be another joint venture between Len Arbery and myself, but Len's personal circumstances eventually precluded him from carrying out our original plans. Nevertheless, his encouragement and assistance have been a staff on which I have leaned heavily. When I stumbled he was always there. Life is partly what we make it, and partly what it is made for us by the friends we choose. And, just as Len wrote no part of this book, so he is a part of it.

I doubt I shall ever write another book of this kind. Occasionally, I flatter myself I am a practical man, so the fatality of modern life drives me to do things which, for want of a better expression, show a good return on investment. My conscience drives me to be cost effective with my 'three score years and ten'. Thoughts of my frail mortality creep up like shadows on a dark night. I have fish-catching ambitions that still burn bright; so I dream of monster carp in some wild, secluded Canadian lake or mighty Russian river. The desire to run with the pack, to join the rat race that English carp fishing has become, is a flame that long ago flickered and died. We are all creatures of our time and it is not for me to judge the morality of modern carp fishing. I am, only just, a part of the carp fishing that this book is about.

When that succumbed, I eventually had to turn away. Perhaps the need to write this book was, in part at least, a last, desperate cry—a yearning—for something that I loved and lost.

So the book makes no attempt to chronicle carp fishing much after the 1960's, except where the continuity of a theme demands it. There will be others, in the future, who will perform this task. They will have the benefit of hindsight as I have had, to determine what they believe to be of relevance. I will have made errors—factual mistakes and erroneous conceptual judgements. I know it, for it is inevitable. I apologise, yet I have done my very best. I realise the responsibility that comes with the task.

I have attempted to remain faithful to the truth. Yet, I have tried to entertain. The two sometimes make poor travelling companions. Embellishment is often the teller's desire to fulfil the need of the listener. And so, perhaps, I have occasionally been party to a little deception. However, where matters of substance are concerned I have adhered as closely as I can to the facts as I know them. A hard-nosed *New York Times* journalist once wrote that what makes a good writer of history is someone who is suspicious. Suspicion marks the difference between a man who wants to write honest history and the one who would rather write a good story. And so, to give the truth I endeavour to make a distinction between facts and beliefs. I try not to disguise my beliefs as truths, for if I think too highly of my beliefs then I am in danger of falsifying the facts. Yet I hope this suspicion does not prove a drawback to the telling of the tale.

I have been acutely aware of the arrogance involved in seeking to write a book that attempts to set out the history of carp fishing. For that reason, if for nothing more, I have chosen the title carefully. It is, in essence, only one man's perception, utilising whatever scant knowledge I have acquired. There will be those who I have failed to mention, or not given enough credit where it was deserved. Perchance I have given some too much, when they merit little or none. Some of the book's personalities are blessed with the privilege of greatness, others, no doubt, found themselves thrust into the limelight by circumstance. Yet one man's influence and accomplishments cast a wide shadow, that many others had to live under. Richard Stuart Walker brought so very much to carp fishing, yet he was the seed of its destruction as he knew and loved it. For all his vision, for all his intellectual prowess, he never saw this until it was too late.

My school-days bring back the words from the Rubáiyát of the Persian poet, Omar Khayyám, who wrote "the moving finger writes; and, having writ, moves on." And it is true in all things, including carp fishing. You cannot relive the time when carp fishers were looked upon, by the angling majority, as harmless eccentrics or a handful of fanatical, patronising elitists. The pioneering, discovery days, that were once part and parcel of embryonic carp fishing, are gone forever in this tiny, over-populated island. The driving forces now are commercially orientated. People earn good livings by catching big carp and selling carp fishing.

It is, perhaps, harder to get as much pleasure from carp fishing as was once possible. But, as always, that lies with the individual's desire. Attitudes in our recreational activities are affected by changes in Society as a whole. We do not keep each part of our lives in separate, isolated compartments. If this book shows another face of carp fishing—a less demanding, less frantic and, dare I say, a happier side—then perhaps the same could be said of life itself.

Chapter 1

The Origins & Introduction of Carp into Britain

The greatest journey must begin with a single step.
   Chinese proverb.

When, exactly, carp were first introduced into this country is uncertain although recent work has shown that it was considerably earlier than had previously been accepted. Thomas Boosey in his book, *Piscatorial Reminiscences and Gleanings by an Old Angler and Bibliopolist,* written in 1835, states that "Carp were introduced into England in the year 1514."

One of the most widely quoted references, and, with justification, some would say hackneyed, to the introduction of carp was Richard Baker's, mentioned in Izaak Walton's *The Complete Angler:*

*'Hops and Turkies, Carps and Beer
Came into England all in a year.'*

Contemporarily, this quote has always been claimed to be full of errors and worthless as a means of determining when carp were introduced. Walton also states that "there was a time, about a hundred or a few more years ago, when there were no carp in England." Since Walton's book was first published in 1653 this would appear to set the date at about 1550. However, Walton was a plagiarist[1] and he cribbed much of the work of one Leonard Mascall, of Plumstead, his book being published in 1590 and titled *The Book of Fishing with Hooke and Line and all other instruments thereunto belonging.* Mascall, himself, has been erroneously credited in the past with being accountable for the introduction of carp into Britain, not least because his book credits a Mr. Mascall, of Plumstead, in Essex as being the person responsible! Mascall translated the book *Planting and Grafting,* in 1589, so it is not improbable that he procured carp from the continent and devoted some attention to their culture. However, large sections of Mascall's book of 1590 were copied, word for word, from part of a much earlier work. This was an appendix to the second edition of a collection of text, which in a later edition was titled *The Boke of St. Albans,* written in 1496 and credited, wrongly, to Dame Juliana Bernes, Abbess or Prioress of Sopwell Nunnery in Hertfordshire[2].

1. Apart from plagiarising much of Macall's work, Walton also cribbed the groundbait recipes from a book discovered in the 1950's titled *The Arte of Angling.* It had been published in 1577 and was written by William Samuel, vicar of Godmanchester. Samuel also states much the same as Bernes about the introduction of carp, that it was a "fish not long known in England." However, he further points out that the shires of Buckingham and Berkshire "are well furnished with carp." It is difficult to know how much credence can be placed on such references made by Walton, Bernes and Samuel. Copying other writers work seems to have been looked upon at this time as an acceptable matter, so the possibility of an erroneous statement being repeated through plagiarism is quite conceivable.
2. Dame Julyans or Juliana Barnes, Bernes or Berners, is supposed to have been the daughter of Sir James Berners, of Roding Berners, in Essex. It has been claimed that Juliana was known for her learning and sporting accomplishments and that she became the Prioress of the Benedictine Nunnery of Sopwell, near St. Albans. However, there is little evidence to support this, indeed her name does not appear in any official records. It seems that previous statements to this effect are based, in the main, on conjecture and inference.

The Origins & Introduction of Carp into Britain

A woodcut illustration from the front page of Bernes's 1496 "lytyll plaunflet" titled a 'Treatyse of Fysshynge wyth an Angle.'

The case against Bernes having been the author was forcibly destroyed by Dr. Andrew Kippis in his *Biographia Britannica*, published in 1784 and again by William Blades in 1881. In fact, there is evidence to suggest that she wrote only the section of the book that deals with hunting. However, tradition has cherished her name and it is the famous quote, that "there be but few in England", that has been given most credence in the past. The year 1496 has therefore been used as a benchmark for the introduction of carp, but in 1883 a substantially different manuscript of Berners' *'Treatyse'*, belonging to A. Denison, was discovered, and scholarly examination has dated this between 1406 and 1450. The fact that hops were initially introduced into Britain for brewing in about 1428 now makes the couplet a little more interesting, although another version, which brackets "Reformation, hops, bays, and beer" together, is clearly intended to refer to the year 1534, when Henry VIII used the principles of the Reformation movement to assert control over the English Church.

Certainly carp were present in Britain, and being farmed, in 1462. In the *Accounts and Memoranda of Sir John Howard, First Duke of Norfolk*, published by the Roxborough Club in 1841, in a volume entitled *Manners and Household Expenses of England in the 13th and 15th Centuries*, there appears the following against a date of 1462:

> 'Item, the same year and the xvi day of Octobre,
> my master putte into the said ponde, in grete carpes.'

and later:

> 'And my master lete owte alle the water, wherefore he
> lete ther in serteyn grete carpets and many odre smale,
> and myche ffyre.'

The earliest mention of carp that the author has come across is found in Arthur Bryant's *The Age of Chivalry*. When John Pechum was made Archbishop of Canterbury, in 1248, he had to provide the following for his enthronement feast:

> '...300 ling, 600 cod, 40 fresh salmon, 7 barrels of salt sturgeon,
> 600 fresh eels, 8,000 welks, 100 pike, 400 tench, 100 carp...'

Further early references, as this one, fail to clarify whether these fish were actually imported from the Continent or bred in England. However, there is good reason to believe that there were connections between the Low Countries and London as regards the dissemination of Continental ideas regarding fish rearing, and it is possible that the introduction and spread of carp were the result of these contacts. It is known that a considerable production centre for freshwater fish existed on the River Thames, at Southwark, as early as 1363. Many fishponds and wharfages were present and this area, known as 'The Stews', backed onto a street aptly named 'Pyke Garden'. It may be more than a coincidence that a man known as 'Frows of Flanders' was leasing The Stews at the time of the Peasant's Revolt in 1381.

Furthermore, when the first English work extolling the virtues of keeping carp was published in 1600—John Tavener's *Certaine Experiments concerning Fish and Fruite*—it went to some lengths to recommend the Dutch cleric, Janus Dubravius, as an authority on the subject. The likelihood, it would seem, is that carp were, therefore, introduced to England, possibly from the Low Countries, sometime in the late-14th or early-15th century and, certainly by the latter half of the 15th century, they were being reared in this country.

By the 1530's they were well established and much sought after, and mentioned in numerous documents. They were not at all hard to come by and records confirm they could be found in Norfolk, Suffolk, Hampshire, London, Surrey, Worcestershire and Gloucestershire.

Treatises such as those written by Tavener (1600) and Roger North *(A Discourse of Fish and Fishponds*—1713) gives them pride of place above all other fish. Indeed, this situation appears to have continued until, at least, the early part of the present century. That noted authority on all matters relating to fish, Frank Buckland, stated in the latter part of the 19th century that "the carp is probably the most widely distributed fish of all the British species." This view was echoed by the knowledgeable editor of *The Angler's News,* A.R. Matthews, when he wrote in 1903 that "The cultivation of this fish became so general, that there is hardly a monastic ruin where the remains of a carp stew or pond is not to be found. The carp is now one of the most common of British fishes; is extremely prolific, and very easily reared."

A large number of pond owners are recorded as keeping carp. The Earl of Rutland bought his supply from a Lincolnshire fisherman, Paul Robinson, who charged 12d. for 10in. fish and 2/- for 18in. fish (Davies 1966). In 1590, John Pyke was accused of having stolen "many and greate carpes" from the Bishop of Winchester's fishpond at Frensham, near Farnham, in Surrey (Baker and Minchin 1948) and, at Cornbury Park, in Oxfordshire, a mid-16th century survey records three fishponds next to a mill which were stocked with bream, carp and eels (Bond and Chambers 1988).

Even in these times there were those who believed that cultivation of fish was being threatened by the increase in number of those who sought to catch them. Thomas Bastard wrote in 1598:

> 'But now the sport is marred, and wot ye why?
> Fishes decrease, and fishers multiply.'

Walton, born in 1593, wrote that the carp was a "subtle fish—nor has he been long in England."

The popularity of carp with pond-keepers is demonstrated in innumerable post-medieval treatises. Tavener and North, noted above, devoted their comments almost entirely to the species, paying scant attention to any other kind of fish in their praises. Amongst others mentioning the carp is Gervase Markham, who records methods used for catching them in his *Country Contentments or the Husbandman's Recreations* (1633), although a substantial part of his book was plagiarised from earlier works. Amongst other things he refers to them as river fish as well as pond dwellers. It would appear from this that sufficient numbers had escaped, or been deliberately stocked, into English river systems, by the early-17th century, for them to be so considered.

North (1713) records that in the early-18th century the London fish market could not obtain enough of these highly-sought fish. In the more remote parts of the country, North comments that the current fashion is to let estates to tenants, who tend to neglect fishponds. Tavener (1600) claims that one of his reasons for promoting the qualities of the carp is that fish keeping is no longer as popular as it once was.

However, this is not always the picture other records give. Fishponds were still popular at the end of the 17th and throughout the 18th century with a great many landowners. Witness to this is the account of Lord Wharton, of Upper Winchendon, in Buckinghamshire, for the year 1686. Literally thousands of "great carp" were taken from a number of ponds on his estates, some for sale and some for restocking other ponds (Croft and Pike 1988). In Sussex, the diaries of one Thomas Marchant show that a large number of ponds in that county were stocked with carp. Marchant spent much of his time in that county, as a fish dealer, travelling from pond to pond to catch the fish (Turner 1873). At various places in Oxfordshire, 17th and 18th century ponds are identified as being systematically managed to produce good sized carp for eating and stocking (Bond and Chambers 1988). In Hampshire, a number of ponds have been identified within the Tichfield area that in the 1740's contained carp. At least a dozen can still be identified today, four of these ponds being those stocked in 1538 by Thomas Wriothesley.

It might be wondered to what sizes these fish attained in comparison with the modern varieties, which can exceed 40lb. in favourable conditions in this country. Roger North noted that his carp could attain 18in. in 5 years. It was not unusual to keep fish much larger than this for the market. Nevertheless, Taverner claims to have seen carp in 1600 that were 33in. from the eye to the fork of the tail. Such a carp, even allowing for a low condition factor of a less-selectively bred carp, might be expected to exceed 15lb.

William Peard gives some idea of the maximum weight for carp in the late-18th and 19th centuries. He recalls how a water known as Stonehead Lake was netted in 1793 to produce 2,000 carp of "large dimensions," including a fish of 30in. length, 22in. breadth and weighing 18lb. In Weston Hall, Staffordshire, he notes there is a painting of a carp of 19½lb. In Sussex, a Mr. Ladbroke presented Lord Egremont with a brace of fish from his park at Gratton that weighed 35lb. It is recorded that Ladbroke made this gesture to demonstrate to the men of Surrey the sort of carp Sussex was capable of producing (Peard 1868).

We have long been informed that carp originated from China and the Far East. Many authors, dating back to the Middle Ages, have postulated this opinion and it has been accepted, uncritically, until fairly recently. Tate Regan, in 1911, added his stamp of approval to this view in his authoritative book, *British Freshwater Fishes.* In 1962 Rudzinski, from Poland, agreed and Butcher (Australia, 1967) and McCrimmon (Canada, 1968) also added their backing. Even C.F. Hickling concluded in his 1962 book, *Fish Culture,* that the species was not a native of Europe but had been transported from the East by way of Cyprus. However, Marcel Huet in his standard work on fish culture, *Traite de Pisciculture,* published originally in 1952, put forward a different view in that "carp originated from eastern Europe (Basins of the Black Sea, the Azov Sea and the Caspian Sea)." More recently, in 1969, Professor Balon has shown almost certainly that the origins of the carp were from central Asia, from the area around the Caspian Sea, some 10,000 years ago. With the ending of the last Ice Age, and the resulting higher temperatures, the species colonised naturally the Black Sea area, the Aral system, eastern Asia including China and, about 8,000 years ago, the River Danube system. In about AD 15 a Roman camp was established near the mouth of the River Morava, which is a tributary of the Danube. From this camp grew a large town called Carnuntum, which was an important resting place on the much used Amber Road. There is strong evidence to suggest that it was from this area that carp were first transported by man throughout Europe. Having first been transferred to Italy, following the decline of the Roman

Empire, the domestication of the species continued with the advent of Christianity, in monastery stew ponds. It was necessary, with the establishment of monasteries from the 6th century, to have a readily available source of fish for consumption during the monks fasting periods, which covered more than 100 days each year. However, undue weight may have been laid on the monastic contribution to the spread of the fish across Europe. A research thesis by Currie, *Medieval Fishponds: aspects of their origin, function, management and development,* has demonstrated that fishponds came to be established by secular authorities as indications of their status as landowners from at least the 1st and 2nd centuries. The first large-scale building of artificial fishponds in Britain was undertaken by members of the Norman secular aristocracy to enhance their status. Indeed, the earliest monastic fishponds were frequently passed on as already existing facilities, given by wealthy secular patrons.

Dendy Sadler's circa 1880 painting of the monks fishing for their supper! Monks had to follow strict fasting regulations, with heavy punishments for violation, for more than 100 days a year. Only crayfish, molluscs and fish (in some areas fowl or unborn rabbit embryos) were permissible. Thus fish became an important source of food. Floods, natural disasters, transportation and wars all influenced the development of artificial stew ponds to provide a consistent supply of fish.

By the time carp were first introduced into England they had been reared in Europe on a large scale for at least 700 years (having originally been domesticated by the Romans in the area of present-day Italy in about the 4th to the 2nd century B.C.). During this period the first selective breeding experiments were taking place which would improve the growth rate and change a number of biological features of the species. Improvements in growth rates, through selective breeding, are not dependent upon variations in scale pattern. In fact, the best growth is achieved in carp which are fully scaled, i.e. the 'common' scaled king carp with a scale pattern the same as that found in the wild carp. Variations in scale pattern correlate to many biological differences in the carp but improved growth is not one of them. Indeed, the overwhelming majority of traits which manifest themselves in reduced scale coverings are unfavourable when compared to those found in the wild carp.

Clearly, since some selective breeding for improved growth was already taking place in Europe, when the first introductions of carp were being made into this country, then the purity of any attributed wild carp must be open to doubt. And, as time went on, the likelihood of

The Origins & Introduction of Carp into Britain

An 12lb. 'wildie' from Brayton Pond, near Carlisle, caught by the son of Fred Sykes. The carp were introduced in 1836, or possibly earlier, but the author doubts that they are genuine wild carp in a strict scientific sense.

further introductions of genuine wild carp into this country clearly diminished. Certainly, it would be hard to imagine that there are any breeding stocks of true wild carp left in this country dating back several hundred years, although it cannot be ruled out altogether. The misconception lays with anglers themselves, for any fully-scaled carp stocks, that are long and thin, have been classified, incorrectly, as wild carp. If there is some historical evidence of carp being present in the fishery for a considerable time, or a passing connection with a monastery, then presumption becomes conviction. Indeed, even carp which showed king carp characteristics, yet were from waters which only contained fully-scaled carp, were deemed to be wild carp. The famed Cheshunt Reservoir was one such water. Richard Walker, in his appendix to Bernard Venables' marvellous book *Fishing*, writes about the members of the Red Spinners catching carp "free from the influence of any domesticated strains." What Dick Walker stated about carp few dared to challenge, and so the myth of the huge 'wildies' of Cheshunt was perpetrated. Jack Hilton compounded this error in his book *Quest for Carp,* and even notable carp historians such as Chris Ball and Len Arbery were consolidating this view in the early-1990's. Chris Currie has also propagated the myth of huge 'wildies' but at least qualified his views in the *Coarse Angler,* in March 1987, by acknowledging that "I do not want to dwell too long on the definition of a wildie...I think for my purposes a fully-scaled fish of long, lean proportions that has not been in contact with known strains of king carp, particularly the mirror or leather varieties, will suffice."

The author has for long been sceptical of the claims of wild carp caught by many of his angling acquaintances. With some he has gently broached his doubts; with others discretion is the better part of valour! He has raised his doubts in print on several occasions, notably in his book *Carp* (Ward Lock, 1989), and subsequently contacted the acknowledged expert on wild carp, Professor Eugene Balon, of Czechoslovakia. Enclosed with the letter were photographs

A 24lb. carp caught in 1887 on Lord Mostyn's Estate, Clwyd. The fish's shape and size, like those caught by the members of the Red Spinners, from Cheshunt, indicates selective breeding.

of Cheshunt 'wildies' including the one-time British record caught by John Andrews, and another, which was claimed to be a record at its time of capture. This is his reply in March, 1991:

"Dear Mr. Clifford,

Your record carp are most certainly not wild forms but feral forms of a domesticated carp. The most visible character to prove this is the clear notch on the forehead or at its dorsum where the head ends and the body starts. The true wild carp has no trace of such a notch. Even domesticated mirror and leather (entirely scaleless) carp, released into natural water bodies, revert ultimately into this form. Other characters, less visible on first sight, are related, for example, to the proportion of red and white muscles, density of blood capillary networks, etc.

Most of it was published by V. Misik and myself in 1958 in *"Biologicke prace"* of the Slovak Academy of Sciences, in Bratislava, volume IV/6, unfortunately in Slovak. Only some of it is reviewed in the essay you have.

At that time we were able to clearly distinguish such feral carp, albeit fully scaled, from the true wild carp when caught together in the Danube River. All the carp captured by us later in the upper Danube and Rhine (see *Env. Biol. Fish. 15: 243-271*) were such feral carp, and so were all the specimens from the U.K. in the collection of the British Museum (Natural History) I looked at in 1971 and 1979. Last year I have seen some true wild carp again in the Zoological Museum in Kiev and so do not believe that its western form exists anywhere but in the tributaries of the Black Sea. It is probably possible to confirm all this with modern techniques like D.N.A. analysis.

Furthermore, we investigated several of the 'wild forms' of carp in North America. All were feral forms. It is hardly surprising as all originated from imports of European domesticated carp.

Sincerely yours,
Eugene K. Balon."

The truth of the matter is that probably no genuine wild carp have been caught in Britain for many generations, if they ever were! The general carp angler's conception of what constitutes a true wild carp is, of course, not the same as that of the biologist, and probably will remain at variance, but that is merely due to ignorance on the part of the angler. If, as Chris Currie seems to imply, anglers wish for the fully-scaled, feral, domesticated carp to be known as a wildie then that's fine—but what then are they going to call a genuine wild carp? A substantial number of knowledgeable carp anglers claim to have seen and caught wild carp but the author remains sceptical, and the famed 'wildies' of Beechmere, Croxby, Wadhurst, Priory Park Lake, Hunstrete, Willowhead Lake, Sawmills Lake and Brayton Pond were almost certainly feral forms of the domesticated carp. The shape of the large Croxby carp, caught by Overbeck, show distinct characteristics that are possessed by domesticated carp.

Mike Winter with 'wildies' from the water B.B. immortalised in his books—The Old Copper Mine—Beechmere.

The Origins & Introduction of Carp into Britain

Further tangible evidence to support this view is that in about 1947 half-a-dozen small, fully-scaled carp were transferred to Woldale from Croxby Pond, and these grew rapidly. Maurice Ingham caught one of these fish, three years later in 1950, which weighed 11½lb. This clearly demonstrates that the Croxby carp's potential fast growth rate derived from their ancestors being carp of a domesticated race.

Richard Walker himself was not consistent in these matters. On one occasion in a letter to Gerry Berth-Jones, in the early-1950's, he pointed out that the carp in Wadhurst "are the original old English wild carp, long, slim and tremendous fighters." Then, later, he went to great length explaining to Maurice Ingham the difficulty in differentiating between them, writing the following:

"These regularly scaled fish are indistinguishable, away from the environment. If I bring you, Maurice Ingham, a bloody great fat sod like Ravioli, you would say king carp with full scaling like a shot. But a naturalist wouldn't dare do so. And if I brought you a long, slim all-scaler, dare you say wild one? I know I daren't. It might be a real king carp underfed. What about a medium-shaped one? Underfed king or overfed wild one?"

The cultivation of carp continued unabated in Europe but fell into disfavour in this country in the early-1800's. Britain, in comparison with other European countries, has a very long coastline in relation to its area and, consequently, with the development of surfaced roads sea fish could be quickly transported considerable distances and still remain fresh. Then came ice, initially imported from Norway, which allowed sea fish to be preserved. By the late-1800's the mechanics of carp cultivation was generally lost in this country, so much so that the noted Victorian ichthyologist, Frank Buckland, wrote the following in 1880:

"There are hundreds of acres of lakes and ponds about in this country which might be readily made to grow fish, if the owners of these waters only knew what to do and how to do it. To many manor houses, and to almost all the ruins of monasteries of England, fish-ponds were formally attached—in most instances they might be brought into work again. The obvious use of these ponds was to supply fish to the monks and others during fast days, for it must be recollected that sea fish could seldom, at this period of English history (owing to the slowness of conveyance and the ignorance of the preservative qualities of ice), be transported from the coast so as to be in a fit state for the table on arrival at inland localities.

The monks of old knew a great deal about the cultivation of fish-ponds, and I am informed that this pond cultivation is still carried on to a great extent in western, central, and southern Europe; in fact, in the very localities where the same conditions of things which formally prevailed in England—viz., fast days and no sea fish—are still to be found."

The term king carp has become associated nowadays with fish which have an enhanced growth rate produced by selective breeding, and which often have some irregular scale patterns. However, it has been demonstrated that some selective breeding for enhanced growth had been taking place in Europe by the time carp were first introduced into Britain in about 1400. For example meaningful carp culture can be traced back to the year 1227 in Austria, and the Emperor Charles IV of Germany, by granting specific privileges, favoured the establishment of carp culture in his country. In about 1367 an extensive carp farm was constructed at Wittingau, in Bohemia, which was maintained by the Barons of Rosenberg for several centuries. In 1670 it passed into the Schwartzenberg family and by 1900 covered an area of some 20,000 acres, with an annual yearly crop of 500,000lb. of carp. At this time it was probably the largest carp farm in the world.

Selective breeding, to produce carp with irregular scale patterns, came after work to improve growth rates and, initially at least, may have been carried out for no more purpose than curiosity value. From at least the 16th century races of carp, with forms where the scales were absent or few, have been recognised in Europe.

Fish with irregular scale patterns occur naturally but very infrequently, the author having seen it in roach and rudd. It is caused by a mutation of the genes which alters the way in which the scales are formed and distributed over the body. The usual cause of such mutations in the past would be the result of irradiation from natural causes. So, these two specific characteristics—improved growth rate through selective breeding and scale patterns—are distinct and not directly related. However, the use of the word king carp came into fashion in the late-19th century and was used to describe carp which possessed improved growth **and** irregular scale patterns and this has not changed during the ensuing years.

Rudd with 'mirror' scaling. The principal genes which effect the size and distribution of scales follow a Mendelian relationship. Rudzinski, in 1928, was the first author to publish data on crosses of carp with different scale cover. Further study by Kirpichnikov, Balkhashina and Golovinskaya in the Soviet Union, between about 1935 and 1948, made it possible to identify the two pairs of independent genes that are located in different pairs of chromosomes, which determine the form that scale patterns will take.

In 1913 the editors of *The Angler's News* received this letter and gave the following reply:

> Sirs,
>
> Mr. Pettit, of the Phoenix A.S., caught a carp in the Thames last Sunday at Windsor, weight 7lb. 15¼oz., on a no. 13 hook, the aspect of which was most peculiar, the skin surface being almost bare of scales, which were placed singly here and there. It was in good condition, and took 45 minutes to get out.
>
> Yours truly,
>
> R. Carr

[We should think that the specimen was a king or Speigel carp. This species of carp was introduced into this country in 'the seventies.' We believe that the carp have bred at Woburn (where they were introduced) and that they are now to be obtained from the fish breeders in this country.]

In the following week's edition the editor, A. R. Matthews, continued:

"Several lots of carp have been turned down in the Thames, but as far as my recollection carries me this is the first of these fish which has been caught with rod and line in that river. I have known of several captures among king carp in the Sussex Ouse (where they have been introduced) and in various lakes in Berkshire, Lincolnshire etc."

The earliest introductions of king carp into the River Thames were in 1895 when 400 were released at Henley, by the Henley Fisheries Preservation Society. Further stockings were carried out by the same organisation in 1902 when "a large number" were introduced; in 1908 approximately 3,500, between 6in. and 10in., were netted in Surrey by the Thames Angling Preservation Society and released at Hampton Court, Thames Ditton and Twickenham, and then a further 500, up to 4lb., were introduced in 1909, although it is not clear whether these subsequent stockings were king carp. Another stocking, this time of "common carp", took place in 1913 when 1,300 were netted from a reservoir at Woodcote, in Oxfordshire. These fish were the progeny of six or seven fish placed in the reservoir nine years earlier.

> **Growth of King Carp.** ANOTHER proof of the rapid growth of king carp was furnished on the 30th ult., when Mr. J. Jones landed at Patricroft one weighing 1 lb. 3¾ oz., which Mr. Baggaley, hairdresser, Patricroft, kindly exhibited in his window, causing a great amount of interest.

An editorial note from The Angler, October 1894, showing that king carp, if not exactly widespread, were subject to considerable interest.

By the end of 1912 Mr. Matthews felt inclined to state that "king, or German mirror carp, are becoming much more common in English waters as time progresses. They are to be met with now in numerous ornamental lakes and private ponds, and some of the rivers also contain these fish. There are king carp in the Thames, Sussex Ouse, Great Ouse, and other rivers I could name." Further captures of the king carp introduced into the Thames at the turn of the century were reported, one example being a fish of 10lb. 7½oz. caught by Mr. F.I. Miles, at Laleham, in September 1922.

The editors of *The Angler's News* were earlier ascribing to the reference by the noted ichthyologist Frank Buckland, who wrote the following in his book *The Natural History of British Fishes*.

"In March, 1873, Lord Arthur Russell was kind enough to bring me up three grand specimens of the looking-glass carp. Sixteen Spiegel[1] carp had been sent alive to his brother, Lord Odo Russell, by Count Maltzan, who lives in Silesia. The three fish which had died in transit weighed 6lb., 5½lb., and 5lb. 2oz., and measured from 19in. to 22in. The greater part of the body of this fish is of the usual carp colour and is quite soft like wash-leather, there being no scales whatever upon it; along the central line on each side of the fish there is a row of very large scales, some being two inches across, some not larger than a sixpence. These are of a golden colour, tinted with opal.

The leather carp is the name given to this fish when the big bright scales are absent, which is sometimes the case.

In May, 1873, Lord Arthur Russell kindly presented to me four living specimens of the Speigel or looking-glass carp. They were presented to Lord Odo Russell, ambassador at Berlin, by Count Munster.

Of these four fish two are now alive and well at my museum, South Kensington.

In October, 1880, Lord Odo Russell brought to Woburn Abbey from Berlin, six Speigel carp bred at Trachenfels, near Breslau, by Prince Herman Hatzfeldt."

Clearly, in this country king carp were initially looked upon as a curiosity, but the continental notion that they represented a viable food source was soon being touted. In the magazine *Fish, Fish Culture and the Aquarium*, W. Oldham Chambers wrote a series of scholarly articles extolling the virtues of the 'German carp'. A little time after these were published, in 1886, a small notice appeared in the same periodical stating:

"In consequence of numerous applications received by the National Fish Culture Association for supplies of leather and mirror carp, the Council have decided to import a large consignment of these species from Germany for distribution amongst those persons desirous of cultivating them, the Association being anxious to encourage the propagation of these valuable edible fishes in the waters of the United Kingdom."

So far, so good. We seem to have a logical and well-founded progression of factual evidence as to when king carp were introduced, backed up by knowledgeable authors of the time. Harry Cholmondeley-Pennell makes no mention of them in his fine book, *Fishing,*

---

1. Spiegel is the German word for 'mirror' or 'looking-glass'.

published in 1889, which suggests they were still a rare commodity. Tate Regan, however, a few years later in 1910, describes the mirror and leather carp in his tome, *The Freshwater Fishes of the British Isles*. The spanner in the works comes in the 1804 edition of George Shaw's *General Zoology,* volume V., part 1, where he writes about the German "Spiegel-Karpe, or mirror-carp", describing them as "mules", and stating that "In some ponds in Lancashire, I have been told by a gentleman of great worth and honour, both these kinds of mules are now and then found." This would, at first sight, appear to undermine the author's proposals as to when king carp were first introduced. However, there is a possible alternative, and that is that the Lancashire carp, assuming they were genuine, were naturally occurring mutations and had not been introduced. The author has mentioned earlier observing roach and rudd with mirror scale mutations and, whilst these do occur extremely infrequently—the author has only come across them in two fisheries—a number of examples were found in each lake.

> **To Secretaries of Angling Societies and Private Gentlemen wishing to Stock Ponds or Aquariums.**
>
> I will send the following Samples on receipt of P.O. for **5s.**, including Bait Can (not to be returned.)
>
> 3 KING CARP,   1 GOLD TENCH,
> 1 GOLDORFEN,   1 GREEN TENCH,
>   12 GOLDFISH.
>
> Also one each of Rudd, Roach, Carp, Perch, and Minnows.
>
> **J. E. CHADWICK,** 10 CITY ROAD, MANCHESTER.

> **STOCKING THE MERE WITH FISH.**—A memorial, promoted by a number of local anglers and others, in which it is proposed to ask the Corporation to increase the stock of fish in the Mere in the Weaponness Valley by 500 tench, 500 perch, and 500 gudgeon, is in course of preparation. About three years ago the Mere was stocked by the Corporation with 2,000 coarse fish, including 1,000 roach, 800 perch, and 200 King carp, and day tickets were sold at a shilling each. Good sport has since been obtained, but the largest "baskets" have fallen to the lot of sea gulls which getting to know the fact of the presence of the fish in shallow water, in hard weather swooped down in hundreds. Despite this inroad of poachers the venture has paid the Corporation at the rate of about 20 per cent. The cost to the Corporation of stocking the Mere on the first instance was £31, and the sale of shilling tickets has averaged about £5 a year.

Above: An advert that appeared in 'The Angler' in November, 1894.
Above right: An 1896 report in a local paper of the stocking of Scarborough Mere with 200 king carp.
Right: Further mention, from 'The Fishing Gazette' in 1894, of stocking with king carp, this time at Roundhay Park in Leeds. These reports clearly demonstrate that king carp stockings were by no means rare events around the turn of the century.

> **LEEDS AMALGAMATED SOCIETY.**
> THE WORK OF STOCKING.
>
> The Roundhay Park Committee are doing their best to make the lakes at Roundhay into one of the best angling resorts in Yorkshire. At their last meeting it was decided to purchase 20,000 one-eyed ova (trout), and a rearing box for the top lake; also 1,000 king carp and 500 rudd for the Waterloo Lake. Mr. James Crampton, the secretary, and a few more members met at the Park at 7 a.m, on Saturday last, to net the canal, when they were successful in landing 10,000 fish, principally roach. There were a few trout, none of them less than 7 in., which were put into the top lake. The others, which included some king carp 2½ lb. each, and a few good tench, were placed in the Waterloo Lake.—W. INGHAM, T. HUNTER, Hon. Secs.

Thomas Ford was the proprietor of the Manor Fishery, at Caistor, in Lincolnshire. His operations began in 1880 and, although his initial occupation was mainly concerned with trout breeding, he clearly was the leading supplier of other species, including king carp, golden orfe, golden tench, goldfish, burbot, salmon, sunfish char and black bass! Indeed, it may very well have been the case that the Manor Fishery was one of very few commercial suppliers of king carp around this time. Certainly, the coarse fish section of his business flourished and, by the early-1900's, it became his principal activity.

> **SEASON, 1889.**
>
> **PRICE LIST.**
>
> The more common kinds of Coarse Fish, viz., roach, dace, perch, carp, tench, gudgeon, bream, gold fish, &c., are supplied at convenient intervals during the autumn and winter, from 20s. to 40s. per 100, according to size. Full Price List on application.
>
> The price of Pike is special.
>
> Fish Meat, carriage paid, 28s. per cwt. 32s. for Fry. Small quantities 6d. per lb.
>
> Terms:—Cash on delivery, and carriage will, unless otherwise arranged, have to be paid by the purchaser.
>
> N.B.—The Manager is prepared to visit and advise with Gentlemen about to lay out Fisheries. Terms on application. Hatching Apparatus supplied.
>
> Address:—THOMAS FORD,
>   Manor Fishery,
>   CAISTOR, Lincolnshire.

ANGLING NOTES.
By W. A. Greensmith.

XV.

I have received several letters this week with reference to the project of placing carp, tench, and rudd in the river Ancholme for the purpose of increasing the variety of fish therein, and at the same time the chance of obtaining a good day's sport on this splendid stretch of water, which is well qualified as a habitat for the above named fish.

Mr Thos. Ford, of Caistor, writes that he would supply 500 carp and 500 tench of from two to four inches long, delivered anywhere between Brandy Wath and Brigg for £11. Carp and tench will travel quite safely in cold weather.

Mr Ford thinks it would be perhaps as well to stick to carp and tench this time. Mr A Mountain, solicitor, Grimsby, reports having taken a carp this week at Croxby pond weighing 13lbs 10oz, and in perfectly clear water, and he also caught one on his last visit there weighing 3lbs. Mr Ford adds that if this can be done at Croxby, surely we may hope for something out of the Ancholme. It rests entirely with the anglers themselves.

I am glad to hear from Mr Alfred Atkinson, of Brigg, that the Ancholme Commissioners do not object to the proposal of placing carp, tench, and rudd in the river for the purpose of breeding, and I hope they will eventually not object to assist us in carrying out this very desirable project.

Mr Alfred Whiteside, of Brigg, kindly writes me on the same subject, and thinks it will be a pity if the matter should be allowed to drop through. As Mr Whiteside is well known to most of the Gainsborough and Sheffield anglers, and is a great lover of the "gentle art" himself, I know he will do his best to further this object, and, indeed, he has kindly promised to do so, and if all the anglers who visit the Ancholme would only assist, the matter would very soon be accomplished. If possible, the fish should be put in this month.

As stated before, the editor of the *Hull News* will acknowledge all subscriptions received for this purpose.

The following amounts have already been promised: Messrs Thos Ford (Caistor) 21s, C E Duncan 5s, E Stubb 2s 6d, J T Tindall 2s 6d, C S Nowell 2s 6d, W Phillipson 2s 6d, Piscator 2s 6d.

Ancholme District.—We have had some delightful showers, and all nature seems refreshed. The angling event of the week has been the capture of another of those large carp at Croxby Lake. This fish was caught on Monday last by Mr. H. Barker, of Grimsby, and weighed just over 13lb. The best dish of trout of which I have heard consisted of eleven fish, weighing just under 7lb.; the two largest fish were about 1lb. each. Prospects are very good for the commencement of coarse fishing on the 16th inst. The Ancholme is exceedingly well stocked; 350 King carp were turned out a few months ago by the Commissioners.—Thomas Ford.

NEWS FOR HULL ANGLERS.

FRESH VARIETIES FOR THE RIVER HULL.

[BY A SPECIAL CONTRIBUTOR.]

Saturday last was a red letter day in the history of the River Hull, from a piscatorial point of view. The Hull Angling Preservation Society having decided to spend a considerable sum of money in the stocking of the above river with fish, arrangements were made with the manager of the Manor Fisheries, Caistor, Lincolnshire, to supply the society with two new varieties of fresh water and sporting fish, and four of Ford's patent fish carriers containing two hundred grayling and one hundred and fifty king carp arrived at the Corporation Pier, and were quickly despatched to the Paragon Station en route for Lockington, with the exception of fifty carp, which were forwarded to the society's ponds in Inglemire Lane. At Lockington Station the fish were placed in a vehicle, and the four miles journey over rough country roads was accomplished in due course, and without the loss of a single fish, which were apparently in the most healthy condition. Several members of the society, together with other angling friends, assisted to get the fish on board the ferry boat, and this was towed to a suitable portion of the river at Wilfholme Ferry, and the fish transferred to their new abode. The honour of placing the first grayling and carp in the river Hull fell to the following Hull anglers, viz., Mr C. Wurr (Victoria Club), secretary of the Society; Mr G. Schofield (Universal), Mr. A. Wrightson (Victoria), Messrs. C. Gamwell and T. Leng (Marlborough), Messrs. F. Christopher, and W. Biglin (Grapes), and Mr J. Walters. The Loch Leven trout will be placed in the river in the same place in about three weeks' time, Mr. Ford not being able to send them at the same time as the above. The best thanks of the society are due to the manager of the M. S. and L. Railway at the Pier, and to Mr. E. L. Davis, of the North-Eastern Railway for the facilities granted in ensuring the quick despatch of the fish; to Mr. W. F. Turner, of the White Horse Hotel, Carr Lane, for providing vehicles; to Mr. Cooper, of Wilfholme, for similar services, and the many willing and interested anglers who generally rendered assistance, and particularly Mr Wurr, the secretary, for the excellent arrangements, which tended to make the whole affair a success.

Left: Reports in 'The Hull News' and 'The Fishing Gazette' of 1893 concerning the stocking of the River Ancholme in Lincolnshire with king carp. Croxby Pond is also mentioned. The details in the 'Fishing Gazette' were provided by Thomas Ford himself.
Top: A further item from 'The Hull News', in the December 19th, 1896 issue, which demonstrates the interest at that time in stocking with king carp. The report also suggests that grayling were not indigenous to the River Hull system as is now believed.

One of the earliest documented accounts of Mr. Ford supplying king carp (2in.-4in. fish) was to Mr. H. Smith-Bosanquet's lakes, at Broxbornebury, in the late-1890's. In 1902 these lakes were netted and 80 king carp, averaging 5lb. were transferred to the Carthegena Weir Pool, at Broxborne, on the River Lee. Also in 1902 Mr. Ford reported that he "had a large crop of these fish available" which suggests that he may have been breeding them himself, although the author has some doubts about this since his farm used water flowing from the chalk downs of the Hundon estate. This cold spring water would have been ideal for the breeding and rearing of trout but less than ideal for carp. It would have been more likely that the fish were obtained from the continent, as clearly must have been the case with the sunfish and black bass. Whatever, Mr. Ford appeared quite proud of his ability to supply king carp and made mention of their fast growth rate, claiming they often reached 6lb. in three years in

England. He further noted that some he had sent to Valencia in Spain reached a weight of 30lb. in five years. The well-known Grimsby carp angler, Harry Sheckell, when writing to Dick Walker in 1950, stated "the only ponds or pits that contain carp in this district were stocked years ago by a Mr. Ford who had fish hatcheries at a village 12 miles from here. He was possibly the best known breeder of fish in the whole country and it was a thousand pities that his place just outside Caistor was not kept up after his death."

Thomas Ford clearly established a flourishing business supplying the demand for carp and other coarse fish. The claim, made by the noted carp expert Chris Yates, that "before....the 1920's there was no real market or special interest in the species" is manifestly erroneous. King carp had been stocked in a great many waters by this time including (in addition to those mentioned earlier) the River Ancholme (1893), the River Hull (1896), the Hampshire Avon (1897), Warren Pond at Chingford (1904), the Great Ouse (1906 by Thomas Ford) and the Crystal Palace Boating Lake (1908), and were growing to a good size.

Aldermaston Lake, near Reading, was found to contain a number of king carp, the largest weighing 22½lb., 19½lb., 16lb. and 15lb. when it was drained in December 1911. Examples of other waters, in which king carp were being caught prior to 1920, were the Burdsley Canal (1901), Stumford Lake (1901), the River Colne at Rickmansworth (1903), Wright's Pit, at Boston (1912) and the Buckshole Reservoir, at Hastings (1912).

Some of the stock ponds at Thomas Ford's Manor Fishery in 1903.

After the death of Thomas Ford, in 1907, The Manor Fishery was purchased by the company which owned, amongst several others, The Surrey Trout Farm and, during the following year, all the farms owned by this company were amalgamated under the title of The Surrey Trout Farm & United Fisheries Ltd. They acknowledged, in one of their annual circulars a little time later, that the experience and traditions regarding the different species of coarse fish handled by Mr. Ford had been of service to the Company in building up this branch of the business. It would appear, therefore, that Thomas Ford was the principle architect of the early commercial introductions and distribution of king carp in this country, and that his comprehensive knowledge and business connections were subsequently utilised by the Surrey Trout Farm.

The Surrey Trout Farm in 1908 when it was under the management of F.G. Richmond. It was formed in 1863 and owned by Thomas Andrews who bred and raised trout, char and grayling on a large scale. He also cultivated vast quantities of snails and shrimps which were sold.

The Origins & Introduction of Carp into Britain

Left: Advert for the Manor Fishery from 'The Angler's News' in 1891. Thomas Ford was possibly importing his king carp from Holland at this time.

Below: Separate adverts for each fish farm in December 1907, just prior to the Surrey Trout Farm taking control of the Manor Fishery shortly after the death of Mr. Ford.

Above: An advert from February, 1908, just after the merging of the two companies.

Above and Right: Sale of some ponds previously leased by the Surrey Trout Farm in February, 1909. There was a dispute in the angling press at the time between the two parties, with their solicitors issuing statements. It revolved around both sites using Shottermill as their postal address and the possible confusion this might create

Left: An advert that appeared in November, 1951 issue of 'The Fishing Gazette', shortly after Bob Richards caught his record carp from Bernithan Court Pool.

14

Another importer of fish, mainly specialising in ornamentals, was L. Cura, who began his business in 1859. He was a pioneer of the goldfish craze, which began in about 1894, importing around 14,000 per week from Italy. The Surrey Trout Farm sometimes obtained fish from Cura & Sons, mainly goldfish, and this memo, enquiring about trade prices for king carp, tench and golden orfe, was addressed to Don Leney's partner, Mr. F. W. Stevens. Cura was charging 50/- for 100 4in. king carp and 4/- per lb. for fish between 5lb. and 8lb. in the 1920's.

This importer, that Don Leney occasionally dealt with, sold king carp up to 5in. in length, as well as other cold-water fish.

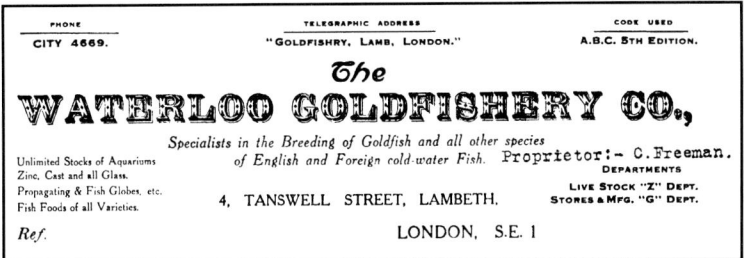

The Surrey Trout Farm & United Fisheries, Ltd.,
SHOTTERMILL, HASLEMERE.

MISCELLANEOUS FISH.

Current Prices on Rail. Carriage Forward. October, 1909.

Fish.	Sizes and Prices.	When Supplied.
Gold Fish	2 to 4-in., 20/- ; 3 to 5-in., 40/- ; 4 to 6-in., 60/- per 100	nearly all the year.
Gold Orfe	2 to 4-in., 20/- ; 4 to 6-in., £5 per 100	,,
Gold Tench	2 to 4-in., 20/- ; 4 to 6-in., £8 per 100	,,
Dace	6 to 8-in., 25/- per 100	Sept. to March
Roach	4 to 6-in., 10/- ; 5 to 8-in., 18/- ; 6 to 9-in., 22/- per 100	,,
Rudd	4 to 6-in., 20/- per 100	,,
Bream	4 to 6-in., 20/- ; 5 to 8-in., 30/- ; 6 to 9-in., 40/- per 100.	,,
Common Carp	2 to 4-in., 15/- ; 3 to 5-in., 25/- per 100	,,
King Carp	2 to 4-in., 20/- ; 3 to 5-in., 40/- per 100	,,
Prussian Carp	2 to 4-in., 15/- ; 4 to 6-in., 30/- per 100	,,
Perch	2 to 4-in., 20/- ; 3 to 6-in., 25/- ; 4 to 7-in., 30/- per 100	,,
Tench	2 to 4-in., 20/- ; 3 to 6-in., 25/- ; 4 to 7-in., 30/- per 100	,,
Pike	About 5-ins., £2 ; 9 to 11-ins., £7 10s. per 100	,,
Burbot	6 to 16-ins., 1/6 each	
Cray Fish	Average size, 20/- per 100	Sept. to Dec.
Minnows	25/- per 1,000 ; £5 per 5,000	Sept. to March
Eels	About 9 to 18-ins., 30/- per 100	May and June

The Surrey Trout Farm's price list for coarse fish, in 1909, not long after they had taken over the business of Thomas Ford.

The Origins & Introduction of Carp into Britain

Donald F. Leney joined The Surrey Trout Farm in 1923, the business having been established since 1867. Initially, he was employed at the Nailsworth site, working under its manager, F.W. Stephens. After a period Leney managed to raise enough funds to purchase a partnership share of the Nailsworth farm and was later joined in the venture by Mr. Stephens. Leney soon discovered that the company had previously been importing carp from Holland but that this had, understandably, come to a halt during the First World War. By 1925[1] Donald Leney had managed to get things going again and had arranged to import carp from a first-class establishment near Vaassen, in Holland, called the Nederlandsche Heidemaatschappij (Donald Leney acknowledged to the author that The Surrey Trout Farm had probably been importing carp from this same source prior to the 1914-18 War).

A netting party at the Nailsworth site in 1947 where the yearling carp for Redmire Pool were collected by Col. Barnardiston and his wife. Second from the right is F.W. Stephens who became a partner of Don Leney in the business. Carp were held at the Haslemere farm and stock was transferred to the others farms when required.

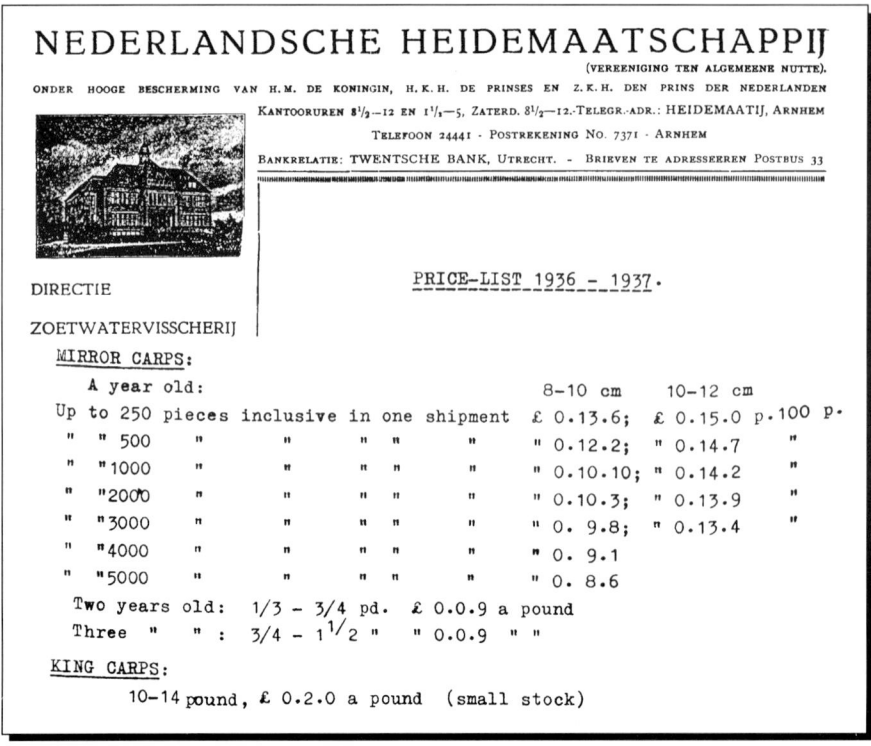

A 1936-37 price list for carp from the Dutch fish farm that Don Leney visited each year.

---

1. Stated as 1925 in a letter to Richard Walker, reproduced in 'Drop Me A Line'. However, the year 1926 was stated in personal communication with the author in 1976.

The Origins & Introduction of Carp into Britain

Don Leney personally visited the Dutch farm each year bringing back his requirements until the outbreak of the Second World War, in 1939. Subsequently, he resumed in 1947 and continued importing from Vaassen, until 1955,[1] when it closed down production. For a while he carried on bringing small carp in from a supplier in Belgium, but he did not feel the fish were of as good quality.

Much has been made of the Galician pedigree of the carp imported by Leney from the Nederlandsche Heidemaatschappij, and there can be no doubt about the quality of such fish. It has already been pointed out that supplies of carp from Leney after 1955 would almost certainly not be of the same stock. But, not all the carp stocked by Leney during the period 1925-55 were of the Galician race. For example, in October/November 1935, The Surrey Trout Farm dispatched, by rail, 110 14in.-16in. common carp to Billing Aquadrome. These clearly did not originate from the Dutch farm and when the author queried this with Donald Leney in 1975 he agreed, writing:

"Thinking back, I now realise that date was just too early to have been able to get them from Holland in the usual batch. These Billing fish would have to have come from emptying some Surrey/Sussex or local water."

The Galician carp is one of a number of well-known European 'races', having evolved over many decades through artificial selection. The term 'race' is used to describe a cultivated species of fish having certain hereditary characteristics and generally originating from the same region. The Galician carps' origins are from an area just north of the Carpathian mountains, in south-eastern Poland and the western Ukrainian region of what used to be the U.S.S.R. Other established races include the Bohemian, Aischgrund, Lausitz, Hungarian and Franconian; and it is simply incorrect to suggest, as has been done many times by Redmire enthusiasts, that the Galician stock is intrinsically superior to these other well-established races.

Perhaps one of the least appreciated aspects of Donald Leney's work was the sheer number of waters stocked with carp by The Surrey Trout Farm whilst it was under his auspices. Many thousands of ponds, lakes, rivers and canals were stocked, in every conceivable part of the country. From the Isle of Wight to Devon and Cornwall; from Worcester to Runcorn and from Todmorden to Dartford. From 250 yearlings to the Surrey Sand & Gravel Co. in December 1930,

The Surrey Trout Farm's lorry being used to deliver a large order of fish in the 1930's. Small consignments could either be collected or they were dispatched in basket cans using the railway system.

to the numerous stockings made by Raymond Perrett in the Bridgewater area. From the 1,600 yearlings for Bromley-Davenport's Capesthorne Hall Lakes to the many thousands purchased by the Essex and Kent River Boards in 1956. From the 36 yearlings sold to Dick Kefford, in April 1951, to the 2,000 sold to the North Harrow Waltonians, in November, 1955.

1. Stockings of carp from The Surrey Trout Farm after 1955 were, therefore, extremely unlikely to derive from the Dutch Galician source. This corrects a misconception, held by a number of people such as Bob Preedy, who stated in the B.C.S.G. magazine, in 1987, that 25 Leney carp of the type that went into Redmire and Billing were stocked into his local gravel pit in 1958.

The Origins & Introduction of Carp into Britain

The Surrey Trout Farm's 12 sales ledgers (now the property of Chris Yates), each holding hundreds of entries, are a veritable Who's Who of carp fishing. On one trip, prior to the Second World War, Leney actually imported from Holland 80 cans, held in baskets, of mainly young carp. The cans were stocked with 250 four-inch fish, so this could have amounted to 20,000 carp! It must have been the case that the vast bulk of the introductions came to nothing. Unsuitable habitats, adverse winters, inordinate predation—these must all have played a part. We now know that the survival of one-summer old carp is not good if they are moved and disturbed unduly during their first winter and, clearly, the bulk of The Surrey Trout Farm's introductions were of this type made at this time of the year.

Donald Leney's trips to Holland, each late-autumn, resulted in 40-60 cans being brought back, depending upon his orders. As a rough guide he charged three times what the fish cost him in Holland. One-third for the purchase of the fish, one-third for transport costs and the final third for his profit! He remembered that "in those days when labour was plentiful and the Railway's staff very helpful, a consignment of 60 fish cans, each weighing 100-112lb., was easily transported, providing one made careful arrangements for handling beforehand—laying-on of goods vans on a pre-set timetable, and even horse-drawn vans to transfer the lot from Liverpool Street station to Waterloo." Most of the fish were delivered fairly soon after arriving in this country, although The Surrey Trout Farm had some small wintering ponds that would hold a limited quantity of carp for distribution throughout the winter.

The Surrey Trout Farm's first coarse fish price list after the First World War. This came about as a direct consequence of Don Leney's interest in re-establishing and developing this side of the business.

Imported fish being checked at the railway station in 1936.

He generally brought back the best grown summer's stock, fish of 4-5in. in length overall (from nose to tip of tail). Occasionally, he included some of the poorer growing fish, 3-4in. but found that these did "not really give good results and survival after wintering unless planted into ideal conditions." Very occasionally, in an exceptionally hot summer, he obtained some 5-7in. fish. He also brought back, to a lesser extent, some two-summer-old carp. These would generally average between 6-9in. in overall length and weigh somewhere between 8oz. and 16oz. (The 3-5in. one-summer fish would weigh about 2oz.). In later years, Donald Leney stocked some local lakes with 4in. fish and cropped them three years later as 2-4lb. fish. At times he managed to get his hands on larger fish and, on one occasion, in 1926, provided the London Zoo Aquarium for its opening with six king carp weighing between 10-20lb. each, which he imported from the Dutch fish farm. The largest, a leather carp, weighed 21lb., and was over 30in. in length. It had been reared on the farm and its age was known to be 30 years. These fish would almost certainly have been breeding stock whose reproductive products, at this age, would be considered less than satisfactory.

Another fish farm that Don Leney occasionally purchased carp from, this one is in France. The company letterhead dates from 1927. Notice the deep, high-hump backed fish that they produced, as distinct from the Galician race that Leney imported from the farm at Vasseen, in Holland.

The small carp obtained by The Surrey Trout Farm from Holland comprised mainly mirrors and leathers, although there were a small number of common scaled carp amongst them. Donald Leney in later years became a bit confused on this point. In 1975 he wrote to the author that "The Dutch Galician carp were **all** leathers and mirrors, but **never** all-scaled." A year later this became "almost all their young stocks were mirrors and leathers, only a very few all-scalers ever resulted." Finally, in 1978 he contradicted himself again writing, "one thing I am positive about—that only mirrors and leathers were ever sent to Redmire, for the Dutch farm only bred that type and from what I can remember I never saw "all-scalers" amongst the yearlings or 2-year olds when I went to select them each winter before bringing them back myself." This should not be taken as criticism of a man whose influence did much to shape the destiny of carp fishing in this country. Memories become hazy, especially in later life, and Donald Leney was 78 years old when he made the last statement. Obtaining factual information from any individual, after a long period of time has elapsed, is fraught with difficulty. When the author pointed out to Richard Walker that he had, over the period of a year, given two differing accounts of a particular event at Redmire Pool, he wrote that, "Memory is indeed fallible, especially when one has to go back 25 years or so! I think you will have to avoid positive statements of your own in some cases and simply write 'according to so-and-so' or 'as far as I can discover'. All historians are faced with such problems and there's only one thing they can be sure of, which is that they can never hope to be one hundred percent right."

One of the most alluring features of the Dutch Galician carp introduced into Redmire was the small percentage of linear carp found amongst them. This rather rare but attractive form is little cultivated nowadays on European fish farms due to its somewhat poorer viability

The Origins & Introduction of Carp into Britain

One of many stockings of carp from The Surrey Trout Farm that took place till about 1968.

and growth rate, yet is often confused by anglers with those mirror carp having an irregular pattern of scales in the general area of the lateral line. The true linear, or line, carp has a continuous, straight and quite regular row of scales along the lateral line. Work carried out at the Department of Genetics and Selection, in Moscow, by Kirpicnikov and Balkasina, as long ago as 1937, on the Mendelian relationship between the principal genes affecting the scaling of Galician carp, show us that for the Dutch fish farm to produce linear carp it must also have produced 'all-scalers'. Now, it is quite possible that, for some obscure reason, the farm decided to destroy as many of the common carp as it could, once it managed to isolate them at the end of the summer, but this would be extremely wasteful both in terms of labour and resources. If the farm had wanted to fully eradicate the common carp from their stocks they could have achieved this simply by using just mirror carp as their breeding stock. Furthermore, when the Dutch Government's Organisatie Ter Verbetering Van De Binnenvisserij (Organisation for the Improvement of Inland Fisheries) took over the management of the Nederlandse Heidemaatschappij fish farms in 1957, it was found that the carp stocks were comprised of common, mirror, linear and leather types, and that some of the brood (parent) stock consisted of linear carp. The use of these would have ensured a percentage of common scaled carp in their offspring. Finally, statements made at the time by recipients of small king carp from The Surrey Trout Farm, introduced prior to 1955, show that common carp did indeed form a proportion of the stock.

There is no doubt that Donald Leney was a very knowledgeable carp culturist, and letters he wrote on the subject, between 1928 and 1950, clearly demonstrate that he was an influential and recognised authority in this country at that time. Dick Walker appreciated this fact, and the detailed correspondence that ensued between them allowed the pervasive Walker to assimilate further information that enriched his understanding of the species.

Don Leney working in his study at Haslemere. His special interest in carp resulted in good quality, disease free stocks being made available.

20

Chapter 2
Some Early Notable Carp Fisheries

If you aspire to the highest place,
it is no disgrace to stop at the second,
or even the third, place.
          Cicero from On Oratory (55 B.C.)

Successful carp fishing has always been dependent upon the availability of a prolific fishery. Indeed, the structure of this book has been laid out in such a way as to show how developments in carp fishing have, until relatively recently, taken place in a series of spasmodic advances on specific waters. But history only shows us what has been remembered or recorded. Influential events have so many times slipped by like fleeting images on a dark night. Ever since the time when carp were first introduced into this country there must have been those who contrived their capture. Many of them went about their quest in isolation, the feats of others have faded with the passage of time. Some received notoriety in angling books and in periodicals, although angling magazines did not become readily available until just before the turn of the century. One of the first, and certainly the longest running, was *The Fishing Gazette* which began on the 26th April, 1877. This was closely followed by *The Angler's Journal* in 1883, *Fishing* in 1886, *Angling and Club Gossip* in 1893, *The Northern Angler* in 1894 and *The Angler's News* on the 1st September, 1900.

So many periodicals have come and gone, and the stories of great battles, of tremendous feats in those distant times, lie dormant in dark attics and on dusty shelves. But some remain to stir the soul and fire the spirit. If we puff away the cobwebs and settlement of years, and turn the ragged brown and brittle pages; if we settle into the seductive embrace of an old, familiar armchair in front of a log fire of dancing flames and, with a glass of fine wine to hand, we can drift back to those bygone times. Give your imagination free rein and taste the excitement as Sir Robert Harvey, fishing the Black Park, at Uxbridge, lands three carp weighing a total of 40½lb., upon a memorable day in 1886. The fish were dispatched to the taxidermist and put on display in the Black Horse Hotel, at Kingston Hill.

A much earlier, prolific fishery once existed in the unusual carp area of Cumbria, situated between the towns of Penrith and Carlisle. In Chaucer's day (1340-1400) the 100 acre Tarn Walding was reputed to hold the largest carp in the county and some of the finest in the whole country.

The River Thames has, since the earliest introductions to this country, held breeding stocks of carp. It has always grown big ones too; in 1739 a 13-pounder was caught near Hampton Court and, in 1883, Travis-Jenkins mentions one of 20lb. in his book, *Fishes of the British Isles*. This was caught at Wallingford, where William the Conqueror received the acknowledgement of the Church after the Battle of Hastings. Patrick Chalmers, in his delightful book about the Thames, *At the Tail of the Weir*, (1932) mentions another carp of 20lb., caught at Benson, which may be referring to the same capture. Chalmers also states that carp were first put in the Thames in 1490 but this is probably attributable to a date given in the

Early Notable Carp Fisheries

work of Berners. Charles Wheeley, a one-time professional fisherman on the Thames, mentioned in his book *Coarse Fish,* two fine carp caught at Shepperton Lock in 1896, and another one a few years later caught nearby, at Halliday's Hole. He also recommends Teddington Weir and Boveney Weir. In 1951 M. Millard had a fine catch of three, weighing 14lb. 2oz., 15lb. and 16lb. 15oz., and in 1961 a 17½-pounder was reported to the angling press. In October, 1965 Major A. Sawyer landed one of 24lb. on breadcrust, from Laleham, followed in December, 1969 by Arthur McIntosh who reported catching a mirror carp weighing 28lb. from the warm water outfall at Sonning Lock, near Reading. Then, in October, 1972, came the first reported 30-pounder. It was caught by Allen Campion, again from the productive warm water outfall at Sonning Lock, and fell for crust on a no. 2 hook to 10lb. line. There is no doubt that London's River still holds some huge carp, fish weighing over 30lb., but they are just as difficult to catch as in Chalmers' day.

The lakes and pools on the Earl of Bradford's estate, at Weston Park, Weston-under-Lizard, also had quite a reputation for big carp during the latter part of the last century. A fish of 22lb. was caught in 1872 and a painting of one of 19½lb., resides in the Hall itself and was caught from the lake called White Sitch.

Another fishery which has a long association with carp is Broadwater Pond, near Godalming, in Surrey. In 1899 a fish of 23lb. 1oz. was caught from this 11 acre, fairly shallow fishery by J. Holden, which was probably a British record. For some reason this fish was ignored a few years later by those who claimed the British record for John Andrews' Cheshunt carp. In those distant days the dissemination of information was rather isolated and restricted. There was no official body set up to adjudicate on, or recognise, record fish. For a fish to become established as a record, it required acceptance by one of the influential angling magazines and, in 1916, this came down to *The Fishing Gazette* and, to a lesser extent, *The Angler's News.* The Highbury A.S., that controlled Cheshunt Reservoir, had many influential members, and their captures received the fullest coverage in the aforementioned magazines.

Kenny Ewington, Jack Hilton's brother-in-law, with an 11¼-pounder from Broadwater Lake. Kenny often fished the lake with Roger Smith in the early 1960's.

Broadwater Lake continued to produce good sized carp; for example F. Johnson caught one of 16lb. 10oz. in June, 1949 and D.W. Holt landed a 19-pounder, taken on paste, in June, 1955. But further stockings of Broadwater Pond, with king carp, saw the lake develop into a very prolific fishery where huge catches, of mainly small carp, have been made.

In about 1904 the small, shallow Warren Pond, which lies in a hollow opposite the Royal Forest Hotel, at Chingford, was drained and restocked with a number of king carp from Germany. The fish were claimed to be "scaleless and weighing up to 5lb." In any event two years later a leather carp, weighing 4lb. 8oz. was caught by A.H. Allen and sent to the taxidermist. The remaining fish continued to grow and breed and, in July, 1918, one of 10¼lb. was landed by C.A. Fisher, then followed, in September of that year, by a larger carp

Early Notable Carp Fisheries

J.T. Fisher's mirror carp of 19½lb. caught in July, 1919 and set-up by Homer's of Forest Gate, London. Epping Forest's Warren Pond first came into existence through gravel excavation in the mid-19th century. It was later enlarged in about 1910-20, after it was taken over by The London Corporation, partly to provide work for the local unemployed. Siltation of the shallow pond has gradually allowed encroachment by reeds, alder and willow shrub.

of 13½lb. caught by Mr. Peters. On the 8th July, 1919 one of 19½lb. was captured by J.T. Fisher and, no doubt, by this time the fishery was the object of considerable attention. A few years later, on the 14th August 1926, A.E. Wyatt caught his 21lb. 10oz. carp which displaced the Cheshunt 'record'. There appears to have been some of those in the Cheshunt club who were not too happy with the Wyatt fish being accepted as the record and, at the following A.G.M. of the Red Spinners claims were made that the fish was "dropsical." In fact, the newspaper reports at the time clearly disprove this, although they remark that the fish "presented a curious appearance being distended greatly, and on being opened up was found to contain 11lb. of ova. It had, it is thought, become spawn-bound."

But big fish remained in Warren Pond for some years after. On Christmas Eve, 1933, a Mr. Cowie and Bernard T. Ward discovered, and removed, a large mirror carp weighing 21lb. from under the ice. The fish was put on display in the Queen Elizabeth's Hunting Lodge, at Chingford. With a remarkable coincidence, 17 years later, Bernard Ward discovered another carp under the ice, again on Christmas Eve. It weighed 16lb., with a length of 29in., and, being alive, was returned to the water. This prodigious, tiny pond was still producing good-sized carp in July, 1949, when F. Alderton caught a 13½-pounder, and demonstrates how king carp can prosper in almost any environment.

The two carp discovered under the ice at Warren Pond. The larger fish, weighing 21lb., was found dead, whilst the 16-pounder was returned alive but died some time later. Both fish are now part of an educational dispaly belonging to The London Corporation. The upper fish is actually a plaster cast, the lower carp being the preserved skin.

Early Notable Carp Fisheries

The Royal Park lakes have always been associated with carp. During the 1st World War, one of the lakes at Hampton Court, built by the authority of Cardinal Wolsey, was drained and a fish of 37lb. was found stranded. This was the largest known example of the species in this country, until Richard Walker's 44-pounder. It was, apparently, eaten by German prisoners. The extensive Virginia Water, in Windsor Great Park, produced another large carp in 1912 weighing 26½lb., and the Long Water, also located at Hampton Court, was renowned for its carp up to about 15lb., which were caught regularly around this time. Probably one of the most picturesque waters in London, the Long Water, which was about 200 yards in length, some six feet in depth and bounded by a magnificent avenue of trees, also had the distinction of producing what must have been, for many years, one of the largest carp caught by a 12 year-old boy—a fish of 16lb. taken in 1927.

An early photograph of Hampton Court's Long Water.

Other popular London carp fisheries at this time were Wimbledon Park Lake, where excessive groundbaiting was humorously suggested to have "altered the depth of 'Carp Corner' of late!" and Rushmere Pond, on Wimbledon Common. The lakes at Crystal Palace and the ponds in Bushy Park were also known to hold carp, and a fish of 20lb. was reported having been caught from the small Diana Pool in 1890. Some 67 years later this same tiny pond also stunned the angling world by producing a 5lb. 12oz. perch.

The Upper and Lower Penn Ponds, right in the centre of Richmond Park, London's largest Royal Park, were also considered excellent carp fisheries at the turn of this century, although its fish were described by the knowledgeable Charles Wheeley (who had a Hardy rod named after him) as "perhaps the shyest in the kingdom—to catch a Penn Pond carp is a feather in your cap." The ponds were regularly visited by a number of dedicated carp anglers, amongst them being Mr. J. Goodwin and Mr. R.W. Wellman, the latter catching one of 9lb. 11oz. in 1908.

The formidable A.R. Matthews, editor of *The Angler's News* described his own efforts so:

"I must confess that, although I have done my best to catch a carp at Richmond Park, I have not gone in for this branch of the art of angling with the cunning and enthusiasm of some of the carp-hunters to be met with there. These anglers are carp specialists. During my various visits to the Penn Ponds I have noticed their many interesting little dodges, their special tackle, and the quiet, careful and deliberate way in which they have participated in their sport. Not a few of the carp anglers are out in the morning by the water, but the majority of the 'old hands' select the

Marjorie Matthews, The Angler's News editor's daughter, fishing for carp in Richmond Park's Penn Pond in 1910.

evening for their operations, fishing right on until nine o'clock, when, according to the park regulations, all rods must be taken in. In September and October[1]—two excellent months for carp—this means that darkness has set in for some time, but unmindful of nightfall, the enterprising anglers continue their lonely vigil.

Big carp, large bait, is the carp angler's motto. Boiled potato, worms, gentles, and other lures are tried at Penn Ponds, but from what I have been able to gather, paste is the lure *par excellence* there."

A list of carp caught from Richmond Park in 1910

10lb. 15oz.	Mr. Light
10lb. 14oz.	Mr. T.H. Needham
9lb. 15oz.	Mr. J. Goodwin
9lb. 14oz.	Mr. J. Goodwin
7lb. 0oz.	Mr. W. Wellman
7lb. 0oz.	Mr. Young
6lb. 4oz.	Mr. W. Wellman

Mr. Goodwin appears to have acquired a notable reputation as a carp catcher around this time, for Francis Francis[2] also mentions him as an authority some years earlier in his 1867 *A Book on Angling* stating: "Mr. Goodwin, of Hampton Court, assured me that he has made some wonderful takes of very large carp, up to fourteen or fifteen pounds weight each, with potato, in the canal in the park there."

Charles Wheeley, a member of the Piscatorial Society, adds in his excellent book *Coarse Fish*, that the carp anglers of Penn Ponds often "throw out a very long way, coiling or spreading the line on the gravel path between the two ponds." Clearly, they believed this was necessary, as Wheeley did himself, because "carp live to a very great age, and the older they are the shyer they get. In shallow ponds their caution is excessive, the largest fish hardly ever moving from the centre, or deepest water, in the daytime, but coming quietly to the sides to feed in the late dusk of the evening."

Mr. J. Goodwin, the Richmond Park carp veteran legering at long range in 1910 with "a piece of paste, not of a marble or pea size, but more the size of a hen's egg."

The Penn Ponds were regrettably drained during the Second World War and their stocks of carp transferred elsewhere.

1. It is interesting to note that many successful modern-day anglers, including Gibbinson and Hutchinson, are in agreement that these months are particularly productive.
2. The highly regarded Francis Francis was actually born Francis Morgan. His mother had a wealthy step-father named Francis Francis, and Francis Morgan became the beneficiary of his estate upon his death, provided he changed his name to Francis Francis when reaching the age of 21. Francis sustained the view that carp could not be caught on coarse tackle, writing that "the angler is compelled to fish as finely as possible." This belief was widely held until Richard Walker came along and convinced the angling public that it was impractical and, in most cases, unnecessary. Walker, however, blamed Albert Buckley for the "shocking blow" his Mapperley success had dealt to carp fishing, when, in fact, Buckley was only accepting the dogma already laid down by Francis Francis, Denys Watkins-Pitchford and others.

Early Notable Carp Fisheries

Another river, which built up a strong reputation as a carp fishery in the early part of the century, was the Somerset Brue. Although never producing very large fish, carp to over 10lb. were being caught reasonably regularly—one of 11lb. as early as 1912, by W.F. Dunkley, at Highbridge, and another of 13¼lb. to H. St. John Durston, in 1915. Several more, in 1918, fell to the rod of M.J. Eddolls, and similar catches continued at least until after the 2nd. World War. Three, out of a total of only seven, reported in the 1941 *Angler's News* Notable Fish List, came from the Brue—the largest weighing 13lb. 12oz., was caught by Mr. King, and was the second best reported that year. Joe Brown, of the Sparkhill A.S., landed several carp over 10lb. in the years 1945 and 1946, and fellow Birmingham townsman, Chas. Green, caught a 14-pounder—at that time only 1½lb. below the River Brue record. A productive area was around Bason Bridge where Brown and Green caught their fish. The outflow from a milk factory, which was situated close by, appeared to be an attraction for the carp. For a number of years it seemed that most of the carp would stay resident in

Mr. Eddolls, who caught a number of carp from the Somerset Brue in the early part of this century.

this area, but by the late-1940's they had changed their habits and spent more time roaming up and down other sections of the river. Spawning time saw a migration of carp to the upper reaches, this being reversed after the reproductive urge had been satisfied. The first three, or four, weeks of the season appeared to offer the best chances of success, as later in the season heavy weed growth and floating duckweed made fishing quite difficult.

Another river in Somerset, that at one time held big carp, was the River Parrett. The knowledgeable Raymond Perrett had weighed a mighty brace, prior to the last War, that went 19½lb. and 17½lb.

There can be few carp anglers who have not heard of Beechmere, the Old Copper Mine near Chagford, in Devon, that Denys Watkins-Pitchford brought to his readers attention in 1950, in a book about obsession, *Confessions of a Carp Fisher*. A sullen, brooding water nestling within the protection of high banks, clothed in beeches and oak, it was for him darkly sinister, yet powerfully fascinating.

The Hertfordshire Lee (nowadays usually referred to as the Lea) also had a reputation for large carp in the early part of this century. A London tackle dealer, L.J. Childs, is seen on the left with a fish of 15lb. 10oz. caught from the Broxbourne area. Mr. Childs, a member of the Clapton Fly Fishers & General A.C., caught the carp on the 6th August 1908, using paste, having his rod and landing net broken in the process.

B.B. was told about it by the well-informed Flt. Lt. Burton and first fished there in 1945 (shortly before Peter Mohan made his initial visit), by permission of the owner, Mr. Palmes.

Ted Burton was very fond of Beechmere, and described it as "the best place I know for carp." He remembered that it was controlled by the Exeter Angling Society who allowed day tickets, and gave the following advice about fishing it (which tells us a great deal about Burton's considerable carp fishing experience and understanding):

Carp fishing at Bradmere in 1946, on an unusually sunny day in a wet and windy summer. The Pool's beauty and sinister fascination exerted upon B.B. the greatest influence of all the carp waters he had known. In 1946 B.B. hooked "the monster of Beechmere."

"The place itself really is a 'picture-postcard' spot, and even one's wife would be content there. If you go to Bradmere you will get the best fish—anything up to 15lb.—with floating crust or flake. Grease a good silk line—say 8lb. b.s.—and tie an eyed hook (no. 6 I have found the best size) direct on the line—no gut at all. Use a fairly whippy (but not too whippy) rod to get the bait out. Have the wind, if any, behind you, and when you see where the fish are make a detour and come up as near as you can to the water under cover of trees or bushes. But don't show yourself at all.

Gently dip the bait in the water before casting—you get a little more weight that way. Cast so that your bait falls a short distance away from the fish, and have sufficient slack line for the drift to do the rest. When the bait is taken **don't strike**—just lift your rod and tighten—then let them run.

Honestly, you just can't hold the big ones at Bradmere. As careful as I've been I've lost more than I've caught—at least I'm honest—because they go off with such a tremendous run at the beginning. But it's marvellous sport and you can be certain of 'runs' which is more than you can say of some places!"

"...watching the hardly visible slender white tell-tale of my quill, I think of what is going on beneath those dark and baffling waters." — Denys Watkins-Pitchford from 'Confessions of a Carp Fisher'

No one now knows for sure when the carp were stocked in the cloudy-blue water of those flooded mine workings, but it would seem to have been somewhere between 1860 and 1900. It is possible that they were transferred from a very old lake nearby which had held carp from about 1760.

Maurice Ingham visited Beechmere during the summer of 1953, and shortly afterwards wrote the following in the Carp Catchers' Club's rotary letters:

"B.B.'s description (in *Confessions of a Carp Fisher*) owes nothing to his imagination, and Bradmere is without doubt the most unusual and attractive water it has ever been my privilege to fish. It had been raining steadily all day when I set off about 4pm on my 70-mile journey to Bradmere, and the prospects were anything but bright. Had I not been returning home a few days later I doubt if I should have gone at all, but the chance was too good to miss, so I decided to brave the elements. The rain fell in torrents throughout the journey but the moment I arrived at Bradmere, it ceased, the sky cleared and the sun shone. My first view of the pool was startling in its suddenness—I was carefully negotiating the hazardous path down the steep, tree-clad slope and then suddenly there was the pool twenty feet below me and a false step would have precipitated me into the dark depths. I chose a pitch at the 'shallow' end, threw out some mashed bread groundbait and some pieces of crust, and set up two rods. The hooks, baited with walnut-sized lumps of bread paste, were cast out to the baited spot and I settled down behind some convenient bushes to await events. I had not been waiting long when there was a terrific swirl out in the middle of the pool and one of my pieces of crust was taken with an almighty cloop. Almost immediately another piece disappeared in a similar manner, and then another; and it was only a matter of minutes before another crust was cast out to replace them, but this time it was attached to my hook! Several carp rose like dark shadows from the depths to inspect my crust and then sank back out of sight, but it was not long before one, perhaps more adventuresome or hungrier than the others, swam up to the bait, nosed it and then dashed off in panic as if alarmed by its own temerity. He did not go far, however, but soon turned round and began slowly, almost imperceptibly, to approach the bait again. This agonisingly slow approach continued

Maurice Ingham with his catch of five Beechmere carp taken on floating crust in the summer of 1953, the trip he remembers as "one of the most enjoyable carp fishing outings I have ever had."

until the fish was about a foot away from the bait, and there it stopped. I am sure no self-respecting insurance company would have issued a policy on my life if my pulse could have been taken at that moment, but, after what seemed hours—but was probably not more than thirty seconds—there was a blurred movement, a loud *sl-o-o-o-sh*, a gigantic swirl, the bread had gone and my line began to flash out through the rings. I tightened on the fish and the battle was joined—and what a battle it was! That fish weighed only 8½lb. but it put up a better fight than any fish of that weight I have caught before or since.

I took another fish of 5¾lb. on floating crust before nightfall and then I reverted to paste bait. During the short period of darkness I had a number of runs but missed all but three, which produced one carp of ¾lb. and five of ½lb. each—the smallest carp I have ever caught—dear little fellows, as bright and clean as a new shilling.

Soon after daybreak the carp began clooping again and I changed over to floating crust. I was obliged to leave Bradmere at 11am but before that time I had taken three more carp—of 10¼lb., 9¾lb., and 9¼lb. As I climbed the steep bank and took a last look down at the water I could see several carp cruising near the surface and I think I might have caught more if only I had been able to stay longer.

Looking back, I think it was one of the most enjoyable carp fishing outings I have ever had. The conditions and surroundings were perfect and although none of my fish was of great size, what they may have lacked in bulk they certainly made up for by their fighting qualities.

I don't know if Bradmere contains any really big carp. I saw none during my short stay, but it is a mysterious water of immense depth, and I would not be surprised to learn that it holds some real monsters."

The pool's character was refined by B.B.'s enthralling stories of its suicides, vast depth, "scurvy tricks" played by the stranger from "furrin parts", a phantom Catholic priest, and his friend, the wise postman, Jim Price. This was all marvellous stuff—grist to the mill for any budding carp fisher. And yet it had crossed the author's mind that, in the interests of historical accuracy, some of B.B.'s romantic licence should be contested. But why should it? This book is brimming with facts and figures, congested with dates and events—and isn't carp fishing more than that? Even for the entrenched cynic surely there is nothing wrong with a little escapism, a dash of mystery in an austere fare of bland documentation. So the real truth of Bradmere Pool will remain locked away, hidden from prying eyes.

"Father Angelus, in shovel hat and cassock, haunted Beechmere for many years."

Some Early References to Big Carp

Month	Year	Weight	Captor	Venue
	1739	13lb.		River Thames nr. Hampton Court
	1779	15½ lb.	John Batten's Master	
	1793	18lb.	netted	Lake at Stourhead or Stonehead (1)
Nov.	1822	21lb. 10oz.	netted	Bayham Abbey lake, Lamberhurst
Nov.	1836	22lb.	netted	Mere at Pain's Hill, Cobham, Surrey (2)
autumn	1858	24½lb.	netted	Great Pond at Harting, near Petersfield (3)
	1872	22lb.		Weston Park, Shropshire
	1872	24lb.		Great Pond at Harting, near Petersfield
	1881	21½lb.		
Nov.	1882	19lb.		Sheffield
Sept.	1883	20lb.		River Thames at Wallingford
	1885	"close on 20lb."		Wimbledon Lake
	1886	3 carp for 40½lb.		
	1887	24lb.		Lord Mostyn's Estate, North Wales
prior to	1889	19lb.	landing net	Captured by H. Cholmondeley-Pennell
	1890	20lb.	rod and line	Diana Pool, Hampton Court (4)
	1892	29lb.	netted	Great Pond at Harting, near Petersfield
5 Nov.	1894	18lb. 1oz.	W. Eady	Private lake at Windsor (5)
3 Jan.	1895	16lb.	H.B. Bowden-Smith	Milford Lake, Highdene
	1899	23lb. 1oz.	J. Holden	Broadwater Pond, Surrey
	1901	16lb.		Hampshire Avon
	1902	17lb.	Otto Overbeck	Croxby Pond, Lincolnshire
Aug.	1903	15lb. 13oz.	H.O. Box	Unknown (6)
March	1903	29lb.	found dead	Wytham Lake, Bourne, nr. Stamford
July	1904	17lb.		Lake at Home Park, Hampton Court
May	1905	27lb.	found dead	Pond near Farncombe, Surrey
	1907	20lb.		Surrey Pond
Sept.	1907	19½lb.	H.S. Locksmith	Weybridge Canal (7)
	1911	22½lb.	netted	Berkshire lake
Dec.	1911	22½lb. (king)	netted	Aldermaston Lake, near Reading (8)
Dec.	1911	19½lb. (king)	netted	Aldermaston Lake, near Reading (8)
Sept.	1912	26½ lb.	netted	Brook connected to Virginia Water
June	1915	18lb. 5oz.	Lieut. O.J. Knudsen	Lake near Grantham
9 Sept.	1916	20lb. 3oz.	John Andrews	Cheshunt Reservoir
	1916	37lb.	netted	Hampton Court
8 July.	1919	19½lb.	J.T. Fisher	Warren Pond, Chingford, Essex
	1920	18lb. 1oz.	J. Crawley	River Adur, Sussex
	1921	24lb.	netted	Birmingham Reservoir
	1922	26lb.	found dead	Kent lake
Dec.	1923	24lb.	netted	Home Park Pond, Hampton Court
14 Aug.	1926	21lb. 10oz.	A.E. Wyatt	Warren Pond, Chingford, Essex (9)
5 Sept.	1926	21lb. 12oz.		Reading
5 Sept.	1926	23lb.		Reading (10)
	1928	18lb.	found dead	Exminster, Devon
Oct.	1928	18¼lb.		Hinkley, Warwickshire (11)
	1928	"almost 30 lb."	netted	Bilsington Priory, Kent
April	1928	23lb.	found dead	Clay pit near Durham

24 July	1930	26lb.	Albert Buckley	Mapperley Reservoir, Nottinghamshire
23 Dec.	1933	21lb.	found dead	Warren Pond, Chingford, Essex
	1937	30-35 lb.	found dead	Mapperley Reservoir, Nottinghamshire
July	1937	21lb.	W. Cooper	Marrott Lake, Horsmonden (12)
Aug.	1937	23¾lb.	Les Brown	Mapperley Reservoir, Nottinghamshire
Aug.	1942	20½ lb.	Les Brown	Mapperley Reservoir, Nottinghamshire
5 July	1946	22lb.	A.G. Horwood	Dagenham Lake, Dagenham, Essex
7 July	1946	23lb.	F. Scott	Dagenham Lake, Dagenham, Essex
1 Oct.	1947	25lb. 9oz.	George Draper	Dagenham Lake, Dagenham, Essex
24 Aug.	1948	20lb. 2oz.	Harry Grief	Dagenham Lake, Dagenham, Essex
11 Sept.	1948	20lb. 6oz.	George Draper	Dagenham Lake, Dagenham, Essex
14 Sept.	1948	21lb. 15oz.	Les R. Singer	Dagneham Lake, Dagenham, Essex
1 Aug.	1949	20lb. 2oz.	F. Steward	Dagenham Lake, Dagenham, Essex
27 June	1950	25lb. 12oz.	Harry Grief	Dagenham Lake, Dagenham, Essex
30 July	1950	21lb. 14oz.	Reg Devonish	Dagenham Lake, Dagenham, Essex
1 June	1951	25lb.	A.A. Slade	Holbrook Park, Horsham, Surrey
22 June	1951	21lb.	A. Barker	Foxon Dam, Sir Osbert Sitwell Estate
2 July	1951	21lb.	J. A. Bentworth	Austin's Pond, Clacton-on-Sea, Essex
22 July	1951	25½lb.	Robert Sinclair	Austin's Pond, Clacton-on-Sea, Essex
before	1951	21lb. 5oz.	E. Eldridge	Colnebrook
3 Oct.	1951	31lb. 4oz.	Robert D. Richards	Bernithan Pool, Llangarron
23 June	1952	28lb. 10oz.	Peter J. Thomas	Bernithan Pool, Llangarron
26 July	1952	20lb. 7¼oz.	Robert T. Atkinson	North Stoneham Lake
28 July	1952	22lb. 8oz.	Robert T. Atkinson	North Stoneham Lake
31 July	1952	24lb. 12oz.	Maurice Ingham	Bernithan Pool, Llangarron, Herefordshire
July	1952	25lb.	Ken J. Drayton	Butt's Pond, North Thoresby, Lincs.
1 Aug.	1952	22lb. 12oz.	Richard S. Walker	Dagenham Lake, Dagenham, Essex
9 Aug.	1952	20lb.	F. Bull	Dagenham Lake, Dagenham, Essex
13 Sept.	1952	44lb.	Richard S. Walker	Bernithan Pool, Llangarron, Herefordshire

1. Variously referred to as Stonehead and Stourhead, the latter probably being correct. Boosey (1835) reports that 2,000 carp were taken from this water, the largest (18lb.) being 31in. long.
2. Accounts sometimes refer to this fish as weighing, probably incorrectly, 26lb. The cased fish was exhibited in 1836 at the Zoological Society and had a length of 30in. and a girth of 24in. and belonged to Mr. Edward Jesse.
3. The length of this fish was claimed to be 34 inches, "not including the tail fin."
4. Reported in the Birmingham Express of September 13th, 1890.
5. Fish set-up by Cooper and the property of the Lychnobite A.S., the members of which worked for a London daily newspaper. Caught on a live 5½in. dace whilst Mr. Eady was pike fishing. It had an overall length of almost 35in. with a girth of 21in. Sometimes incorrectly stated as being caught from the Thames at Windsor. Caused considerable excitement at the meeting of the Piscatorial Society on the 5th November, with several members expressing the opinion that it was a record fish.
6. This fish was described by the secretary of the captor's angling society as "a very handsome fish of the good old English breed, measuring 31in. in length and 21in. long." This statement possibly suggests that some discrimination against the more corpulent king carp already existed.
7. This fish was stated at the time to be dropsical as over 3lb. (alternatively reported as 5lb.) of liquid was found in its "stomach" by W.F. Homer, the famous taxidermist who set it up. The fish, nevertheless, was accepted as the largest carp caught in Britain, by the influential editor of the Angler's News, up until September, 1915. It was taken on honey paste whilst night fishing. Since carp actually lack a true stomach the liquid would have been found in the abdominal cavity.
8. The lake was run down to allow repairs to the pen-stocks and revealed a number of large king carp. The largest fish was exhibited in the Department of Zoology of the British Museum (Natural History).
9. This fish was stated to be a king carp and to be "eggbound" containing 11lb. of ova.
10. Stated to be 30in. in length.
11. A king carp caught on rod and line.
12. Won the prize rod in the News of the World Fish of the Week award—July 18th, 1937.

Carp Reported to The Angler's News

The following is a list of the total number of carp reported to the Angler's News Notable Fish List, above its qualifying weight of 8lb., for the years 1938 - 1948.

Season	Number Reported	Smallest	Largest
1938-39	42	8lb.	15lb. 5oz.
1939-40	8	8lb. 6oz.	18lb. 8oz.
1940-41	11	8lb. 8oz.	16lb. 8oz.
1941-42	7	8lb. 7oz.	20lb. 8oz.
1942-43	6	9lb. 2½oz.	13lb. 1oz.
1943-44	10	8lb. 8oz.	16lb. 12oz.
1944-45	2	9lb.	14lb.
1945-46	20	8lb.	14lb.
1946-47	16	8lb. 4oz.	23lb.
1947-48	4	10lb. 13oz.	25lb. 9oz.
1948-49	17	8lb.	21lb.
1949-50	5	11lb. 6oz.	20lb. 2oz.
1950-51	16	8lb. 4oz.	25lb. 12oz.
1951-52	18	8lb. 2oz.	31lb. 4oz.
1952-53	13	8lb. 1oz.	44lb.
1953-54	34	8lb.	23lb. 10oz.
1954-55	17	8lb.	27lb. 5oz.

COMPLETE LISTS FOR THE LAST SIX SEASONS OF THE ANGLER'S NEWS

20-02-0	F.C. Steward	Aug. 1949	Dagenham Lake
16-10-0	F. Johnson	June 1949	Broadwater Lake
13-08-0	F. Alderton	July 1949	Warren Pond, Chingford
12-08-0	R.C. Vivash	Aug. 1949	Horton Pool, Colnbrook
11-06-0	L. Singer	Sept. 1949	Dagenham Lake
25-12-0	H. Grief	June 1950	Dagenham Lake
21-14-0	R. Devonish	July 1950	Dagenham Lake
20-06-0	H. Stanbridge	Sept. 1950	Dagenham Lake
15-14-0	H. Poole	June 1950	Dagenham Lake
15-14-0	C. Stevens	July 1950	Dagenham Lake
15-09-0	G. Rousell	Aug. 1950	Dagenham Lake
15-06-0	G. Banham	June 1950	Dagenham Lake
15-06-0	C. Thompson	July 1950	Dagenham Lake
14-14-8	J.E. Watson	Aug. 1950	Benniworth Haven *(Woldale)*
14-06-8	G. Draper	Aug. 1950	Dagenham Lake
14-02-0	W.G. Tinsley	Jan. 1951	River Lea
13-12-0	C. Stevens	July 1950	Dagenham Lake
11-15-0	H. Stanbridge	Sept. 1950	Dagenham Lake
9-08-0	S. Tickle	Aug. 1950	Tunbridge Wells
8-15-0	A.E. Seddon	Sept. 1950	Private water, Sussex
8-04-0	A.E. Seddon	Sept. 1950	Private water, Sussex

31-04-0	R.D. Richards	Oct. 1951	Bernithan Pool *(Redmire)*
15-08-0	R. Walker	June 1951	Private water, Lincolnshire *(Woldale)*
14-04-0	R. Walker	June 1951	Private water, Lincolnshire *(Woldale)*
14-02-0	M. Millard	July 1951	River Thames
13-15-0	W. Hockley	Sept. 1951	Badshot Lea
13-12-0	R. Walker	June 1951	Private water, Lincs. *(Woldale)*
12-10-0	R. Walker	Oct. 1951	Lake, near Herts. *(Temple Pool)*
11-07-8	P.R. Smith	Sept. 1951	Private lake, Pylewell
11-00-0	R. Walker	June 1951	Private water, Lincolnshire *(Woldale)*
9-12-0	H.R. Hill	July 1951	Wadhurst Lake
9-07-0	E.R. Wood	Sept. 1951	Private Lake, Lymington
9-00-0	C.A. Stone	Aug. 1951	Wadhust Lake
8-09-0	M. Shields	June 1951	Denton Reservoir
8-08-0	H.R. Wood	July 1951	Wadhurst Lake
8-05-0	R. Walker	Sept. 1951	Private lake, Herts. *(Temple Pool)*
8-04-0	R. Walker	Sept. 1951	Private lake, Lincolnshire *(Woldale)*
8-02-0	E.R. Wood	Aug. 1951	Private lake, Lymington
44-00-0	R.S. Walker	Sept. 1952	Redmire Pool
28-10-0	P.J. Thomas	June 1952	Redmire Pool
18-08-0	J. Norman	Aug. 1952	Mapperley Reservoir
14-00-0	J. Chandler	Aug. 1952	Tarn Pond *(Cutt Mill Pond)*
11-12-0	B. Evans	Sept. 1952	Private lake
11-11-0	K. Downer	Aug. 1952	Crystal Palace Lake
11-06-0	R. Willsher	Aug. 1952	Crystal Palace Lake
11-05-0	Mrs. J. Steytler	July 1952	Crystal Palace Lake
11-00-0	J. Chandler	Aug. 1952	Tarn Pond *(Cutt Mill Pond)*
9-12-0	C.A. Stone	July 1952	Keston Pond
9-08-0	Mrs. M. Berth-Jones	Aug. 1952	Wadhurst Lake
9-04-0	H.R. Hill	July 1952	Wadhurst Lake
8-01-0	H.R. Hill	June 1952	Wadhurst Lake
23-10-0	G. Berth-Jones	Aug. 1953	Dagenham Lake
17-00-0	K. Drayton	Aug. 1953	Private pond, Lincs. *(Butt's Pond)*
16-04-0	K.W. Clower	July 1953	Mapperley Reservoir
16-00-0	B.H. Payne	June 1953	Private lake
15-04-0	J. Champion	Sept. 1953	Private water, Sussex
15-00-0	G. Berth-Jones	July 1953	Mapperley Reservoir
14-07-0	K.W. Clower	Aug. 1953	Mapperley Reservoir
13-04-0	D.L. Steuart	Aug. 1953	Private water, Staines *(Horton Pond)*
13-00-0	D.L. Steuart	Aug. 1953	Private water, Staines *(Horton Pond)*
12-0-12	J. Bridger	Dec. 1953	River Arun
12-00-0	W.A.M. Le Feuvre	Aug. 1953	Cheshunt Reservoir
11-04-0	E.J. Opie	Sept. 1953	Oare
11-03-0	K.W. Clower	July 1953	Mapperley Reservoir
10-12-0	A.W. Lewis	Aug. 1953	London Colney
10-12-0	D.L. Steuart	July 1953	Private water, Staines *(Horton Pond)*
10-10-0	R. Chadwell	Aug. 1953	Private water, Sussex
10-00-0	B.A. Jewel	Aug. 1953	Private water, Staines
10-00-0	P.R. Smith	June 1953	Private lake, Lymington
9-12-0	J.G. Howe	Oct. 1953	Kodak A.S. water

9-08-0	J.D. Nixon	July 1953	Lenwade
9-04-0	H. Bennett	Nov. 1953	Private water, Kelvedon
9-04-0	Mrs. Berth-Jones	June 1953	Wadhurst Lake
9-04-0	H. Kingsley-Kefford	Sept. 1953	Private lake, Lincs. *(Woldale)*
9-00-0	G. Berth-Jones	Sept. 1953	Private lake, Herts.
9-00-0	P.R. Smith	Aug. 1953	Private lake, Hants.
8-10-0	E.A. Reed	June 1953	Dam Pond, Farnham
8-09-0	C.P. Wait	July 1953	Private water, Sussex
8-8-10	D. Clark	Nov 1953	Kodak A.S. water
8-08-0	B.H. Payne	June 1953	Private lake, Tunbridge Wells
8-06-0	B.H. Payne	July 1953	Private lake, Tunbridge Wells
8-03-0	G.H. Berth-Jones	June 1953	Wadhurst Lake
8-02-0	A. Hill	June 1953	Claydon Lake
8-00-0	G.H. Berth-Jones	June 1953	Wadhurst Lake
8-00-0	R.W.K. Kefford	Aug. 1953	Hullbridge
27-05-0	E.J. Opie	Sept. 1954	Private water, Sussex *(Redmire)*
22-00-0	A.W. Albutt	July 1954	Leighton Buzzard *(Tiddenfoot)*
15-06-0	J.D. Nixon	June 1954	Parkdene Pool
15-03-0	D.L. Steuart	July 1954	Private water, Staines *(Horton Pond)*
13-12-0	D.L. Steuart	July 1954	Staines *(Horton Pond)*
12-00-0	D.L. Steuart	July 1954	Staines *(Horton Pond)*
11-12-0	R.H. Stearman	Sept. 1954	Private water, Sussex
11-08-0	R.W.K. Kefford	Sept. 1954	Hullbridge
11-04-0	D.L. Steuart	July 1954	Staines *(Horton Pond)*
10-00-0	D.L. Steuart	Aug. 1954	Staines *(Horton Pond)*
10-00-0	W.E. Tonkin	Aug. 1954	Private water
9-08-0	B.A. Jewel	Aug. 1954	Staines
9-04-0	Miss K.M. Holmes	Aug. 1954	Staines *(Horton Pond)*
8-00-0	M.K. Higgins	June 1954	Keston Lakes
8-00-0	C.A. Stone	Aug. 1954	Keston Lakes
8-00-0	R.W.K. Kefford	June 1954	Private water
8-00-0	R.W.K. Kefford	June 1954	Hullbridge

Chapter 3
Croxby Pond & Otto Overbeck

*Black are the brooding clouds and troubled the deep waters,
when the Sea of Thought, first heaving from a calm,
gives up its Dead.*
　　Charles Dickens from *The Chimes*.

One of the earliest carp fishing pioneers was Otto Overbeck. His very name has a mystical ring to it and fuels the imagination. He was certainly respected as a master carp fisherman by notaries of his time. Robert Bright Marston, editor of *The Fishing Gazette,* wrote in 1904, that "Probably one of the most skilful and enthusiastic carp anglers in the world is Mr. Otto Overbeck, of Grimsby" and, a few years later, the editor of *The Angler's News,* A.R. Matthews, followed this up with "Overbeck is one of the most successful carp anglers in England."

Otto Christopher Joseph Gerhardt Ludwig Overbeck was born in 1860 a British subject, but was descended from a distinguished Dutch family. His parents were of mixed nationality—his mother Prussian/French, and his father Dutch/Italian. His father had been a researcher at the Vatican but, after his conversion from Catholicism to Protestantism, he moved to England. Otto had two sisters and a brother, and his parent's wealth and cosmopolitan background endowed him with a wide variety of interests, and he gave much support to local angling organisations. He was a patron of the Grimsby & District Amalgamated Society of Anglers and the president of the West Marsh Angling Club. Furthermore, he was attentive of all forms of sport but particularly swimming, and started an annual scholarship scheme to enable youngsters to continue, free of charge, with swimming lessons after they left school. He was educated at University College School and Bonn University; and became a respected research chemist, a geologist, accomplished linguist and artist. He then settled

Otto Overbeck at the time he fished Croxby Pond.

in Grimsby and worked for some years as an analytical chemist at Hewitt Bros., the brewers, and, in 1911, invented a non-alcoholic beer. This he hoped would be acceptable to the temperance societies, but its success depended upon various changes in the statutory Excise Regulations which were not forthcoming. In 1924 he patented his electronic rejuvenator. The principles behind this rather dangerous contraption are explained in his book *Electronic Theory of Life,* published in 1925. He believed, along with others (this type of machine was not at all uncommon prior to the Second World War) that the nervous system and the brain could be stimulated and improved by passing electricity through the body. The Overbeck Rejuvenator, which sold at £6 6s. for the standard model rising to £10 10s. for the 'High Power Model de Luxe', was taken quite seriously by the public at large. Nowadays, few would be taken in by its claims but a full page report given in *Tit-Bits,* in November 1928, clearly demonstrated that it had widespread acceptance. Indeed, its popularity resulted in employment for over 40 people in his Chantry House Factory and brought him considerable wealth.

When Overbeck first fished for carp at Croxby is not clear, but it was certainly prior to the turn of the century. He was not alone in his quest, either; Richard Mason, the County Coroner, who was a well-known Lincolnshire angler and angling journalist, also spent some time there and mentions in one of his articles, in 1890, that "Mr. Arthur Mountain has very kindly placed in the *(Grimsby)* Park lake the *(very fine specimen)* carp[1] which he caught at Croxby Pond about three weeks ago." That Mason himself was successful was confirmed in a contribution to *The Angler's News* written much later by his friend 'A.S.' in 1951:

"The late Richard Mason experienced great sport at times fishing Croxby Pond—it held enormous carp—great fat fellows. Occasionally, Mr. Mason got to grips with them; on one outing he had the luck to take three carp weighing in the aggregate 42lb. from this water." It is interesting to note that A.S. wrote about the "enormous carp" in the past tense, which suggests that at the time of writing *(1951)* he felt this no longer was the case. We shall see later that others agreed with him.

Mrs. Joyce Marriott with the Overbeck Rejuvenator that belonged to one of Joseph Clayton's children. Overbeck often stayed at the Clayton's cottage when he was fishing at Croxby Pond.

Otto Overbeck mentions further carp fishermen by nickname. There was 'Norway' whom Overbeck acknowledged was a "great carp angler" having caught Croxby carp up to 13lb. 2oz., and there was 'Negative', who was described, somewhat obliquely, as "a positive fisherman," with carp to his credit of 13lb. 10oz. No doubt the significance of the nicknames was not lost to those in the know! A report in *The Fishing Gazette,* for June 10th, 1893, refers

One of Overbeck's Croxby carp, weighing 12½lb., caught on the 20th September, 1895. It was 28½in. long with a girth of 18in. Two other carp, weighing 10lb. 4oz. and 8lb. 7oz., were also caught during the same visit and their dorsal fin bones are in the top left-hand corner of the case. There is a note from Overbeck, pasted on the backboard, explaining that the serrated edge of these bones often caused the loss of fish due to the line coming into contact with them and being damaged. Note the missing pectoral fins—Chris Yates' first 20lb. Redmire common also had this abnormality.

1. The weight of this fish was just under 13lb. and a further carp weighing 12lb. was subsequently caught and transferred to Grimsby Park Lake, from Croxby Pond, as a companion to the first.

to a Mr. H. Barker, from Grimsby, as catching a carp from Croxby Pond weighing just over 13lb. Perhaps this was Overbeck's "Norway." However, Overbeck was clearly regarded as the first fiddle when it came to Croxby carp. Mason, writing in one of his newspaper articles in 1896, mentioned the experiences of a Mr. Underbrook yet was obviously meaning Overbeck, and gives us a rare insight into his angling character:

"Did any *(Grimsby anglers)* read about two months ago in the columns of *The Sportsman* of that wonderful struggle of 5½ hours duration of Mr. Underbrook with a mighty carp of the estimated weight of 25 pounds? The *locus in quo* was Croxby Pond. It is well known that big carp are the most shy and suspicious fish that swim in the lakes and ponds of England. Mr. Underbrook's experience was a peculiar one, and, no doubt, he now feels he can honestly say,

*'Of all the fish that swim the watery mead
Not one in cunning can the carp exceed.'*

Mr. Underbrook is a cute and determined angler of the most persistent and dogged sort. He knows full well from his previous experience in carp fishing that coarse tackle is useless in angling for so a wary a gentleman as *Cyprinus Carpio*. No! Mr. Underbrook is a knowing card, and he bears in mind the following line:

*'The carp whose wary eye, admits no vulgar tackle nigh,
Essay your art's supreme address, and beat the fox in sheer finesse.'*

Mr. Underbrook has a large stock of patience, as the readers of these notes will admit, when they learn that for 5½ hours he used every artifice he could think of to land the 25-pounder, even going into the mud (and there is **some** mud in Croxby Pond) up to his waist, but all to no purpose, for Mr. Carp eventually, after this abnormally long struggle, managed to get the gut trace across his huge back fin and severed it in two."

Overbeck's largest carp weighed some 17½lb., which took him over four hours to land, and formed part of a three fish catch in 1902, the others weighing 14lb. 5oz. and 10¼lb.

Overbeck's largest carp, weighing 17½lb., from Croxby Pond. The other of the brace weighed 14lb. 5oz., with a further fish of 10lb. 4oz. being caught later in the day. The length of the 17½-pounder was, to the fork of the tail, 24½in. and all three fish were taken on "sweet paste" on September 26th, 1902. The fish were set-up by the famous taxidermists, J. Cooper & Sons, and this magnificent case is arranged with a quite unique setting. The painting of Croxby Pond, on the backboard, was possibly done by Overbeck.

Croxby Pond & Otto Overbeck

He caught a considerable number of fish but the majority of them appear to have weighed between about 7lb. and 14lb., although Overbeck states quite categorically that 20-pounders had been caught from Croxby and that he, personally, saw one weighed. Many years later it was claimed by Raymond Rudd that the largest carp ever caught from Croxby weighed 25lb. and was taken by a local vicar. Whilst all these fish were of the common scaled variety, and have been accepted contemporary as genuine wild carp, the author feels there is reason to regard this with caution. The evidence for this is given earlier in the book.

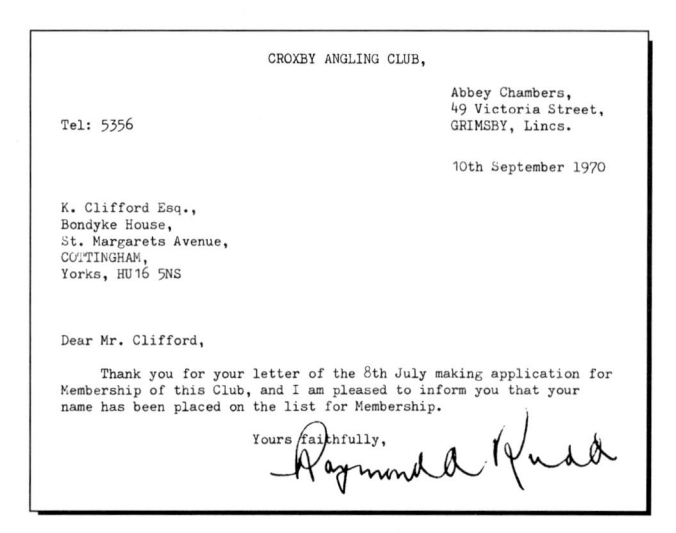

```
                    CROXBY ANGLING CLUB,
                                    Abbey Chambers,
                                    49 Victoria Street,
        Tel: 5356                   GRIMSBY, Lincs.

                                    10th September 1970

K. Clifford Esq.,
Bondyke House,
St. Margarets Avenue,
COTTINGHAM,
Yorks, HU16 5NS

Dear Mr. Clifford,
     Thank you for your letter of the 8th July making application for
Membership of this Club, and I am pleased to inform you that your
name has been placed on the list for Membership.
                              Yours faithfully,
                              Raymond A. Rudd
```

The author's own flirtation with Croxby Pond and its famous carp came to nothing. After this letter from the secretary in 1970 no more was ever heard.

Croxby Pond, at the time of Otto Overbeck, was an artificial lake of about 14 acres belonging to the Earl of Yarborough. It lies about five miles east of Caistor, in a steep-sided valley formed by the action of a tributary of the Waithe Beck cutting into the chalk Wolds. The Beck's headwaters rise in Caistor town and once formed a vigorous stream supplying the pond with a constant flow of fresh, alkaline water. The whole pond was, and still is, surrounded with an impervious bed of what Overbeck described as "bulrushes" but which is, in fact, reedmace (Typha latifolia). In places these stretched out 20ft. to 30ft. into the lake. The bottom consisted of about 3ft. of "rich, black mud" often covered with weed. The lake was possibly constructed in the 18th century as part of the landscaping of the Brocklesby Estate and, by 1824, a substantial wood had been cultivated on the higher ground on its south side. Overbeck, however, believed that the carp, and by implication the lake, had existed "since the Middle Ages and even pre-Elizabethan days, when the monks of an abbey (whose name only remains and whose very ruins have vanished long ago) placed them there." The author is a little confused by this statement since the Middle Ages are classified as the period between about 1000-1400 and Elizabeth I lived between 1533 and 1603. However, it has been generally accepted by those associated with the Croxby fishing in the past that the pond was stocked by monks, and an example of this belief was a letter written by Robin Fowler, one of the Croxby members from about 1950, stating:

" It was originally constructed by the monks of Ravendale in the Middle Ages in order to provide a supply of carp." Contrary to this view is the fact that a recent enquiry to the British Museum Map Room found that Croxby Pond was marked on maps after 1779 but not before that date. Whatever, we know that the pond existed at least by 1779, and sometime around 1860 a shooting lodge was constructed adjacent to the wood and overlooking the lake, and this, in later years, was used as a gamekeeper's cottage. Overbeck stayed at this cottage on many occasions, being looked after by the gamekeeper, Joseph Clayton, and his family.

Occasionally, Overbeck was accompanied by a friend, Mr. Openshaw, who also stayed at the cottage and fished for the Croxby carp. The gamekeeper's family was a big one, ten children all told, six being born at the cottage. Mrs. Marriott, a grand-daughter of Mr. Clayton, recounts how some of the children had to move out of their room and sleep in the loft when Overbeck was in residence. The older children also had to serve breakfast for their guest and take lunch down to the lake for him when he was fishing, and their mother had a whistle with which she would let Overbeck know when the evening meal was being served. Ah, what hardships the pioneer carp fishermen had to endure! One of the boys, Jack, spent many hours in Overbeck's company and was 'allowed' to mix the paste for the carp. Mrs. Marriott still remembers the reek of aniseed which was often left on her uncle's hands! Jack, who was given a present of a fishing rod by Overbeck, was, clearly, privy to many of his secrets but unfortunately died just before the author managed to make contact with him.

Joseph Clayton and his wife, Nancy, outside their cottage where Overbeck often stayed when he fished at Croxby.

There can be little doubt, however, that Overbeck was way ahead of his time and that he went to great lengths in his desire to understand and outwit his quarry. For example, he examined, with the aid of a microscope, the stomachs of carp to ascertain what they had been feeding on. He kept carp weighing 5lb., 4½lb., and 3¾lb. in a large concrete tank outside his home, Chantry House, in Grimsby, studying their habits and, subsequently, is reputed to have trained them to ring a bell when they required feeding. With the aid of opera glasses,

A photograph of the lake, with very low water level, at the time when Otto Overbeck was fishing there. The gamekeeper's cottage, where Overbeck stayed, is at the top of the hill.

Croxby Pond & Otto Overbeck

Overbeck spent a considerable amount of time observing the habits of the Croxby Pond carp. He concluded that a bunch of gaudy flowers tied on the line brought the fish from all directions to investigate (he wasn't sure if the scent of the flowers was responsible). He also noticed that if the carp moved the line "in bright sunshine, and see the glitter they are all off at once." At one stage, in an effort to conceal his line, he dried some mud from the lake bed, varnished his line and, when the varnish was tacky, covered it with the fine mud dust. His list of favourite paste baits also makes interesting reading, and there is more than a passing comparison to some of our modern baits:

1. Pound up half-a-pint of clean maggots with clean white bread crumb (no water). The resulting paste smells strongly of high cheese and loses its original scent. The only drawback is that perch attack it.
2. White crumb, strawberries and sugar (no water).
3. High cheese and white bread crumb.
4. Brown bread, sugar and wild peppermint.
5. Bread crumb, glucose and brandy (or sherry).
6. Bread crumb, glucose and aniseed oil.
7. Sponge cakes pounded into a fine crumb, mixed with fine loaf sugar powder and real, not artificial, honey. Before casting each bait is dipped into liquid honey.

Another bait that Overbeck used for catching carp was bumble-bees. He often sent Jack Clayton, the son of the keeper, into the woods to collect them paying him a penny for each one. He realised the desirability of using groundbait, squeezed-flat, to prevent it sinking into the mud and was prepared to use a boat for groundbaiting accurately and "even for laying out the line." Clearly, he was ready to try almost anything if it led to the downfall of his quarry. Yet, in other areas of carp fishing Overbeck was obviously regressive. He believed any rod would suffice as long as enough line was available (often displaying pride at having played fish for a considerable time), and the use of three or four baited, treble hooks, all attached to the same line at intervals, was recommended. He did realise, no doubt learning the hard way, that the use of more than one hook was a risky option. He qualified its use in the following manner—"Note in this method the danger of a fish being hooked on the nearest triangle and your having to drag the other hooks (three of them) bare, endangering your chances badly." However, he clearly felt the risk worthwhile stating that "I invariably run that risk; one hook and groundbait makes too little show." We are also told by Bob Lincoln in *50 Years of Angling* that "on three parallel rods he once caught two carp simultaneously, and they fouled all three lines. A friend held the free rod whilst Overbeck played his fish, despite the tangle, and landed him, 10lb., and then got the other, 8lb. It was a *most exciting time, and it took him ages to untangle 12 triangles.*" He also appreciated the hazard loose hooks could present in netting and the following short quotation tells us much about his tackle and the man himself:

"The landing net is two feet across, folds up, and has a ten foot handle. Trust no one to use it unless you know him to be cool angler. For a mad dash and a lost fish and broken tackle really are beyond human endurance. I know of nothing more difficult than to be alone with one's rod and a big fish on and have at the same time to land him up to your armpits in mud and water. It requires a world of patience and tact, for remember the rest of those triangles!!"

Overbeck recognised the value of pre-baiting, suggesting that this be "carried out regularly for some days before fishing." He firmly believed that the rod and angler should be hidden from the fish and that there should be no talking. He also felt that smoking was best avoided if at all possible. And, furthermore, he was of the opinion that boat fishing was a worthless occupation, suggesting that "a boat is useless to fish from, no carp will go near it."

He conceded, though, that "one can, however, use them comfortably for taking out the line, and groundbaiting accurately, and then coming away (a long way away), leaving the rod on the bank." He would, with this latter conclusion, find many allies in today's carp fishing scene! Similarly, he would accommodate a knowing wink and a wry smile with his views on 'leaving the rods to fish for themselves.' He wrote the following in 1908:

"The really monster carp, however, are the most chary, and the largest keep always well out, and seldom approach the banks; even from daybreak to dusk. I have caught carp from daybreak up to quite late on summer evenings (9.30pm); but whether they really sleep or not I cannot say. In returning at 3am, when the mist lay in a solid bank of cotton-wool over the pond, I have found them on already. How long they have been hooked I cannot say, for the last thing I do on retiring is to bait up, groundbait and cast out, trusting to luck. Many times have I found the line quite in another direction with 50 or 60 yards taken out; but no fish."

Otto Overbeck died in 1937, having moved down to Devon after purchasing a large house there, called Sharpitor, in 1928. During his period of residence he became a recluse with few outside contacts. There is some evidence to believe that he may have become a recluse through being shunned by his acquaintances and local society, after reports of criminal impropriety with juveniles appeared in the local newspapers. He left a substantial estate, having become a wealthy man through the financial success of his 'Rejuvenator' which was still in production at the time of his death. Shortly before his demise he had another book published, this one titled *The New Light: A Scientist's Philosophy of the Universe*.

He was, without doubt, a man with many original and novel ideas, and the renown he received as the leading carp expert of his time was largely deserved. He dismissed many of the fallacies surrounding carp fishing and his scientific background allowed him to perceive carp and carp fishing methods in a more logical manner than had hitherto been done. He, and many of his contemporaries at Croxby, were in no doubt that catching carp was a feasible occupation.

Part of Otto Overbeck's fabulous collection of cased fish that he caught and which decorated his large home, Sharpitor, in Devon. He was an avid, if idiosyncratic collector, particularly of natural history items.

During the 1920's and 1930's the fishing at Croxby was granted on a permit basis by the Estate agent. Generally, this consisted of one permit being issued per person, per month, but some concessions were made in certain cases. One of the largest carp caught during the 1930's was landed by George Butt and weighed 16¼lb. As a matter of interest there is made mention in *Drop Me A Line* of a water in Lincolnshire called Tubb's Pit, which was carp fished successfully by Harry Sheckell (who is also mentioned in *Drop Me A Line*) and Ken Drayton, the latter having caught a 25-pounder from there in August, 1952. The author queried this with Dick Walker who replied—"Actually, we coined the name 'Tubb's Pit' so

Croxby Pond & Otto Overbeck

An early member of the Croxby A.C., John Watson, who was an undertaker by profession, fished the lake in the 1940's successfully for its carp.

as not to attract undue publicity; the pit in fact belonged to a gentleman rejoicing in the name of W.W. Butt." During the research for this book it became apparent that the Butt's who fished Croxby for carp and who owned the pond were part of the same family, well-known Grimsby trawler owners. In fact Walter Butt and Harry Sheckell were good pals and fished together a great deal. Others who fished Croxby during this period were Oscar Cleave and Jack Smith—the latter, as a 15 year old, catching his first (9lb.) carp in 1920.

In 1943 Croxby Pond, as part of the surrounding 155 acre property, was sold for £18,500 to help pay for the 4th Earl of Yarborough's death duties. Coincidentally, Overbeck could just have afforded this had he lived, for his total assets six years earlier amounted to £19,375, the bulk of which was given to the National Trust. It was estimated that by 1981 the Trust's bequest had increased in value to about £2 million.

Croxby Pond was purchased by Arnold Hastings Laver, a wood merchant, who harvested most of the mature timber on the Estate, much of it being used for pit props in the coal mining industry. In 1959 the property was again offered for sale at auction and was bought back by the Yarborough family for £13,250. Early on in Laver's ownership the fishing on the Pond was leased to a club, which became known as The Croxby A.C. With some 30 members it was almost exclusively comprised, in the beginning, of reasonably wealthy individuals, many of whom were often connected with Grimsby's fishing industry. George Parker was the first secretary, being followed by Raymond Rudd in about 1950. Arthur Wright was one of the very few early members who was not affluent, yet he was fully accepted as an equal within the confines of the Club. On one occasion, very early on in the life of the Club, he remembers it was agreed that each member should donate £50 (a very substantial sum as Mr. Wright only earned £2 per week), for repair work around the pond. George Parker, the secretary, knowing that it would be impossible for Arthur Wright to meet this requirement paid Arthur's share out of his own pocket, without letting the other members know.

A photograph of John Watson at Croxby Pond, with the rod and reel he used to fish for the carp. He was first introduced to the lake by another member, Johnny Willerton, who is reputed to have been responsible for stocking the fishery with roach, which he brought from the River Glen, at Surfleet.

42

Croxby Pond in the 1940's. The trees on the left were planted by Joseph Clayton in 1907.

This was a marvellous gesture and demonstrated the comradeship that existed at that time amongst anglers. Arthur Wright only remembers one occasion when he had a strong disagreement with another member. He arrived at Croxby one day to find that George Butt had made use of five jetties fishing a rod from each one—it was necessary to fish from the jetties because of the considerable beds of reedmace which surrounded the pond. No amount of persuasion would make him remove one of the rods, so Mr. Wright had to solicit the assistance of the keeper, Mr. Brown, who came down from his cottage and read the Riot Act to the reprobate!

Soon after the Club was formed the lake was netted and many of the smaller fish removed, as it was recognised that the average size of the carp had fallen. This seemed to have little impact as by 1950 Maurice Ingham and Dick Walker both had the impression "that at the present time Croxby is greatly overstocked." Certainly the carp that Walker and Ingham caught in 1949 never amounted to much—fish of between 1½lb. and 8lb.—although a carp of 14lb. had been reported by one of the members the previous season, and another of 15lb. had been caught in August, 1943. Yet, in 1991, Maurice remembers the Pond with affection writing that:

"I was only a member of the Club for one year, after which I did not renew my membership—being, at that time, more attracted by bigger carp elsewhere—but my impression was that it was heavily overstocked with 'wild' common carp that bred prodigiously. They were real 'torpedoes'—built like greyhounds—very, very fast and tremendous fighters, but I never caught, or saw, one much in excess of 8lb. to 10lb., though some of the Club members spoke of specimens in the teens of pounds.

Having read of Overbeck's exploits, Dick Walker was very keen to 'have a go' at Croxby and I took him along with me a couple of times during my membership. Like me, he was impressed with the speed and fighting qualities of the fish, but I think he came to the conclusion that there were bigger and better carp to be caught elsewhere. At that time we were obsessed with sheer size alone, but if I had my time over again I think I would appreciate the Croxby carp more highly, for their sporting qualities alone. I think, now, that I would prefer to catch three or four hard fighting Croxby 'torpedoes' in an afternoon than to wait, perhaps for days for a much bigger, though less attractive king carp. Our attitudes and values change over the years!"

A photograph taken by Maurice Ingham showing the Pond in 1953. The relentless encroachment of the reeds have reduced the water area and the Tea Room, installed by Arnold Laver at the suggestion of his gamekeeper as a money making scheme, had been dismantled, moved, and rebuilt to be used as the Angling Club's hut.

Croxby Pond's more recent past has been calamitous. The low level of the lake has often given cause for concern, but gradual siltation and reduced flows of the feeder stream, due to water abstraction, have aggravated the problem. During the severe drought of 1976 the lake almost dried up. A mechanical digger was employed to dredge a trench alongside the dam wall and only here did water remain until the October rains. Sadly, most of the carp and other fish succumbed, even though a pump was used to increase the oxygen content of the water in the trench. The Croxby Pond A.C. lease ran out in 1979 and there remained little enthusiasm amongst the members to continue. The secretary, Raymond Rudd, personally renewed the lease and operated a trout syndicate at the fishery. This was always going to be a doubtful venture, as trout cannot thrive in this type of habitat and, in 1987, the trout fishing project came to an end. However, during the intervening years the few fish which had survived the 1976 drought had successfully reproduced, and it had become a viable coarse fishery again. In 1988, a local police angling club took over the fishing rights but further problems were lurking just around the corner. In the summer of 1991, water levels again became dangerously low and, with the assistance of the local N.R.A., 1,500 carp, having an average weight of 4lb., and several hundred small roach, bream and tench were netted and removed to another lake on Lord Yarborough's estate. Further, substantial dredging work was carried out in the autumn of that year and we can only hope the legacy of Overbeck, Croxby and its carp can live on for future generations.

Chapter 4
Cheshunt Reservoir

*A little after half-past eight
this tip trembled and then disappeared.....*
      Hugh Tempest Sheringham writing in *The Field* (1911).

Less than a dozen miles from the centre of London, hidden and enclosed from the outside world by a dense band of mature trees, lies Cheshunt Reservoir. Even today, with the hustle and bustle of city life all around, once you walk down the long flight of steps, under an archway of trees, and gaze upon the lake stretching away into the distance, you are lost in another age, another time and you are at peace with your indolent surroundings. That sense of stepping into a secret world, that every special carp water possesses, must have been so much stronger in those long ago, Victorian times. As the mind wanders to those bygone days, an idle moment can be passed musing on the reasons why carp were released into Cheshunt. Did the aura of the fishery itself drive someone to stock it, or was it the casual introduction of carp that cast the lotus spell? Truly there is a magic at Cheshunt, every real carp angler who has walked down those steps has felt it. You can hear it in the whisper of the trees and the lapping of water; you can smell it in the thick, black, oozy mud and crushed water plants; and when you close your eyes you can hear it on those dark, still, midsummer nights. Jack Hilton sensed it and described it in his book, *Quest for Carp* so:

"There was an air of mystery about the place, as with most of the old carp waters....it was like entering another world where only the leap of a big carp could interrupt one's tranquil thoughts."

Cheshunt already held carp when the Highbury A.S. took on a lease in 1910. They proudly pronounced the fact in July of that year with this notice in *The Angler's News*:

"It is with very great pleasure that we announce that the Society has been successful in acquiring a lease of the big reservoir at Cheshunt. The reservoir, which is a disused one, is delightfully situated in a well-wooded and picturesque district and surrounded by fine timber. It is only 14 miles from London and the nearest station being Cheshunt, on the G.E.R. It contains some immense carp and tench, numerous pike, perch and other general fish and may safely be stated to be the best fishing near London. The water comprises nearly 10 acres and the extent of bank is 1,147 yards. Boats will shortly be put upon the water and the weeds cut in the selected spots for angling."

*"...down a long flight of steps, under an archway of trees..."
Cheshunt Reservoir stretches away before you.*

Cheshunt Reservoir

That Cheshunt Reservoir held big carp was no secret, indeed they had been caught prior to the Highbury A.S. lease by, amongst others, Mr. Kelly who, apparently, after casting out his bait would slam the gate in an effort to delude the carp into believing he had left the water! As a matter of fact William Senior, the much-loved president of the Highbury A.S. had fished the Reservoir in about 1874 for its carp. On one occasion he espied an old gentleman fishing under a shady tree. He got into conversation with him, and learned that he was none other than Calcraft, the famous hangman, whose designs were also on the downfall of a Cheshunt carp!

The lease was advertised in *The Fishing Gazette* and the fact that its editor, Robert Bright Marston, was a member of the Society probably helped immensely. The following is a transcript of the letter from the Highbury Angling Society to the owners:

"In response to the advertisement in *The Fishing Gazette*, I beg to repeat my previous offer on behalf of the Highbury Angling Society of the £25 per annum for a lease of the South Reservoir at Cheshunt. As mentioned in the advertisement the lease to be granted for a period of seven years, terminable by either party at the end of the third or fifth year. The offer to be inclusive of rates and taxes and subject to minor conditions to be mutually arranged.

I enclose a copy of the rules of the Society and also a list of members to give some idea of the social standing of our subscribers. These include Mr. R.B. Marston, editor of *The Fishing Gazette* and Mr. H.T. Sheringham, angling editor of *The Field,* under the direction of whom the reservoir will not only be fished in a sportsman-like manner but should considerably improve in value."

The Highbury A.S. was formed in 1868, by a well-known angler who lived in this rural London suburb. He called his angling friends together at a tavern, known in those days as the 'Cock', at a corner of Highbury where later the railway station was built. By the turn of the century the club had attracted many more members, from a much wider area, many of

R.B. Marston, founder and editor of 'The Fishing Gazette'.

A typical Victorian angling club meeting from around the time the Highbury Club was formed. Although angling clubs had been established since 1792 (The Leckford Club in Hampshire in 1796, The Waltonian Society, formed in Newcastle in 1820, and The Houghton Club in 1822) it wasn't until around the mid-1800's that they became abundant. Several of the members of the Highbury A.S. played a prominent role in the establishment and administration of the London Anglers' Assocation and the National Federation of Anglers.

46

The president of the Red Spinner A.S., William Senior, whom Sheringham often referred to as 'The Master' and himself as 'Your Scholar'. They first met on the Kennet at Newbury in 1895.

whom were very influential. In 1917, because of these reasons, the Society decided to change its name. At that time the Society had as its president the well-known and respected angling author, William Senior, whose nom de plume was 'Red Spinner'. As a compliment to their much-loved president this title was adopted as the Society's new name. For the period of Cheshunt's fame the secretary was first George Rayner (until 1914) and then W.T. Attwood.

It is probably true to say that Cheshunt came to prominence, as the pre-eminent British carp water, with H.T. Sheringham's 'tongue-in-cheek' critique in *The Field* on July 1st, 1911. For about 20 years Cheshunt held the crown, often producing the biggest fish of the year in *The Angler's News* Notable Fish List, that is until Albert Buckley succeeded at Mapperley. Strangely, the decline in the size of Cheshunt's carp became apparent around the time Mapperley took over. But let us go back to the afternoon of June 24th, 1911 as Hugh Tempest Sheringham made his way along the little lane, up towards the gate that leads to Cheshunt Reservoir, and listen to his marvellous story:

"To begin with, I very nearly did not go at all, because it rained furiously most of the morning. To continue, when towards noon the face of the heavens showed signs of clearness and my mind swiftly made itself up that I would go after all, I carefully disentangled the sturdy rod and the strong line, the triangle-hooks, and the other matters that had been prepared the evening before, and started armed with roach-tackle. The loss of half a day had told me that it was vain to think of big carp. You cannot, of course, fish for big carp in half a day. It takes a month. So subtle are these fishes that you have to proceed with the utmost precautions. In the first week, having made ready your tackle and plumbed the depth, you build yourself a wattled screen, behind which you may take cover. By the second week the fish should have grown accustomed to this, and you begin to throw in ground-bait composed of bread, bran, biscuits, peas, beans, strawberries, rice, pearl barley, aniseed cake, worms, gentles, banana, and potato. This ground-baiting must not be overdone. Half a pint on alternate evenings is as much as can be safely employed in this second week. With the third week less caution is necessary, because by now the carp will be less mindful of the adage concerning those who come bearing gifts. You may bear gifts daily, and the carp will, it is to be hoped, in a manner of speaking, look these gifts in the mouth—as carp should. Now, with the fourth week comes the critical time. All is very soon to be put to the touch.

On Monday you lean your rod (it is ready put up, you remember) on the wattled fence so that its top projects 18 inches over the water. On Tuesday you creep up and push it gently, so that the 18 inches become 4 feet. The carp, we hope, simply think that it is a piece of screen growing well, and take no alarm. On Wednesday, Thursday, and Friday you employ the final and great ruse. This is to place your line (the depth has already been plumbed, of course) gently in the water, the bullet just touching the bottom so that the float cocks, and the 2 feet of gut which lie on the bottom beyond it terminating with a bait in which is no fraudful hook. This so that the carp may imagine that it is just a whim of the lavish person behind the screen (be sure they know you are there all the time) to tie food to some fibrous yet innocuous substance. And at last, on Saturday, the 31st of the month, you fall to angling, while the morning mists are still disputing with the shades of night. Now there is a hook within the honey paste, and woe betide any carp which loses its head. But no carp does lose its head until the shades of night are disputing with the mists of evening. Then, from your post of observation (50 yards behind the screen), you hear a click, click, which tells you that your reel revolves. A carp has made off with the bait, drawn out the 5 yards of line coiled carefully on the ground, and may now be struck. So you hasten up and strike. There is a monstrous pull at the rod-point, something pursues a headlong course into the unknown depths, and after a few thrilling seconds there is a jar, a slackness of line, and you wind up sorrowfully. You are broken, and so to home.

I mention these things by way of explaining why I had never before caught a really big carp, and also why I do not deserve one now. As I have said, I took with me to Cheshunt Lower Reservoir roach-tackle, a tin of small worms, and an intention to try for perch, with just a faint hope of tench. The natural condition of the water is weed, the accumulated growth of long years. When I visited it for the first time some eight years ago I could see nothing but weed, and that was in mid-winter. Now, however, the Highbury Anglers, who have rented the reservoir, have done wonders towards making it fishable. A good part of the upper end is clear, and elsewhere there are pitches cut out which make excellent feeding-grounds for fish and angling-grounds for men. Prospecting, I soon came to forked sticks, which have the satisfying significance to the ground-baitless angler. Someone else had been there before, and the new-comer may perchance reap the benefit of another man's sowing. So I sat me down on an empty box thoughtfully provided and began to angle. It is curious how great, in enclosed waters especially, is the affinity between small worms and small perch. For two hours I struggled to teach a shoal of small perch that hooks pull them distressfully out of the water. It was in vain. Walton must have based his 'wicked of the world' illustration on the ways of small perch. I had returned about twenty and was gloomily observing my float being to bob again when a cheery voice, that of Mr. R.G. Woodruff, behind me observed that I ought to catch something in that swim. I had certainly fulfilled the obligation; but it dawned on me that he was not speaking of small perch, and then that my rod was resting on the forked stick and myself on the wooden box of the hon. secretary of the Anglers' Association. He almost used force to make me stay where I was, but who was I to occupy a place carefully baited for carp, and what were my insufficient rod and flimsy line that they should offer battle to 10-pounders? Besides, there was tea waiting for me, and I had had enough of small perch.

R. G. Woodruff, Secretary, London Anglers Association. One of the Original Founders of the N.F.A. at Birmingham, 1903

So I made way for the rightful owner of the pitch, but not before he had given me a good store of big lobworms, and also earnest advice at any rate to try for carp with them, roach-rod or no roach-rod. He told me of a terrible battle of the evening before, when a monster took his worm in the dark and also his cast and hook. Whether it travelled north or south he could hardly tell in the gloom, but it travelled far and successfully. He hoped that after the rain there might be a chance of a fish that evening. Finally, I was so far persuaded that during tea I looked out a strong cast and a perch-hook on fairly stout gut, and soaked them in the teapot till they were stained a light brown. Then, acquiring a loaf of bread by good fortune, I set out to fish. There were plenty of other forked sticks here and there which showed where other members had been fishing, and I finally decided on a pitch at the lower end, which I remembered from the winter as having been the scene of an encounter with a biggish pike that got off after a considerable fight. There, with a background of trees and bushes, some of whose branches made handling a 14-foot rod rather difficult, it is possible to sit quiet and fairly inconspicuous. And there accordingly I sat for three hours and a quarter, watching a float which only moved two or three times when a small perch pulled the tail of the lobworm, and occupying myself otherwise by making pellets of paste and throwing them out as groundbait.

Though fine, it was a decidedly cold evening, with a high wind; but this hardly affected the water, which is entirely surrounded by a high bank and a belt of trees. Nor was there much to occupy attention except when a great fish would roll over in the weeds far out, obviously one of the big carp, but 100 yards away. An occasional moorhen and a few rings made by small roach were the only other signs of life. The black tip of my float about 8 yards away, in the dearth of other interests, began to have an almost hypnotising influence. A little after half-past eight this tip trembled and then disappeared, and so intent was I on looking at it that my first thought was a mild wonder as to why it did that. Then the coiled line began to go through the rings, and I realised that here was a bite. Rod in hand, I waited till the line drew taut, and struck gently. Then things became confused. It was as though some submarine suddenly shot out into the lake. The water was about 6 feet deep, and the fish must have been near the bottom, but he made a most impressive wave as he dashed straight into the weeds about 20 yards away, and buried himself some 10 yards deep in them. 'And so home,' I murmured to myself, or words of like significance, for I saw not the faintest chance of getting a big fish out with a roach-rod and a fine line. After a little thought, I decided to try hand-lining, as one does for trout, and, getting hold of the line—with some difficulty, because the trees prevented the rod-point going back far—I proceeded to feel for the fish with my hand. At first there was no response; the anchorage seemed immovable.

Then I thrilled to a movement at the other end of the line, which gradually increased until the fish was on the run again, pushing the weeds aside as he went, but carrying a great streamer or two with him on the line. His run ended, as had the first, in another weed-patch, and twice after that he seemed to have found safety in the same way. Yet each time hand-lining was efficacious, and eventually I got him out into the strip of clear water, where the fight was an easier affair, though by no means won. It took, I suppose, from fifteen to twenty minutes before I saw a big bronze side turn over, and was able to get about half the fish into my absurdly small net. Luckily, by this time he had no kick left in him, and I dragged him safely up the bank and fell upon him. What he weighed I had no idea, but I put him at about 12 pounds, with a humble hope that he might be more. At any rate, he had made a fight that would have been considered very fair in a 12-pound salmon, the power of his runs being certainly no less and the pace of them quite as great. On the tackle I was using, however, a salmon would have fought longer.

The fish knocked on the head, I was satisfied, packed up my tackle, and went off to see what the other angler had done. So far he had not had a bite, but he meant to go on as long as he could see, and hoped to meet me at the train. He did not do so, for a very good reason: he was at about that moment engaged in a grim battle in the darkness with a fish that proved ultimately to be one ounce heavier than mine, which, weighed on the scales at the keeper's cottage, was 16 pounds 5 ounces. As I owe him my fish, because it was by his advice I put on the strong cast, and the bait was one of his lobworms, he might fairly claim the brace. And he would deserve them, because he is a real carp-fisher, and he has taken great pains to bring about his success. For myself—well, luck attends the undeserving now and then. One of them has the grace to be thankful."

Cheshunt Reservoir

Although Sheringham states he was using a 14ft. rod it is interesting to note that in his book, *Coarse Fishing,* wherein the article from *The Field* is reproduced, there is an advert from the old London fishing rod and tackle manufacturers, Messrs. J. Gillett & Son, which states:

"Feather-weight roach-rod, 4 Joints, 15ft., 2 Tops, in Bag, 8s. 6d. It was on this rod that Mr. Sheringham caught his 16lb. 8oz. carp." Even in those days fish put on weight after capture and in this case the exaggeration also included the rod! Or, as the famous Thames angler A.E. Hobbs once put it, "I wish fish grew as fast in the water as they do out." In actual fact Sheringham's fish was cased and was on show for many years at the offices of *The Field* bearing the inscription of 16lb. 5oz. The cottage, mentioned by Sheringham, where the Cheshunt fish were usually weighed and recorded, belonged to Mr. Barrett.

From what Sheringham says we can determine that Woodruff was the first member of the Higham A.S. to be successful in deliberately fishing for carp at Cheshunt. Woodruff's own account of his capture appeared in *The Daily Mirror* at the time and is reproduced here:

"My fish was caught from a swim which had been baited up for ten days previously. The carp bait had not been touched for two days. For the purpose of catching a tench lighter tackle and lobworms were being used. It was on this tackle at 10pm that I had a run and in the dark, and without any assistance, had a very keen fight with my prize.

Without any knowledge of where the fish was and with only the rod point against the skyline to guide me in my actions, the fish was slowly but surely prevented from getting into the weeds. It was turned, and made for the open water. When thoroughly under control, I was looking for signs of the fish at 30 yards, but to my astonishment what I took to be a patch of weed was the fish not more than five yards away.

Three times I got the carp over the net, but each time it got away, the net being too small. At last, with rod and net-handle in one hand and the ring of the net in the other, I lifted him out.

I was lucky to land such a fish on such a light running tackle, as I have lost many carp on heavier tackle. I was fishing with a Lee roach pole, fitted with running tackle, and was using a heavy roach line and a no. 4 hook."

R.G. Woodruff with his 17lb. 2oz. Cheshunt fish in 1911.

R.G. Woodruff was an all-round angler, highly respected and well-loved by his fellow anglers. He was the secretary of the London Anglers' Association for 25 years and held the presidency of the National Federation of Anglers for six years. He organised the very first National Championship, on the Thames, in 1906, after the proprietors of *The Daily Mirror* presented the L.A.A. with a magnificent cup to be used for a competition. To give the reader some idea of the esteem in which he was held, the following is from Calcutt's *History of the London Angler's Association* written in 1924:

"On countless occasions, the secretary of the L.A.A., Mr. R.G. Woodruff, has been hard at work, in the interest of his fellows, when the iron tongues of church bells have tolled the hour of midnight.

From the time he accepted the office of secretary, in 1900, until the present day, he has been constantly engaged in working, scheming, and helping to improve the conditions of anglers, and angling.

The methods adopted by R.G. Woodruff were unusual in character. There was no ostentatious display, no striving for notoriety, no flights of rhetoric, and yet the inspired enthusiasm of other men was not one whit superior to the deeply sincere, but unpretentious, action of Mr. R.G. Woodruff.

His temperament was inclined to be phlegmatic, and by reason of this, he was often misunderstood. The ease with which he overcame difficulties only served to encourage his associates to impose further tasks, which were already much more than the average angling secretary would care to undertake.

He knew not the meaning of defeat. Provided the result to be attained was for the benefit of anglers and angling, he used his best endeavours to secure that result, and if opposition was encountered on the way, he put machinery in motion, which could be likened to a strong never-ending pressure, continued until the opposition was overcome.

His ideals were based on the broadest principles, and he aimed at accomplishing all. If discovered to be in the wrong, he willingly and readily gave way, but his opponents would have to satisfy him of their being in the right.

On such principles as these, and by such labours, he attained an unassailable position of popularity. His name became a household word with London anglers. He travelled North, South, East, and West, to develop and encourage the sport of angling.

He interested himself in, and obtained a proficient knowledge of, matters pertaining to rivers, railways, fish preservation, piscary, and angling organisation, so that his name, to a great extent, added to the goodwill value of the L.A.A.

He was, however, unaffected by praise, he simply just went on with the work in hand as if nothing had happened. He knew everybody worth knowing in the angling world, and everybody knew him, and he would rather give praise than be praised. The nature and the volume of the work undertaken, and completed by him became known only to his close friends. Few indeed are aware of the debt they owe to Woodruff for his efforts in protecting their sport on the Thames.

Woodruff, in addition to being a capable secretary, was an angler of no mean ability. He tasted the giant carp from Cheshunt Reservoir, and of the Loch Leven trout. He was English Champion in 1908, for casting a distance of 175 feet, with a 1¾ ounce weight and also for light float, casting 99ft. 6in., with 1¼ drachm."

In the winter of 1913 the Highbury members were dismayed to learn that three large carp, several pike, and a few tench had been killed and partly eaten by otters. The carp were estimated at 14lb. in weight, measuring some 29in. It was reported that "steps were being taken to put an otter pack on the track of the destroyers." Indeed, it is quite evident that otters were ruthlessly slaughtered by any means during this period and that anglers were regularly involved in their destruction.

After Woodruff, John Andrews became acknowledged as the carp expert in the Highbury club, as this report in the September, 1915, issue of the Angler's News demonstrates. His tally of nine carp over 10lb., would only be surpassed by Mummery's total of twelve.

The Highbury Angling Society.

CARP and tench fishing at Cheshunt is still attracting the members, and since last report three great carp have been hooked; two regained their liberty by getting the best of the anglers and the third was captured by Mr. J. Andrews. This fish put up a good fight for half an hour before being brought to the net. It was a handsome specimen, and scaled 12lb. 9oz. It is reported that Mr. Andrews was smashed up by a very big fish the following day. This member has now five large carp over 10lb. each standing to his credit, viz., 17lb. 2½oz., 16lb. 11oz., 16lb. 8oz., 12lb. 9oz., and 10lb. 12½oz., which is a record for the British Isles.

Cheshunt Reservoir

A List of Carp caught from Cheshunt Reservoir

Date	Weight	Captor	Bait
24/05/1911	16lb. 5oz.	H.T. Sheringham	lobworm (30in. x 21in.)
24/05/1911	16lb. 6oz.	R.G. Woodruff	lobworm (29½in. x 20½in.)
July 1911	13lb. 10oz.	H. Dunn	small potato
01/08/1911	8lb.	T.H. Openshaw	potato
27/08/1911	17lb. 2oz.	R.G. Woodruff	potato (31½in. x 21½in.)
09/09/1911	12lb. 4oz.	G.H. Rayner	potato
Aug. 1912	14lb. 9oz.	G.H. Rayner	potato
04/08/1913	11lb. 8½oz.	A. Piercy	small potato
05/08/1913	16lb. 11oz.	J. Andrews	potato
Aug. 1913	14lb. 11oz.	R.G. Woodruff	potato
July 1914	16lb. 8oz.	J. Andrews	potato (31in. x 21in.)
02/08/1915	17lb. 2½oz.	J. Andrews	potato (30in. x 21¾in.)
Aug. 1915	12lb. 9oz.	J. Andrews	
pre-1916	10lb. 12oz.	J. Andrews	potato
pre-1916	11lb. 4oz.		potato
pre-1916	11lb. 8oz.	J. Andrews	potato
06/09/1916	20lb. 3oz.	J. Andrews	potato (31in. x 23in.)
Aug. 1918	15lb. 15½oz.	F. Jones	potato
Aug. 1918	14lb. 5oz.	W. Bain	potato
1921	14lb. 12½oz.	J.C.S. Mummery	potato
06/08/1922	18lb. 4oz.	J. Andrews	potato
07/08/1922	15lb. 15oz.	J.C.S. Mummery	potato
Sept. 1928	15lb. 12oz.	J.C.S. Mummery	potato
Aug. 1929	13lb. 2½oz.	E. Cant	potato
Aug. 1929	14lb. 8oz.	J.C.S. Mummery	potato
Aug. 1929	11lb.	J. Andrews	potato
July 1932	12lb. 5oz.	J.C.S. Mummery	potato
Sept. 1932	11lb. 15oz.	J.C.S. Mummery	potato
Aug. 1932	10lb. 6oz.	J.C.S. Mummery	potato
Aug. 1933	11lb. 13oz.	J.C.S. Mummery	potato
Aug. 1933	12lb. 12½oz.	J.C.S. Mummery	potato
Aug. 1933	10lb. 3oz.	J.C.S. Mummery	potato
Aug. 1934	11lb. 1oz.	J.C.S. Mummery	potato
July 1935	9lb. 1oz.	J.C.S. Mummery	potato
July 1935	10lb. 3oz.	W.E. Perks	potato
Aug. 1935	9lb. 14oz.	J.C.S. Mummery	potato
Aug. 1935	10lb.	J.C.S. Mummery	potato
Sept. 1935	8lb. 10oz.	J.C.S. Mummery	potato
Aug 1939	8lb. 6oz.	O.G. Edwards	
Aug. 1939	10lb. 5oz.	R. Crebbin	potato
July 1940	9lb. 4oz.	L.C. Pagniez	
Sept 1941	8lb. 7oz.	G.F. Thompson	

The list of early carp caught from Cheshunt is comprehensive and shows that Woodruff was the most effective carp angler during the early years. Following on from Woodruff, the next successful carp angler at Cheshunt was John Andrews. (In early September, 1916 Woodruff had to leave London to take up an appointment for the War Department in Manchester. His job as secretary of the influential London Anglers' Association being performed by his brother, William Woodruff, in his absence.)

The following is Andrews' story leading up to the capture of Cheshunt's largest ever carp in 1916, which was acclaimed as a British record at the time:

"There is carp fishing, and carp fishing. In some carp lakes and waters carp of 6lb. or 7lb. are looked on as leviathans, but when one fishes in the Highbury Angling Society's fishery, noted for big carp, fish of the same weight are reckoned babies, and, as one American said to another, 'only baits.' I may tell those not acquainted with the Highbury's fishery that there are hundreds of carp over 8lb. and many over 20lb. there.

I have now been a member of the H.A.S. about six years, and it was my intention when joining to do my best to get a record carp. I knew very little about carp fishing, but soon learnt from others the way to do it, and knowing persistence was the game, I determined to set all my wits to work to circumvent one of these monsters. First of all the great difficulty in landing a carp was the weed which had increased for years and years until it had become a matted mass, so that no one could get a bait into the water without being hung up; and if one was lucky enough to get a potato bait to the bottom, it was a thousand to one chance it would never be seen by a carp.

The first thing in my mind was to work out how to get a clear space or swim in which I could fish. Several of the members held consultations, and various devices were tried for the purpose of clearing spaces, but not very satisfactorily.

This year, with the aid of a device invented by Mr. J.T. Potter, I prepared a new swim at the top in the thickest part of the weeds, where I and others had seen a number of very big carp rolling over from time to time. It is no light matter clearing out a space amongst weeds as thick as they are at Cheshunt. I estimate the amount of weed taken out of this swim—25 by 50 yards—at three tons, and if anything this is under rather than over the weight. Having cleared the swim thoroughly in the early part of the year, and everything being ready for carp fishing, I was anxious for the time to come when I would try for the great fish. New lines and tackle were purchased, and everything was prepared for 'The Day'. At last it arrived, and the first week-end found me at Cheshunt sitting at the new swim with my eyes glued to the line, wishing for a run. The carp for some unknown reason prefer a boiled potato to anything else— why I don't know; but potato they want, and potato they'll have.

Nothing happened for the first two week-ends except an occasional false alarm through the wind shifting the line or something of that sort, the weather being quite against carp fishing. At last there was a very hot spell which seemed to be the proper carp weather. It was so good that even Mr. A.R. Matthews (The editor of *The Angler's News*) wrote to the secretary of the H.A.S. to know if any carp had been taken. Although nothing had been caught I can tell you confidentially, Mr. Editor, that I had three of those big fish on; two of which smashed me like tinder, and the third came unstuck. What awful luck! Just imagine it, three fish, and good ones, gone in one season. They may have all been records, but one can never say. I had landed carp up to 17lb. 2½oz., and those that were lost certainly seemed heavier. Oh misery me. The day I caught the record carp was a day no one in this world would have thought possible—climatic conditions for capturing a carp were out of the question. Wind north-west, very gusty, almost a gale, and a dull leaden sky, late in the season, really past the time one fishes for carp, and yet I was fortunate enough to get the monster. I had been fishing overnight, and thoroughly baited the swim. I rose about 4am on September 9th, had a cup of coffee, and went to the swim about 5am.

I had hardly settled down before I had a run. I struck, and was fast in a big fish. It was an exciting moment for me, as directly the fish felt the hook go home, he made a terrific dash, and tore fifty yards of line off the reel, and then turned to the right for some yards, and buried himself in the matted weed, and fortunately for me lay there and sulked, thinking he was safe. I yelled to another member fishing on the other side of the lake for help, and as the fish kept in the weeds it gave me time to get the punt, and fight him yard by yard in the weeds, until I got him into the open again, where after some time (quite an hour) I brought him to the landing net. As he lay in the bottom of the punt he was a carp to be proud of—a perfectly-shaped golden bronze fish—31 inches in length, 23 inches in girth, and over six inches through the shoulders. The carp weighed 20lb. 3oz. and is, I believe, the record carp for English waters.

I have not got the biggest fish I have seen at Cheshunt by a long way, and next year will

John Andrews' record Cheshunt carp of 20lb. 3oz. The photograph shows the cased fish after it had been refurbished by the well-known London fishing tackle dealer, Dave Steuart, himself a successful carp angler and gifted taxidermist.

try again, and see if I can't capture one quite 25lb., if not more."

Although Andrews' achievements, in terms of the size of carp he caught from Cheshunt, were never bettered (he landed the three largest carp of that period) he was not to be recognised as the carp supremo. This crown was to be the property of J.C.S. Mummery. He was, without doubt, the most successful carp angler of that era and, of the 35 double-figure fish caught between 1911 and 1939 at Cheshunt, he accounted for 12, more than one-third of the total—a remarkable achievement. Unfortunately for

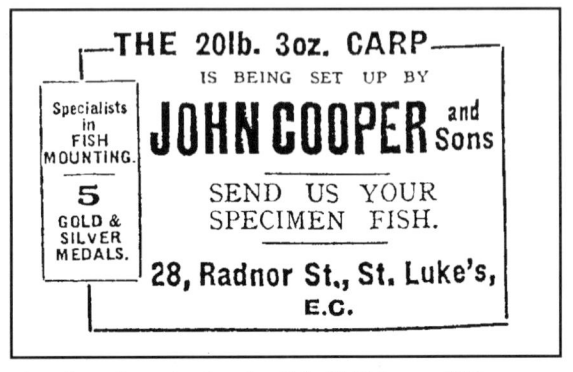

An advert from the October 7th, 1916 issue of 'The Angler's News. The taxidermists, John Cooper & Sons, rarely engaged publicity so they must have considered the commission of the 'record' carp a noteworthy event.

him, by the time he came to grips with the water the size of the carp was undoubtedly on the decline. Mummery's tackle was a light, split-cane pike rod, an 'Aerial' centre-pin reel and a plaited, undressed silk, pike line of about 12lb. breaking strain. The end tackle consisted of about 4ft. of gut substitute mounted with a small treble. Like several of the other members who **seriously** fished for carp at Cheshunt he had no truck with the use of a float, believing that his line would be less conspicuous if it were lying flat on the lake bed. No lead was added for casting, distance was achieved by weighting the cast with groundbait which consisted of soaked bread and bran, stiffened with pollard (a type of bran containing flour) until it was tough enough to use in the following manner.

The cast was soaked until it was very pliable, and the triangle was then baited with a small par-boiled potato being placed on the hooks by means of a baiting needle. Then enough line was drawn from the reel to reach the desired spot and laid out on a groundsheet to avoid tangles. Now came the most difficult part of the preparation. A good lump of groundbait was moulded into a sausage-shape, and then the softened cast was wound about it from end to end. The groundbait was then pressed into a globular shape leaving the potato a few inches from it. After casting out, two yards of line were coiled on the groundsheet so that the carp felt no resistance from the reel after picking up the bait.

It is interesting to note that Mummery, and the other Cheshunt anglers who were fishing seriously for carp at this time, did not favour the use of a float. This was also the way of other acknowledged carp experts at about this time. Otto Overbeck, whom the celebrated editor of *The Fishing Gazette,* R.B. Marston, held in high esteem for his carp catching prowess, did not use one; nor did Mr. J. Goodwin at Richmond Park, whom Francis Francis and the editor of *The Angler's News,* A.R. Matthews, regarded so highly. Now this is quite contrary to the impression that has been given in recent years by the majority of modern historical angling writers. We are led to believe that float fishing for carp was practised almost universally in the past. Dick Walker stated as much in *Angling,* in 1979, writing:

"It is surprising how new ideas become traditions and, from then on, become hard to shake. When at the tender age of ten I began trying to catch large carp, I never heard of anyone who fished for them other than with float tackle. Hadn't Sheringham caught his 16lb. 5oz. carp from Cheshunt by float-fishing, and written a classic account of the capture."

But Sheringham wasn't a serious carp angler, and so the claims by Richard Walker and others, that float fishing was the only method used in the past, has itself turned into a "tradition, and, from then on, become hard to shake." In the same article Walker continued in the same vein, adding:

"Didn't all the textbooks, with few if any exceptions, assume that float-fishing was the way to catch carp?" Yet, even in Sheringham's *Coarse Fishing,* only a few pages further on, after the description of the capture of his only carp, he wrote:

"In some cases where you have to cast a long way it may be better to use a leger, and in that case the bullet or lead should be on the reel-line, three feet of gut below it being enough. Some anglers get over the lead trouble ingeniously by squeezing a lump of stiff ground-bait on to a couple of split-shot, and using that as the weight to carry out their line."

When Gerry Berth-Jones joined the Red Spinner's A.S. in 1955 he felt that fishing Cheshunt was like stepping into another world. The tackle hut was an antique shop. Old landing nets and ancient lanterns lay about—strewn with cobwebs, their owners long since passed on. One remaining old fisherman, who was in his late-eighties, told him that a particular dusty lamp was the one Hugh Sheringham had used, to shine on his float, on his nights after the carp.

There have long been several misconceptions about John Andrews' 20lb. 3oz. carp. Firstly, it has been accepted by almost every contemporary angling writer that it was a pure wild carp, the original phenotype, unadulterated by selective breeding—yet none of them have offered evidence to support this claim. In fact the evidence supports the opposite. The shape and dimensions of the fish are strongly suggestive of a domesticated carp and the size, in itself, makes the premise extremely questionable.

Secondly, it clearly was not the largest carp caught on rod and line. At that time there were no official lists or bodies adjudicating on the validity of claims, and the general acceptance of a fish as a record depended upon its cause being taken up by the editor of either *The Fishing Gazette, The Angler's News,* or *The Field.* The Highbury A.S. and, subsequently, the Red Spinner's A.S. had many well-known and prominent members and friends (indeed, the editor of *The Field,* up until 1909, had been William Senior himself), and I'm sure these factors, no doubt unwittingly, had an influence upon Andrews' fish being accepted as the record. Whatever, it was generally looked upon as the record until A.E. Wyatt caught a 21lb. 10oz. mirror carp from Warren Pond, at Chingford, in Essex. Wyatt was a London angler and was legering with paste on a small treble hook, a usual practise when fishing for carp at that time (the hook incidentally was made by the famous firm of T.H. Sowerbutts & Sons). The fish was weighed at the headquarters of the Izaak Walton A.S., and was subsequently put on view at Sowerbutts' premises. It was greatly distended and when opened up was found to contain 11lb. of ova, and it was stated in the angling press at the time that the fish had probably become 'spawn-bound'. Interestingly, at the following Red Spinners' 59th Annual General Meeting, in April, 1927, Wyatt's fish was disparagingly referred to as "dropsical"—perhaps they felt upset at losing the record?

With the benefit of hindsight it is clear to see that Cheshunt started to decline sometime in the 1920's. Although more double-figure carp were caught during the 1930's than in the previous decade, they were of a smaller average size (the largest being only 12¾lb.), and substantially smaller than those caught in the golden years between 1911 and 1918. After 1939 the size and numbers reported dropped dramatically—the numbers perhaps being a reflection of the lack of interest. One member who did carry on carp fishing was Doctor Norman Bengarfield. He had been a young man when Cheshunt was in its heyday and had fished with John Andrews and Mummery. He was known, in latter years, simply as 'The Doc' and even though he was in his 'eighties' during the 1960's he still made regular visits to the lake, accompanied by his nurse and his dog, Rufus. He had been an eminent gynaecologist and one of two brothers who had raced Bentley's at Brooklands. Clearly, he was a man of many, enviable talents!

However, the Society gradually realised something was amiss in the 1940's and, in 1949, one of the members, Mr. G.W.S. Ingram, kindly donated some 'new blood' in the form of 70 king carp up to 4lb. in weight. Promoted by Archie Fielding, further stockings with 'Leney' carp took place with 500 6in. fish on the 17th November, 1951 and 1,000 4in.-5in. fish on the 4th December, 1954. With the new fish the water gradually changed, the assiduous weed disappeared and was replaced by vast beds of water lilies. Yet still the lake still retained a feeling of hypnotic

"With the new fish the water gradually changed, the assiduous weed disappeared and was replaced by vast beds of water-lilies."

mystery, and it inexorably drew many famous anglers to its historic swims in the 1950's and 1960's—Jack Hilton, Alec Lewis, Gerry Berth-Jones, Mike Winter, Don Wheeler, Roger Smith, Dave Steuart, Pete Frost and Bill Keal; but let Bill tell you of his first impression:

"I got to know Cheshunt in about 1956. I fell in love with it straight away. Everything about it seemed special. You walked up to it along a little lane, unlocked a gate and went down some steps. And there before you in all its beauty lay the lake. Completely surrounded by 70 foot trees, it stretched away from you for a quarter of a mile. Clumps of lilies and beds of weed

Bill in the mid-1950's, with a carp that looks as if it may have been one of the, by then, few descendants of the original fish.

showed through the sepia coloured water and the air hung with the smell of carp. It was like stepping into another world. A vastly better world at that.

The fishing, one soon discovered, was a little different from the old days. The carp were mostly mirrors, with a liking for margin fished crust at night and a bunch of worms lobbed to them during stalking sessions at dawn and after rain showers. They were pretty fond of potatoes too, though more in the daytime than at night.

The fish were a pretty high average size, about 14lb., but they never quite made the 20lb. mark. And I began to suspect that there wasn't a very big head of fish there either. About 30, I thought. After a time I became so desperate to catch a 20-pounder that I began to treat Cheshunt only as a reserve water—for rainy weekends and those long, long nights in October. It was particularly good as a reserve water, because I had built a hut there with my friend Alec Lewis, where we could leave cooking gear and extra blankets. And in the rain we could watch our rods from the veranda. All very lah-de-dah, it was.

But then came the great freeze-up in the winter of 1962-63. After ten weeks of ice every carp was dead—and pretty well everything else in the water too. Cheshunt had no great depths, eight feet at the most and no natural in-and-out flow. It is in fact a reservoir, though in its lengthy history it has never been used as such. Any water that comes in, comes through a small pipe at one end. And any water which is let out goes out through another small pipe—at the same end. With no movement in the water the build-up of gases from decaying leaves and rotting vegetation must have killed off the fish long before the thaw. We had many times attempted to break the ice, but in that Arctic period the water froze even as we broke it.

I went up to Cheshunt, to help bury those fish. It was a pitiful site. Thousands of bream, pike, eels and fry lay bloated on the surface, together with our carp. There was just about the number of double-figure fish there that I had suspected, all mirrors, with the exception of two commons. None looked any bigger than I had ever caught. I realised that, save for the commons, I must have caught all of them at some time or other and some at least twice.

There was no feeling of pride at that moment. There was work to be done. The water had to be built-up again, I was the warden for the water. I went to the club and asked for money and a free hand to do what must be done. I got both with no set limit to the amount to

Cheshunt Reservoir

be spent. But what's the good of money if there aren't any fish to be had?

I was in immediate touch with every fish farm in the country and with every private dealer I could discover. It became obvious that it was going to be no easy task. Nobody had fish for us at that moment.

The first actual stock were a gift from that splendid carp man from Wickham Market, Dick Kefford, whose records have kept us so well informed for so many years. He heard of our plight and told us of a little stock pond of his.

In due course, about Whitsun I think, Alec Lewis and I motored up and collected from Dick a bonny batch of 18-month-old mirrors. There were 51 in all and when we put them into Cheshunt Alec and I looked at each other and Alec said: 'Well, it's a carp water again.'"

Bill Keal sitting on the steps of his fishing hut at Cheshunt. Bill was responsible for re-developing Cheshunt as a carp fishery after its disastrous fish kill of the 1962/63 winter. He obtained 'Leney' carp from Dick Kefford, Israeli carp from a fish farm, Dutch carp up to 8lb. from the Billingsgate fish market and unwanted stocks, up to 16½lb., from local waters, which he caught on rod and line.

Chapter 5
Mapperley Reservoir & Albert Buckley

Constant labour of one uniform kind destroys the intensity and flow of a man's spirit, which finds recreation and delight in mere change of activity.
   Karl Marx.

If you walk down the valley with Mapperley Reservoir before you, the high dam wall stretching across the centre of your vision, you can gaze all around as far as the eye can see and everything, for almost two centuries, was owned by the Miller Mundy family. Over 2,000 acres was their domain. They possessed unimaginable wealth and great influence, and feudal rights over the common man. Albert Buckley was a common man. A quiet, unassuming, modest man. He gave his very life hewing the coal from the colliery pits under the Shipley Estate. And as you walk down that valley and sense the Miller Mundy riches and power of those long ago days all around, you wonder who in the length and breadth of our land remembers this once mighty family dynasty. Yet that common man, that lowly coal miner, whose love and pleasure was to fish in his employer's reservoir, will never be forgotten because of the fish he caught on July 24th, 1930.

The Shipley Estate dates back to Medieval times and was given to various noblemen as a reward for military service to the Monarchy. The Domesday Survey of 1086 records Shipley as being owned by Gilbert de Gand. By 1210 the Strelly family were in possession of the estate and used it for sporting purposes. There were vast areas of woodland, and deer and wild boar were hunted. In 1610 family debts resulted in the Strelly family selling the estate to George Peckham for £8,000. The park and Hall were valued at £550, the woodland £4,000 and the coal deposits £3,000. During the 16 years that George Peckham owned Shipley he cut down most of the woodland and sold it for a profit, a practice known today as asset stripping. This changed the character of the land forever. In 1626 Peckham sold Shipley for £6,100 to Sir Edward Leche, Master of Chancery and Knight of the Realm. Unfortunately, the Leche family fortunes changed for the worse and by 1710 the estate was completely mortgaged. Then, Hester Leche married Humprey Miller and he redeemed the mortgage. The daughter of this marriage, also called Hester (Miller) married Edward Mundy, of Markeaton Park, in 1734 and the Miller Mundy dynasty began. Their son, Edward Miller Mundy, was the first Squire of Shipley. Between 1734 and 1922, whilst the Miller Mundy family owned the estate, they developed and maintained the property in a first class way. Changes were made to the landscape, such as the creation of lakes and the expansion of collieries, but care was taken not to create unsightly pit spoil heaps or alter the general beauty of the land. Shipley Estate also became largely self-sufficient. It had 14 farms, its own railway station, water supply, gas works, canal and wharf.

Edward Miller Mundy (the 1st) M.P. took up his rightful place as Lord of the Manor of Shipley in 1767, on the death of his father. His succession coincided with a huge nation-wide

Mapperley Reservoir & Albert Buckley

increase in the demand for coal which was satisfied by the development of canals, railways and steam powered colliery mills. During the next 55 years he made profound changes on the Estate. He enlarged the Hall and gardens, increased the output of coal, promoted the Nutbrook Canal and had two large reservoirs, Shipley Lake and Mapperley, constructed to supply water for the canal. It was in 1793 that Edward, along with several other influential local landowners, decided a canal would be the answer to the problem of transporting coal from the mines of Shipley and West Hallam. A year later work began on the construction of Shipley Lake and the Nutbrook Canal. Although the canal initially prospered it suffered from a shortage of supply water, so that in 1821-22 the 29 acre Mapperley Reservoir was constructed.

Edward Miller Mundy (2nd) inherited Shipley Estate in 1822 and died in 1834. He was succeeded by Edward Miller Mundy (3rd) who was a sickly individual and died in Barbados in 1842. His younger brother Alfred returned to Shipley from Australia, looking after the property for 28 years until 1877. It was then taken over by his son, Alfred Edward Miller Mundy, who owned Shipley until 1920. He was the last Squire and with his death the estate passed to Godfrey who sold it to the Shipley Colliery Company in 1922. There then came a dramatic change for the worse in the running of the estate, and resulting subsidence caused Shipley Hall to be demolished in 1944. On January 1st, 1947 the Shipley Colliery Company was taken over by the National Coal Board and, in 1976, the site was acquired by Derbyshire County Council which developed it as a Country Park with access to the public.

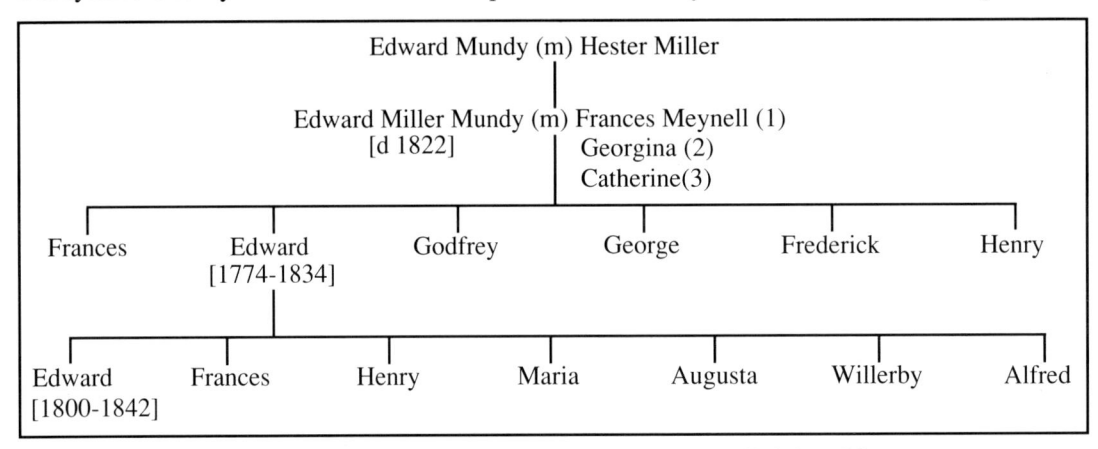

Edward Miller Mundy(1st) who was responsible for the construction of Mapperley Reservoir in 1821-1822.

```
Edward Mundy (m) Hester Miller
            |
Edward Miller Mundy (m) Frances Meynell (1)
     [d 1822]           Georgina (2)
                        Catherine (3)
   ┌──────┬──────┬──────┬──────┬──────┐
Frances  Edward  Godfrey  George  Frederick  Henry
        [1774-1834]
   ┌──────┬──────┬──────┬──────┬──────┐
Edward  Frances  Henry  Maria  Augusta  Willerby  Alfred
[1800-1842]
```

The Miller Mundy family tree — their wealth and power rivalled that of Croesus.

Mapperley Reservoir was constructed by the damming of a valley, which formed a large body of water in the shape of an elongated triangle. At the widest point, along the dam wall, it is about 280 yards. In total length it is some 700 yards. Two small feeder streams enter at the very top of the lake and at this point a silt trap, covering several acres, was constructed. This shallow weedy area, which became known as the Inlet Pool, is cut off from the main lake by two promontories. Built of huge stone blocks, they reach out towards each other from either bank. On all but the dam the lake is surrounded by trees, mainly self-setting willow and alder, but in places, growing a little further back on higher ground, ornamental trees and shrubs have been planted. The many rhododendron bushes add a blaze of colour at the start of each season. Over the years the fluctuating water level has left a wide margin of submerged trees, some dead whilst others, mainly of the willow family, thriving in the wet conditions. A rough track spanned the top of the dam connecting Mapperley village to Shipley Hall and the estate grounds. It was along this track that Albert Buckley was to walk many times little knowing what fate had in store for him.

Robert Albert Buckley was born on the 27th April, 1888, and named Albert after his father who was a keen fisherman (as was his father's brother, Harry). Albert married Annie Elizabeth Papworth and had three children. His first son, Ephraim, was a fine artist and was born in about 1911. A daughter, Daisy, and another son, Eric, followed. It is difficult to imagine nowadays the hardship suffered by a coal miner and his family in the early part of this century. Strikes and the Great Depression of the late-1920's and early-1930's must have spelt a meagre existence; and for a man who lived half his life in those dirty black bowels of the earth, then just the thought of spending a few hours by a peaceful lake, breathing and seeing and sensing, must have given him the will to carry on.

The rough track along the dam, which Albert was to walk many times, little knowing what fate had in store for him.

Looking right, from the dam, towards the boathouse and the Pond House, where the keeper lived, in about 1928.

Albert, like his father, developed a fondness for pike fishing and had spent several seasons in their pursuit around the lakes of Shipley Estate. His best catch, taken in 1924, consisted of nine pike weighing 156lb., the smallest being 15lb. and the largest 22lb. (Two of Albert's pike were set up together in the same case and were on sale for £200 at the Nottingham Antique Centre in 1987. They were purchased by a friend of the author, Brian Culley of Quorn. Some two years later they came into the possession of an antique fishing tackle collector, John Stevenson, of Stoke-on-Trent).

Part of the catch of pike made by Albert Buckley from Shipley Reservoir on 20th September, 1924. The pike were set-up by taxidermist Arthur Rogers, of Nottingham, and weighed 19½lb. and 15½lb.

The author has often wondered how it was that Albert Buckley, and his friends,[1]

---

1. Albert's "three friends" who could fish the lakes as and when they pleased, as opposed to guests who had to be accompanied, were Albert Innocent and probably Amos Chambers and Albert's father. Early guests included J. Harriman, Joe Beaumont, F. Hardvick and Albert's other friend, who successfully fished for carp, Les Brown. The latter was the publican at The Colonel Burnby public house, in Hartley Road, Nottingham. Albert Buckley was in the habit for many years of visiting this pub on a Saturday night and talking to Les Brown, when that gentleman was not attending his customers.

Mapperley Reservoir & Albert Buckley

had, to quote Albert, "secured the privilege of angling" at Mapperley Reservoir. It might be reasonable to assume that Albert and his friends were not in a position to offer a substantial financial inducement, so there had to be some other reason. In August, 1990, the author met Ted Meakin, who had fished at Mapperley Reservoir for much of his life. As a boy he was taught to fish by Joe Beaumont, a coal-face worker and a contemporary of Albert Buckley, who fished the Reservoir in Albert's company. Interestingly, Ted recounted the story, told to him by a friend of Albert Buckley called Mr. Kidd, that "the reason why Albert received permission to fish at the Reservoir, was that Albert had been walking through the Estate and had seen a child in difficulty in one of the lakes. He dived in and pulled him out. It turned out that the child was the young son of some official of the Estate, possibly the Estate Manager, and because of that he was given permission to fish in the lakes on the Estate." Subsequently, the author managed to obtain Buckley's personal effects that relate to his fishing, including scrapbooks, newspaper cuttings, letters and a notepad which contains the draft of a book on carp fishing, intended for publication in collaboration with B.B. (Denys Watkins-Pitchford). It is in this notebook that Albert writes the following:

Joe Beaumont, a friend of Buckley's and one of the first anglers to hook a carp at Mapperley Reservoir.

"Mapperley Lake is a beautiful stretch of water covering round about 30 acres. It is a distance of about 4 miles from my home and to get there I travel 2 miles by bus and the rest I walk. It is on the border of Derbyshire, in the Shipley Estate, together with two more large lakes about the same size. These other two are open for public fishing and contain a variety of fish including pike, perch, roach, bream, tench and eels but no carp. In the grounds, standing at the summit of a tree-covered hill, are the ruins of a once great building called Shipley Hall which are entirely surrounded by old, massive trees of oak, elm, ash, beech and with rhododendron bushes everywhere. A long time ago the Hall was owned and occupied by the late Squire Mundy. This was more than 20 years ago but it now remains a decayed shell through which the four winds of heaven may roam.

From the village of Mapperley a private road winds up the hill to the Hall gates which face north and south of the grounds. A lodge house is built at the side of each entrance gate. The gates were once well kept and painted gilt but now they are rusted

A Mapperley Reservoir carp fisher in the 1930's.

and moss green and Virginia Creeper trails across the porch of the little lodges. Through these gates the now grass and weed covered gravel drives wind their way through the great trees to the Hall itself. They are seldom trod upon by the hunters and foxhounds which met at the Hall winters long past. There are also several collieries and farms on the Estate that were once owned by Squire Mundy but now have changed hands. It is since the Estate has been turned over that these lakes have been open for public fishing. Mapperley Lake since 1930 has been rented by myself and a few fishing friends."

The statement is unambiguous, and was repeated in several newspapers which gave reports of his catches, that he and his friends rented the fishing rights on Mapperley Reservoir. However, the likeliest explanation is that Albert did save the child from drowning and that, in return, he and his friends were allowed to retain the fishing rights for a small rent. It is a story, however, that was unknown to Albert's son, Eric. He told the author that he was "never aware of such an incident or that it might have explained why my father succeeded year after year in gaining the fishing rights. But I must admit I have often wondered how my father came to secure those rights at what seemed to me, even for those days, a very reasonable rent. That he knew one of the Estate administrators (the Estate Agent, as I always understood) was undoubtedly true, and every year my father visited the Agent's house to negotiate the fishing rights."

It was early July, 1930. Two years earlier British women had been given the right to vote. The previous November had seen the Wall Street crash and soon Hitler would be gaining influence in Germany. But the carp in Mapperley were still impregnable, their habits a secret known to no one. They had been stocked in 1911 by the owner, Alfred Edward Miller Mundy. It has been written that they came from Burton-on-Trent in horse-drawn vehicles and were all small fish, but Ken Clower was informed by an old estate worker in the 1950's that he had helped to release the carp into the lake. They had reputedly come from a private estate lake in the Midlands and were shipped, in tanks, by train to the local station and then by horse and cart. Some of the fish "would weigh around 10lb.", the old boy claimed.

News of Albert Buckley's record carp first appeared in *The Nottingham Guardian,* of August 9th 1930. Not seeking publicity for his achievement it was left to Mr. F.T. Heald, the Clerk to the Trent Fishery Board, to make contact with the national angling press. The initial details of the capture appeared in *The Angler's News* of August 16th and then, by making contact with the captor directly, the editor was able to extricate the story from Mr. Buckley himself.

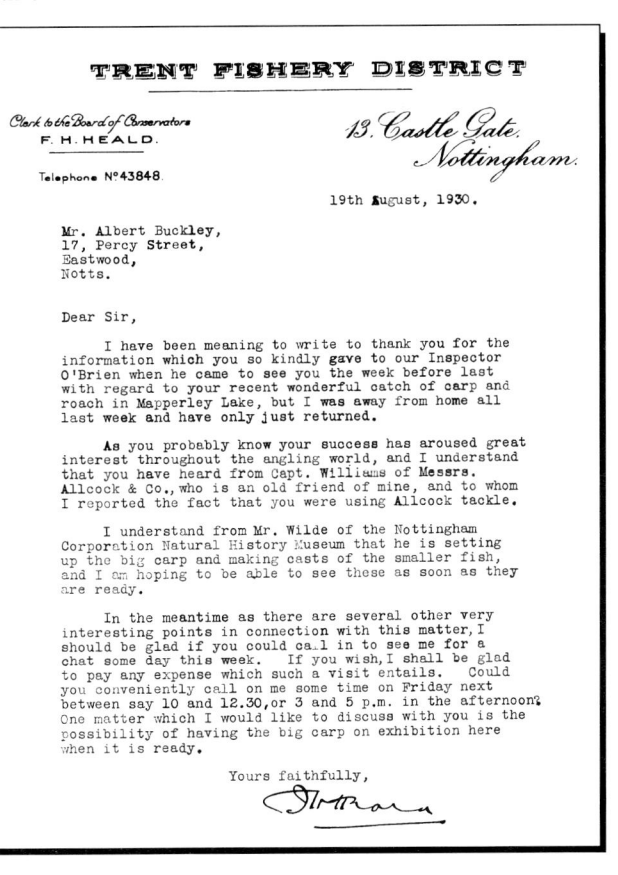

A much fuller account was given in *The Fisherman's Bedside Book* by B.B., published in 1945 at the end of the 2nd World War. This marvellous book, an inspiration to so many, was incidentally given to Dick Walker, by his mother, for Christmas 1946. He enjoyed the book so much he wrote to the author as soon as he had finished it and so a bond was formed which resulted in, amongst many other things, the formation of the Carp Catchers' Club. The book was printed on prayer book paper due to the restrictions and rationing of the War and it gave the only detailed account of Albert Buckley's historic capture—that is until now. For amongst Mr. Buckley's angling notes, now in the possession of the author, is

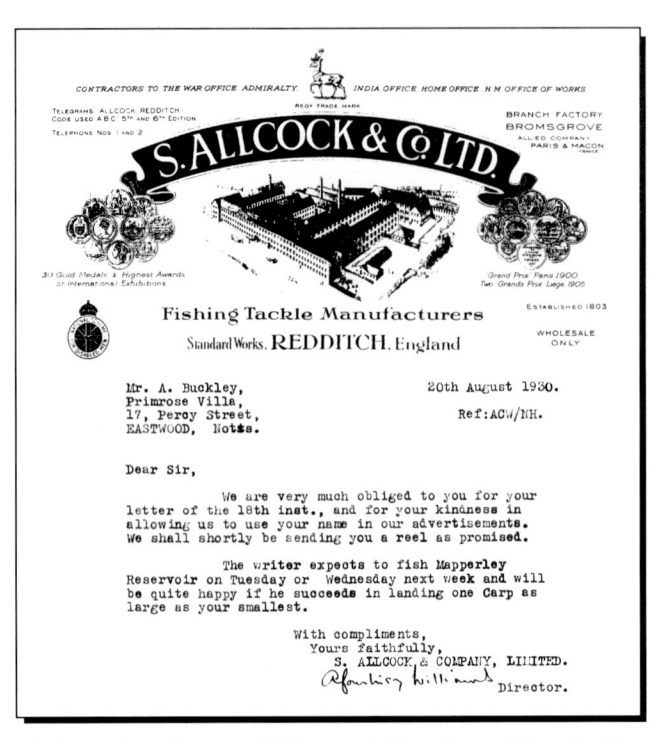

The letter from Courtney Williams, of Allcock's, to Albert Buckley.

written the complete version of the events leading up to the landing of his record fish. Here is Albert's complete story:

"The lake lies in a valley between the Hall and Mapperley village. Shaped like a massive pear it has a sunken bridge at the tail-end which once had a road over it leading from the town of Heanor, a distance of 2 miles to Mapperley village, and dates back nearly 100 years since it was last used. The lake is partly surrounded by woodlands and during the summer months is an ideal beauty spot for the photographer and artist.

Among the watersides grow reeds, bulrushes, water irises and various other water plants, giving home to numerous waterfowl including moorhens, coots, wild duck, grebes, kingfishers, snipe etc. During the winter flocks of wild geese, as many as 200, live and feed on the banks and field sides of the lake. It is certainly a quiet and very lonely spot. At one side of the lake, on the roadside at the deep end, facing the west an old wood and tiled boathouse reaches out into the water. Directly behind this stands the old gamekeeper's house and garden, where I very often spend many an hour should the weather turn out to be very wet.

During the early opening of the 1930 fishing season I had been told that the lake held some monster carp, whom nobody had ever had the good luck to catch on rod and line. *(It is recorded that one of 19lb. was shot during the days of the last Squire Mundy—author's note.)* It was early July, and we were all fishing for roach one day when one of my companions nearby hooked a fish which he said was one of the big carp. However, shortly afterwards he was broken by it and lost a considerable portion of his line and tackle. He reported this incident to me who, aware of the legend that the lake contained carp, watched carefully what happened when my friend had renewed his gear and recommenced his efforts. Sure enough, in a very few minutes off went his float again and the fish set off, at a great pace, for 40 or 50 yards up the lake then stopped suddenly. The fish turned and rushed back to the wall side whereupon it shot off parallel along the wall side, on the bottom in about 15ft. of water. It continued for over 200 yards, as fast as we could run up the road to keep in contact, then it stopped again suddenly, about three yards from the wall-side. The water was clear and I could just perceive the end of its tail. The fish appeared to be head downwards and seemed to be continually rubbing its head into the mud bottom. After a considerable time off went the great carp at a terrific speed straight up the lake and took all of my friend's line, about 150 yards. Fortunately the line broke near the hook. The fish was on for over 2½ hours and we never really saw it. This was the first encounter with the big carp of Mapperley Reservoir and my friend estimated it to be a 30-pounder.

After all this I really thought these carp would not bite again, but my friend believed they would. During the time when these first carp were hooked, there was a westerly wind blowing towards us and several carp were heard and seen near us plunging out of the water. Since then, after carefully studying these carp, I know now that this shows they are on the feed.

The following Saturday my father and I were fishing, but not for carp because I did not think they would bite again. There was a strong westerly wind coming down the lake so we fished on the boathouse side which was sheltered from the wind. About 11am my friend, who had lost the two big carp, came to fish and he asked if we had seen or heard any big carp jumping up. We said we sure had, and I told him we had seen them at the head end, that is on the wall side. Immediately upon hearing this he went over there to fish. He was fishing for about half-an-hour when suddenly his float slid off, under the water. He touched the fish which set off at a great speed but eventually it broke him. That day he hooked and lost 11 big carp and never even had a glimpse of any. The reason I did not fish for them myself was because I only had between 20 and 30 yards of line on my reel. After he had been broken 4 or 5 times I walked across to him and watched him get smashed up three more times. It was from this experience that I eventually learned the ways and habits of the monster carp. About half-a-dozen of these carp took all the line off the reel but, as luck would have it, my friend managed to recover all his line as the fish broke just the gut bottom. No doubt the majority of carp fishermen would have thought the place had been baited up a day, or so, previously, but there had been no groundbait thrown in at all. The only time my friend threw in any was when he commenced fishing, and that was only five or six pieces about as big as a marble, and a few at intervals. The bait was comprised of brown bread paste mixed with honey. This same friend of mine has lost over 30 big carp during 1930 and did not get a good view of any of these fish, never mind land them!

The penstock platform, close to the dam wall at Mapperley Reservoir. It was near this spot that Albert Buckley caught his fish, and it is surprising that the majority of his carp were not lost considering the frail tackle he was using. This photograph was taken in the 1940's.

Mapperley Reservoir & Albert Buckley

After seeing all this happen to him, I told him that the following Saturday would see me prepared to fish the same place for them. At this idea he laughed and remarked that I should get smashed up just the same as he did if I used similar tackle. From that day's experience it altered my opinion about these carp. However, due to unforeseen circumstances, I was unable to fish the lake until the week following Saturday, but my father and I had been preparing all the tackle necessary. We had a large salmon net, a collapsible one but somewhat heavy, yet big enough to land a 30-pounder, a gaff hook, a rod of 3 sections, with a split-cane top and 300 yards of Allcock's No.1 silk line on an Allcock's Popular Aerial reel.

At last, Saturday July 19, came. We caught the tram to Heanor where we alighted and walked the rest of the way which is over 2 miles. As we walked I noticed the wind was blowing rather strongly from the west again and it had been like that for the past week or so.

Heanor village at the time when Buckley first fished Mapperley Reservoir for carp. He would have disembarked from the tram where the man is standing on the left of the photograph, and walked towards the right, in the opposite direction to the group of three youths. On his return he would have caught the tram to Eastwood at the point where the tram is in the photograph.

We arrived and I decided to fish the same spot as my friend had previously. The wind was blowing straight down the lake towards us. The distance across the dam is roughly about 300 yards and my father was fishing about 100 yards away. He was also fishing for the carp but with much stronger tackle as he thought it was impossible to land one on the flimsy tackle I was using. I cast out in about 12 feet deep, well on the bottom. I then threw in 4 or 5 pieces of paste all around my float. I was using a crow quill, with just one shot about 12in. from the hook.

It was now about 8am. Nothing happened for about an hour then suddenly I saw, about 80 yards away, a great carp roll on the surface of the water. After seeing this I was on the lookout for more. A few minutes later I could see several of them coming up to the top of the water and gradually getting nearer, and nearer, to my float. After witnessing all this I can admit I felt thrilled. I crouched low-down and threw in a few more bits of paste around my float. Then suddenly it was gone. His first wild dash, after being hooked, sent him tearing up the lake about 150 yards. The fish then stopped and very slowly came back towards me. As time wore on I eventually got him nearer the wall-side, but he still remained close to the bottom of the lake. In the last quarter-of-an-hour, or so, he continually circled round and round, about 8 yards from the wall. During this time I gently tried to raise him off the bottom till at last I did get him to the surface. Here he gave 4 or 5 more circles round but these were much weaker until, finally, he came within reach of the landing net which my father had ready. He netted him close to the wall and eased him out onto the bank.

So that was my first carp, and it was also the first one to be caught on rod and line from Mapperley Lake. I was exactly 55 minutes in getting him. We carried it over to the keeper's house, which was close by, where he scaled 16lb. The keeper was surprised at seeing the fish and remarked, saying that after being over 30 years employed on the Estate, it was the first carp to have been caught on rod and line from the lake."

Albert went back and within ten minutes had hooked another carp. A similar waiting game ensued and almost 50 minutes later his father wielded the big, two-handed salmon net and lifted a 14-pounder out. The second fish proved that Albert was able, even accounting for his light tackle, to successfully land the Mapperley carp. What he was doing differently to his friend, who had repeatedly lost so many fish on similar tackle, remains a mystery to this day.

On the following Thursday, the 24th July, Albert returned. It had rained very heavily for several days and the water, which was normally very clear, was highly coloured. A report in a Nottingham newspaper was headed **'Trent Near Flood Level—2,670,800 Tons Fall on Nottingham in the Past Five Days.'**

Albert was fishing alone on this occasion and wrote the following, which appeared in *The Angler's News,* soon afterwards:

"On July 24th I got four carp and two roach—the carp were 9lb., 11lb., 15lb., and 26 lb.; the roach were 2lb. 12oz. and 3lb. 6oz. *(They were later shown to be hybrids—author.)* I caught them all with brown bread paste mixed with honey. I was using Allcock's No. 1 silk line and no. 10 hook to very fine gut.[1] It took me nearly an hour and a half to land the 26-pounder. I have a very large landing net, but I could not use it, so I had to use the gaff, which broke, so I had to finish up getting him out with my hands. As soon as I got the carp on the bank I conveyed it to the gamekeeper's house nearby. His scales weighed up to 25lb. but these would not weigh the fish. At this the keeper guessed it to be between 28lb. and 30lb. but I think it was about 26lb. Because of the gash in the side of the fish, where my gaff had pierced it, the carp had lost a good deal of blood, and unfortunately I could not get it weighed properly until 8.30pm. when I was at the house of Mr. Leonard Wilde, of Nottingham Natural History Museum, who is setting the fish up to accompany two of the big pike I have at my home.

Local Rainfall	
Friday, 18th July	0.355in.
Saturday, 19th July	0.161in.
Sunday, 20th July	0.980in.
Monday, 21st July	0.411in.
Tuesday, 22nd July	0.684in.

Details from the Nottingham Evening News of the 23rd July, 1930.

---

1. There seems to be some misunderstanding regarding the tackle Buckley was using. Mike Wilson, writing in *The Carpworld Yearbook* in 1992, stated that Buckley's Allcock's No.1 Lincoln silk line was actually 8lb. breaking strain and not the 3lb. as reported by Buckley. In fact, it was reported in *The Angler's News* at the time of capture, by the manufacturers themselves, S. Allcock & Co., that the guaranteed breaking strain of Buckley's silk line was 4¼lb., which was variously reported in a number of local newspapers. For some reason Buckley later claimed it was actually 3½lb.

    Mike Wilson also claimed that Buckley's 4X gut leader had a breaking strain of 1lb., and he possibly obtained this figure from a table supplied by Messrs. S. Allcock & Co. (which probably related to silkworm gut), reproduced in E. Marshall-Hardy's *Angling Ways.* However, it is not quite as simple as this. There was some considerable variation in the breaking strains of a particular gauge of natural silk gut, and it was by no means unusual for gut dealers to overstate the fineness of their product. The Pilot Gut Company wrote in one of their catalogues that "Frankly, there is no unalterable standard on which the sizing of gut can be based, but nevertheless there is comparative uniformity in the gradings adopted by most of the reputable manufacturers. There are unscrupulous dealers, however, who exploit the gullibility of their clients by offering them so called 9X and even 10X gut. The writer has seen such gut offered which in reality could not be fairly described as 5X. Similarly, at the other end of the scale the stouter sizes are frequently undergraded."

    A. Norman Marston, in *The Newnes Encyclopaedia of Angling,* gives an average breaking strain for 4X natural gut as between 2lb. and 2¼lb. Furthermore, in 1932 synthetic gut, the most popular being Ja-Gut or Jagut, was available and this offered higher breaking strain than natural gut for any given diameter. We don't know whether Buckley was using natural or synthetic gut since he only ever described it simply as gut.

Mapperley Reservoir & Albert Buckley

The other three carp and the two roach are going to Nottingham Museum, where Mr. Wilde[1] hopes to make a display of them. The first two carp I got I cut up and gave them away. I should have had them set-up, only I felt sure of getting one larger. I caught the 26-pounder and other fish between 9am and 1pm, and so I thought it would be best to pack up, because I was wondering how I was going to get them home, as I had to walk two miles to Heanor to get the tram. But, as luck would have it, I saw a boy with a wagon[2] and gave him a shilling to take them to Heanor for me. And so, after a great struggle, I got them home."

One of the early reports of Albert Buckley's record carp. A great deal of the information that appeared in the press derived from F.H. Heald, of the Trent Fishery Board, who took a personal interest in the capture.

Some years later three members of the Carp Catchers' Club (Walker, Ingham and B.B.) were to speculate on the length of Albert's record fish when they visited Wollaton Hall museum on June 20th, 1951, two days after the historic formation of this illustrious group. Walker stated that its length "looked no more than 30in." However, its dimensions were recorded shortly after its capture by officials of the Trent Fishery Board. It had a length of 32in. and its girth was 28in.

Albert Buckley's record carp. The cased fish was sold by a relative of the Buckley family and now resides in a fishing tackle shop in South Wales.

Albert Buckley and his friends held the exclusive right to fish Mapperley for many years. The number of carp they caught was very few and Albert believed that the best opportunities arose when the weather was rough and wet. He was, of course, limited in his experience to this one water. The character of this reservoir, and his acceptance of the widely-

1. Leonard Wilde was the taxidermist at Wollaton Hall between 1926 and 1961. Born in 1904 he began work as an apprentice gardener on Lord Middleton's Estate, Wollaton Park, at the age of 15. Leonard enjoyed the outdoor life and an interest in wildlife was encouraged by Bernard Rose, the professional taxidermist whose shop was in Mount Street, Nottingham. In due course Leonard helped in Mr. Rose's shop in his spare time. At the age of 22 he was appointed taxidermist of the newly formed collection at Wollaton Hall. Although the number of specimens he mounted during his years at Wollaton Hall did not exceed 200, the quality was very good. He was a fine craftsman with fish mounting and painting, one of the best of that period. He accompanied Albert Buckley on several trips to Mapperley, in the unsuccessful attempt to catch a large carp himself.
2. The "wagon" was in fact an orange box fastened to four pram wheels.

Reproduced from an old newspaper, this photograph shows Albert Buckley's fish caught on the 8th Sptember, 1930.

held view that carp could only be caught on light tackle, led him to the opinion that fishing the snag-free, deep water dam area, when the wind was in a westerly direction, offered the only profitable means of landing a hooked fish. He was well aware that the Mapperley carp spent much of their time in the shallow water and correctly concluded that they could not be beaten on fine line in the confines of the submerged trees and prolific weed. He also rightly demonstrated that during periods of strong wind the carp moved into the deeper water near the dam. His major failing was to believe that carp could not be hooked on strong tackle. Dick Walker felt very strongly that Albert Buckley's catches, and his views on light tackle, had set back the development of carp fishing. In 1952 Dick wrote the following:

"A method was evolved which had purely local application, depended on abnormal weather conditions, had a very low scoring rate and was not generally applicable. The tackle used was totally inadequate for general carp fishing, and Buckley, though a fine angler, never really understood carp, though he made important observations on the effect of weather. Buckley's success dealt a shocking blow to the spread of carp fishing, from which it has yet to recover completely."

A year later Walker made similar public criticisms of Buckley but was, at that same time, generous in his praise. Dick wrote:

"He *(Buckley)* was pretty dogmatic about his methods, and I have always suspected that he was not necessarily on the right track. Buckley was a very great angler; he caught a great many specimen fish of all kinds. If he were still alive, we should be honoured to have him accept an invitation to become a member of the Carp Catchers' Club. His observations on carp have proved of enormous help to us; but I think his method of fishing was basically unsound, and that it had a bad influence on carp fishing everywhere." And then, a little later, Dick concluded by writing:

"Then the late Albert Buckley caught a carp weighing 26lb. at Mapperley, using fine tackle, which

Albert with his daughter, Daisy, and his grand-daughter, in July, 1941.

there is little doubt had the effect of causing many anglers to conclude that correct tackle for carp fishing must be superfine; the right bait a small one; and that the most effective method was float-fishing in deep water. Every one of these suppositions is wrong on nine occasions out of ten; and it is little wonder that in the years following 1930 a great many anglers came to regard carp fishing as a waste of time."

It is probably fair to assume that Dick Walker made the conscious decision to refrain from public criticism of Albert Buckley's methods until after his death on the 15th August, 1949, at the age of 61.

Mapperley Reservoir & Albert Buckley

The death certificate gave the cause as pneumonia, but a lifetime spent in the coal mines is, almost certainly, what really killed him. Although Dick's criticism was probably factually correct it does seem more than a little unfair in retrospect. It could equally be claimed that Dick's opinions on the feeding habits of carp in cold water *dealt a shocking blow to the spread of winter carp fishing*. Buckley never actually propagated his views in the angling periodicals and only wrote of his methods when pressed to do so by B.B. for his book. Had not Francis Francis, of whom Walker had much regard, written "The carp is very wary, so one must—despite his great size—use light tackle." If anyone is to blame for, as Dick Walker puts it, Buckley's "bad influence" then that can only be Denys Watkins-Pitchford. In 1950, at the time of the publication of *Confessions of a Carp Fisher,* B.B. had been a friend of Dick Walker's for three years. They had corresponded a great deal and carp fished together during this period. Yet B.B. agreed with Buckley, writing in *Confessions of a Carp Fisher,* that "no self-respecting carp of any size will ever be captured on gut stouter than 3X in clear water." There is little doubt in the author's mind that, even by 1950, B.B. felt more 'in tune' with the methods and achievements of Albert Buckley than he did with those of Richard Walker. I think this can be demonstrated by the inscription B.B. wrote in a complimentary copy of *Confessions of a Carp Fisher* that he sent to Buckley in 1950[1] which stated "To Britain's Premier Carp Fisher, Albert Buckley, from the author B.B."

Buckley's reels with his float and hook wallet. The books are complimentary copies from B.B. with the inscription in 'Confessions' from the author dated March, 1950.

A very good friend of Albert Buckley was Arthur Walkington, who lived at Burton Joyce, near Nottingham. He wrote under the pen name of 'Idler' for many years in *The Fishing Gazette* and *The Angler's News,* and also had one small book published in 1937, about fishing in Norfolk. In late 1952, Dick Walker caught his 44lb. carp from Bernithan Pool and there was, naturally, a great deal of attendant interest and praise. In November 1952, 'Idler' wrote the following about Mapperley in his weekly column:

"That there are carp here to beat the recent record 44-pounder is the firm opinion of those who should know, and also this fish from the photograph published is a common carp, and not a mirror carp, which leaves apparently the Buckley fish of 26lb. as the record mirror carp."

This notion was soon corrected and it was pointed out that apart from the 44-pounder, Bob Richards had caught a 31¼lb. mirror and Buckley's fish had also been beaten by Pete

---

1. B.B. sent the book in March, 1950 unaware that Albert had died the previous year.

Thomas with his 28lb. 10oz. mirror.

But Idler wasn't to be subdued easily and soon countered with:

"My remarks about the late Mr. Albert Buckley's record mirror carp stand, the fish was caught unaided, and any record fish should be so caught. I fancy recently in a description of big carp caught (Walker's fish), two anglers were involved."

This sparked a fiery debate. John Norman and others sprang to Dick's defence whilst opponents sought to discredit his capture. Mr. W. Park, of Doncaster, felt that:

"In reference to carp fishing in Mapperley Reservoir, J. Norman ignores the fact that Albert Buckley caught his 26lb. carp on roach tackle during daylight. A 26lb. carp caught during daylight is a better performance that one of 30lb. or 40lb. caught in the dark by any member of the Carp Catchers' Club."

Idler then appeared to justify his claim that Buckley still held the mirror carp record with the following letter in early January, 1953:

"Mr. Buckley had a mirror above 33lb. but did not wish it recording. His big carp (26-pounder) was caught and landed by himself, a great feat and to me it is the mirror record still. Mr. Walker's 44 lb. carp is a magnificent fish, but I don't like the poor old chap in the Zoo—put him back is my idea!"

The matter was not allowed to rest there, however, and Idler took Walker to task at every opportunity. No doubt he felt honour bound to defend his deceased friend against, what he almost certainly saw as, unjustified criticism from the 'young upstart' Walker. More light was shed on the astonishing claim about Buckley's 33lb. carp in a letter from Idler not long before his own death in December, 1955:

"I consider the late Albert Buckley's capture of a record carp by fishing with rod and line in daylight, still the best feat. He was alone, and landed the great fish himself. He took another one out of Mapperley alive and very much heavier, but made no claim to fame with it because it was not on rod and line." The mystery of this fish appears to have died with Idler. Mapperley undoubtedly held fish of this size, for in 1947 a fish, varyingly estimated at between 33lb and 35lb. was found dead and John Norman wrote the following in August, 1951:

"Dead fish were found three winters ago after a thaw following a heavy snow fall. They were swept down the left-hand spillway and found stranded. One was estimated at 30lb. and there were many small ones of only a few pounds in weight so that Mapperley carp do breed." Further reports of very big carp from Mapperley were given to the author by Tom Duro, the chairman of Cotmanhay Angling Club, whose family has known Mapperley intimately. His father remembered that during the 1926 General Strike two miners speared a very large carp for food, from the inlet pool. During this period other large carp, destined for the pot, were also poached from Mapperley. On another occasion, in the month of May in the early-1950's, a mirror carp weighing over 30 lb. was found dead at the reservoir and was taken to the Black Horse pub in Mapperley village. It was hung up and displayed for some time, causing a great deal of local curiosity, before being buried.

Buckley and his friends continued their exclusive fishing at Mapperley after 1930, until the nationalisation of the coal industry in 1947. Their catch rate was poor with just six fish landed in 17 years, although Les Brown became the first man to take two carp over 20lb.[1]

With the formation of the National Coal Board, fishing on the Shipley estate became more widely available and, in 1951, John Norman, of Nottingham, obtained a permit. At one minute past midnight on June 16th he commenced fishing.

1. It was rumoured that one of Les Brown's carp was caught on a mussel and one caught from a boat.

Mapperley Reservoir & Albert Buckley

For almost two days he tried everything he knew—"floating bread, paste and worm hard on the bottom, night fishing and dawn all drew a blank." He never even saw a carp. So, at 5pm on the Sunday, when the rules stated that fishing had to cease, he went on a further reconnaissance. And there, at the head of the lake, he discovered just what he had been searching for. In a previously unpublished article, uncovered by the author, John describes seeing the Mapperley carp for the very first time:

"And there, at the head of the lake he discovered the carp." The Mapperley shallows, in the early 1950's, looking from the islands.

"I leaned against a long dead willow and searched the shallows with binoculars for a sign of the carp. Nothing moved for some time and then I saw them. Out in the lake, cruising just beneath the surface were fifteen ghostly blue, grey shadows. They moved slowly, ponderously. They looked immense. At over one hundred yards range they still looked huge and I was determined to catch one of them, however long it took."

The next day, on Monday June 18th, 1951, four carp anglers met at Mapperley. They were Maurice Ingham and Richard Walker, who had travelled over from Woldale (Benniworth Haven), B.B. and John Norman. They sat on the dam, near the spot where Albert Buckley had caught the record carp and talked about carp fishing—what else! They bemoaned the scarcity of suitable waters and the possibility of overcoming this by future introductions of carp. They talked about tackle, bait and technique. The idea of a carp-catchers club was also discussed and it was agreed amongst them to take the necessary steps to form it. Soon Jack Smith, of Bradford-on-Avon, and Harry Grief, of Dagenham were invited to join. Then, in August, 1951, a rotary letter, for the exchange of ideas and experiences, was started.

The concept of a carp club was, according to Dick Walker many years later, first suggested by B.B. during the Mapperley visit. ("It was B.B.'s idea to form a club—nobody else's.") Dick agreed that it was a good idea and proposed that it be called the Carp Fishers' Club, but B.B. countered with the title of the Carp Catchers' Club. However, at the time of this statement (1983)[1] Dick claimed that Pete Thomas was also present at the Mapperley meeting, and this is clearly erroneous. Another version of the formation was given by Edward Ensom (Faddist) in *The Angler's News,* in 1952. He stated that the idea of a carp club had come about by way of an exchange of letters between Maurice Ingham and Dick Walker in 1950, and that this suggestion was brought up again during the bankside discussion at Mapperley and put into operation.

But Dick, Maurice, John and B.B. had also come to fish Mapperley. Dick remembered they had gone well prepared:

"Our tackle included six split-cane carp rods, of the type developed by B.B. and I in previous years. John Norman had made his own to our dimensions, and a most creditable job it was. Maurice had made himself a fellow to the first which he made last season, and I had

---

1. Interviewed by Kevin Maddocks and Peter Mohan in 1983, two years before Dick's death on the 2nd August, 1985, and reproduced in the *5th British Carp Study Group Book.*

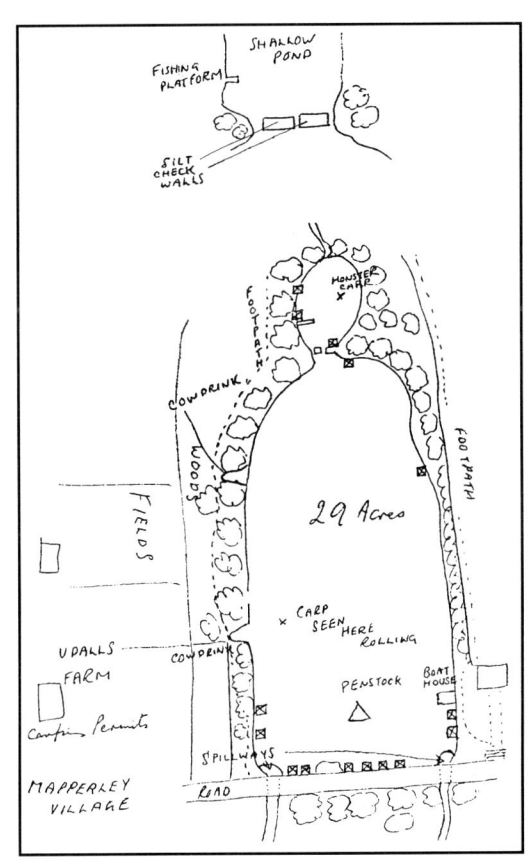

A map of Mapperley Reservoir drawn by John Norman in the early 1950's.

brought my original one, plus two new ones, for B.B. and a second one for my own use."

John Norman had tried to prepare for the onslaught under "clear instructions from B.B. and Walker." However, the heavy rains of spring had flooded the lake and had put paid to any hope of swim clearing and pre-baiting prior to the start of the season. They walked round the lake and as they approached the Inlet Pool, Dick again takes up the story:

"Up at the head of the lake are two artificial islands which appear to have been designed as a silt trap[1]. These can be reached by wading, and we found that in the shallow water at the head of the lake the mud had been stirred up considerably, in a way which might well have been due to carp. Accordingly, we decided to clear out some of the fallen timber, lop off obnoxious willow branches, to groundbait some 20yd. or 30yd. out from the island, and to fish over the groundbait all night and through the early morning. This programme was carried out faithfully, and paste, potato and worm were put out on three rods."

After two days with no sign of carp, Dick, Maurice and B.B. decided to make a dash back to Lincolnshire and Woldale. Whilst they were packing their gear Dick realised he had left his knapsack on the island and, at about 2pm, he went off to retrieve it. In the baited swim were "two mighty carp. I cannot attempt to estimate their weight," he wrote shortly afterwards, "the water there was 3 ft. deep, and when they up-ended to grub amongst the bait, their tails broke surface."

That magical day in July, 1930, when Buckley caught 4 carp, would never be repeated given all the efforts of the Carp Catchers' Club. Dick Walker wrote this in May 1952:

"The work John Norman must have put in at Mapperley is tremendous, and if he even gets one decent carp out of it we shall all have to take our hats off to him; it's the most difficult water I've ever seen."

John responded to Dick's challenge, for that is what it was, a challenge which would encourage and spur him on, with a plea that Mapperley be renamed 'Norman's Folly'. He told the other C.C.C. members that there were now two Mapperley's, "one the Folly and the other a suburb of Nottingham in which there stands a lunatic asylum. If I persist in fishing the former with as little results as I have experienced to date I shall, undoubtedly, finish up in the latter, in a violent ward."

Yet, reward was just around the corner. Many wish for good luck, and assuredly luck often plays its part in angling. But what many perceive as luck is often toil; Fortune's expensive smile is sorely earned.

---

1. John Norman later found out these islands were actually once the ramps that led to an old bridge, as described earlier in the chapter by Albert Buckley. These spanned the stream prior to it being dammed and the Reservoir being formed.

Mapperley Reservoir & Albert Buckley

In August 1952, John Norman caught his Mapperley carp. This is John's story:

"Carp like a bolt hole, and they feed more freely in the shallows when there is deep water nearby. It was tedious work finding such a place with a plummet and float, but I searched the bed of the lake on many occasions. I finally found what appeared to be the ideal spot, namely a 2ft. shallow area which sloped away to 6ft. on either side of an extensive, but thin, weedbed where, I reasoned, both food and shelter were available to the fish. I baited up this swim carefully and although the place was too difficult to fish at the time, since it was necessary to wear gum boots to bait it, I resolved to fish it when the water level fell. But burglars intervened. Three of my neighbours were robbed and, clearly, I could not go off on night fishing expeditions until my wife's peace of mind was restored, by which time that particular season was over."

John Norman night fishing at Mapperley Reservoir in 1952.

In late July, 1952 John began baiting this spot again. A fortnight later he settled down for a night session and cast out a large ball of paste, made with brown bread and honey. He groundbaited with about five dozen balls of similar paste bait and a honey bomb.

"These bombs contain liquid honey in a cardboard carton which is sealed with a thick cellophane top. This cellophane disintegrates in time and the honey oozes out slowly. With my rod on its rest I hid myself and listened all night to huge carp as they splashed and wallowed nearby.

Then at 5.15am I had a run! The line whipped through the rings and it wasn't until seconds later that I heard the buzzer. I leapt up and ran to my buzzer like a rheumatic crab. I was stiff with cramp."

John did everything right. When 80 yards out the fish kited towards a tangle of dead willows on his left, but, by running along the bank, John was able to keep in contact with the fish and turn it from danger. Soon it was in the net and he had his long sought after prize. It weighed 18½lb., was 27½in. long and was a fully-scaled mirror carp.

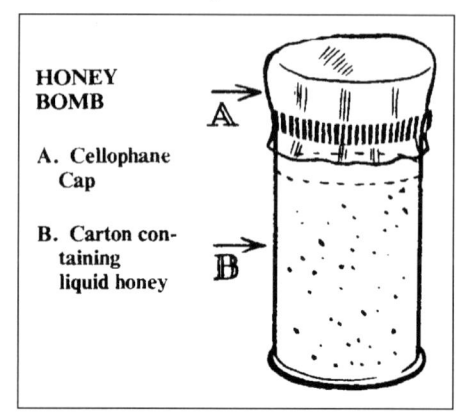

HONEY BOMB

A. Cellophane Cap

B. Carton containing liquid honey

John Norman's drawing of his 'honey bomb' which appeared with the story of the capture of his 18½lb. carp, in the August 1953 issue of Angling magazine. In later years Richard Walker often stated that Norman's capture was far more noteworthy than his own success at Redmire that same year.

A year was to pass before another carp was caught from Mapperley. Success was to come to an old school-pal of John's, called Ken Clower. They had lost touch after their boyhood days although both had served as Gunnery Officers in the Royal Artillery throughout the War. Ken was having a look round Mapperley one day, checking out its carp potential, when he bumped into his old friend actually carp fishing at the top end of the lake. They, there and then, decided to join forces. This is John's story of their campaign and Ken's triumph reported in the C.C.C. rotary letters:

"One evening in July after a really warm, still afternoon Ken went down on his own to the Inlet Pool. For four weeks, prior to the 16th June, we had baited both Inlet Pool and the main lake, an average of four times a week, with at least five loaves each time. Fishing from the wall, with two rods out, Ken settled down well behind cover and fished with large balls of paste on the fringe of the weeds. These cover the middle and top end of the pool, except for a narrow channel down the centre. At 8.30pm he saw a big, grey shadow steal through the gap that connects the pool with the main lake. A small boy, fishing from the wall on the other side of the gap, nearly fell in. The fish was followed by several more soon after the boy departed at 9.30pm, and the bubbles and undulations in the weeds caused by feeding carp became very pronounced. Shortly afterwards came our first run of the season. Ken struck and the fish ran straight up the clear channel between the weed beds. Then it ran under the floating weed, gradually slowing down through the combined resistance of

John Norman's 18½lb. fully-scaled mirror.

weed drag and Ken's finger on the lip of the spool. The carp ran back towards him and the floating weed fell off the line in great streamers. Two dangerous rushes at the fallen timber and rubbish, which is such a feature of the pool early on in the season, were both stopped and soon he controlled his wobbling hands and knees enough to net it. It weighed 11¼lb.

Nothing happened during the night, except the rolling and splashing of big carp further up the pool. At 4.30 next morning another run came and a short, but nevertheless dangerous, fight resulted in a carp of 16¼lb. Well done Ken!

Ken Clower's Mapperley carp weighing 11¼lb. and 16¼lb. Ken was to become well-known as an expert at catching Hampshire Avon barbel and chub, and an angling broadcaster and journalist.

Ken tried to keep them alive in a forty gallon drum but they both, unfortunately, succumbed. Since he has put 200 carp in Mapperley this March I think he is entitled to two fish."

Ken Clower first obtained permission to release more carp into Mapperley from the Estates Officer of the N.C.B. Then on the 26th February, 1953 he liberated 200 4in. yearling carp. A further consignment of 200 5in. yearlings were released during December, 1953. On the 17th November, 1954, the third and final stocking took place. These again were 5in. yearlings, some 120 mirror carp and 180 common carp.

Mapperley Reservoir & Albert Buckley

Of this last batch 275 were placed in Mapperley and 25 in Hogg's Pond. All 700 fish were supplied by The Surrey Trout Farm—Ken purchasing 500 and John Norman the remainder.

On July 17th, 1953 the Carp Catchers' Club's group assault on Mapperley began. Ken Clower had baited up several swims daily for a week prior to their visit. John Norman again takes up the story:

"Pete, Dick and Maurice came down and fished with Ken in the Inlet Pool but without result. I fished the main lake until 12pm and then had a couple of hours sleep in the car whilst waiting for Berth-Jones and his wife, who were due to arrive very late. Round about 3am, since they hadn't arrived, I went back to my fishing.

The next evening the Berth-Jones arrived and we had a concentration in the main lake. Only Dick and Ken remained at the Inlet Pool. At about 2am there was a little tea brewing, and a carp gossiping session going on with Mrs. B.J. and I in

The Carp Catchers' assault on Mapperley. Pete Thomas and Maurice Ingham decide what to have for breakfast!

the centre. This was bad carp fishing since lights were undoubtedly shown, but it taught us a lesson. We were listening to Gerry B.J. telling us that, although he had caught many carp up to 9lb. in his lake, he had never had one over this weight. He was just saying this when his buzzer went. He struck and was into a good fish. He waded out to keep the fish away from the weed fringe and after some heavy boring and runs, he brought a carp of 15lb. to the net. He was delighted, and we all were for him.

Pete got the next fish. It weighed 16lb. and we were very doubtful about landing it since in its first rush it went into a weed bed. Handlining did not work. Maurice heaved in two huge bricks—no good either. Then a final try by Pete at handlining produced a wriggle from the fish, and it came free. What a great spectacle that was. Pete thigh deep in water and weed, the eerie silhouette of the trees in the beam of Maurice's big lamp as it followed the twist and turns of the big carp, myself crouching with the big net and in the background the 'Bee Jays' and Dick. At last it came to the net and everyone cheered loudly."

Here at last was the final confirmation that the Mapperley carp could indeed be caught by design. First John Norman, then Ken Clower and now a joint effort by 'the team'. Dick produced a centre page, picture spread for *Angling Times* detailing the success of their trip. It appeared on August 21st, 1953 and was titled, somewhat sensationally for those days, DICK WALKER EXPLODES THE MAPPERLEY MYTH.

The 'team' in good spirits at Mapperley. Gerry Berth-Jones and his wife May, with Pete Thomas. Maurice Ingham keeps a watchful eye on the proceedings from on high! There is a story, typical of the old reprobate Walker, regarding this particular Mapperley trip. He apparently gathered the 'clan' together and told them he had a master-plan to defeat the Reservoir's carp. Maurice and Pete would fish on the north bank, John and Ken on the south bank, Gerry away at the far end on the dam and himself and May on the stone island!

Maurice Ingham fishing a low-water Mapperley Reservoir in the 1950's.

Sadly John Norman, who was a talented angler and journalist, a gifted artist and a brave individual (he served for three years in the Bomb Disposal Squad of the Royal Engineers before being commissioned into the Royal Artillery), died suddenly at the age of 38. He began to complain of head pains that eventually led to brain surgery. He recovered well from the actual operation but collapsed and died from a chest infection in July 1957, just before the publication of his third angling book, *Coarse Fishing with the Experts*. With the loss of his friend, Ken Clower "no longer had the zest to fish Mapperley on his own." For most of the other members of C.C.C. Redmire Pool was now the focus of their attentions, and so another era at Mapperley Reservoir came to an end.

John Norman getting ready to land Gerry Berth-Jones' 15lb. mirror carp from Mapperley Reservoir in July 1953.

In the late-1950's and early-1960's a new breed of carp angler, the progeny of the writings of Dick Walker and his contemporaries, was making its presence felt up and down the country. At Mapperley these included Alan Otter, Archie Braddock, Ray Longland, Geoff Eddowes, Eric and Arthur Beal, Reg Norgrove, Tom Duro, Dave Allen, Ted Brown, Garth Harrison, Derek Bridges and Roy Crosby.

Tom Duro with his home-made landing net at Mapperley in 1955. Buckley fished from the top of the wall on the right due to higher water levels. The penstock is in the background.

Mapperley even drew the young southern gladiators, eager to do battle with the famed Mapperley monsters. Kenny Ewington, Alec Lewis, Roger Smith and Bill Keal all gave it their best shot. But their success rate was no better than those who had gone before them. They tried all sorts of ingenious ploys and went to great lengths to outwit the Mapperley carp. But the most amazing device was invented by Alan Otter. He knew that honey had been used in the past with success, by both John Norman and Albert Buckley, but he felt there were serious drawbacks in their methods. So this is what Alan dreamed-up:

Nottingham Specimen Group member Archie Braddock standing by the big weedbed on the southern bank of the Reservoir, in August 1960. He lost a huge carp in this weedbed fishing a 'surface-lobworm' and, the following month, landed a 16½-pounder about 200 yards further along the bank whilst using a surface-fished swan mussel.

Below: *Archie Braddock playing his 'huge' carp which he unfortunately lost.*

"After a lot of thought I came up with the idea of a permanent, built-in honey feeder. During the close season, armed with a spade and 20ft. of polythene tubing, I set about laying my pipe. The idea was to carry one end of the tube out along the ledge, secure it, and bury the pipe in the bottom mud, fastening the other end to the platform, where a pump of some sort could be attached for pumping a strong dilution of honey water through the pipe and into the swim. The ramifications involved in this were hilarious. Clad in bathing trunks, spade in one hand, tube in the other I carefully waded along the ledge to the full extent of the tube. I had previously fixed a nozzle to the end of the tube, at right angles, to act as a sort of fountain and to prevent the end of the tube getting buried in the mud. Having selected the spot for this fountain of honey I placed the blade of my spade on the hard clay bottom, taking meticulous care that it was at the correct angle to the bank, and then completely forgetting my buoyancy in the water I pushed on the spade. I did a beautiful forward roll over the handle and plunged head first into 6ft. of water.

After spending the next couple of hours groping for the spade which belonged to my father-in-law I finally managed, a spade's width at a time, to bury the tube along the ledge and secure the other end under the platform out of sight.

The pump presented no problem at all. I got hold of a complete windscreen washer assembly from a friend in the motor trade and it worked admirably. The quart capacity reservoir was filled with strong honey water, the pipes connected up and after a few pumps a small patch of bubbles could be plainly seen out in the swim, subsiding as the air in the pipe cleared and was replaced by honey. Here then was a perfect way of introducing honey into the swim without the disturbance of throwing things out into the night."

Unfortunately, things did not quite go according to plan for Alan. Although the carp in Mapperley have a sweet tooth, so do the bream. This is was happened to Alan at midnight on June 15th:

Everything was quiet; the calm before the storm, I thought to myself as I carefully cast as near as I could to my honey fountain. I did not have long to wait. I had hardly attached my line to the buzzer before it was singing away, frightening me half to death. Even in my most optimistic moments I had not dreamt of success quite so soon. Alas, it was not to be. As soon as the line tightened I recognised the dead weight, the feeble flap of a 4lb. bream hooked on carp tackle. I re-baited, cast again, another flow of honey, short wait, and the same thing happened again, and again and again. It was painfully obvious that a bait must be found that was immune to anything other than a large fish like a carp."

Alan's search for a means of deterring the bream and tench led him to the use of swan mussel as bait. A few weeks before the start of the 1966 season he started introducing the chopped up insides of swan mussels, about 2 or 3 times weekly. A few minutes into the start of the new season and Alan had a run. After a 20 minute fight the first carp over 20lb. from Mapperley for 35 years was landed. He wrote afterwards that "the confidence with which that fish was picking up the mussels meant almost certainly that it had been used to doing so for quite some time. So regular ground-baiting over the past two or three weeks had got the carp into the habit of finding mussels in that particular place and it had eaten so many its natural fears and suspicions were gone. A classic example of the benefits of long term pre-baiting. Unfortunately, I was unable, through pressure of work, to carry on baiting the swim regularly and further visits produced nothing. I do remain convinced however, that given the necessary time and using a natural bait which is more or less immune to the tench and smaller fish, then the odd carp can be tempted."

One-time secretary of the National Carp Club, Alan Otter with his hard-earned 20lb. carp. The Reservoir, which became known as 'Heartbreak Lake', never really produced comparable fish to those that were subsequently caught from Redmire, Billing or Dagenham, but it gained a formidable reputation for uncaught monsters.

Clearly, Mapperley could never have been considered prolific—somewhere in the region of 32-35 'double-figure' carp between 1930 and 1966 works out at about one per year. But the changes that recent times have brought have done nothing to improve the situation. The inlet pool is silted-up and choked with weed; well-worn, permanently numbered swims replace tiny gaps in the bankside vegetation, and the crystal-clear water is now a muddy-brown colour. Buckley would be hard pressed to recognise the lake that once seduced the minds of carp anglers for over twenty years. The inexorable march of progress created Albert's paradise and also destroyed it.

Mapperley Reservoir & Albert Buckley

A List of Carp caught from Mapperley Reservoir

Date	Weight	Captor	Bait
19th July 1930	15-8	Albert Buckley	honey paste (1)
19th July 1930	14-8	Albert Buckley	honey paste (2)
24th July 1930	9-8	Albert Buckley	honey paste
24th July 1930	11-8	Albert Buckley	honey paste
24th July 1930	15-8	Albert Buckley	honey paste
24th July 1930	26-0	Albert Buckley	honey paste
1930	16-8	friend of Buckley's (probably Amos Chambers)	
1930	12-0 (plus 3 others)	W.E. Davis	honey paste (3)
8th Sept. 1930	14-12	Albert Buckley	honey paste
8th Sept. 1930	11-4	Albert Buckley	honey paste
5th Aug. 1931	18-8	Albert Innocent	
11th July 1932	19-8	Albert Buckley	honey paste
August 1937	23-12	Les Brown	mussel (4)
August 1941	20-8	Les Brown	mussel (4)
1946	15-0	ref: *Fishing Gazette*	
June 1947	13-2	Albert Buckley	small red worm
August 1952	18-8	John Norman	brown honey paste
1952	5-4	Ken W. Clower	
July 1953	16-4	Ken W. Clower	paste
July 1953	11-3	Ken W. Clower	paste
July 1953	15-0	Gerry Berth-Jones	
July 1953	16-0	Pete Thomas	
August 1953	14-7	Ken W. Clower	
1954	14-0	friend of Dick Walker	
after 1957	15-0	Ken W. Clower	floating crust (5)
12th Sept. 1958	20-8	Ted Meakin	flake
13th Sept. 1958	17-8	Ted Meakin	flake
Sept. 1958	14-0	Ted Meakin	flake
September 1960	16-8	Archie Braddock	surface mussel
September 1960	16-8	Geoffrey Eddowes	freelined flake
16th June 1966	20-0	Alan Otter	mussel
23rd June 1969	28-0 (common)	Ted Brown	
23rd June 1969	18-8	Ted Brown	
1985	21-0	A. Blanchon	
1985	28-0	Phillip Mead	

1. This fish reported also as 15½ lb. in various publications.
2. This fish reported also as 14½ lb. in various publications.
3. The first carp reputedly to be caught from the shallows. Taken by W.E. Davis, the author of a number of angling books.
4. Rumoured to be caught on mussel and that one of these fish was taken whilst boat fishing.
5. Estimated as no balance was available.

Note: In the April, 1971 issue of the British Carp Study Group magazine, Dick Walker claimed to have caught two double-figure carp from Mapperley. In 1983, Peter Mohan and Kevin Maddocks interviewed Dick at his house and extracts of that tape were published in the 5th British Carp Study Group Magazine. During that interview Dick stated he caught "seven or eight carp out of Mapperley." It is a matter of record that Dick only fished at Mapperley on a few occasions in the 1950's so, clearly, these two statements cannot be reconciled. Furthermore, the author can find no independent reference to any Mapperley carp caught by Dick and can only conclude, therefore, that he is mistaken.

Chapter 6
Dagenham Lake

I'm only halfway to paradise,
So near yet so far away.
         sung by Billy Fury.

The Becontree and District Angling Society was formed in Devonish's Timber Yard on the evening of September 23rd, 1932. Ten local anglers were present and, after electing John Landy as secretary and James Walker as chairman, they agreed to advertise for further members in the local press and hold a General Meeting two weeks later. At that meeting it was proposed by J. Grourk and seconded by E. Devonish that steps be taken to lease Boyer's Pit, in Dagenham, and this was carried unanimously by those present. Some sort of gentleman's agreement with the owners must have been reached as the club erected notice boards around the pit shortly afterwards.

Barely a dozen miles from Charing Cross, Boyer's Pit was still being worked for sand and gravel at that time; it was about five acres in size and seemed to offer excellent potential as a fishery. It contained few fish, if any, and the club determined to acquire stocks from wherever they were able. Mr. C. Single, the Society's president, kindly started the ball rolling by purchasing 750 fish—200 perch, 200 carp, 200 rudd and 150 tench—for £7 16s. 0d. in November of that year. The following March a pond at Ockendon, owned by a Mr. Hawkins, was netted and this resulted in 134 carp, "every one a specimen" according to the Society's minutes. And in 1935 further stocks were purchased from the Thames Angling Preservation Society, although this caused a slight problem as the club had insufficient funds at that time to pay the bill!

Everything appeared to be going well with the Society. The membership was gradually increasing and all the signs suggested that Boyer's Pit was developing into a fine fishery. Then, on January 7th, 1936, at the monthly meeting held at the Railway Hotel, the secretary read out a letter he had received from William Boyer & Sons Ltd. to the effect:

"We (Wm. Boyer & Sons Ltd.) do not understand where you obtained the information that the fishing rights at Dagenham are let, as our manager gave permission to Mr. Walker for the police to fish these waters. We return herewith Postal Orders value £2 0s. 0d."

This clearly caused consternation in the club, but the matter was resolved by the chairman, Jim Walker, who by a strange coincidence just happened to be a policeman, and he approached the local works manager, Mr. Vanner, with the proposition that the Society be allowed to continue fishing and that they recruit 25 police officers as members. Clearly, a bit of 'kidology' had taken place when Jim Walker had initially approached Boyer's about permission to fish the water. In fact, the club attended many meetings with William (Bill) Boyer over the years in an attempt to get a lease, or some form of secure agreement, but he would not oblige them. Boyer would listen to all the club's arguments but his answer was always the same—"If you don't like what you've got you know what you can do!"

In 1936 the largest carp caught weighed 1lb. 5oz. Two years later a batch of specially imported Hungarian carp were added to the existing stocks but, unfortunately, many of them soon perished. Nevertheless, the fishery developed, particularly after 1939 when the gravel extraction on the eastern bank ceased, and the fish grew well in their new, rich environment.

Dagenham Lake

Fish were continually being stocked by various members on an ad-hoc basis, bringing whatever they could catch from local ponds. At that time none of the members seriously fished for carp or even dreamed what lay ahead in the years to come.

Boyer's Pit, or Dagenham Lake as it later became known, is about 11 acres in extent, with the majority of the lake approximately 4ft. deep; the deepest water being about 12ft. At the western end substantial weedbeds existed up until 1964, including water lilies, but the remainder of the lake was clear of weed except that much of the bottom was covered with a rich blanket of silkweed. There can be little doubt that the inter-relationship between the very shallow, crystal-clear water and the prolific silkweed, which is extremely productive in terms of insect life, was the main reason why Dagenham lake produced so many big carp. There probably were other contributory reasons, too; for instance, the club stopped the removal of any of the large carp after three of the first carp over 20lb. had been taken away to be set up. The Society had always discouraged the removal of the carp, with the president, H.L. Bradbury, stating in 1948 that, "We have the welfare of present and future members in mind, and if I am lucky enough to get a carp the right side of 20lb., it will go back into the water. I prefer live fish to glass-case specimens, and that is the opinion of most of our members." It is likely that the Becontree members attitude on this point influenced Dick Walker when he fished the lake in August, 1952. A few days after his visit he wrote in a letter that "I'm not going to stuff any more. I'd rather have a photograph and leave the fish for the next chap to catch. My Dagenham carp was only 11 years old and may one day be a 30-pounder, and if it does, I hope Harry catches it."

The Society also insisted, after 1946, that all pike be returned and this most probably stopped the lake from becoming severely over-populated. The members attitude towards pike was almost unique around this

Harry Grief's 25½lb. Dagenham pike, caught on the 21st December, 1941, before the Society introduced its rule banning their removal.

time, with notable exceptions being writers such as Arthur Walkington and Cecil Plimsole pleading for an end to their "massacre".[1] Unintentionally, this probably also helped to reduce the stocks of small carp that had been introduced. Between 1946 and 1951 around 5,000 small carp and tench were released, and if 20% of these had survived it would have had a serious impact on the lake's ecology at that time.

Dagenham Lake started to gain national prominence in about 1946. The membership had grown from the early days, when it consisted of about 40 members, to somewhere in the region of about 300. For a number of years many of the members had been aware that the water now held large carp. Indeed, several had been caught (with many more being lost)—the best being a fish of 16lb. 12oz. caught in 1943 by Harry Evans which, at that time, was considered a very fine specimen indeed. The story of its capture appeared in B.B.'s *The Fisherman's Bedside Book* published in December 1945, as did the capture of Harry Grief's 25½ lb. pike. However, few, if any, of the members fished seriously for them at this time. There were decent roach and big crucians to be had instead, which offered far more consistent sport. If a big carp came along and the angler was very lucky then, perhaps, just perhaps, it

---
1. Pike should be Protected—by Idler (*The Angler's News* 19th March, 1949).
   Plea for Pike—by Cecil Plimsole (*The Angler's News* 19th February, 1949).

might be landed. One member, called Cornelius, played a carp for over five hours on 2½lb. b.s. line before losing it. But slowly this was changing. In about 1946 three, or four, anglers began specifically fishing for the carp. Major George Draper was the first, then soon followed by Harry Grief and Ernie Pallant. They, and particularly George Draper, brought a fresh approach. They employed adequate tackle for a start. Draper initially used a 9ft., 2-piece Tonkin cane, with a split-cane top, rod. However, he lost no time in instructing an Austrian rod-builder called Myseik, who subsequently caught a Dagenham near 20-pounder himself and who made rods under the trade name of 'Marvellor', to build him a three-piece split-cane model (actually whole Tonkin cane for the first 3ft.) with a test curve of about 2lb.

Harry Grief, in about 1951, made his own split-cane rod and Dick Walker, writing in June, 1952, said of it:

"I have handled Harry's carp rod and for Dagenham I consider it superior to the Mk. IV. At Dagenham a line of 6lb. to 8lb. b.s. is strong enough and with a rod like Harry's it would be possible to keep more out of the water when playing a fish a long way off. The rather easier action would also help with lighter lines. For more snaggy or weedier waters I prefer the Mk. IV, but on the water for which it was designed it would be difficult to better Harry's. It is 11ft. and is about half-way between the Avon rod and the Mk. IV in power." They had trouble with various makes of hooks, so Major Draper made his own from hand-forged, surgical steel which they attempted, unsuccessfully, to get Hardy's to reproduce. Draper had been stationed in New Zealand with the Royal Artillery Corps., and he had spent a fair amount of time fishing for the huge rainbow trout in Lake Tarpo, so he had considerable experience in handling big fish.

George Draper mainly used soft bread paste as a bait, which he made up at home and brought in a stone jar. He was meticu-

Harry Grief photographed in 1985 with the rod he and Arthur Higgins designed for carp fishing at Dagenham. It was described as being stiffer than the Wallis Wizard —"more akin to the Slater's Newark Perfection."

lous and precise in everything he did—one of his hobbies being model making—and this resulted in a number of his items of tackle being self-made, with great care and attention to detail. Whilst Harry and his friend, Ernie Pallant, float fished, using a narrow-beamed torch after dark for illumination, Draper invariably light-legered, fishing at short range. They also started, at Major Draper's instigation, recording water temperature and wind direction to see if there was any relationship with the carp's feeding habits. In 1950 Draper wrote the following:

"During the season of 1948 I was able to fish quite regularly, at least twice every week on our club water from the opening day of the season until the end of October, so have chosen the appropriate entries for that period. I was fishing for carp, and more especially for large carp, so the scope of this contribution is somewhat limited with regard to quarry, period and locale, although it has the advantage of being a careful record covering a full season's fishing under variable conditions."

Dagenham Lake

Date	No. of fish	Weight	Water Temp.	Wind
23rd June	4 commons	4¼, 3½, 3½, 2¾lb.	63°F	S.E., almost flat calm
30th June	1 mirror	16¼lb.	58°F	N.W., strong in gusts, rain squalls
5th July	1 mirror	16lb. 7oz.	59°F	N.W., to S.E., slight and variable
5th July	1 common	2lb.		
12th July	1 common	2¾lb.	58°F	West, moderate
19th July	1 common	3¼lb.	64°F	West, moderate to fresh
20th August	1 common	2½lb.	60°F	S.W., almost flat calm
30th August	1 common	3¼lb.	61°F	S.S.E., almost flat calm
8th Sept.	1 common	3lb.	62°F	S.E., almost flat calm
11th Sept.	1 mirror	20lb. 6oz.	64°F	S.E., slight
29th Sept.	1 common	2¾lb.	58°F	S.W., slight
3rd Oct.	1 common	3lb.	57°F	West to S.W., slight

George Draper's weather records for the visits to Dagenham Lake in 1948 when he caught carp.

"Whilst is would be presumptuous to be dogmatic on the strength of such slight evidence I am of the opinion that wind direction is of little or no importance, although its nature might be.

During the long spell of prevailing north-easterly wind in 1947 I had excellent sport with carp. The weather was bright and settled and the wind itself was certainly not cold, just a pleasant mild breeze. Water temperature on the other hand might prove to be of the greatest importance.

During hot spells, with the water temperature over 68°F, the carp seemed very listless and choosy, and below 58°F were inclined to be sluggish. A hot spell like this occurred halfway through July and lasted until towards the end of August, whilst the water temperature started to drop rather abruptly at the beginning of October, sending the fish completely off feed. The ideal water temperature seemed to be about 62 to 64°F, bites came more frequently and with greater zest.

All fish of the smaller size were weighed on my pocket balance to the nearest ¼lb., whilst those over the 10lb. mark on the club scales, most meticulously to the uttermost ounce. All water temperatures were taken at the bottom of the pond in about six feet of water."

Dagenham Lake in the late 1940's.

It is clear that this small group, and particularly Major Draper, displayed considerable perseverance. It is much easier, nowadays, to carry on fishing in a certain way when you have the knowledge that what you are doing has produced a great many fish in the past. For those pioneers at Dagenham that luxury didn't exist. It is to their credit that they stuck at it, and caught huge carp not by luck, but by intention.

Probably somewhere in the region of only 15 to 20 carp over 20lb. had ever been caught on rod and line in Britain up until this time, and the largest was Buckley's fish of 26lb. By July, 1946 the largest carp landed at Dagenham was 16¾lb., yet bigger carp could often be seen in the shallow, clear water and there was a great deal of speculation amongst the members that a new record might one day be caught. Then A.G. Horwood, fishing maggots, caught a leather carp which weighed 22lb. Two days later, Frank Scott, using an old 3-piece, 12ft. greenheart rod, beat that by a pound. The time for conjecture was over; here was the proof that Dagenham definitely had the potential to produce a new record carp. That must have been a considerable fillip to the handful of serious carp anglers who fished there at that time. Unknown to them, however, a lot of blank trips lay ahead before they would reap their justly deserved rewards. Major Draper fished two, sometimes three nights a week, usually arriving about 10pm and leaving for home, which was at Ilford, on the early morning milk train. Harry Grief usually carp fished in the evenings, starting about 7pm and carrying on through until about midnight. Sometimes he stayed longer if the prospects seemed good.

Frank Scott's 23lb. carp caught on the 7th July, 1946.

An early Dagenham carp fisher. His choice of tackle was based partly on the belief that carp could only be hooked on fine line and also on the idea that other species might as well be caught during the prolonged periods of inactivity. In spite of these handicaps some success was forthcoming due to the general lack of snags and weeds in the Lake. These concepts were to change, first with the specialisation of George Draper and Harry Grief, and, later, through the visits and influence of Dick Walker.

But it wasn't until October the following year that all the effort paid off. George Draper then landed the second largest carp ever seen in this country. It was caught at 3am and not weighed until several hours later when it registered 25½lb. It was suggested that it may well have weighed over 26lb. at the time of capture and would have broken the record. This may indeed be true, but by the same token Buckley's fish was gaffed, lost a lot of blood, and was not weighed until 7½ hours later.

1948 saw Dagenham claim the crown as Britain's premier carp water; three fish over 20lb. were caught, in addition to a number of other very large fish. Harry Grief caught his first 20-pounder and Major Draper landed his second, but the largest fell to Len Singer. This is his story written in 1953:

"It was a very warm evening, calm with no wind whatsoever. The water temperature was 56-58°C and had been so for the preceding week. I was tackled up with 6lb. Luron line,

Dagenham Lake

four-inch centre-pin reel and a no. 8 hook, Model Perfect. I had fixed a small split-shot nine inches from the hook which stopped a home-made, cork-encased lead, which just sank. This gave enough weight for casting but very little resistance in the water. It also clears the bottom weed when reclaiming line from a cast. The rod was 12ft., split-cane from butt to tip, built in three sections and the bait was very soft bread paste.

My first cast was made without bait allowing the line to sink and take up water. The line was then wound in and approximately thirty yards was pulled off the reel (the same amount was pulled off every cast) and coiled at my feet. Soft paste, the size of a walnut, was placed on the hook and cast out. By aiming at an object on the opposite bank, and with the same amount of line pulled off the reel each time, I am able to hit the same place within a few yards every cast. I then threw in half-a-dozen knobs of paste, as near as I could to where the hookbait sank. The line was then gently tightened against the lead, two yards pulled off the reel, and a small piece of paste placed six inches from the bottom ring with the rest of the two yards coiled beneath it. Some time later, in fading light, my tell-tale paste jerked up to the bottom ring and stopped. I, too, had jerked upright, waited for some further indication but then assumed nothing was doing. Then suddenly I saw my coils of line moving through the ring. I grabbed the rod and with a long, backward, follow-through (nylon will not stand shock tactics) drove home the hook by the weight of the check only. After twenty minutes, in which time I had to climb on top of the bank and raise the rod vertically with extended arms to allow Johnnie and Mary (the swans) to pass under the line, the fish was on the bank—a common carp of 21lb. 15oz."

The fat 21lb. 15oz. common carp caught by Len Singer in September, 1948. It was probably the largest caught in the country that season.

Serious carp fishing from a popular swim on the south bank of Dagenham Lake.

Around this time several letters appeared in *The Angler's News,* promoting the view that the carp caught from Dagenham Pit should really not be eligible for entry into that newspaper's renowned competition. The gist of the argument was that because Dagenham was private, and the fishing unavailable to all and sundry this constituted an unfair advantage. The correspondence dragged on for weeks with even Dick Walker wading in. However, the saga was finally closed by the editor, no doubt in the interests of social diplomacy, realising that it is unwise for Englishmen to discuss politics, religion and fishing in private waters!

The beginning of the following season understandably started with eager anticipation. Big carp could be seen frolicking in the open water, taking free offerings completely bereft of caution. Then, as if they somehow understand the angler's intentions, when the season begins the carp are gone like some ethereal will-o'-the-wisp.

The days came and went, weeks drifted by, and still no carp of substance were caught. It wasn't until August that F.C. Steward caught the first carp, another magnificent common carp, weighing just over 20lb. As the season faded perhaps there were some who wondered, maybe even a few who spoke aloud, that Dagenham was in decline. Had the chance of breaking the carp record slipped by; even if monster carp still languished in the lake, had they become too cunning to be tempted?

But with a new season comes fresh hope. Gone are the long, cold nights of winter when dreams slowly rebuild desires. Soon eager anticipation washes away lingering doubts. So it was that the carp fishers

F.C. Steward with his 20lb. 2oz. carp.

of Dagenham made plans for another assault on their mysterious and secretive quarry. Many big carp were caught that year and Buckley's record so nearly tumbled. It shook, it rocked, it trembled but just a few ounces lay between Dagenham's best and the 20-year-old Mapperley giant. Few fanatical anglers can ever experience the thoughts and emotions that must have raced through Harry Grief's mind as he clambered up the bank with his prize and carried it to the hut to be weighed. Had all those countless hours finally brought their reward? The cold, clinical scales said 25lb. 12oz.—just 4oz. short. So near yet so far away! It is easy to be overwhelmed in such situations. Time can stand still for the captor, whilst all around there is a buzz of chatter from other excited anglers. Someone tried to push an orange in the carp's mouth to make the scales register over 26lb. Another said, "Come on Harry, we'll all say it weighed over 26lb." But Harry would have none of it, his first concern was for the welfare of the fish. So Ernie Pallant and Harry carried the fish carefully back to the water's edge and gently released it. A wonderful gesture from a fine sportsman.

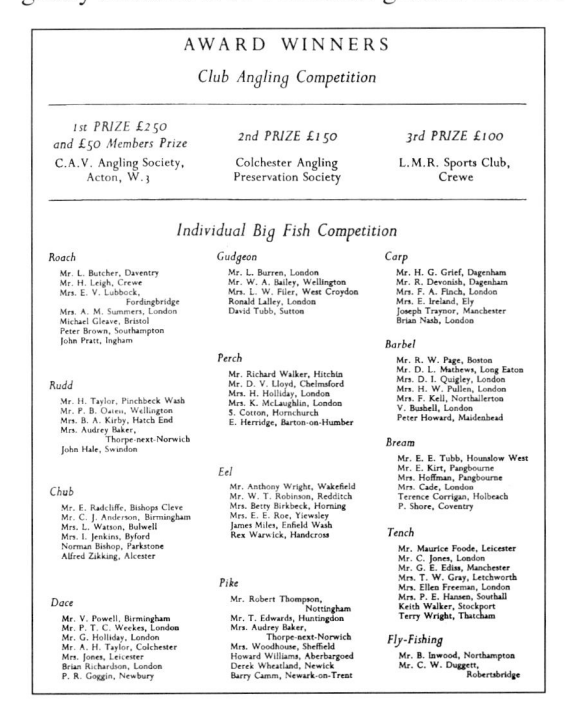

The Daily Mirror Award Competition presentation that Harry Grief attended for catching his 25¾lb carp. Many famous names were also in attendance: Ernie Tubb, who fished for the Wadhurst carp; Dick Walker, who had caught a 4lb. 2oz. Arlesey perch; Hampshire Avon supremo Humprey Lubbock's wife, even a young Ron Lalley, later to fish at Bracken Lake and Redmire.

Dagenham Lake

Harry's fish was, of course, the second best carp ever caught at the time and the story of its capture is now told for the first time in Harry's own words, written shortly afterwards:

"Away in the heart of an industrial town in Essex lies a famous carp fishery, known to anglers throughout the country as Dagenham Lake. It is a lake with a difference, a complete contrast to a carp fisher's dream of the remote, mysterious pool, far from the maddening crowd, where absolute peace and quietness reign supreme. A contrast so marked, that an angler here fishes to the accompaniment of the thunderous roar of trains that skirt the lake, which vibrate and shudder the very ground he sits upon. Vivid flashes of light from the conductor rails of the electric trains slice the night sky as they stream by incessantly; brilliant arc lights from the nearby factory buildings cast crazy reflections upon the water during the dark hours and yet, under circumstances such as I have described, the simple fact remains that probably more 20lb. carp have been taken from this fishery than any other in the country.

This achievement is mainly due to the combined efforts of the Becontree and District A.S. who, during their 20 years of existence, have exercised their good judgement and care to preserve sport for the future, with the possibility of a record carp in the offing. Much effort has been made to attain this end, as records show, and the credit must belong to the officers and members of the club as a whole.

The 27th was a typical June day, hot and sunny, with a cloudless sky. Thoughts of an evening's fishing were naturally with me throughout the day and, in consequence, as soon as my business was concluded, I promptly made my way to the lake. Pausing to discuss the prospects with a colleague, he informed me that he had taken a 15lb. carp the previous evening when conditions seemed identical.

Equipped with suitable tackle for large carp, a 9½ft. built-cane rod[1], 6lb. monofilament line, peacock quill, together with a no. 5, specially forged, hand-made hook I proceeded to a swim where I had previously observed carp feeding just before dusk.

I quietly cast in a large piece of breadflake, which sank slowly into about 5ft. of water, coming to rest on a ledge about 12in. wide. In a fairly short space of time my float dipped sharply, and was away. The culprit proved to be a common carp of about 3lb., which was immediately returned.

I re-baited, again with flake, throwing in a few pieces as groundbait, and cast to exactly the same spot. As the light began to fade I switched on my hand-lamp and shone it on my float. Suddenly, the silence is shattered as a train roars by on the other side of the lake, then, just as quickly, all is quiet again. The patient watch on the float is resumed and then I am startled again as a large carp leaps from the water, not 20 yards away, and crashes back into its element, leaving a cascade of water to follow, each drop glistening like a jewel in the reflection of the many powerful arc lights opposite.

I thought I detected a slight movement of the float, and surely enough it is moving— very, very slowly along the surface. My hand steals instinctively towards the butt, the float

---

HOMERS, Fishing Tackle Specialists
135, Woodgrange Road, Forest Gate, London, E.7

USING A HOMERS "Dagenham" Three piece Split Cane 11ft. 6in. Rod, and a MILWARD "White Spider" new Terylene Line, 6 lb. breaking strain, Mr. H. Greif landed another magnificent CARP of 25 lbs. 12 ozs.

MILWARDS NEW BLACK OR WHITE SPIDER LINES made from TERYLENE POLYESTER YARN, the new super strong waterproof, rotproof material. The greatest discovery yet made in the field of line making.

Prices per 100 yds.
lbs. breaking strain.

3	4	6	8	11	15	21	30
18/4	19/7	20/10	23/3	28/2	33/8	39/10	45/11

SEND FOR HOMERS NEW 1950 CATALOGUE
An excellent guide for all Anglers. Price **6d.** inclusive of Postage.
ESTABLISHED 1887

---

1. There is a question mark regarding the actual tackle used. Although Harry Grief wrote the above shortly after the capture, an advertisement appeared on the front page of *The Angler's News,* on August 19th, 1950, which stated that the fish was caught "on a Homers 'Dagenham' 3-piece, 11ft. 6in. split cane rod and Milward's 'White Spider' new Terylene 6lb. line."

finally submerges and the hook is firmly driven home. The next second my reel check was shrieking as the fish tore off about 80 yards of line before I managed to slow it down. Anglers along the bank reeled in their rods and began offering the usual well-meaning advice. The fish was slowly circling with the top rod joint twitching like a needle on a weighing machine! I increased the pressure but the carp responded by streaking off to my left along the bankside. Side-strain at last turned its head and this time it shot off towards the centre of the lake. Suddenly it bored deeply, causing me to apply all the pressure I dare. Then a few yards, precious yards, of line are recovered and so, back and forth, the tussle went on. I began to think in terms of a record fish and half-glanced at the size of my landing net. Suddenly, the rod sprang back and the line fell slack. My heart sank and I frantically reeled in, desperately hoping against hope. Despair was just as quickly replaced with elation as I re-made contact and realised the fish was charging directly towards me. At the last moment it veered sharply to my left, like a car skidding around a corner. This last effort exhausted both the fish and myself and, with my heart pounding like a piston, I again applied the deadly side-strain and finally stopped my gallant adversary. I gently reeled it, completely spent, into the net. There, after 30 minutes of thrills, lay a beautifully proportioned common carp. Willing hands bore the capture to the club hut for weighing which, after a re-check, proved to be 25lb. 12oz.—just 4oz. less than the record. I lifted it from the scales and gently carried it back, where I returned it to the water and stood watching it slowly recover from its ordeal. Then, with a defiant flick of its tail, it disappeared from sight leaving me alone at the bankside with my thoughts."

No photograph was taken of Harry's near record carp, but this is his 23½-pounder caught on the opening day of the 1958 season.

And so Dagenham's great chance, its crowning moment in history, slipped away. The following year Redmire would be discovered and its shadow would obscure all other aspirants for the next forty years. Many more big carp would still be caught from the Becontree water and many great battles would take place, but none would provide a better example of the friendly and helpful atmosphere that this club engendered than that of a young, enthusiastic teenager.

"Many more big carp would still be caught from the Becontree water and many great battles would take place" ...Len Singer with his 22¼-pounder. Len experimented with all sorts of baits during his carp fishing visits to Dagenham, including sausage, macaroni and even bluebell bulbs.

Dagenham Lake

This is Raymond Piper's story that appeared in the September, 1955 issue of *Angling Times*:

"To experienced carp angler Harry Grief there seemed little hope of taking fish on the day he acted as host to the 12-year-old son of a friend. For the temperature was 76 degrees and the water on the lake was perfectly calm.

But Harry took the youngster, Raymond Piper, out on his boat accompanied by another angler. Into the heat of the afternoon they boated, across the lake into a dense patch of weed stretching 100 yards by 50 yards. And here they surprised a shoal of carp. Back they pulled gently to decide a plan of action.

Raymond was by now so excited that, rather than disappoint him, the others—despite the obvious difficulties—agreed to try for carp. If one was hooked they would up anchor and follow it to clearer water.

And Raymond was the one to get the bite. Down went his float and a big carp was on. Up came the anchors as the fish bored away steadily through the masses of weed whilst Raymond held the rod manfully. The two men with him, time after time, cleared off the weed around the line—some of it in very heavy bunches, but the carp refused to leave the weed and Raymond refused to give in.

It was now decided to move the boat away and try and drag the fish into clear water. Slowly this was achieved. Inch by inch the boat moved, and four times the carp dived under the boat so that Raymond was obliged to leap along the boat and pass his line underneath to avoid a break.

Eventually, they cleared the weeds and landed Raymond where, 150 yards from the spot that he first hooked the fish, he played it out and won the battle.

When it was landed the carp weighed 22lb. It had put up a tremendous battle but had been beaten by Raymond's skill and determination, despite his 7lb. line and size 8 hook. Raymond is believed to be the youngest angler ever to catch a carp over 20lb."

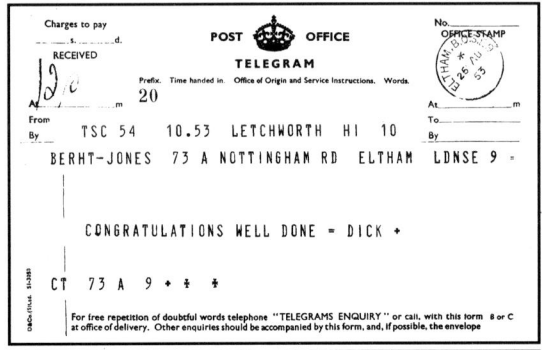

Right: Gerry Berth-Jones with his 23lb. 10oz. carp.
Top: Walker's sent this telegram to Gerry as soon as he heard about the capture of the only 20-pounder that year.
Above: The Carp Catchers' Club were closely involved with the Dagenham Lake at one stage. B.B., and later Dick Walker, were both made honorary vice-presidents.

Dagenham Lake

In 1978 the author wrote the following about his own early carp fishing:

"The next year we started exactly were we had left off. We were at a loss to understand why we failed to get bites. It was a story which has been repeated time and time again, since the Red Spinners first fished at Cheshunt and their captures petered out as did those of the members of the Carp Catchers' Club at Redmire after 1960. It was a failure to keep one step ahead of the fish." With no disrespect to the anglers who fished for carp at Dagenham they, too, fell into the same trap. They continued with the same tried and tested methods and baits. Richard Walker saw the problem and wrote in private correspondence about Dagenham to Ken Sutton that, "Only a very few people fish for the big carp and even then little imagination is used, they never try to think ahead of the carp, and persevere instead of thinking, with the same methods that were to some small degree successful in 1946." Yet, with the benefit of hindsight, exactly the same could be said of Walker himself and his efforts at Redmire. Dogmatism is a symptom of growing old, yet truth is the arrogance of youth! I guess the great man realised this in his later years and wrote this to the author shortly before he died:

"To quote Tennyson:
'Our little systems have their day.
They have their day and cease to be.'
Or, if you prefer another bit of Tennyson:
'The old order changeth, yielding place to new.'

The time comes in all fields of human endeavour when older men should get out of the way and let the younger and more energetic chaps take over."

Issac Newton said that, "If I have seen a little further, it is by standing on the shoulders of giants." Truly, so many stood on Dick's giant shoulders.

Dick with his first 20lb. carp—a Dagenham common weighing 22¾lb. The fish was caught at 1.05pm and the 17½lb. mirror at 4.45pm on the 1st August, 1952. His intellectual prowess occasionally led him to be arrogant which surfaced after these impressive captures, distinguished by the fact that he used logic rather than perseverance in their downfall. Being caught at distance and during a hot afternoon created a considerable amount of speculation and admiration amongst some of the club members, several of whom soon acquired fixed-spool reels. Walker was doubtful these would achieve the desired results, writing to Gerry Berth-Jones at the time that "the trouble about those chaps at Dagenham is that they only know what I did, not why I did it."

Dagenham Lake

But at Dagenham, as with the rest of the country, an infusion of new blood and fresh ideas came through the popularisation of carp fishing. The 'old order' was indeed changing. The dominant, and historically consummate, magazines had been *The Fishing Gazette* and *The Angler's News*. The 55-year-old *Angler's News* ceased on the 2nd March, 1956, almost three years after *Angling Times* was founded. *The Gazette,* which stretched back to 26th April, 1877, struggled on for a little longer until its 4,445th issue on the 30th June, 1962. But new hopes require fresh illusions and, so, following *Angling Times* we had *Angling* (June 1959), *Angler's World* (June 1962), *Fishing* (22nd February, 1963), *Creel* (July 1963) and *The Angler's Mail* (11th June, 1964)—a plethora of imagery, of dreams and ambitions! The proliferation of periodicals between 1959 and 1964 was a result of demand and, during this period, as an integral part of that growth the appeal of carp fishing began to mushroom also. The 'baby boom' which followed World War II had led, by the early-1960's, to large numbers of teenagers with unprecedented affluence and leisure, and open and impressionable minds! This also coincided with a greater availability of carp fisheries, many of them maturing gravel pits created as a by-product of the post-war building boom and the stockings during the early-1950's, promoted vigorously by Dick Walker and his friends. And John Lenton was one of these 'young, enquiring minds'. He began concentrating on carp in the late-1950's and spent his time studying Dagenham Lake. Few big fish were now being caught, indeed some members suggested they were no longer present in the same numbers. Only one carp over 20lb. had been caught in 1956, none in 1957, two in 1958 and three in 1959. In 1960 John Lenton alone caught five, plus another 11 over 14lb.—a quite outstanding performance. He put part of his success down to his method of groundbaiting. This consisted of trails of very stiff paste all leading to the same area. A short distance away soft bread was then introduced to concentrate the attention of the numerous small bream away from the main baited area. It is interesting to note that most of the early members who fished specifically for the carp refrained from using groundbait. Harry Grief "didn't agree with excessive groundbaiting" and, more often than not, they felt that it would only encourage the attention of unwanted species.

Lenton continued to reign supreme at Dagenham for the next few years, even becoming the club's secretary and treasurer. But in 1964 disaster struck. Boyer's started working the site again and the gravel washings were discharged into the lake. Harry Grief sadly remembers the "black, filthy ooze" being pumped into his lovely water and knew it was the end of an era.

In later years Dick was to be very critical of the 'numbers' syndrome that had become widespread throughout carp fishing. This letter, written shortly after his Dagenham capture, confirms that he also could be a slave to vanity!

Right: *John Lenton returns a 19-pounder to Dagenham.*

A List of Carp caught from Dagenham Lake

Date	Weight		Captor	Details
	9-0		H. Evans	
27/10/43	16-12	mirror	H. Evans	Story in B.B.'s *Fisherman's Bedside Book*
July 1944	14-0		H.J. Grief	
17/6/45	10-2	mirror	F.E. Bull	
2/7/45	13-8	mirror	H. Evans	
23/7/45	10-1	mirror	A. Monk	
1/8/45	10-3	mirror	S. Bradbury	
13/8/45	9-0	mirror		
16/8/45	8-1	common	R. Dick	
16/6/46	14-11½		R. Dick	
17/6/46	13-5	mirror	F. Bull	
29/6/46	10-12	mirror	A. Archibold	
5/7/46	22-0	leather	A.G. Horwood	maggot; 28½in. x 28½in.; set-up
7/7/46	23-0	mirror	F. Scott	30¼" x 28"; set-up
6/9/47	16-12	leather	A. Wisland	
1/10/47	25-9	mirror	G. Draper	33½in. x 30in.; fish set-up
16/6/48	11-3½	mirror	L. Bidgeway	
19/6/48	15-4	mirror	H.E. Davis	
19/6/48	14-12	mirror	G. Austin	
29/6/48	18-4	common	H.A. Poole	float/leger; 12 lb. line; no. 4 hook; paste
30/6/48	16-4	mirror	G. Draper	
3/7/48	18-6	mirror	J. Stephens	
5/7/48	18-14	common	A.E. Cutts	
5/7/48	16-7	mirror	G. Draper	
24/8/48	20-2	leather	H.J. Grief	
11/9/48	20-6	mirror	G. Draper	
14/9/48	21-15	common	L.R. Singer	30in. x 27½in.
27/9/48	11-7	mirror	W. Chivers	
1/8/49	20-2	common	F.C. Steward	small red worm on 4½lb. line.
22/9/49	11-6	mirror	L.R. Singer	
25/6/50	11-0½	common	H. Thompson	
26/6/50	15-4	mirror	H.A. Poole	
27/6/50	25-12	common	H.J. Grief	flake; float tackle; 9.30pm
27/6/50	15-6	mirror	G. Banham	
July 1950	15-6		C. Thompson	
23/7/50	15-14	mirror	C. Stephens	
28/7/50	13-12	mirror	C. Stephens	
30/7/50	21-14	common	R.G. Devonish	Caught in all-night competition—largest ever caught in a match at time; breadflake
12/8/50	14-6½	mirror	G. Draper	
27/8/50	15-9	mirror	G. Rousell	
12/9/50	20-6	mirror	H. Stanbridge	28in. x 25½in.
15/9/50	11-15	mirror	H. Stanbridge	
5/10/50	19-12	mirror	R. Myseik	
12/10/50	16-2	mirror	E. Pallant	Spinning for pike from boat; foul-hooked
12/10/50	24-8	mirror	E. Pallant	Spinning for pike from boat; foul-hooked
29/10/50	15-3	mirror	L.R. Singer	
19/1/50	19-12	mirror	E. Pallant	Foul-hooked

Dagenham Lake

Date	Weight	Type	Angler	Notes
28/6/51	17-8	mirror	H. Poole	
3/7/51	15-2	mirror	L.R. Singer	
1/8/52	22-12	common	R. Walker	1.05pm; sunk crust
1/8/52	17-8	mirror	R. Walker	4.45pm; sunk crust
9/8/52	20-0	common	F. Bull	6am; sunk crust
Aug. 1953	23-10	leather	G. Berth-Jones	
1954	14-2	common	Mr. Mansell	12 hook; mid-water, roach fishing
17/6/55	15-4	common	F. Piper	crust
17/6/55	21-12	mirror	F. Piper	crust
19/6/55	22-4	mirror	L.R. Singer	paste
19/6/55	24-12	common	S. Manning	worm; 7lb. line; size 12 hook (3)
17/7/55	23-0	common	E. Pallant	flake
6/8/55	21-10	common	H. Bamford	maggot
19/8/55	22-0	common	R. Piper	aged 14; crust
7/8/56	21-9	common	C. Mansell	flake
1956	18-9		R. Baker	
1957	19-4	common	C. Mansell	
1957	18-12		C. Mansell	
16/6/58	23-8	mirror	H.J. Grief	paste
8/7/58	19-10	common	R. Baker	paste
27/7/58	12-6		C. Mansell	
30/7/58	14-5		C. Mansell	
2/8/58	21-0	common	J. Key	11.05pm
23/8/58	16-12		Members guest	
20/6/59	19-7½	mirror	F. Bull	size 12 hook; 3½lb. line
4/7/59	11-8¼	common	G.B. Smith	
21/7/59	11-9	common	B. Livsey	
27/7/59	14-8	mirror	G.B. Smith	
13/8/59	21-15	common	J. Key	
27/8/59	14-8	mirror	J. Key	
15/9/59	20-7	mirror	J. Hollick	
23/11/59	20-12	mirror	J. Mansell	size 12 hook; 3½lb. line; flake

Some Carp over 20 lb. caught after 1960

Date	Weight	Angler
9/7/60	21-8	J. Lenton
22/7/60	20-3½	J. Lenton
30/7/60	23-14	J. Lenton
3/9/60	21-7	J. Lenton
17/9/60	21-0	J. Lenton
1960	20-12	J. Mansell
30/9/61	22-5	J. Lenton (1)
6/10/61	22-9	L.R. Singer (2)
1962	23-4	J. Lenton
1963	21-14	C. Everitt
1963	21-10	J. Lenton
1964	23-1	J. ?
1964	21-1	R. Snaith

Len Singer with his 22lb. 9oz. carp caught in 1961. After Lenton, Len was one of the most successful carp anglers in the early 1960's.

1. Also caught a further seven carp over 17lb. that season.
2. In addition also caught five over 12lb. that season.
3. Won a prize rod in the 1955 *Angling Times* Specimen Fish Competition.

Chapter 7
Redmire Pool

*There's a spot in my heart which no colleen may own,
There's that depth in my soul never sounded or known,
There's a place in my memory, my life that you fill,
No other may take it, no one ever will.*
         sung by John McCormack.

The influence of Redmire Pool and what happened there in the development of carp fishing cannot be overstated. For a quarter of a century, from 1951 until the end of the Jack Hilton period, Redmire was in the mainstream of the evolution of carp fishing methodology. The magnetism of the Pool drew many of the innovators of carp fishing and they developed, honed and perfected their original ideas there; and many of them fell in love with the place. For these reasons, and also because of its history, the productiveness of the water in terms of big carp, and its utter enchantment, Len Arbery and Kevin Clifford wrote their book, *Redmire Pool,* published in 1984 by Beekay.

The main problem when writing a book containing a lot of factual information, as *Redmire Pool* does, is trying to verify that what you are told, and read, is correct. The preparation of *Redmire Pool* confirmed many things. People sometimes embellish the truth; with the passage of time they often forget, or make mistakes, and so the authors got a few details wrong in the book. Some of the errors are not that important although it is always preferable, with a book of this nature, to be factually correct, whilst others are matters of substance. For instance, whilst researching the book, K.C. checked the Meteorological Office's weather records for Ross-on-Wye, on Wednesday, the 3rd October, 1951—the day Bob Richards caught his record fish, and noted it was foggy and overcast. After the book was published he managed to get hold of Bob Richards handwritten account of the capture and Bob stated it was bright and sunny! Yet, a Miss M. Wight, who interviewed Bob shortly after the capture commented that the fish was caught on a "dull, foggy day." Most would agree that getting the weather wrong is an occupational hazard of fishing but more serious is the following. On information received, as the police often say, the author wrote to Richard Walker in 1984 asking him if Bob Reynolds had ever been a member of the Carp Catchers' Club.

Dick with Bob Richards' record carp just prior to setting it up.

Redmire Pool

Dick replied bluntly, "Bob Reynolds was never a member of the C.C.C." In fact, Bob was invited to join by Dick himself, on behalf of the C.C.C., at the same time as Fred J. Taylor and Dick Kefford. They all accepted and a notice to this effect appeared in the *Angling Times* of November 8th, 1957. I think I can guess why Dick denied Bob Reynolds was ever a member of the C.C.C. and when I queried another discrepancy, he wrote:

"Memory is indeed fallible, specially when one has to go back 25 years or so! I think you will have to avoid positive statements of your own, in some cases, and simply write 'according to so-and so' or 'as far as I can discover'. All historians are faced with such problems and there's only one thing they can be sure of, which is that they can never hope to be one hundred percent right."

So in an attempt to 'set the record straight', and shed a little light on new information about the very early days of Redmire, this chapter will cover the pool's history when it was just starting to make history.

The Pool, as part of Bernithan Court Estate, was owned by the Hoskyns family for about 150 years, until around 1830. The property then passed to Mr. Phillips, of Worcester, and later a Mr. Rudge. In about 1890, it was purchased by the Drinkwater family. During this period the Estate fell into decay, with turkeys being reared in what is now the drawing room of the house. In 1926 is was bought by Lt. Colonel Barnardiston. Action was now taken to repair the damage brought about by years of neglect. In 1951 the property was sold to Mrs. Amy Simmons, great aunt of the Richardson brothers and Simon Bailey who now own it. Mrs. Simmons let the house to Captain John Francis Maclean until his wife's death in 1966.

In early March, 1934 fifty 5½-8in. carp were stocked in the Pool. They were purchased from the Surrey Trout Farm. Lt. Col. Barnardiston and his wife collected them personally from the Midland Fishery, at Nailsworth, which is about 30 miles from Ross.

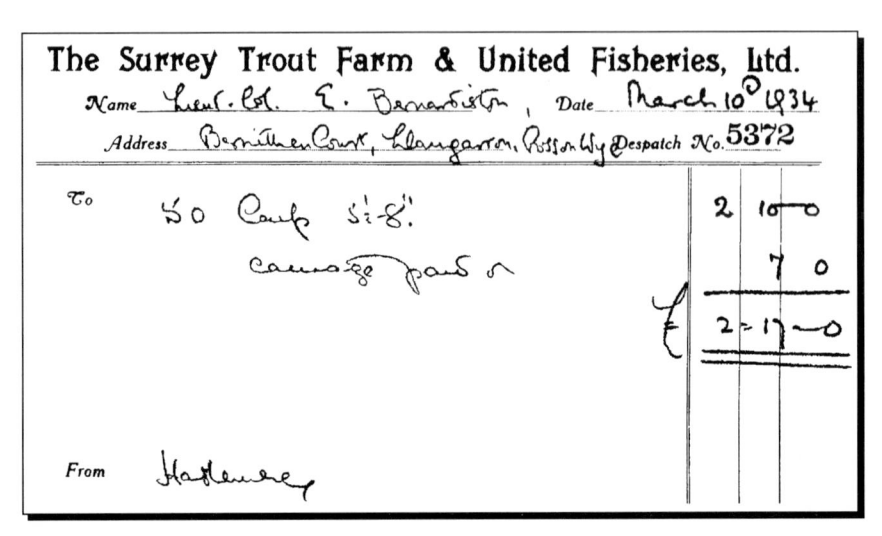

The original invoice issued to Lt. Col. Barnardiston for the Redmire stocking. The invoice shown in the Redmire Pool book was actually a mock-up copy, prepared by Don Leney in the late-1970's for the authors.

Although it has been stated on many occasions, by such notables as Dick Walker, Jack Hilton and again, in 1990, by Chris Yates, that these fish were yearlings, the author was always a little sceptical. Marcel Huet in his *Textbook of Fish Culture* states that the average weight for yearling carp, raised on carp farms in Europe, is 1oz. to 2oz. and the length would be 9cm. to 12cm. (3½-5in.) The information that the Redmire stocking were yearling fish came, in the first place, from Don Leney and, indeed, this appeared in various Surrey Trout

Farm advertisements at the time of Bob Richards' record carp capture, in October, 1951, and was also claimed in a subsequent letter to *The Fishing Gazette*. However, the author raised this matter with Don Leney in 1978 and he replied:

"You are right. Their size 5½-8in. in March, 1934 would have meant that they would almost certainly have been spawned in Holland in 1932, which I would have imported direct myself during the 1933/34 winter. In those days one very seldom could buy fish of the summer's spawning any larger than 4-5in." Don Leney had already confirmed as much in an earlier letter in August, 1977 when he told me the following: (However, the author felt such an important point required clarification.)

"Each late autumn I used to go over to Holland to inspect the summer's crop and buy the best grown, usually 4-5in.—but I also bought some of the slower growth rate 3-4in. I found that the 3in. fish really did not give good results and survive after wintering unless planted into ideal conditions."

On the basis of this information the author assumed that the Redmire introduction consisted of 2-year-old fish and stated this in the book, *Redmire Pool*.

However, since then, during the research for this book, the author has obtained documents which show that the Dutch farm, from whom Don Leney obtained his carp, were in fact claiming to occasionally have yearling carp available which were up to 17cm (7in.) in length.

The invoice from the Dutch carp farm for the carp purchased by Don Leney in the winter of 1933/34. It was probably from the batch of 300 15-17cm one year old fish that the Redmire stocks derived.

Redmire Pool

The yearling carp were normally graded by the farm into 8-10cm. (3-4in) and 10-12cm. (4-5in.) fish but, sometimes, a larger size, 15-17cm (6-7in.) was offered.

Investigation by the author has shown that during recent exceptional warm summers, yearling carp, grown on European carp farms, can achieve a length of up to 7in. Furthermore, it is likely that the lower stocking density in the carp growing ponds, used by European carp farmers in the past, compared to what is the normal practise nowadays, would have assisted in increasing the maximum sized achieved by the yearling carp. It is probably the case, therefore, that the information given in *Redmire Pool* is incorrect. The Redmire stock were, more than likely, yearling carp, as originally stated—spawned in 1933 and not 1932. However, on the 1st December, 1956, 80 king carp were released into Woldale. These were a gift from Don Leney, obtained through the good offices of Dick Walker. The fish were 7in. long and documents at the time confirmed that they were two-summers old.

There has also been some confusion about whether Walker's 44-pounder could have been one of the original stock fish, introduced in 1934. Again, this derives from statements made by Don Leney about the carp supplied by the Surrey Trout Farm. Mr. Leney had formed the opinion, even as long ago as January, 1953, that Walker's carp was the progeny of the carp he had imported. He wrote "The famous Ravioli of 44lb. in The London Zoo—may she prosper there on doughnuts etc.—was one of these all-scaled fish, bred from typical mirror or leather fish, some 100 x 6in. *(this is incorrect—the invoice shows fifty)* which I handled in 1934 before sending them over to our Nailsworth, Glos. fishery, whence they went to the lake which produced this historical lady."

Dick Walker viewing Clarissa at London Zoo. "...may she prosper there on doughnuts etc."

Don Leney initially was quite persistent in this view, pointing out in 1976 that "the Dutch Galician king carp were **all** leathers or mirrors, but never all scaled" and, in 1978, "One thing I am positive about—that only mirrors and leathers were ever sent to Redmire, for the Dutch farm only bred that type and from what I can remember I never saw all-scalers amongst the rising yearlings or rising 2-year-olds when I went to select and order fish each winter." However, after gentle prodding by the author he revised his previous statements and conceded that a small percentage of them could have been 'all-scalers'. Evidence obtained by the author from various Dutch authorities does show that small common carp were being produced on the Dutch carp farm, and Richard Walker, writing to the angling press, in June 1953, regarding the stocking of Arlesey Lake with 1,000 king carp from The Surrey Trout Farm, clearly makes the point that carp with common type scaling formed a significant part of the consignment. Furthermore, a letter from S.W. Bradbury, the secretary of the Becontree & District A.S., written to *Angling* magazine, in April 1953, regarding a delivery of 1,000 6in. carp on the 3rd December, 1952 from the Surrey Trout Farm, states that "I doubt if two of them are alike, they varied from leather to common." So, the weight of evidence would indicate that, at least some Galician "all-scalers", were being imported by the Surrey Trout Farm from Holland. The comparison of the growth characteristics of the scales from Eddie Price's 40½lb. carp and Richard Walker's 44-pounder, carried out by George Sharman, strongly suggested that they were contemporaries. This leads to the conclusion that Walker's fish was, indeed, one of the fifty 5½-8in. yearlings introduced in 1934.

The Dutch fish farm visited by Don Leney was situated north of Vaassen, on the road to Emst. It was part of a company called De Nederlandsche Heidemaatschappij, which translated means The Dutch Moorland Reclamation Society. The Company began breeding carp in 1899, having imported its brood stock, since there were no known selectively bred races of carp in Holland at that time. The first batch were raised in the moat of a historic castle, De Cannenburgh, situated just outside Vaassen. That first attempt produced just 4,850 mirror and leather carp, of between 4in. and 8½in. in length. Production then moved to the purpose-built site near Emst, that Don Leney was to subsequently visit. In 1901 some 28,000 carp were produced, of an average size a little smaller than those from the moat, and in 1902 the total amount produced had risen to 36,000 fish. The company soon started breeding other species of fish and it wasn't long before they had outgrown the small site at Emst. This had been foreseen as in 1900 construction of a very much larger site had started at Valkenswaard, south of the large town of Eindhoven, not far from the Belgian border. Construction of additional ponds carried on until 1930, when a total area of about 300 acres was under water. In 1919 the first carp were produced at Valkenswaard and it was not long before the site at Emst, which only covered a few acres and consisted of just 4 small ponds, was relegated to a distribution role, holding carp for shipment to the northern part of Holland. In 1957 the Dutch Government's Organisatie Ter Verbetering Van De Binnenvisserij (O.V.B. which means The Organisation for the Improvement of Inland Fisheries) took over the control and operation of the fish farm at Valkenswaard. They found a mixture of common, mirror, linear and leather carp present on the site, and removed all the brood stock which carried the genetic traits that were capable of producing carp other than common or mirror scaled off-spring.

The site of the fish farm at Emst. Since 1975 it has been developed as a recreational park, with its main theme being put-and-take trout fishing. Some 40,000 people a year now visit the ponds where Don Leney once collected his carp for stocking into waters all over Britain.

In 1986, Pat Russell, who had fished at Redmire during the period of the Carp Catchers' control, visited Holland and, after considerable investigative work, managed to speak to 72 year-old Mr. J. Dokker, who had been the foreman of the Emst fish farm. He told Pat Russell that De Nederlandsche Heidemaatschappij "had imported two strains of carp."

Redmire Pool

(Strictly speaking this should be races). The first were Eisgrunder *(actually named Aischgrunder)* from southern Germany and also Kaliser from central Poland" and brood stock from these two distinct types, with their own hereditary characteristics, had been crossed to produce the company's own variation. This revelation, published in *Coarse Fisherman,* raised a few eyebrows. So what of Leney's long-standing assertion that the fish were of the Galician type, another famous race deriving from the carp farms of south-east Poland and its border with western Ukraine? But, hold on, the mystery deepens. The Nederlandsche Heidemaatschappij company's fishery manager, at the Emst farm, was A.J.L. Looijen, under whom Mr. Dokker worked. He wrote a chapter in a Dutch book about the history of the company's fish breeding work. The author managed to get hold of a copy of this work through the kind services of H.J.G. Bloemen, the chief fishery officer at Valkenswaard, when he visited the farm in 1989. After arranging for Mr. Looijen's work to be translated it seemed that it only created further confusion, for he stated unequivocally that the company's brood stock came from Lausitz, a region of south-eastern Germany, around the Polish and Czechoslovakian border, which is some 400 miles from Galicia. Further enquiries with Mr. C.M. Bungenberg de Jong, Head of Production at the O.V.B., elicited the forthright statement that the "Valkenswaard and consequently the Redmire carp are certainly not crosses with the thick-set Aischgründer carp and belong to the wide-spread Galician race." Additional investigation showed that research carried out by the famous German zoologist, Professor Schäperclaus, on the German carp races, demonstrated that only two distinct types had been introduced into that country. These were the Aischgründer and the Galician races. So, it would appear that the Dutch carp were, indeed, obtained from Lausitz, but that the stock obtained derived originally from Galicia. Supplementary evidence to support this proposal comes from Professor Wunder, a well-known carp specialist who worked prior to the Second World War in Silezia. He examined the Valkenswaard carp and believed that they were descended from the carp farm at Trachenberg, which was north of the former town of Breslau. This is close to the Lausitz region, as proposed by A.J.L. Looijen. So the evidence would seem to bear out the fact that the Redmire carp were of the Galician race, their predecessors brought to Holland in 1899 from a carp farm situated somewhere in eastern Germany or western Poland. The German/Polish stock had also been imported, at a much earlier date, from the Galician region, just north of the Carpathian Mountains.

The Valkenswaard fish farm in the 1930's.

Pat Russell at Redmire, who, in later years, was told that the fish stocked into the Pool were bred from two, seperate races of carp.

Bob Richards was the manager of Frederick Wright's tobacconist's shop, in Westgate Street, Gloucester. In about 1950 he became interested in fishing and came across a copy of B.B.'s *The Fisherman's Bedside Book*. When he read the chapters on carp fishing he was captivated and became determined to catch one. It was not long before he had landed his first, a 2lb. 'wildie'. But rather than satisfying his ambition it only made him, like so many before and since, crave for more. About this time he joined the Gloucester Anglers' Association and made friends with an experienced angler called Harold Boulton. Bob was talking to some fishing friends one day about Albert Buckley's record carp, and Harold suggested that the only place he knew where a carp, larger than Buckley's, could be caught was Bernithan Pool. He told Bob he had fished there once, in 1949, and although he had caught nothing he took the punt out and saw some monster carp. Bob telephoned the owner that very evening and obtained permission to fish the pool the following Thursday. This first, and only, trip for that year was in late September, 1950 and Bob was accompanied by his friend John Thorpe. They first called at the home of the owner, Mrs. K. Barnardiston, and she kindly took them down to the pool and showed them where she had seen the carp feeding. Bob and his friend spent most of the afternoon exploring and, whilst out in the boat, they saw a monster carp.

Between June and October, 1951 Bob visited Redmire on about ten occasions. Only once did he have a bite, during September in the late afternoon, but the fish broke him in the weed. His next visit, on Thursday, September 27th, was another blank day, and as he knew his final visit for that year was to be on the following Wednesday, during his holidays, he arranged for some groundbait to be introduced. Eric Higgs, the young son of one of the estate workers, agreed to "bait up two spots each morning, with a handful, or so, of bread, hand rolled into balls the size of marbles." (Here again a discrepancy, albeit not significant. The foregoing was written in December, 1951 but Bob then wrote in 1953 that "I told him to put in about half a loaf of bread, each evening, till Tuesday evening, explaining I wanted it put in small pieces as large as walnuts.")

Wednesday, October 3rd was an exceptionally mild day, indeed it had been so for several days past. A mild spell, such as this, often occurs during October and B.B. says, in his book about Wood Pool, that country people often describe it as "the Little Summer of St. Luke." He writes in one of his books that "these mellow warm days bring the carp on to rove for the last time." No doubt that is what Bob was hoping as he travelled from Gloucester on the bus. Arriving at the pool at about 11am he assembled his tackle in the Willow pitch. His rod was an Allcock's Lancer,[1] which was attached to an Ambidex No.1 reel holding 6.1lb. breaking strain Platil line. The end-tackle consisted of a small running bullet ledger, stopped by a split-shot about 2ft. from the hook, which was a no.10 tied directly to the line. A small cork float was set at about 5ft. The bait was paste, about the size of a walnut, made from a new loaf and dipped in honey before being cast out.

Bob Richards fishing the Willow Pitch a few days after catching the record carp. The photograph was taken by Miss M. Wight, a friend of the owner.

1. Bob described the rod as an Allcock's Lancer in a letter to the *Fishing Gazette*, shortly after the capture. Dick Walker received the rod from Bob to try and repair it, as it had an "almighty set in it — even the ferrules were bent." The mystery is that Dick described it, in correspondence, as a "Milward's version of the well-known Wallis 11ft. 3-piece rod."

Redmire Pool

Eric showed Bob where he had been baiting and they noticed that the water was very coloured in this particular spot. What happened next changed the course of carp fishing history. Within 15 minutes of casting out Bob hooked and landed a carp of 5lb., his biggest at that time. A few minutes later he landed another, this time weighing 4lb. 5oz. At 12.30pm he lost a much better fish when the line caught around his reel pick-up. Soon another was lost, this one Bob estimated at about 9lb. Almost immediately another was hooked but soon became stuck solid in weed. Eric was despatched to find some stones and after an age returned with his arms full. The carp refused to budge so Bob resorted to hand-lining. All this proved to no avail and the fish broke free once again. After all the disturbance Bob decided to move to the opposite side of the lake, just above the boat house. The time was about 2.30pm. For a while he fished without a bite and then began to think how foolish he had been to move away from his baited pitch. At about 3.15pm he collected his tackle and moved back to the Willow pitch. In the time it took Bob to light his pipe he had another bite. This time everything went right and before he knew it he had the fish under his rod tip. Realising that his net was totally inadequate he got Eric to fix his gaff together. On his second attempt the fish was gaffed and with one strong heave it was lifted onto the bank.

And there it lay, gasping and heaving in the long grass, a carp so monstrous Bob could only begin to guess what it might weigh. The ripples across the pool faded away as the life ebbed from that wondrous creature. In the quiet and silent way it had lived so it died, the fight for its life, and that alone, breaking the link. A moment in time when destiny grants a man his hearts desire and the shadow falls far and wide. Great glory for Bob Richards, yet he would later sincerely regret the death of the fish, though no blame could be attached to his use of the gaff for it was the way of things in those days.

Still in a daze Bob and his young assistant carried the fish up to the owners house. There it was weighed by Mrs. Barnardiston on Avery Platform scales, with a graduated balance-arm. The weight of 31¼lb. was confirmed back in Gloucester by John Thorpe, and also by fishing tackle dealer Fred Harvey, who had the carp on display in his shop in Barton Street for a few days. By a strange coincidence Bob's young son, Christopher, was just leaving the annual Barton Fair with his mother when dad, on his fateful return from Redmire, staggered off the bus with the great carp in his arms. The *Daily Mirror* were quickly contacted and soon enough a reporter and photographer turned up on Bob's doorstep. Unable to get their 'scoop' picture of Bob with his fish (it was at Fred Harvey's tackle shop) the *Mirror* hacks made do with second best—a full frontal of Christopher's goldfish! The subtlety of Fleet Street! A friend of Bob Richards telephoned B.B. (Denys Watkins-Pitchford) the morning after it was caught with details of the capture. B.B. advised him that the fish should be preserved and suggested that it should be sent direct to Dick Walker.

Bob had, rather foolishly, given details that the fish had been caught from Bernithan Pool, at Llangarron, to any interested party, including the local and national press. Then, a few weeks later, Don Leney inadvertently mentioned the owners

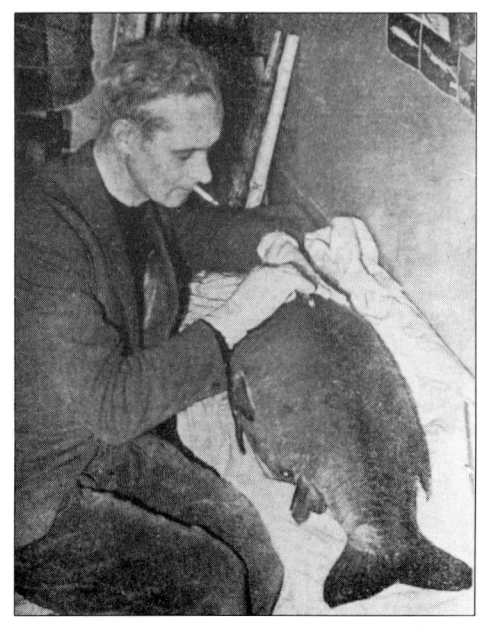

Dick, in his workshop, about to make the first inscision into Bob Richards' record carp.

name, Mrs. Barnardiston, in a letter to the *Fishing Gazette*. So, although Bob Richards had made it clear that the fishing was strictly private, as indeed it was, a couple of very keen individuals independently set about making the necessary enquiries to establish if, and how, they could fish this fabulous new carp water. Those individuals were Richard Walker and Dick Kingsley Kefford. Dick Walker did his best to make friends with Bob Richards. He made a superb job of setting his fish up, considering the state it was in, and by building him a Mk. IV carp rod. Dick, as secretary of the Carp Catchers' Club, also lost no time in inviting Bob to become a member. However, the real breakthrough came from Dick Kefford. He was a keen carp angler and had corresponded with B.B. and Dick Walker around December 1951. He had an influential friend, who lived at Ross-on-Wye, and the friend managed, during the early part of 1952, to supply the name and address of the new tenant of Bernithan Court, for Mrs. Barnardiston had now left the property. His name was John Francis Maclean, later, in 1953, to become Lord Lieutenant of Herefordshire. In early May, 1952 Dick Kefford wrote to John Maclean, who at that time had not yet moved into Bernithan Court and lived at Llangrove, and received by return of post the following reply:

"Dear Sir,
I thank you for your letter of yesterday's date and I shall be pleased to reserve the lake at Bernithan Court for you and your friend to fish from Friday evening the 4th until Sunday the 6th July.
I gather there are a good many carp in the pool, but not many trout. Before the last war the late owner used to stock it every two years with trout, but nothing has been done in this respect in recent years.
Yours truly,
J.F. Maclean."

One can imagine Dick Kefford's elation when the answer he had so desired came. Unable to contain his excitement, two days after receiving the permission, he penned the following to Dick Walker:

"Dear Richard Walker,
You may remember we corresponded one to another last December when B.B. sent on to you a letter I wrote to him.
I have made preparations for a carp fishing expedition to Bernithan Court, having received permission for myself and a friend. The permit is granted from Friday July 4th until Sunday July 6th (both days inclusive). Then I have the notion of going on to Hunstrete and (or) Lymington, returning home on Friday July 11th. Provision has been made for camping at all venues.
The point of my writing is that my friend who usually accompanies me on my week's summer carping cannot now manage the trip. I wonder whether it would appeal to you to take his place and come with me, either for Bernithan only, or for the whole trip? I should very much like you to, and if you thought favourably of my idea, I would come over to Hitchin and have a chat in the afternoon of Sunday May 18th.
I have an 18 h.p. Vauxhall Velox car which as you probably know is fairly roomy—it should accommodate ourselves and our paraphernalia satisfactorily. My way would pass through Hitchin so that I should be 'passing you door' as they say.
I do hope my proposal appeals to you and that you will reply in the affirmative.
Sincerely,
Richard W.K. Kefford."

Redmire Pool

Dick Walker didn't need to think twice about an offer like that and wrote back immediately. This is his reply written on the 8th May:

> "Dear Mr. Kefford,
>
> I should like to go to Bernithan with you very much, and it is most kind of you to involve me. Unfortunately I am not free during the week following the weekend you have planned; I have to attend a Horticultural Show on July 8th, 9th and 10th on behalf of my firm, so should have to be home by the evening of July 7th.
>
> I was planning to go to Bernithan on June 20th, but have so far been unable to contact the new owner. Can you help over this? A preliminary recce would greatly improve our chances on a subsequent visit.
>
> By all means come over on May 18th, you will be very welcome. I have an engagement in the morning but shall be free during the afternoon and evening. Perhaps you could then give a professional opinion on our Siamese she-cat, which refuses to have any more kittens!"
>
> Sincerely,
> Richard Walker."

Dick Kefford then wrote back on the 9th May:

> "Dear Richard Walker,
>
> Thanks very much for your prompt reply. I am of course delighted that you can make the trip with me to Bernithan on July 4th.
>
> I was fortunate in having a 'contact' living near Ross-on-Wye who knows the new owner at Bernithan Court. Certainly I will tell you the owners name and present address, or what it was last week, as I understand he will be moving into Bernithan Court in the near future. However, I would prefer that you left me unmentioned as being the source of this information. Here it is: J.F. Maclean, Thatch Close, Llangrove, Nr. Ross-on-Wye.
>
> I am please that you can see me on Sunday May 18th. With ordinary luck I should be along about 2pm having of course lunched en route.
>
> Much looking forward to meeting you.
> Richard W.K. Kefford."

Once in possession of the new owner's name and address Dick Walker lost no time in dispatching one of his most persuasive letters. The reply from John Maclean was written on the 14th May. It said:

> "Dear Mr. Walker,
>
> It was my intention only to allow those persons to fish the pool at Bernithan Court who had done so in the past, but in view of what you write I have reserved the pool for you and your friend from June 20th to 23rd.
>
> Yours sincerely,
> J.F. Maclean."

On the day of his return from this visit, Dick Walker wrote the following letter to Dick Kefford:

> "Dear Dick,
>
> "Bernithan is terrific. I don't know how or where to begin!
>
> We began fishing on Saturday morning. Pete Thomas caught a carp in the first hour, 8¾lb. Then rain and wind until Sunday, mid-afternoon, and fish pretty well dormant. I got a

4-pounder at 2am Sunday morning, in the rain, and another around 9 or 10 am.

On Monday morning, 4 am, Pete got one, 28lb. 10oz.! Length $33^5/_8$ in. to tip of tail, $31^3/_8$ to fork, girth 27 inches. One of the medium sized ones, Dick, for we saw several which were every bit of 10lb. heavier than that. Bait, plain breadpaste, bantam-egg size, on No 3 'Quickstrike' hook, 11lb. b.s. perlon monofil, Mitchell reel, and one of the Mk. IV carp rods, which I had ready just in time for the trip. This tackle **controlled** the fish with **power in hand**. (You really must have one of these carp-rods, which I think we can fairly say have been proved, not only by this fish but by Maurice Ingham's getting a 16¼lb. fish on June 17th., as well as the fair quota of 14 and 15-pounders we have had in the past two seasons.) Pete brought the fish to net in under 10 minutes and of course I was there waiting with my big net and had him in before he realised what was happening. He got really cross then, and I had to hang on to the net with both hands, or we should have lost fish and net as well.

Every cupful of Bernithan water, no matter where taken or at what depth, contains hundreds of protozoa, mostly daphnia. But the carp will take bread and paste, which can be used as there are no other fish except eels. I have arranged for baiting-up every evening between now and July 4th. I also memorised the route carefully and we can go straight to the pool; campsite is good and you could fish from the car if you wanted. Weed is bad—no sort of water for lines under 9lb. b.s., and I advise 11 or 12lb. at the very least.

Maclean says the pool must be a 'Lake in the West of England' from now on. He says permission to fish is to be limited to Carpcatchers' Club and a few who have permission in the past, and of course you.

I am very excited about our trip there; as I told you our first visit consisted in finding our way about the job of catching carp there, and it took us right up to the last morning. But given good weather conditions and 'knowing the drill' as I think I do now, plus the baiting-up, ought to add up to results next time, and since the pool contains **numbers** of fish of 20, 30 and even 40lb., the possibilities are immense. I've been after carp too long to be over-optimistic, and we may be beaten by weather or some other highly unfavourable factor; but given the right conditions, angling history could be made there, and you and I may be the ones to make it.

Best wishes,
Dick."

And so the die was cast. What happened at Redmire Pool during the next 25 years was to be the main influence in the direction taken by carp fishing. But it could have been very different. A mere chance, an idle word, an insignificant act and the cards are dealt; then win or lose you must accept fate's decision. Denys Watkins-Pitchford wrote the following shortly after the Carp Catchers' Club were first given permission to fish the Pool: "It was brought home to me very forcibly how important it is that members of the C.C.C. should take care whom they ask to fish these waters. I was told by someone I will not name (not a member of our club) who has fished Bernithan that he took his .22 rifle along and tried to poach the ducks. This sort of thing is absolutely disastrous on private waters and could lead to the closing down of all operations against the carp there."

John Francis Maclean became Lord Lieutenant of Herefordshire in 1960. He was wicket-keeper for Gloucestershire and Worcestershire, and went on the M.C.C. tour of Australia in 1922-23.

Redmire Pool

Then, some time later, Walker had cause to make a strong condemnation in the rotary letter:

"I am very sorry to have to say that a lot of litter has been left at Bernithan, including bottles, paper and tins. This is a very bad thing. I know who is responsible, and if it occurs again I shall ask Mr. Maclean to refuse permits to the members concerned. I should be sorry if ill-feeling arose out of this, but sorrier still if we lost the privilege of fishing at Bernithan because of the bloody disgusting behaviour of some C.C.C. members, who ought to know by now that shoving their rubbish into a leafy hedge doesn't mean that it will never be apparent when the hedge isn't leafy."

In 1956 a problem which had been simmering for some time came to a head. Walker wrote the following in the rotary letters:

"Gentlemen, you will no doubt wish to know about the trouble with Davies, the farmer at Bernithan. My first intimation of it was when Mr. Maclean wrote telling me that Davies had asked that no cars be taken down to the lake without his permission. Apparently someone had a row with the shepherd who is agin anglers. There is a feud, apparently, between the Higg's and this chap, and as the Higg's are friendly with the anglers, the shepherd tries to get the anglers kept out. He has in the past tried to convince Maclean that we scare away the ducks and poison the water and goodness knows what. This latest line, about a row with one of the anglers whose car was bumped by a sheep, seems to be part of the same business.

Anyhow, I wrote a very conciliatory letter to Davies, enclosing a stamped addressed envelope, but got no reply. Before next season opens I'll write again, and if I still get no reply I'll go and see him personally. He cannot prevent us from fishing, only from taking cars down to the lake, and if he insists on banning the cars, I'll make a handcart and leave it with Maclean. But I think all will turn out right."

And so it did, for Dick's persuasive powers could even manage to beguile a 'hard-nosed' Welsh farmer like Davies.

That Redmire meant different things to different anglers in not in contention, but what is undeniable is that it captivated just about everyone who ever fished there. Many were lured into its web by the tales of its ghostly leviathans. The sightings have been many and varied. From Walker, Ingham and B.B.; from Eddie Price to Jack Hilton and Bill Quinlan; and from Len Arbery, Rod Hutchinson, Bob Jones, Chris Yates and Tom Mintram. A vast litany of stories and sightings. So let us slip back in time, to the early-1950's, and consider the words of one Richard Walker written in the Carp Catchers' Club's rotary letters:

"The largest carp at Bernithan is well over 60lb., in fact I hesitate to say what I think it might weigh. It makes Ravioli look like a youngster. I don't think any member who hasn't seen it

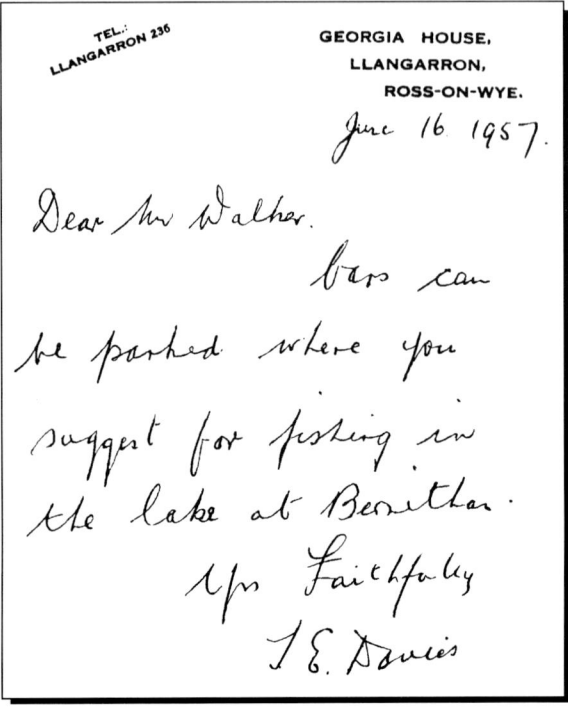

Farmer Davies' reply to Walker's 'persuasive' letter resolving the problem of car parking at Redmire Pool.

can even imagine what a fantastic animal it is. I have had some excellent close views of it this year and I say emphatically 60lb. is a most conservative estimate of its weight. I'd say there are about 50 carp upwards of 25lb. at Bernithan, perhaps 20 over 35lb."

The above was written in 1953 and Walker had no reason to change his mind two years later:

"What sort of place is Redmire? No photograph that I have been able to take does justice to its beauty. It is so pleasant to be at Redmire that one does not mind failing to catch fish; which is just as well because failing to catch is easily the most common way of spending time there. In fact, very few carp, large or small, are caught. The exact number taken since the opening of the 1952 season is 18, of which ten were over 20lb. That includes my foul-hooked 23-pounder. That is the catch for upwards of 3,000 fishing hours by members of the C.C.C. and guests; an average of 300 fishing hours per 20lb. carp.

In the plan of the Pool, X marks where fish upwards of 18lb. were caught; O marks where undoubtedly big carp were hooked, and, for one reason or another, lost. It will be seen that the Willow Pitch appears to have fished best, but I am inclined to think that this is simply because a lot more time has been spent there than anywhere else. The favourite haunt of the monsters—the three or four big fish that would make my big fellow look like a well-grown youngster—seems to be the region of Pitchford's Pit.

On one memorable morning Pete Thomas hooked two fish in Pitchford's Pit within 10 minutes or so. Both escaped, alas, for they were the real grand-fathers, sixty pounds, perhaps more. Bob Richards got into another of them in the same place. It went over to the islands, 150 yards away; then swung round into the weeds opposite the islands. The hook came back bent and twisted."

By 1962 the estimate had crept upwards. Dick wrote this in his *Angling Times* column:

"At Redmire Pool, I saw Pete Thomas hook a carp that would have made my record one look small. It was a fantastic fish, so big that no one who saw it cares to put a figure on its weight, but I don't think it was less than 60lb. and it could have been 80lb."

The beauty of Redmire Pool—sunrise from the Willow Pitch captured by Maurice Ingham in the early 1950's.

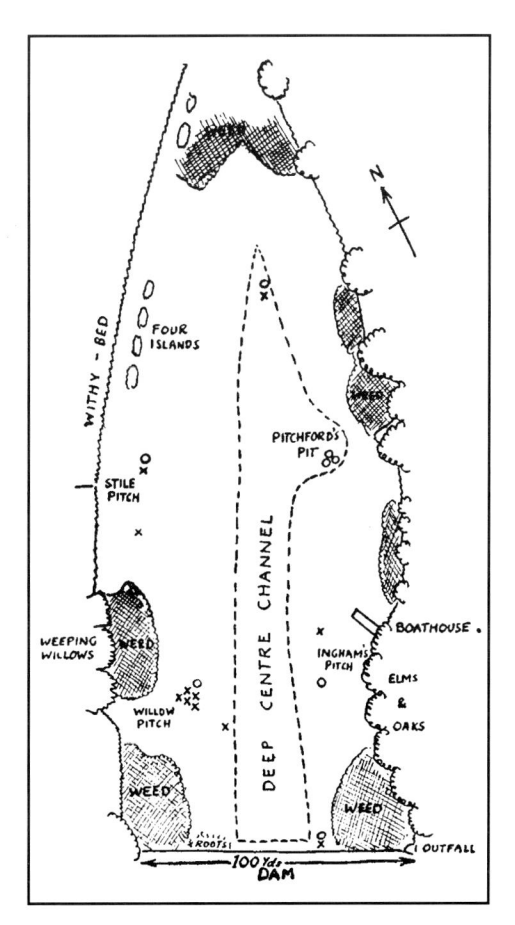

Dick's 1955 drawing of the Pool's captures.

Redmire Pool

The next year Dick wrote about the occasion again in *Angling Times*, but this time the biggest fish Pete lost was "getting on for 60lb." and the two carp together "must have weighed upwards of 90lb."

One hot afternoon, in August 1954, Maurice Ingham remembered being at Redmire with Dick Walker. He wrote the following shortly afterwards to the other members of the Carp Catchers' Club:

"I spotted some carp basking close in to the east bank just above the boathouse, and walked round to have a closer look at them. There was about half-a-dozen fish, not one less than 30lb.—two, I feel sure, were nearer 50lb. than 40lb., and the biggest one Dick, for once at a loss for a suitable adjective, described simply as 'a bugger'! I thought I could no longer be surprised by the size of the fish at Redmire, but this was positively breathtaking. It was cruising slowly around with its back well out of the water, and I watched it for at least half an hour from a distance, at times, of not more than fifteen feet. It was an all-scaled fish—like Ravioli—and I would estimate its length at 3ft. 6in. to 4ft. and the width across its shoulders at 14in. Its weight—your guess is as good, probably better, than mine, but if I was asked to hazard a guess I would say 70lb. at least and possibly more. Dick cast a floating crust out to them but although they passed within inches of it many times, they showed not the slightest interest in it."

No monster this—Dick returns a 'double-figure' carp to Redmire Pool in 1956.

Like Maurice, Jack Hilton (as well as Rod Hutchinson, Chris Yates and Bob Jones) claimed to have seen a carp 4ft. long at Redmire. Jack watched the fish for over half-an-hour in June, 1969 and wrote that it was "every inch of four feet long." But Dick Walker believed such a length impossible and, in retrospect, was appearing conservative as regards the weight of the monsters he had seen, writing, "Neither Jack Hilton nor anyone else ever saw a carp four feet long at Redmire. Several of us saw fish appreciably bigger than my 44-pounder but nothing like four feet. I think it is possible that the biggest I saw might have reached 60lb., but appearances in the water are deceptive."

Yet there is no denying that a great many anglers claim to have seen carp much larger than 50lb. in Redmire. Some are down-to-earth, plain-speaking men; some of high breeding; some of learning with academic qualifications; whilst others are day-dreamers who perceive record-breakers in every farm pond in the land. The evidence seems overwhelming. But yet, but yet, the maggot of doubt still lingers in the cynic's mind. Have not 50-pounders been also seen in Ashlea Pool, in Boxmoor, in Billing Aquadrome and Savay, in Linton Park and Hollybush Pool and Wraysbury—and somehow, as if by magic, they manage to evade capture; whilst the same old relics get caught time and time again. Ah, but yet, dear reader, what is life without a dream, for Somerset Maugham has truly told us that "man has always sacrificed truth to his vanity, comfort and advantage. He lives not by truth but by make-believe."

So when you peer into those shady pools and search those secret, silent depths; and as you see a shadowy apparition glide subtly into your consciousness, remember well that your eyes are not responsible when your mind does the seeing.

Redmire Scrapbook

Remember well that your eyes are not responsible when your mind does the seeing!

Bob Richards was there to show Dick Walker and Pete Thomas the Pool during their first visit on the 21st June, 1952. It was during this weekend that Pete landed the second biggest carp ever caught in Britain.

Redmire Pool

Pete Thomas lands a 20lb. carp from the Willow Pitch in 1961. Bob Rutland helps.

Pete Thomas gets the bird! Fishing the famous Willow Pitch with Dick Walker in late-1955.

Bob Richards at Redmire Pool in July, 1956.

> 11, Bearton Avenue
> Hitchin
> 21.8.52.
>
> Dear Gerald,
>
> Your knot looks a good one. I haven't had time to test it yet, but provided the ABCDE turns are made good and tight it looks as if it will be the best yet. Meanwhile, as I am going after Bob Richards' record at the weekend, I have whipped a N° 2 Model Perfect to each of three 300 yd. lengths of perlon, each disposed on a "Mitchell" spool.

There have been those that have said that Dick must have sold his soul to the Devil to catch the fish he did! Indeed, Walker made a great many predictions, a quite remarkable number which turned out to be correct. On the 3rd September, 1952 he wrote to Ken Sutton telling him of his intention to visit Redmire on the weekend of the 13th - 15th. writing, "I like tench, and when I've broken the carp record I shall have to set about these tench." Walker's 44-pounder was his 76th over 10lb., his first double being taken in 1933.

Pat Russell and Pete Thomas having a 'fry-up' in the Willow Pitch in 1954.

Redmire Pool

HITCHIN ANGLING CLUB
DAILY MIRROR COMPETITION WINNERS 1951

President:
FLY FISHING Section
G. P. ROBERTS, Esq., J.P.

President:
GENERAL FISHING Section
A. TURNER, Esq.,

General Secretary:
S. KING
17, Heathfield Road,
Hitchin, Herts.

Hon. Vice Presidents:
Individual Achievements:—
British Records:—
Richard Walker
Common Carp, 44lbs., 1952
Peter Thomas
Mirror Carp, 28 lbs. 10ozs., 1952

Chairman: MAJOR R. B. FRENCH, Hon. Vice President

HOME WATERS:—ARLESEY LAKE,   OFFORD, RIVER OUSE,   TROUT—RIVER OUGHTON, HITCHIN

Certificate of Appreciation

Awarded to Pat Russell for Services to the Club and to record his Carp of 27lbs & 18½lbs.

W. R. French
Chairman

1956

For the Members

A very rare photograph of B.B. at Redmire.

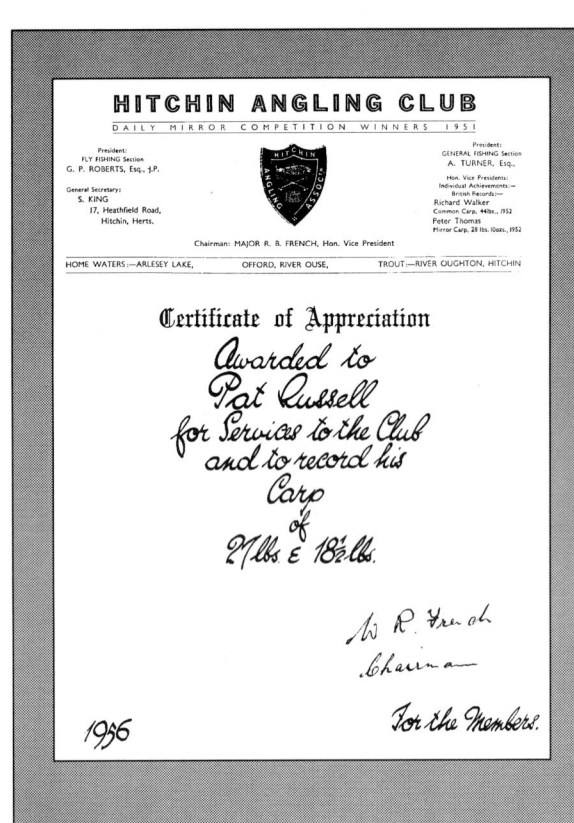

11 Bearton Avenue,
HITCHIN,
Herts.

5th December, 1957.

Dear Denys,

    Mr. Maclean, of Bernithan Court, Llangarron, Ross-on-Wye, has had a serious operation, and although now returned home, will have to take things very easy for several months.

    Pete Thomas and I have sent him some books, and I thought it might be a nice idea for every C.C.C. member to send him one - which need not be new.

    If you have a book you think he would enjoy reading, and which you can spare, would you like to send it to him, making it clear that he is not to bother to return it?

    His interests are in golf, cricket, wildfowl, shooting and Natural history generally.

    Yours sincerely,

Dick

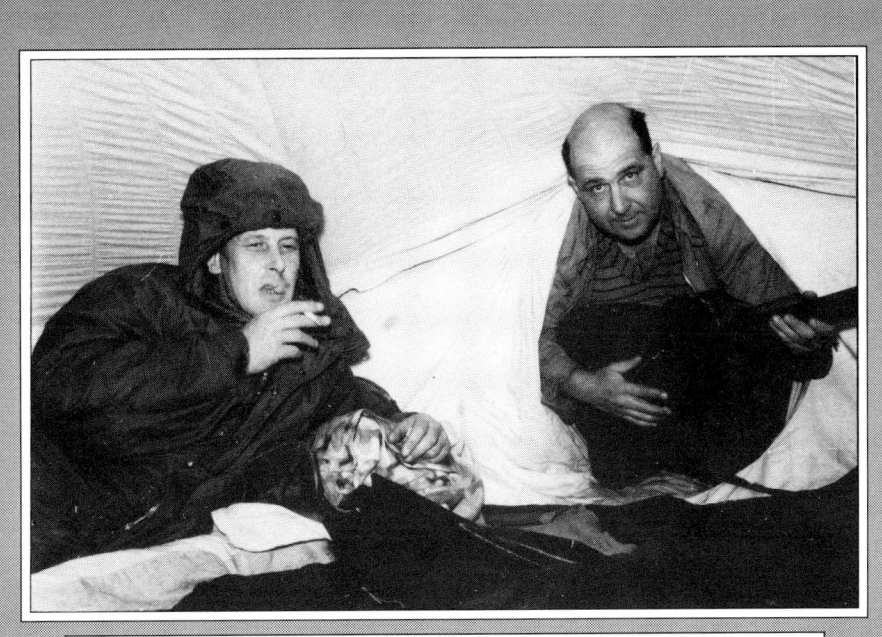

Fred sings his favourite 'country and western', but Dick isn't impressed! He reckons a fish whose dispersement throughout Europe was due to the Romans will only respond to opera! Walker and Taylor at Bernithan in August, 1960.

A trip to Redmire for Pat Russell and Pete Thomas in June, 1967, whilst Redmire was under the control of John Nixon and the fishing was available to members of recognised specimen groups.

Redmire Pool

> THATCH CLOSE,
> LLANGROVE, ROSS-ON-WYE,
> HEREFORDSHIRE.
> LLANGARRON 232.
>
> 14 May 52.
>
> Richard Walker Esq.
> 11 Bearton Avenue.
> Hitchin.
>
> Dear Mr Walker.
>
> I thank you for your letter of yesterday's date.
>
> It was my intention only to allow those persons to fish the pool at Bernithan Court who had done so in the past, but in view of what you write I have reserved the pool for you and your friend from June 20th to 23rd.
>
> Yours sincerely
> J. F. Maclean.

The letter that changed the course of carp fishing history.

Joe Taylor plays his 26-pounder in June, 1962.

Pete Thomas, Bob Rutland and Ron Chapman during a sleepless weekend at Redmire. But it wasn't the carp that kept them awake—it was floating weed, 'pigeon scarers' and a lost Rolex watch!

May Berth-Jones and that prodigious big-fish angler, Derrick Davenport, with a Redmire carp in June, 1955.

11 Bearton Avenue,

Hitchin.

Phone 1833

Dear *Gerald*

June 12th & 13th seem the most useful days for the weedcutting at Redmire, but before organising this I await a report from J.F.Maclean,Esq. on the state of weed-growth, which is backward this year and may be too little to be worth cutting before the season begins.

Should this be so, I suggest we meet in London on June 12th, in the evening or afternoon, and defer the weed cutting until later. Much of this might be done if members visiting the pool each spent a few hours at it before leaving. It is my intention to provide, and leave at Redmire, equipment for the purpose.

May I have members' views on this matter as soon as possible, please?

1944

Dick Walker

Secretary.

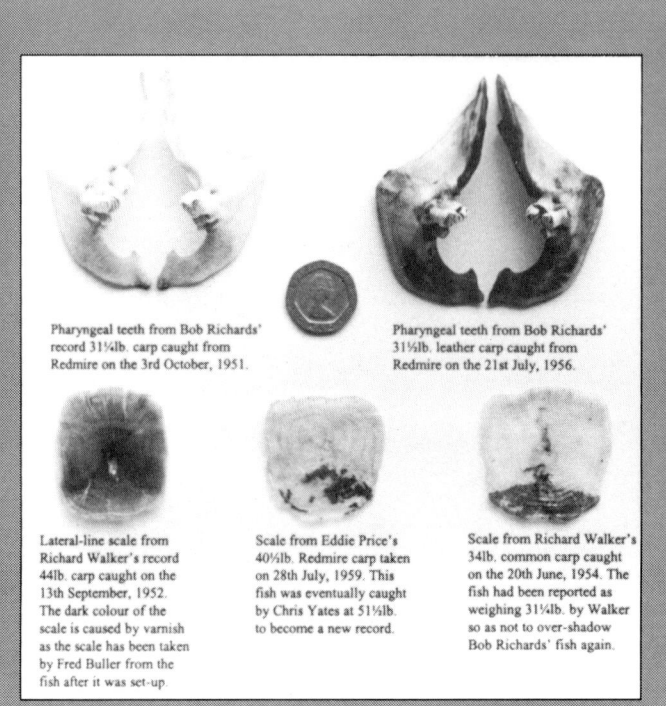

Pharyngeal teeth from Bob Richards' record 31¼lb. carp caught from Redmire on the 3rd October, 1951.

Pharyngeal teeth from Bob Richards' 31½lb. leather carp caught from Redmire on the 21st July, 1956.

Lateral-line scale from Richard Walker's record 44lb. carp caught on the 13th September, 1952. The dark colour of the scale is caused by varnish as the scale has been taken by Fred Buller from the fish after it was set-up.

Scale from Eddie Price's 40½lb. Redmire carp taken on 28th July, 1959. This fish was eventually caught by Chris Yates at 51½lb. to become a new record.

Scale from Richard Walker's 34lb. common carp caught on the 20th June, 1954. The fish had been reported as weighing 31¼lb. by Walker so as not to over-shadow Bob Richards' fish again.

Redmire Pool

Pete Thomas with his 20lb. common caught in September, 1963.

Derrick Davenport fishing the Redmire dam in the mid-1950's.

Redmire Pool

"Now see here Russell, you'll do no good taking flashlight photo's of fires."

Joe Taylor's largest carp—a 26-pounder caught at the start of the 1962 season.

May Berth-Jones and Derrick Davenport plotting the Redmire carp's downfall over a 'cup of tea'.

Redmire Pool in July, 1956. Bob Richards is stowing his tackle away in Alan Hinde's A30.

Redmire Pool

Zoological Society of London,
Regent's Park,
London, N.W.8.

TEL. ADDRESS:
ZOOLOGICAL-PHONE-LONDON
TELEPHONE:
PRIMROSE 3333
HON. SECRETARY:
THE VISCOUNT CHAPLIN, F.L.S.
DIRECTOR:
L. HARRISON MATTHEWS,
Sc.D., F.L.S

OUR REF.
YOUR REF.

28.10.52

Dear Sir,

I am please to report that the large carp in question is now on show and doing well. If you ask one of the Keepers if he will take you behind the "scenes" I think you will find he will be only too pleased to do so.

Ask for Mr Arkhurst.

Yours sincerely,
H. F. Vinall

H. F. VINALL,
Curator of Aquarium

Chapter 8
Billing Aquadrome

*I was a lonely, teenage, bronking-buck
with a pink carnation and pick-up truck
but I knew I was out of luck
the day the music died.*
    Don McLean from *American Pie.*

There was a time, in the years following the severe winter of 1962/63, when Billing Aquadrome was considered Britain's premier carp water. Many well-known anglers believed that Redmire Pool had died in the desolate months of that cruel winter and, although the fishing at Billing was considered very difficult, its pedigree was such that Bill Keal headlined his weekly feature in *The Angler's Mail,* in June 1966, with "Billing Is Still Our No. 1 Carp Water!" The basis for this reputation was based around the captures made by one man—Bob Reynolds.

Billing Aquadrome is, in fact, a pleasure park containing a number of gravel pits. It is situated at Little Billing, just outside Northampton, and the site lies adjacent to the River Nene. However, it is the 16 acre Willow Lake (sometimes referred to as the Willow Pool or the Willow Tree Lake) which was the attraction for the dedicated carp enthusiast.

Willow Lake, in Billing Aquadrome, at about the time when Bob Richards first began fishing for its carp.

Billing Aquadrome

The pit is old; certainly by 1920 it was in existence when it was stocked with trout by the owner, Colonel Elwes, of Billing Hall. Shortly after this the site was purchased by the Mackaness family and the first stocking of carp took place in 1935. Further introductions were carried out in the two subsequent years, all of which came from The Surrey Trout Farm.

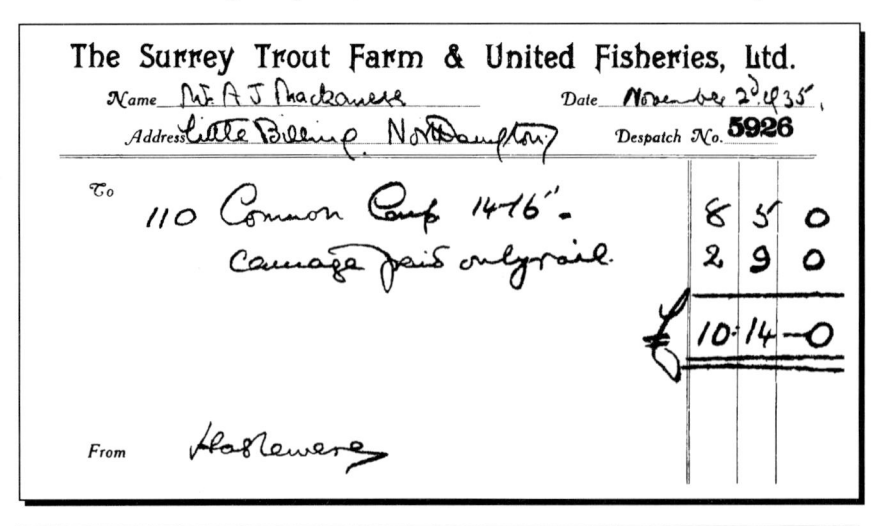

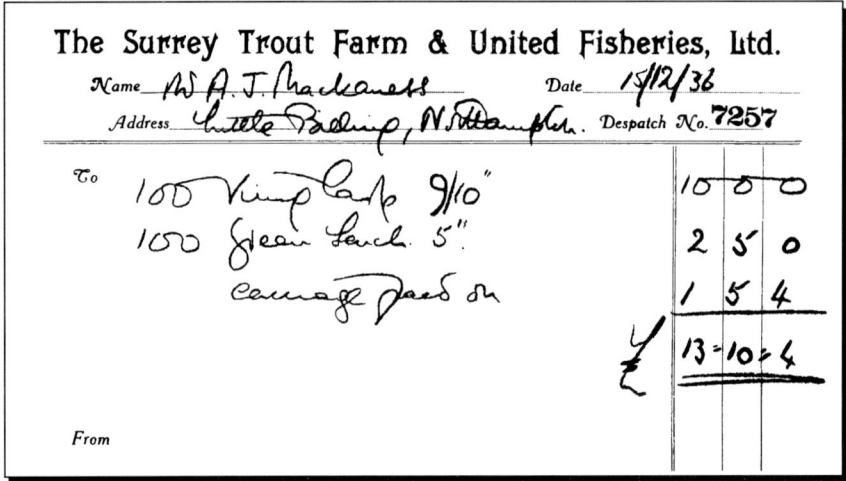

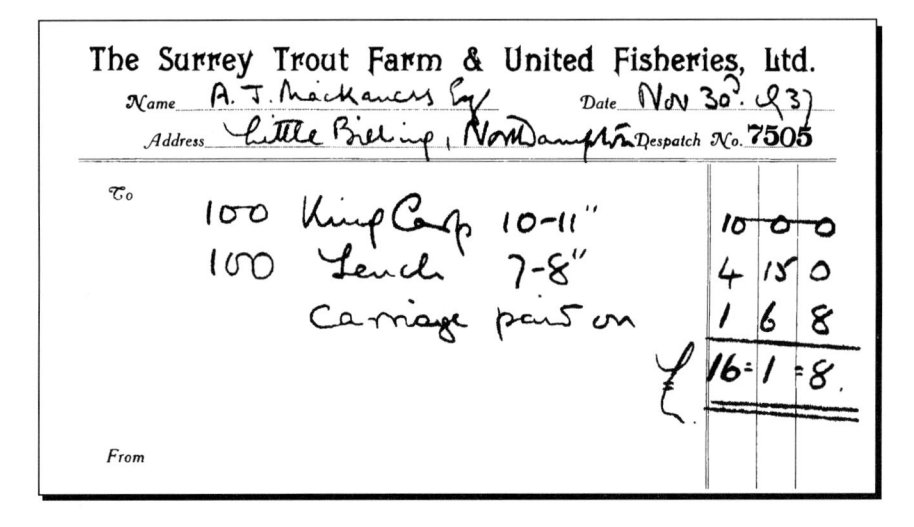

The Surrey Trout Farm & United Fisheries, Ltd.
Name: W.A.J. Mackaness Date: November 2nd 1935 Despatch No. 5926
Address: Little Billing, Northampton

To		£	s	d
110 Common Carp 4-6"		8	5	0
Carriage paid only rail		2	9	0
		£10	14	0

From: Haslemere

The Surrey Trout Farm & United Fisheries, Ltd.
Name: W.A.J. Mackaness Date: 15/12/36 Despatch No. 7257
Address: Little Billing, Northampton

To		£	s	d
100 King Carp 9-10"		10	0	0
100 Green Tench 5"		2	5	0
Carriage paid on		1	5	4
		£13	10	4

From:

The Surrey Trout Farm & United Fisheries, Ltd.
Name: A.J. Mackaness Esq. Date: Nov 30th 1937 Despatch No. 7505
Address: Little Billing, Northampton

To		£	s	d
100 King Carp 10-11"		10	0	0
100 Tench 7-8"		4	15	0
Carriage paid on		1	6	8
		£16	1	8

From:

The stockings of small carp were shared between several of the lakes on the site and by the early-1940's the heaviest carp reported was 13¼lb., the captor landing another of 8¾lb. on the same day. Another angler, Mr. Blundell, caught fish of 13lb. 1oz. and 11lb. 7oz. on successive days in October, 1937. Fishing at that time was allowed on the pits known as Jungle Lake and the Angler's Lake, but perhaps an indication of what was to come was the discovery of a dead carp which weighed 20¼lb., in the late-1940's. A few years later another fish estimated to weigh 30lb. was found dead in a spawn-bound condition.

By the early-1950's the complex was well developed as a pleasure park and advertised as the 'Playground of the Midlands'. There was a swimming pool, next to the Willow Pool, a restaurant, donkey-rides, swings, slides and paddle boat, as well as a variety of rowing boats, punts and canoes for hire. But the greatest attraction was a miniature model of the 'Royal Scot', pulling five small coaches and capable of carrying 60 passengers. The 'holiday camp' and 'fun-fair' attractions gradually increased during the intervening years with a children's zoo, neon signs, petrol pumps, amusement stalls and the loudspeakers blasting out the latest renditions from the Hit Parade. Willow Pool was far removed from the vision of secluded perfection that its name suggested. With flashing lights filling the sky as darkness slowly wrapped the solitary carp angler in this foreign land, the overworked loudspeakers were no match for the music of Buddy Holly, Ritchie Valens and The Big Bopper. But out there in the darkness, somewhere in that oblivious deepness, monstrous carp lived and entrapped the mind of a young man.

It was 1957, and Jack Good had brought the message to the younger generation with *Six-Five Special*, his programme devoted to rock and roll. That same year Buddy Holly and The Crickets had shot from obscurity to top the British Record Charts with their record, *'That'll be the Day'*, but Buddy's meteoric rise to fame would soon lay shattered amongst the wreckage of a plane crash.

Bob Reynolds was a 24 year manager of a shoe shop, but he lived and breathed for carp fishing. For him the medium was not in radio waves—he didn't have time for rock and roll. He had an inventive imagination and was very practical. He designed and built much of his own tackle, which included his rod, rod-rests, bite alarm and an ingenious landing-net cum carp sack! Bob's carp fishing had begun some two years earlier at a small park lake in Northampton, but his attention was soon transferred to Billing Aquadrome when he was invited to fish Willow Lake. The owners, having been told that the big carp which were known to inhabit the lake were almost uncatchable, suggested to Bob that he might like to try. Bob agreed, but only on the condition that he was allowed to night fish and could use a boat.

The lake at that time was crystal clear and full of weed, and the bottom was, as many gravel pits tend to be, undulating. Bob first tried floating crust but the hoards of small rudd and ducks scuppered this idea. Then he spent a considerable time sounding the various depths and, after finding a weed-free area near a tiny island, he embarked on a regular baiting campaign for two weeks. Every night he rowed out and baited up with two loaves.

Bob Reynolds carp fishing on his tiny island.

Billing Aquadrome

Bob's first couple of fishing trips suggested that carp were present in the swim, which no doubt encouraged him in his efforts.

The morning of his third attempt, August 10th, was wild, with the wind gradually increasing to gale force throughout the day and, by the time Bob was ready to depart for Billing, persistent rain had also set-in. Who but a carp fanatic would relish sitting on a minute stump of an island in the middle of a raging, windswept lake? There is a loneliness associated with the true kernel of carp fishing; in its essence it is a solitary pursuit where a man's thoughts stray down many avenues. And, although it may be true that you find in solitude what you take to it, there is the conviction that long exposure isolates the soul.

But the rain poured down, lashing the tiny, inhospitable island where the destiny of the young carp fisher was to be shaped. Is it really true that our destinies are decided by nothings, helped along by some insignificant accident — as a drop of rain falls upon an acorn, so may rise the tree on which our morality is crucified?

Bob comforted himself with the fact that the inclement weather meant the lake would have been hardly disturbed throughout the day, yet the practicalities of setting-up in those extreme conditions would have deterred all but those whose bravery borders on the foolhardy. Bob's father assisted but implored his son to show good sense and return home. Yet the craving has to be indulged; there is no drug that assaults a man's good sense as that of carp fishing.

Then he was alone with the wild darkness all around. At midnight he had his first run but it came to nothing. Then, an hour or so later, another. Now a shadowy figure crouched against the un-fettered, thrashing storm; a straining rod backlit by the glow from nearby Northampton town, and then blurred, stinging eyes straining to glimpse the swirling form as it is drawn towards the waiting net. Ah, yes, Bob's ingenious 'bicycle wheel rim attached to a hessian sack' landing net was lifted around the gasping fish. He weighed sack and fish and found it to be well above the limit of his 25lb. balance. What emotions flooded Bob's mind? If you are one that has been touched by Fortune's hand you have the means to imagine, the rest of us shall never know.

A further hour passed and then Bob hooked another monstrous carp. Stumbling into the water he went to his left as quickly as he could, straining against the determined rush of the fish to reach some snags. Only just in time he turned it and then the battle was fought out in deeper water until, thirty minutes later, the rusty bicycle rim again served its unintended purpose.

It was now almost 2.45am and, whatever fate had in store for the remainder of the night, history had been made. Never before had an angler caught two carp over 20lb. in the same session. Indeed, only a handful of anglers existed at that time who had caught more than one 20lb. carp in their lives.

Bob's ingenious landing net. The rim of a bicycle wheel to which was tied a large sack. When the carp had been successfully netted, the sack was detached from the wheel-rim and another attatched.

And now the weather began to change. It was as if the gods had somehow admitted that they had failed. This time the young warrior Ajax, son of Oileus, had overcome the storm and the raging sea on his tiny rock. The rain eased, the wind abated and a pale moon shone its light on Willow Pool.

At 4.30am Bob's father returned. He had slept a fitful sleep worrying about his son.

The front pages of Angling Times. The story of Bob Reynolds' amazing catches also appeared in the national newspapers creating a tremendous amount of interest in Billing. This publicity seriously backfired, so much so that Bob eventually gave up carp fishing at the lake for several years.

During these successive trips Bob had caught the 6th, 7th and 8th largest carp ever, and became the only person to have caught two 20lb. carp in a sitting—and he had achieved this twice! A few years later he was to record the country's 4th largest carp before turning his attention to pike fishing.

One by one three fish were ferried across to be admired by both of them. Some time later they were weighed on commercial scales. The first was a 24lb. 12oz common, the second a 27lb. 13oz. mirror and the third, a truly wondrous 28¼lb. fully-scaled mirror.

The following Sunday Bob returned to Billing and his tiny island. He again night fished and caught a further two carp over 20lb.—a leather carp of 26lb. 10oz. and a mirror of 27lb. 9oz. Bob continued fishing during the following day and hooked a fish, in the early afternoon, that was bigger than anything he had caught so far which, unfortunately, broke his 9lb. b.s. line.

It is difficult to now convey the astonishment and wonder that these catches made on the angling public at that time. In one week Bob had caught the 6th, 7th and 8th largest carp ever landed in this country. It was a quite outstanding achievement by an angler who planned and fished in isolation.

Billing Aquadrome

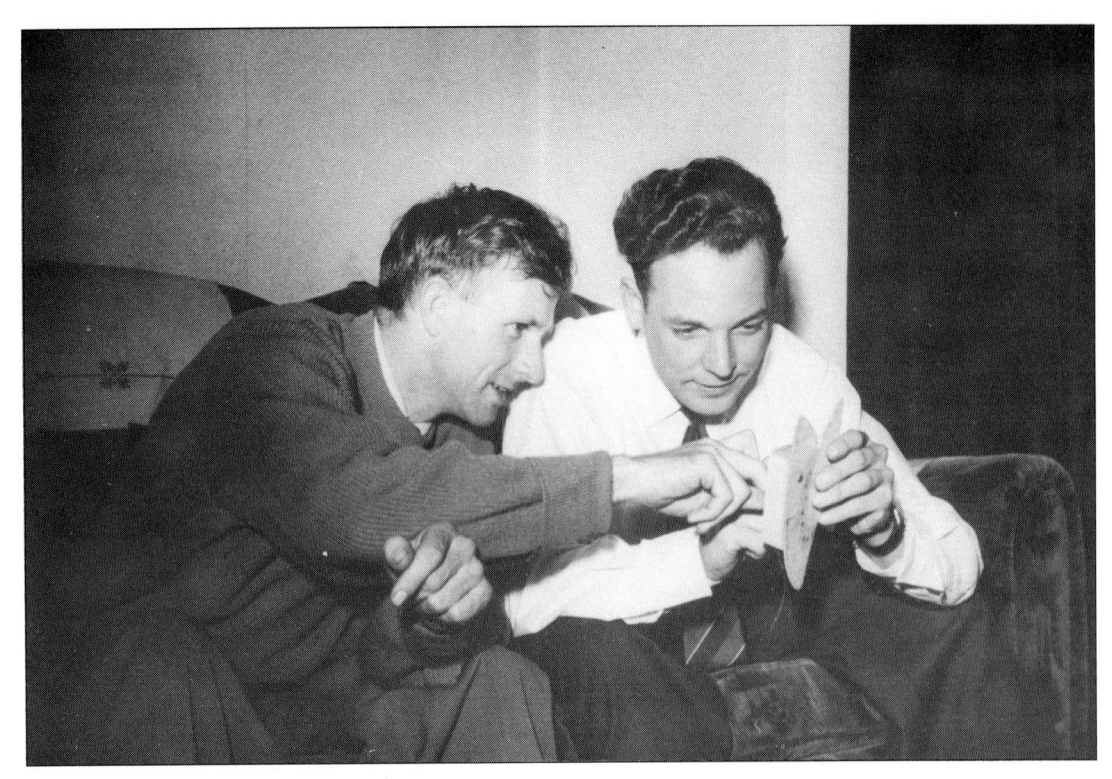

Bob Reynolds was presented with a carp landing net, made by B. James and Son, for his remarkable catches. Dick Walker went to Bob's house to make the presentation, and this photograph taken by Dick at the time shows Bob demonstrating his experimental bite alarm to Pete Thomas.

For various reasons Bob was invited to apply for membership of the famed Carp Catchers' Club which, at that time, had fallen into the doldrums. He was accepted in October 1957, at the same time as Dick Kefford and Fred J. Taylor, and a press release to this effect appeared in *Angling Times*. However, the publicity given to Bob's tremendous feats, and his disclosure that the fish he lost, nicknamed Big Ben, "would beat Dick Walker's 44-pound fish," brought problems. Some years later Bob Reynolds acknowledged that "he revelled in the publicity and glory, but paid the price of fame." The weekend following his second blitz at Billing found one angler fishing in Bob's swim, the next weekend there were five! Bob recalls

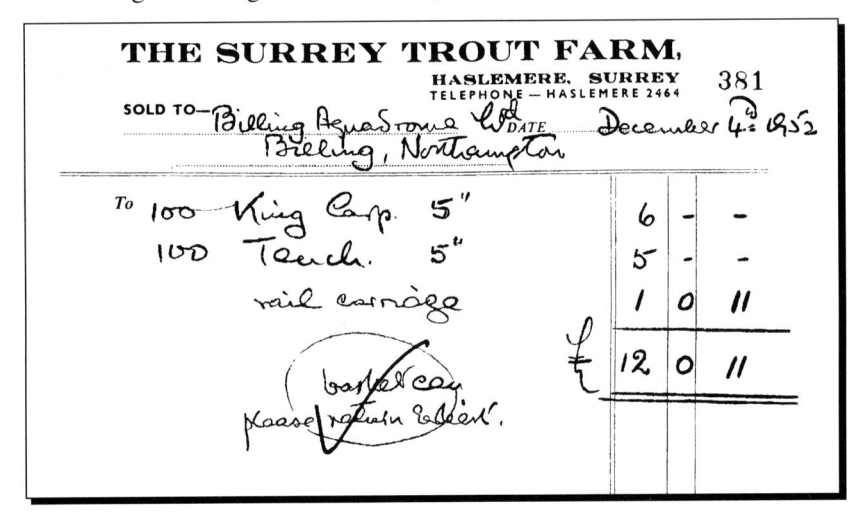

A later stocking of carp from Don Leney's Surrey Trout Farm.

that the following season, "1958, was a disaster. No sooner would I settle somewhere than I would have company. Every swim I pre-baited was fished by someone else before I was ready and my preparations were complete. Half-way through the season I gave up." He spent the next three seasons fishing other carp waters and then "returned to the rat race of Billing a wiser and more experienced carp angler."

Billing was never to again so readily give up its secrets. It justifiably became known as one of the most difficult carp waters in Britain. The early rush of eager hopefuls were gradually replaced by a handful of 'weathered' die-hards, whilst the holiday camp amenities increased making serious carp fishing evermore difficult. In 1961 the owners decided to make night fishing available to the general public at 7/6p per rod and this resulted in a number of good carp being caught. For a while luminaries such as Fred Wagstaffe, Johnny Bingham, Phil Shatford, Bill Keal, Alec Lewis and Jim Gibbinson gave it their best shot, but it was an uphill struggle. One amusing anecdote was made by Alec Lewis, when asked about his time spent at Billing and who else was carp fishing there during the same period. His reply was enlightening—"Well, there were chaps like Fred Wagstaffe who used to fish there, which was all right if there wasn't a full moon."

Other, lesser know mortals also succumbed to the formidable problems of Billing and associated hazards! That maestro of Dagenham, John Lenton, had good reason to remember a trip he made. He wrote the following letter to a friend in 1962:

Alec Lewis, inseparable fishing pal of Bill Keal since their school-days, with a 23lb. 13oz. carp from Billing Aquadrome.

"Now about that Billing trip! I'm afraid we didn't even **see** a carp. The chaotic side of the story is as follows—Bob Reynolds called here on the Thursday morning on his way to the Docks. He told me to go out to the lake, contact a man called Joe and tell him we would be fishing that evening, then to go to Bob's home and await his return. Exit Bob. I caught a coach to Northampton, took a taxi to the lake only to find (a) Joe didn't work there any more; (b) the owners frowned on night fishing; and (c) it was not possible to get permission till the afternoon and then only if it was possible to contact the company secretary! I went to Bob's house—only to find one wife, three children with whooping cough, a blocked washing machine, a broken front door and a broken back door! Bob did not return that day, he had broken down (like his washing machine and doors) in London, and I spent the time helping where I could. I slept in the front room that night and after I was sure there was nothing more I could do I went to the lake about mid-morning on the Friday. I managed to get permission and started fishing at midday. Nothing moved! At 4.30pm Bob arrived and we fished through the night without a run! Next time I hope we have warmer weather (and no whooping cough!)."

Billing Aquadrome

Perhaps a measure of the effort put in by Shatford, Wagstaffe and Gibbinson was that a total of 200 nights resulted in just five carp, with only one weighing over 20lb.! Jim Gibbinson summed up his feelings about the place in the following paragraph:

"My own affair with Billing was quite brief—it started in July 1965 and ended in July 1966. In that period just one carp was caught, an 11lb. fully-scaled carp that was taken one dawn by Phil Shatford. Fred Wagstaffe, Phil and I rented a chalet in the grounds of the Aquadrome to enable us to devote as much time to the water as possible. I came away beaten, not by the carp—they would not have made me admit defeat—but by Billing Aquadrome itself."

Jim felt that one of the major handicaps was that the 16 acre lake held very few carp, resulting in location being one of the difficulties that had to be overcome. It is interesting to note that Wagstaffe concurred, stating in 1966 that he too believed the water held very few carp, "no more than 50 or 60." Nowadays this stocking density would be regarded as quite reasonable and would not be looked upon as being a problem.

But it was to be Bob Reynolds who would once again stun the angling world with a Billing carp. In August, 1961 Bob landed a mirror carp weighing 33lb. 2oz. The newspaper reports stated that Bob had baited up for a month prior to this, his first visit and hooked and lost two other carp. His companion for the night, Peter Andrews, who had never fished for carp before also lost two fish, one of which was estimated to be around 28lb. A report in *Angling Times* quoted Bob as saying, "I think my catches in 1957 made Billing so popular that I could no longer be sure that no one would fish the swim I baited up. So I decided to use a different smelling bait." The bait was claimed to be banana-flavoured bread paste. In the next issue of *Angling Times* Bob was interviewed and reported as follows:

"Bob was a wind-up merchant," according to his pal Fred Wagstaffe. Was the fish really caught on just plain bread?

"So Bob, who believes in mammoth groundbaiting for big carp, was faced with a real problem. How could he groundbait a certain spot for a month and then fish it, and be certain that even if other anglers pitched in his swim, they could not take advantage of his groundbait?

He decided that both the hookbait and the groundbait would have to differ from the normally accepted ones. So Bob first of all discarded bread and potatoes, and went to work on vegetables. By using broad beans, runner beans and peas as both hookbait and groundbait he took carp to 10lb. from a number of heavily fished waters in the Northampton area.

Fish other than carp found them to their liking so Bob decided to switch from vegetables to fruit. He chose bananas as being the least acid fruit, and set to work. And on slices of banana Bob took carp to over 10lb. last season. Then another problem arose. Even using hooks with barbs on the back of the shanks failed to grip the banana as well as Bob would have liked. So Bob came back to bread, flavoured with banana essence."

However, in 1978, Bob wrote an article for the British Carp Study Group magazine

A sketch of Willow Lake drawn by Bob Reynolds.

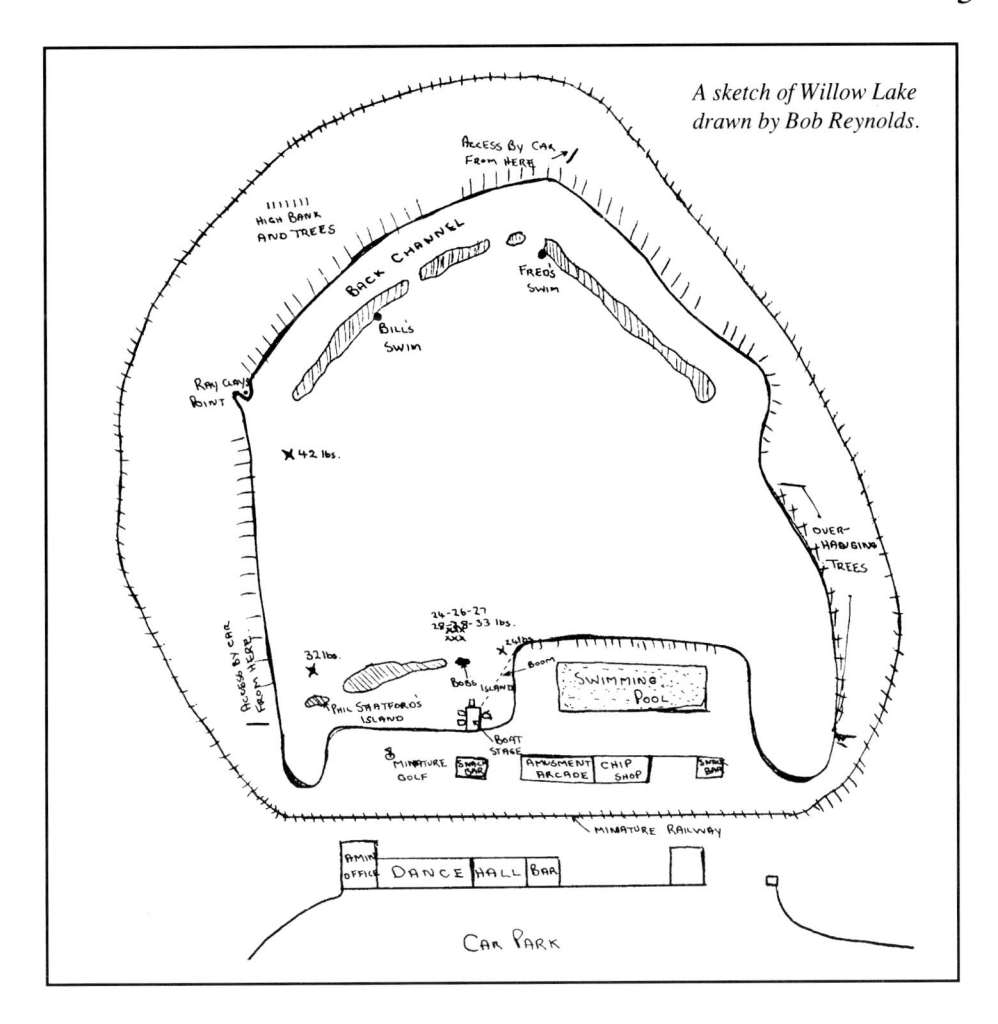

entitled 'Carp Can Be Educated To Eat Anything'. In it he tells rather a different story!

"At Billing I started baiting up with banana, and after two weeks I found someone fishing my baited swim—using banana also! He told me that he had watched me baiting up, had retrieved one of my bricks, and examined the bait (Bob often attached bait samples to a brick with fishing line and then retrieve the brick later to see if the bait had been taken).

So I started again, this time with flavoured bread. I used the double-bluff now, so that anyone checking would find me apparently using bread.

I decided not to use banana flavour because of the anglers who were already doing so and instead I used aniseed. I only fished twice, on successive weekends in August. The first was a blank and the other produced the 33-pounder."

The mystery is compounded further when the author recently interviewed Fred Wagstaffe, who fished with Bob for many years both in this country and in Ireland. Fred commented, "Bob said he caught it on banana flavoured paste, but he didn't. That was a wind-up. Bob was a wind-up merchant." Fred confirmed that Bob was, indeed, experimenting with flavours at the time but assured the author that Bob's fish was caught on plain bread flake.

Nevertheless, Bob's 33-pounder, the 4th largest carp ever caught, ensured that his stunning Billing captures would be acknowledged as some of the greatest-ever witnessed in the annals of carp fishing history.

Two years passed and Phil Shatford was rewarded for his perseverance and tenacity. Fred Wagstaffe recently recalled the occasion:

Billing Aquadrome

"There was an area in the north-eastern corner of the lake—a little narrow bay, all full of weed, scum, pop bottles, tin cans, newspapers and God knows what, where the prevailing wind used to blow it all. There was one time when we used to see no end of carp in this bay and we thought, well, we'll night fish for them. The only fish I caught out of there was a tench of about 4lb. on floating crust. But the carp were there and what we figured out they were doing was this. When they were taking the piece of crust from within a mass of rubbish, they suck the lot in, blow it out and then select the one piece that they want. This was the conclusion we arrived at, rightly or wrongly. We'd get this movement and then nothing because by sucking it in and the blowing it out the hook had come out of it.

Phil Shatford and I had fished quite a few nights for these carp in this bay, so we decided we'd fish the area that the fish would have to pass over as they approached. The carp either came down a deep channel into the bay, or they came round this little island and down the shallow part, which was only about 2½ft. deep. So we sat on this little island, which was just a few feet wide, and sat back to back with a tree between us. Just as it was getting dark we realised we were sitting near a wasp's nest and we almost decided not to bother. But anyway, we spun a coin to decide who was going to fish the deep channel and who was going to fish the shallow channel. I span the coin and I won so I fished the deep channel. I felt sure they would come up the deep channel—they didn't, they came up the shallow side. I had two rods out and I remember standing up to speak to Phil. He was using the Heron bite alarm and the light came on and I said, "Phil, you've got a run." He reached forward to his rod as his buzzer started to sound and I looked up and I could see the great mass of this carp's back, and I thought it had swam through the line. But it had actually taken his bait and that was the 32lb. common."

After trying heavy pre-baiting, with about 400lb. of potatoes, and landing only bream, Phil Shatford tried a different approach to catch his big carp.

Both Phil and Fred had previously followed the dogma laid down by Bob Reynolds, in that success was dependent upon heavy prebaiting. But this had only brought subjugation of the bream, that Billing held in great numbers. Finally, they had decided to "search for the carp, rather than draw them to us with groundbait."

Another two years of little activity followed, then Billing so very nearly came up with the jack-pot. Ray Clay was a 42-year-old steward at an ex-servicemen's club who liked to take his family to Billing Aquadrome, and they often stayed in a caravan on the site. He was a casual angler who spent many a happy hour filling his keepnet with the Willow Pool's small roach and bream. Then, one fortuitous day, he saw a large carp in his swim. He rigged up some heavier tackle and cast a piece of floating crust to it and was soon admiring a 24lb. carp. Ray was impressed! He decided there and then he would become a proper carp angler. He went out and bought all the right gear, read what he could, and returned to Billing for an 'all-nighter.' At 11pm, four hours into his first-ever carp session, his "bread paste dipped in honey" was taken by a huge 42lb. common carp!

What a fickle mistress carp fishing is, a capricious enchantress whose charms beguile us and destroy us. Pity those who had fished their hearts out, season after season for, at best, a few crumbs from the lady's hand. What momentary despondency the silly *Angler's Mail* headline "Cassius Clay Carp is Best for 14 years" must have brought to the 'Billing regulars.'

Ray Clay's landing net handle broke as he attempted to lift this 42lb. common carp.

Sacked until the following morning, the fish itself proved difficult to weigh. The first set of scales used only went up to 20lb. and were totally inadequate. A second set, which weighed up to 30lb., also proved deficient and it wasn't until the owner of the Aquadrome, Sam Mackaness, took the fish off to a wholesale greengrocer that its weight was established.

Perhaps 1970 was a year that saw something of a renaissance in terms of carp caught at Billing, although this has to be seen in relative terms. A new breed of carp angler was emerging at about this time and Billing was receiving fresh attention and new approaches. One of this enthusiastic band was Peter Chillingsworth. He dismissed the reason given by many of his predecessors for failure at Billing. In the early-1970's he stated that "most carp anglers I meet and get talking to at Billing realise the problems of catching carp there, but they always add a virtually non-existent problem. I refer, of course, to the holiday camp atmosphere which exists and causes most serious carp anglers to fail there. They say 'how can carp be caught when trains are running around the lake and people are splashing about in boats above your bait?' Well, I have hooked carp at midday on a sunny Whit Tuesday, amid the boats and despite the trains. The real problems of catching the carp at Billing are the age-old ones of location and persuading the fish to take your bait when you have found them."

Billing Aquadrome

Forthright views, but what evidence can Peter produce to substantiate his claims? Shall we let him tell, for the first time, the story of his huge Billing carp?

"I arrived at about 4pm. The sun was shining and a moderate north-easterly breeze was blowing. To be quite honest I had no idea where to fish, as I had not seen any tendency for the fish to show in a particular area this season. Two trips round the lake and no sign of carp left me in a quandary.

Thinking back over the years I remembered seeing carp in two areas very occasionally, and so I picked a swim where I could cast to both spots. One of these required a 40 yard cast, at 45 degrees to my left, and the other a maximum cast straight out in front.

A corner of Willow Lake. Did uncaught monsters once live here? This idyllic scene from the 1960's masked the true face of the real Billing!

By now the clouds had gathered and a storm was imminent, so I positioned my brolly and was arranging my tackle when the storm broke at about 5.45pm. Cowering under my shelter I set up three rods and just lobbed out two of them, using flake as bait, and left the other handy should it be needed. The rain gradually eased off and stopped altogether at about 8pm. This gave me an opportunity to catapult a number of pieces of flake, encased in groundbait, to my left-hand swim. I then made-up a quantity of cheese-paste and began catapulting small balls of this into my second swim. It was whilst this was happening that I noticed a small patch of bubbles appear about 10 yards from the bank, at about 45 degrees to my right.

I picked up my spare rod and baited the hook with a large lobworm. I walked along the bank until I was opposite the bubbles and attempted to cast it out, freelined. Unfortunately, I could not quite reach. I then tried encasing the worm in a ball of mud, but due to the storm the mud was too wet. Feeling in my pocket I found a two-swanshot link leger and I attached this to my end tackle. I cast again, well past the bubbles, and drew the bait back then let it settle directly amongst them. I walked back to my swim, paying line out, and placed the rod in a rod rest with the tip pointing upwards to stop the line fouling the bankside rushes.

I had just started to bait up my other rod when it happened! The rod baited with the worm shot forward and jammed the butt ring against the rod rest. The clutch started singing as my hand reached forward. I struck and hit something solid which I expected to rush off across the lake. However, after taking only two or three yards of line it stopped and thrashed on the surface. My initial estimate was that it weighed about 12lb. and I bent into the fish expecting it to come in fairly easily. No effect. It just continued to wallow where it was. I gradually gained about three yards when the fish began to kite towards a gap in the reeds. I decided to change the direction in which I was pulling, hoping that this would make the carp move away from the bank. It didn't, the fish just stopped! I slid down the bank and waded to the edge of the rushes. Slowly I gained line. I pushed my net forward into the water as I drew the fish closer. Then I saw it properly, it looked enormous."

Peter attempted to weigh it with his scales but it took them down to their limit of 32lb. He tried to estimate how much more it weighed and guessed at about 36lb. After sacking the fish he went to the bar and ordered a pint of Double Diamond and in a shaky voice asked if they had any scales available to weigh a large carp. It transpired that none could be obtained until the following morning and it is to Peter's credit that he decided that he was not prepared to keep the fish sacked up for that length of time. Then, suddenly, he remembered the scales in the public toilets and, carrying the fish there in the sack, these revealed that its weight was somewhere between 34lb. and 35lb.

Today big carp still remain in Willow Pool, but for many anglers the surroundings just cannot be reconciled with their concept of what carp fishing should be about. Duncan Kay summed up his feelings about Billing in 1971, and what he wrote is no less valid today:

"Slowly, over the years, the Aquadrome has become more and more commercialised, resulting in more buildings, more people and consequently more disturbance. Now, due to blind organisation and the desire for money, the management has destroyed the atmosphere of Billing, and along with it nearly all chance of it producing its former catches again.

One good thing comes out of all this, and this is that the large, old carp will be able to live out their lives in relative peace from carp anglers. I know of one fifty-pounder that will be relieved for that.

So I say good-bye to the Billing carp."

Top: Pete Chillingsworth with his 'Double Diamond' 34-pounder, weighed on the Aquadrome's toilet scales.
Middle: "Today big carp still remain in Willow Pool"— but they seem just as difficult to catch. Mark Harrison spent 12 months before he landed this carp in 1989, weighing 36lb. 2oz. It turned out to be the same fish that had been caught by Bob Reynolds almost 28 years earlier.
Left: The solitude of carp fishing! Duncan Kay with an army of 'interested parties' admiring his 20½lb. mirror, caught at Billing Aquadrome in June, 1970.

Some Carp caught from Billing Aquadrome

Date	Time	Weight	Type	Captor	Bait
11/8/57	(12.45am)	24lb. 12oz.	common	Bob Reynolds	flake
11/8/57	(1.45am)	27lb. 13oz.	mirror	Bob Reynolds	flake
11/8/57	(3.15am)	28lb. 4oz.	mirror	Bob Reynolds	flake
18/8/57	(4.15am)	26lb. 10oz.	leather	Bob Reynolds	flake
18/8/57	(8.00am)	27lb. 9oz.	mirror	Bob Reynolds	flake
6/8/61	(3.30am)	33lb. 2oz.	mirror	Bob Reynolds	flake
-/9/61	(1.00am)	24lb. 4oz.	mirror	Johnny Bingham	balanced crust
-/9/61	(4.45am)	22lb. 8oz.	mirror	Dick Tebbutt	flake
1961		4 fish to 17lb.		Phil Shatford	
1961		23lb. 13oz.	mirror	Alec Lewis	potato
1961		9lb.	common	Alec Lewis	potato
1962		14lb.	mirror	Fred Wagstaffe	
1963		9lb.		Fred Wagstaffe	paste
1963		8lb. 12oz.	common	Bill Keal	paste
1963		9lb. 12oz.		Fred Wagstaffe	
30/7/64	(9.50pm)	32lb.	common	Phil Shatford	balanced crust
-/8/66		26lb.		E. Bailey	flake
1966		24lb.		Ray Clay	floating crust
-/9/66	(11pm)	42lb.	common	Ray Clay	honey paste
-/6/70		11lb. 8oz.	common	Duncan Kay	flavoured paste
-/6/70		20lb. 8oz.	mirror	Duncan Kay	flavoured paste
1970		16lb.		Alf Engers	
-/6/70	(8.30pm)	34lb.	common	Pete Chillingsworth	cheese

Frank Guttfield fishing for carp in July, 1968, at one of the other lakes on the Billing Aquadrome complex. Although carp had been stocked in several of the pits, it was the Willow Lake, in the 1960's, that anglers such as Bill Keal, Fred Wagstaffe, Alec Lewis, Phil Shatford and Jim Gibbinson believed offered the best chance of catching a carp to beat Walker's record.

Chapter 9
The Peterborough Cut

*We dug a tinfull of worms and tied my rod to the crossbar,
and, evading questions with the suppleness of long practice,
we set off down Broad Lane to join Joe at the cut.*
    Maurice Wiggin from *Troubled Waters.*

The design of a coal-fired electricity generating station, built within a short distance of the centre of Peterborough, required that a constant supply of water was always available to cool its turbines. The source of the water was to be the River Nene, so the station was sited close by, a short distance upstream from the main town bridge. The temperature of the discharged cooling water could be as high as 85°F so a canal was constructed, some 20 yards wide and a third of a mile long to return the warmed water into the main river well away from the station intake. They were separated by about 15 yards of bank until the canal kinked left and opened out into a concrete basin before joining the river. At this point a bridge was built over the 'Cut', as it became known, to allow pedestrian access along the river bank. It was about as far removed from the vision of what the ideal carp water should be as is possible. Even on the darkest nights it was impossible to dream away the industrial landscape which lay all around: the power station belching out its sulphur-laden fumes, tirelessly pumping its lifeblood to the factory machines and houses of Peterborough; the powerful, rhythmic, yet not unfriendly sounds of the railway and the sickly-sweet smell drifting across from the sugar factory on the south bank of the river; headlights cutting through the swirling steam from traffic rushing backwards and forwards over the Nene road bridge, its occupants completely oblivious to the microcosm of the Cut.

The microcosm of the Cut, surrounded by a sea of industry.

The Peterborough Cut

Construction of the electricity generating station took place in about 1936/37 during a period, just before the Second World War, which saw numbers of, what are now, small generating stations being built up and down the country. Large cities such as Manchester and Leeds often had three, or four, such local stations supplying the electricity requirements of the local community. The National Grid did not exist and the amount of electricity produced was tailored to local demand and apparently varied, insomuch that in Leeds, for example, different light bulbs were required depending in which part of the city you lived. The Peterborough station produced 38 megawatts (million watts) compared to the 4,000 megawatts produced nowadays by the Drax power station in Yorkshire. The life span of these small generating stations was between 30 and 40 years and the Peterborough site was closed in October 1976, although the discharge of warm water had become erratic from about 1968 onwards. In actual fact the Cut was built some years after the station was operational, in 1954, as its initial design allowed for the discharge to be made directly into the River Nene.

In 1952 the Nene and Welland Fishery Board decided to stock some of the waters under their jurisdiction with king carp. These were purchased from the Surrey Trout Farm and arrived on the 18th March, 1952 on the back of a converted ex-army truck. They were of the excellent Galician race, deriving from the same bloodstock as the Redmire leviathans. Some 3,200 of these fish were distributed into various pits, lakes, drains and canals in the area with the remaining 1,800 being released at five points along the River Nene. Approximately 200 were put in at Northampton, 400 near Thorpe Waterville, 400 at Ashton Lock, upstream of Oundle, 400 at Nassington and 400 in the lower reaches of the river around Peterborough. Only this last stocking met with real success and undoubtedly the influence of the warm water of the Cut was crucial.

The Surrey Trout Farm invoice. Part of the consignment was destined from the Peterborough Cut.

The years slipped by. During that time a sprinkling of carp had been landed from the Nene, many more had been lost on the inadequate tackle of the 'pleasure angler'. One of the first fish reported in the press was a carp of 17½lb. caught in October, 1956. Then, the Friday, January 9th, 1959 issue of *Angling Times* arrived in the newsagents shops up and down the country, and the headlines declared 'HUGE NENE CARP ON ONLY 4 lb. LINE'. The lead story reported what was "believed to be the largest carp ever taken from a river, a 20lb. 6oz. specimen landed by a Peterborough angler from a cut off the Nene after a three-quarters of an hour battle on 4 lb. b.s. line. The angler, Don Barnes, was laying on with bread paste hoping to catch bream. Then the carp took his bait and ran straight up the Cut away from the main river. The fish went under a bridge and he followed it along the bank in order to keep his line from snagging on the bridge. He played the fish up and down the Cut for over half-an-hour before he and a Sheffield angler, holidaying at Peterborough, could get it to the bank. Neither angler had a landing net big enough to cope with the fish. The one they tried to use buckled under the fish's weight, and the carp went off again. Mr. Barnes by this time was getting almost as tired as the fish. When he succeeded in bringing it to the bank again, his fellow angler scooped it out on to the bank by netting its tail and lifting it from the water. Mr. Barnes then sent his son looking for a place to weigh the fish, but was unlucky. So he wrapped it up in a wet cloth, mounted his cycle, and tucking the fish under his arm, pedalled the mile-and-a-half home. He put the fish in the bath while he looked about for a shop that would weigh it. Eventually, a corn merchant was found and the fish was weighed and verified. Mr. Barnes then wrapped up the carp again, cycled back to the river and returned the fish to the spot he had taken it from."

"The fish went under a bridge..."

No doubt the *Angling Times* reporter listened to this story with fascination. The thought of a cyclist riding through the bustling centre of Peterborough, trying to steer with one hand whilst holding a lively carp with the other is an angling journalist's dream. It is to *Angling Times* what Watergate was to the *Washington Post*.

By 1961 the area around the Cut saw regular visits from anglers whose tackle was more suited to landing their intended quarry. Peter Nisbet, a 34-year-old schoolteacher from Norfolk, had caught a 16lb. carp from the Cut earlier in the season and was determined to catch another. He returned at the beginning of September and, after baiting a swim for two evenings, he tackled-up using a built-cane roach rod, 9lb. line and a size 4 hook. The bait was ordinary bread paste almost the size of a golf ball.

Nothing happened for a long time. Small fish flipped on the surface as dusk fell. In the distance the disturbance created by a bigger fish caused heads to peer into the gloom. Gradually, most of the other anglers reluctantly gathered their belongings and made their way home along the well-worn banks, disappearing into the steamy gloom. The bats began their nightly aerobatics and the Cut's infamous rat population scuffled about in the undergrowth looking for the angler's discarded bait. Time slipped by until 1.30am and then suddenly, without warning, Peter found himself playing a monstrous fish. There was almost a disaster as the reel jammed solid, but by keeping a cool head he gradually managed to gain ground by pulling the line in by hand. After a heart-thumping 30 minutes it was finally landed and proved to be a new record river carp weighing 21lb. 5oz.[1]

1. This fish was incorrectly credited, in the summer 1989 issue of *Carpworld*, as being the first 20-pounder caught from the Cut.

By 1962 there was a regular group fishing specifically for the Cut's carp. Being within easy cycling distance of a large population some of the Cut's most successful carp anglers of this period were barely into their teens. Between January and November 1962, 14-year-old David Olson caught 13 carp. A measure of David's enthusiasm for carp fishing was the fact that the largest, a 20lb. mirror, was caught on Guy Fawkes night when the majority of youngsters were preoccupied with other activities! During the same month 11-year-old Peter Hall, on the eve of his 12th birthday and fishing with his 14-year-old brother David, caught a 22-pounder.

Interest in the Cut began to spread far and wide. *Angling Times* had by now realised what a little gold-mine they had, literally on their doorstep, and ran several features about it. Centre page spreads and articles in the *Angling Times* sister publication, *Fishing,* meant trip after trip down the icy, muddy banks for staff photographers Sonny Cragg and Bill Goddard. If anyone was left in the slightest doubt about the Cut's credentials, after all this publicity, it was dispelled in early July, 1963.

Using an old rod, Peter Hall, of Peterborough, landed this 22lb. carp.

A 29-year-old research chemist from Loughborough, Mike Smith, settled down at 10pm with his friend Don Lawson for a night after the carp. Fishing with potato as bait, Mike hooked and landed a 13¾-pounder around midnight. He could hear carp moving all around the margins so he changed over to floating crust. At about 2am his silver paper indicator twitched forward and, after a short fight, what was to become the Cut's most celebrated carp was on the bank. It weighed a staggering 29½lb., the 10th largest ever caught. At about 5am Mike had another take on crust, and this one put up a really tremendous battle. It weighed 19¾lb. A move along the bank saw yet another fish hooked but that one broke him in the weeds. His friend, fishing nearby, had to make do with a consolation 9¾lb. common.

Mike Smith's carp was to become the Cut's most famous resident. Here it is caught by Peter Hemingway 18 months later, in 1965.

The Peterborough Cut

This period, around 1963/64, saw the Cut start to come under intense angling pressure, perhaps to a greater extent than any other water had previously experienced. Names which were to become part of carp angling folklore, such as Fred Wagstaffe, Jim Gibbinson, Dave Goodrum, Stan Hill, Alf Engers, started to appear. These were anglers who already were experienced in catching carp but the Cut was unlike other carp fisheries—feeding habits were very often determined by electricity demand! During the night electricity supply was at its lowest but around 7am usually started to increase. This was not always the case, however, and the vagaries of the power station's operational procedures meant that warm water discharges could not be predicted with any degree of certainty. On other occasions the warm water was discharged directly into the river (it has been suggested that this was to stop the intake freezing over), at a point just downstream of the intake, so wasted trips to the Cut had to be accepted as a matter of course.

Above: 15 year old Peter Harvey has a 17-pounder witnessed by Mike George of Angling Times. During the fight the agate lining fell out of Peter's rod ring and the line became dangerously frayed. After carefully playing the fish for 15 minutes it was netted by fellow Peterborough Specimen Group member Larry Mould.
Above right: Grantham angler, Dave Goodrum, caught this 24lb. mirror at about 5am on a freezing January night in 1965. The fish put up a tremendous fight, forcing Dave to follow it along the bank.
Right: Dave Goodrum with his 21¼lb. mirror carp caught at 3am on October 1st, 1965. Bait was the ubiquitous potato.

The Peterborough Cut

The next three years saw the Cut in its prime. It was constantly mentioned in the angling press and this notoriety brought anglers from far and wide to tread its barren, austere banks. But the aforementioned difficulties, combined with the prolific rat population and the very real hardship of cold-weather carp fishing saw the majority of young hopefuls quickly become disillusioned and admit defeat.

Perhaps one fish alone did more to elevate the Peterborough Cut into the consciousness of the angling public, than all the others put together. Its début, as mentioned earlier, was when Peter Nisbet caught it in 1961, at 21lb. 5oz. Destined to become the Cut's most famous inhabitant, it broke its own river record on a further four occasions.

Sept. 1961	21 lb. 5 oz.	Peter Nisbet
July 1963	29 lb. 8 oz.	Mike Smith
Oct. 1964	31 lb. 12 oz.	Stan Hill
Dec. 1964	33 lb. 12 oz.	Peter Harvey
Feb. 1965	33 lb. 12 oz.	Peter Hemingway
June 1965	34 lb. 4 oz.	William Beta

Bud Jessop, fishing pal of Stan Hill, and both members of the Denton Carp Catchers, caught this 21½-pounder using floating crust on the 10th October, 1964.

On the last capture it unfortunately perished in William Beta's sack. The weave of the hessian sack, and perhaps the high water temperature, resulted in its demise. The fish was set-up by *Angling Times* and many years later sold by them to the well-known carp angler and tackle manufacturer, Kevin Nash.

Jack Thorndike admires William Beta's record river carp at the Angling Times offices.

Born in Hungary in 1944, William Beta often travelled up from London to fish the Cut for its carp with his mother, Iona, and their chaplain, Dr. Bela Ispanki. On this occasion he baited up with a few small potatoes and was using a small ball of cheese, on a size 6 hook, as bait. His line was 8lb. breaking strain. Fishing close to the footbridge nothing happened during the first night and the next day. But about 11pm, on the second evening, William had a run and landed a 10-pounder. No sooner had he cast out again to the middle of the Cut than he had another bite and this time history was about to be made.

Caught near where the Cut enters the River Nene, William Beta, of Neasden, with his 34¼lb. carp, taken shortly after the start of the 1965 fishing season.

The bleak Orwellian landscape of the Peterborough Cut.

The Peterborough Cut

These golden years saw regular success come to a few hardy individuals who could put up with the perverseness of the fishing. Dave Moore, Elliott Smith, and other members of the Peterborough S.G. and the Denton Carp Catchers Club, reaped their well-earned rewards.

After about 1966, both the numbers of carp caught from the Cut, and their average weight, diminished. Whatever caused this decline no one ever discovered, but the Cut's demise was ultimately sealed a couple of years later by operational decisions made by the Electricity Generating Board.

The final chapter in the Cut's history is taken up by the highly-respected carp angler Elliott Symak, who, when he fished the Cut, was known as Elliott Smith:

"I entered the Peterborough Cut carp scene a few months after William Beta's fish had been caught and winter fished there a great deal. I enjoyed a certain amount of success, but my chance of a genuine 30-pounder died with that fish, I am sure. Quite a number of 20lb. carp were being caught between 1965 and 1967, and I landed my first in January 1966. Although I can't remember much about the 22lb. fish I do remember it came from the grotty old 'basin', at the mouth of the Cut, and took about 3 fags to land!

One of the most notable captures, also during early January 1966, was of three fish over 20lb. caught in a couple of days by Dave Moore, of Peterborough.

With freezing winds and snow sweeping across the country, 16 year old British Railways clerk, Peter Harvey, caught this 33¾lb. river record using a groundbaiting method suggested by Fred Wagstaffe. A later claim-to-fame came when he landed a 6lb. zander from the Cut, on catfood paste, in the mid-1970's!

Stan Hill with the result of many weeks effort after the Cut's carp. A member of the Denton Carp Catchers, named after Denton Reservoir near Grantham, he often fished the Cut with his fellow-members Bud Jessop and Dave Goodrum. The carp was caught at about 2am by 24-year old Stan, using a freelined potato on size 2 hook tied to 8lb. breaking strain line. Stan and Bud were fishing just about half-way along the Cut, in an area known as the 'Bush Swims' whilst Dave fished the 'Lower Pipe Swim'.

Fishing conditions on the Cut were pretty grim. A long, almost featureless bank stretched before you—there was little cover. As the most productive times were during the winter months, so, inevitably, the conditions were usually damp, the banks drab, the rare beds of reeds brown and uninteresting. The uniform length of water gave little indication where

The Peterborough Cut

carp might be found and they rarely bubbled or leapt. It was more often than not a question of guesswork, with a bit of intuition thrown in. We knew, though, that under the steaming surface swam lots of carp, both large and small, alongside bream, chub and millions of bleak. The place was alive with large rats, and anything edible had to be kept packed away otherwise the rodents would help themselves.

The 'Bushes Swims' about half-way along the Cut.

The basin, which must be the most 'uncarpy' swim in the entire country, was an area of concrete and steel which was fished from either the bridge or from the sides, off the railings. The importance of the basin, however, was that the carp had to pass through it to get in or out of the Cut, and I am in no doubt that it was here that the best catches were made. When the Nene was in flood, and a foot, or more, of extra water rose up those vertical concrete sides, then I knew I was in with a great chance of hooking some of the Cut carp.

Of all the many problems associated with the Cut, though, the one which always loomed largest for me, at any rate, was trying to keep warm. For three, or four, winters I fished the Cut in a dedicated manner; namely as often as I could make it—during which times, of course, there was ice, snow, rain, gales. I've more than once fished in a foot of snow, or watched the thermometer drop well below freezing during the course of a night. We didn't have bivvies or

Elliott Smith's largest carp from the Cut weighing 26lb.

Two famous Cut characters. Elliott and 'Lumpy'—weighing 24½lb.

143

The Peterborough Cut

thermals, or Skeetex boots. We used wellingtons or waders, anoraks, 45in. brollies and as many blankets as we could carry. Some of us wore army-surplus tank suits. Often I stood in the warm waters of the Cut to 'un-solidify' my frozen feet!

Despite all this hassle, I guess through the resilience of youth and the companionship of some marvellous mates, I got by—we all did—and also managed to enjoy ourselves a great deal.

Unfortunately, a decision was taken by the C.E.G.B. that the power station, which had for so many years burnt its coal and belched its smoke over the Peterborough landscape, was to be phased out and then, suddenly, round about 1968, the flow of the warm water became irregular. It really only became a worthwhile proposition at this point for locals to continue and myself, along with a few others, such as Nigel Bryant, continued to fish the Cut up to about 1972.

In the winter of 1967 a fish of 30lb., caught by Don Hepworth, was reported and, then, in August of the following year, the same fish, it is believed, was landed again in the main river. This fish could possibly have featured as a new river record had the warm water remained flowing down the Cut, but it was almost certainly one of the many carp which joined the exodus into the seven mile stretch of the River Nene between the Dog in a Doublet and Orton Locks.

Lumpy again! This time caught by Dave Moore from the Cut bridge, in September, 1966. Its deformed mouth and repeat capture led Elliott Smith to write an article, in 1966, putting forward the idea, although actually dismissing it himself, that there might not be as many carp in the Cut as originally believed. This possibility was given further scope for development by Terry Eustace, in a feature for Angling magazine, in May, 1970, which suggested for the first time that carp could be identified by their scale patterns.

After the power station closed down there was a plan to completely fill the Cut in, but an alternative was finally implemented whereby only the section from the station's outfall to the first bridge was covered over.

And so an era in carp fishing came and went. Tales of rats, and mud, and sugar-beet factory stink, were told on dark winter nights when all but the bravest souls were sat in front of warm fires. I was lucky enough to be part of this piece of carp fishing history and, although I suffered along with those other mad souls, I wouldn't have missed it for the world."

Yet what became of the Cut carp? Were they destined to roam endlessly the mighty River Nene, or did they find a new home, some secret hideaway, safe from the inexorable pursuits of man? A handful perhaps still roam their past haunts, lost souls longing for the winter warmth amongst the discarded prams and supermarket trolleys. One of the old stalwarts, a fish of 26½lb. was caught by David Williams (who also caught a 12lb. barbel from the Nene in 1969), from the mouth of the Cut in July, 1977. It had been landed by Dave Moore some 10 years earlier, in the same spot at almost the same weight. But carp rarely seek to hide their presence, and for those determined enough even this slow and dreamy river cannot give them sanctuary. It is a little know fact that a few dedicated individuals tracked their whereabouts down and, during the last ten years, two fish—a mirror and a common—were landed in excess of the old Cut record. The common, in fact, was caught twice weighing 34½lb. and 35½lb. The mirror weighed 36lb.!

Dave Moore, who later became a fisheries officer with Anglian Water Authority, holding a beautiful linear carp that epitomizes the Dutch Galician stockings of Leney.

The catch that brought the Peterborough Cut into centre-stage for a few years in the 1960's. Don Lawson (left) caught the 9¾lb. common, whilst Mike Smith rocked the carp world with fish of 29½lb, 19¾lb. and 13¾lb.

The Peterborough Cut

A List of Carp caught from the River Nene at Peterborough

Date	Weight	Captor	Location	Bait
Jan. 1959	20lb. 6oz. (m)	Don Barnes	Cut	bread paste
Sept. 1961	21lb. 5oz. (m)	Peter Nisbet	Cut	bread paste
Sept. 1961	20lb.	Ted Hill	North Bank	bread paste
June 1962	20lb. 8oz. (m)	Phillip Buck	Orton nr. Peterborough	cheese
Aug. 1962	23lb. 8oz.	Edmund Hobbs	Cut	bread
Nov. 1962	20lb. 2oz. (m)	David Olson (14yr.)	Cut	bread paste
Nov. 1962	22lb. (m)	Peter Hall (12yr.)	Cut	bread paste
1962	22lb.	Joseph Caffrey	Cut	
Jan. 1963	20lb. 1oz. (c)	David Olson	Cut	crust
July 1963	29lb. 8oz. (m)	Mike Smith	Cut	floating crust
July 1964	21lb. 8oz.	Barry Hulme	Cut	bread paste
Oct. 1964	21lb. 8oz.	Bernard Jessop	Cut	floating crust
Oct. 1964	31lb. 12oz. (m)	Stan Hill	Cut	potato
Dec. 1964	23lb. (m)	John Howsen	Nene nr. Peterborough	maggot
Dec. 1964	33lb. 12oz. (m)	Peter Harvey	Cut	potato
Dec. 1964	24lb. (m)	Fred Wagstaffe	Cut	potato
Feb. 1965	33lb. 12oz. (m)	Peter Hemingway	Cut	potato
Jan. 1965	24lb. (m)	Dave Goodrum	Cut	potato
Jan. 1965	23lb. (m)	Jack Howson	Nene at Peterborough	single maggot
Jun 1965	34lb. 4oz. (m)	William Beta	Cut	cheese
Sept. 1965	22lb. 8oz.	Geoffrey Rothery	Nene at Peterborough	bread paste
Oct. 1965	21lb. 4oz. (m)	Dave Goodrum	Cut	potato
Oct. 1965	25lb. (m)	Ilona Beta	Cut	bread paste
Dec. 1965	23lb. (c)	Dave Goodrum	Cut	potato
Jan. 1966	22lb. (m)	Elliott Smith	Cut	bread
Jan. 1966	24lb. (c)	Stuart Ellis	Cut	bread
Jan. 1966	20lb. 8oz.	Dave Moore	Cut	bread paste
Jan. 1966	22lb.	Dave Moore	Cut	bread paste
Jan. 1966	23lb. 4oz. (c)	Dave Moore	Cut	bread paste
Feb. 1966	26lb. (m)	Elliott Smith	Cut	bread paste
Feb. 1966	24lb. (c)	Elliott Smith	Cut	bread paste
Feb. 1966	25lb. (m)	Dave Goodrum	Cut	floating crust
March 1966	24lb. (c)	Jim Gibbinson	Cut	sunk crust
March 1966	20lb. (c)	Graham Igglesden	Cut	bread flake
June 1966	21lb. (m)	Ilona Beta	Cut	floating crust
March 1966	27lb. (m)	Fred Warwick	Cut	paste/crust
Sept. 1966	24lb. 8oz. (c)	Dave Moore	Cut	crust
March 1967	24lb. 8oz. (c)	Elliott Smith	Cut	
March 1967	25lb. (m)	Elliott Smith	Cut	crust
March 1967	30lb. (m)	Donald Hepworth	Cut	bread flake
Aug. 1968	30lb. 8oz. (m)	David Wesley	Nene at Peterborough	paste
July 1970	20lb. (c)	Robin Stone	Cut	potato
Feb. 1971	22lb. 8oz.	B. Davies	Cut	
June 1971	24lb. (c)	Mike Nickels	Cut	breadflake
July 1971	26lb. 12oz. (m)	Ray Peckett	Nene nr. Peterborough	

Chapter 10
Nothing New under the Sun

You see the ways the fisherman doth take,
To catch fish: what engines doth he make!
    John Bunyan

The relationship between man and fish began at the dawn of history, and carp at first were looked on as no more than a food source. We do not know exactly when man first turned the occupation of his mind to catching them for pleasure, rather than securing sustenance, but it was long, long ago. By the time carp were introduced into this country the recreation of angling was well developed and convoluted carp baits, not unlike those which are used presently, were advocated. Richard Frank proposed in 1658 that an excellent paste for carp could be made if you "Take fine bean-flour, English honey and poudred sugar, amalgamized or mingled with the yolk of an egg; and if the fat of a heron be supperadded to it, it makes it not the worse. Besides, sometimes he loves a taste of the dairy-maid." The carp's liking for dairy products and its sweet-tooth were clearly appreciated by Frank, whereas James Chetham's brew, given in 1681, suggests that you should "Take Man's Fat and Cat's Fat, of each half an ounce, Mummy finely powdered three drams, Cummin-seed finely powered one dram, distilled Oyl of Annise and Spike, of each six drops, Civet two grains, and Camphor four grains...." Colonel Robert Venables was much less adventurous when he suggested, in 1676, that "Carp love the largest red Worms....Paste also of all sorts made with strong-scented Oils, Tar, Bread-grain boiled soft, Cadbait, Gentles, Marsh-worm and Flag-worm especially...."

Over 200 years earlier, what possibly could be the first written account of groundbaiting for carp was described (Sloane 1118—fol. 30). In modern English it suggests that "To take carp and make them multiply get new cow dung and mould it with loam like a loaf; then make holes and put into them the innards of chickens or capons or of any other fowl and throw the ball into the water, or let it down in a basket." A not dissimilar idea was suggested by Richard Blome, writing in *The Gentleman's Recreation* in 1686, whereby a board is covered with clay, in which is mixed a lot of beans. This is then sunk to the bottom and, as the clay slowly dissolves, the beans are made available to the fish. The carp's reputed fondness for cow dung was also repeated by the plagiarist Nicholas Cox, in his book of the same title, printed in 1674. In fact, plagiarism seems to have been a common occurrence in these early works and perhaps was socially acceptable.

For all our modern arrogance that we have developed deadly methods and baits which our angling forbears would never have considered in their wildest fantasies, we find that in truth very little is new. The imagination imitates and innovation germinates only with the nutriment of knowledge. In 1835 Thomas Boosey wrote the following, which would be no less perceptive if written today:

"*(The)* carp is a very wary fish, and requires the angler's utmost patience to ensnare. The biting time of this fish, (particularly of large carp) is very early in the morning. They delight in still water, where there are large flags and weeds, with broad leaves. One of the best methods of angling for carp is to gently drop in a line leaded with a single shot only, which will be sufficient to sink the bait. Do this in the following manner—let the bait so fall, that itself, and a few inches of line, with the shot, may rest on one of the large leaves, the bait itself hanging within the water, over the edge of such a leaf; this bait must be a red worm, with a gentle to cover the point of the hook. When you observe the shot drawn from the leaf, give the fish time to swallow his bait. You are enabled to judge their haunts when you hear them smack, or suck, as it is sometimes called. Throw in some slices of bread as ground-bait, on the over-night: and cast in, whilst angling, some small pieces....but the ground-bait is sufficient to entice them to the place." Boosey's advice, whilst having an authoritative ring to it, was no doubt influenced by the earlier work of Richard Brookes, who writes in his book *The Art of Angling* (1743) that "A carp exercises the angler's patience as much as any fish, for he is very sly and wary. They seldom bite in cold weather, and in hot, a man can not be too early or too late for them.

Proper baits are the red-worm in March, the cadew in June, and the grasshopper in July, August, and September. But a recent discovery has proved a green pea to be a bait inferior to none, if not the best of all; and that the best method to prepare them for use, is by half-boiling a sufficient quantity, and covering them with melted butter.

In hot weather, he will take a lob-worm at top, as a trout does a fly: or, between the weeds, in a clear place, sink it without a float, about eight inches in the water, with only one large shot on the line, which is to be lodged on the leaf of some weed. Then retire, keeping your eye on the shot, till you see it taken away, with about a foot of the line, and then you may venture to strike. Great numbers of carp have been taken this way."

Brookes goes on to describe what must be one of the first, if not the first, references to the use of floating crust as a bait for carp. He recommends that "In ponds, the best method is to throw six or eight slices of bread, to be carried with the wind, and in a short time, it is probable, you will see many fish feeding on it. If not, crumble a little very small, and cast it were the slices rest; which will be a means to make them find the pieces at top, which when you have suffered them to feed on, take a very long rod, strong line, middle-sized hook, and one shot fixed just above the hook, and baited with about the size of a large horse-bean or the upper crust of a rasped Fruit Roll, and you may pick out what size and quantity you please by dropping your bait before the largest fish, as he is feeding on the slices at the top. This is a sure means of getting sport, and but little known."

A note in *The Fishing Gazette,* in 1893, draws the reader's attention to the use of bread crust in the following manner:

"Has anybody tried the following method of catching carp? Plumb the depth of the pond, and bait with cubes of bread. Fix your bullet so that the bread will float on the top of the water, the lead, of course, being on the bottom. Small fish proceed to nibble the bread, and so attract the larger fish, one of which at last runs off with it. Then hit him!"

Let us follow this line of inquiry a little further. In the April, 1952 edition of *The Angler* Richard Walker stated that "I invented a method, known as margin-fishing, which consists of using a floating bait fished directly under the rod-point, with no line touching the water." This claim was perpetuated by many notable commentators, including Edward Ensom, and Bernard Venables who wrote that "a method, almost without parallel for innovation and ingenuity, was invented by the astonishingly fruitful Richard Walker—he calls it margin fishing." In *Drop Me A Line* Dick believed that "the only real contribution I have been able to make to our sum of carp-lore is the technique of margin-fishing, and this is only useful when there is no likelihood of disturbance from other anglers."

But let us turn the clock back to 1863, and read Cornwall Simeon's *Stray Notes on Fishing and Natural History* where we find the following:

"If on a fine calm summer night you visit a piece of water well stocked with Carp, especially if its sides be perpendicular and faced with brick, and the fish be numerous in proportion to the feed, you will probably hear every now and then a long-drawn sucking noise, followed by one as of blowing. They are, I have no doubt, ascribable to the Carp's habit, while 'priming' along the edges of ponds at night, of sucking in from the interstices amongst the bricks, of any insects which may be lurking there, and which he could not otherwise get within reach of his mouth, and afterwards rejecting any substances which may not suit him, all 'between wind and water,' as a sailor would say. When feeding carp with bread, you may often see this power of suction exercised by one as he rises almost perpendicularly under a piece floating on the surface, and draws it down in a little vortex to his scarcely visible mouth, which, by the way, is thus enabled to take in much larger morsels than it otherwise could. I have no doubt that, owing to this habit of Carp in thus priming along the sides of ponds at night, a night-line set with the bait hung on the surface of the water, close to the edge, would be a very killing dodge for them."

Undoubtedly, Richard Walker, along with some help from his Hitchin A.C. carp fishing friends, independently developed and honed the method of margin fishing at Bearton Pond. Clearly, Dick popularised the method and deserves credit for doing so, but it is unlikely he was the first to devise it. A similar situation existed when Jack Clayton, the Boston tackle dealer, was credited in 1957 with inventing the swing-tip, and Dick, himself, was amongst the first to point out that it had been described some 152 years earlier in *The Complete Troller*.

Nevertheless, with the help of Bernard Venables and his *Daily Mirror* features in early 1951, margin fishing was popularised and resulted in a number of fine carp being caught. Notable at that time were a 21-pounder caught by T. Bentworth and a 25½-pounder by Robert Sinclair from Austin's Pond, at Clacton-on-Sea.

The first mention of margin fishing in Bernard Venables' Daily Mirror strip feature. It appeared in June, 1951, shortly before Bob Sinclair caught his 25½-pounder using this method. Bernard's endorsement had the effect of popularising the technique and making Walker the object of considerable attention.

The 'revolution' of the early-1970's, in using particle baits for catching carp, was laid out by Rod Hutchinson in his expansive discourse in the December, 1975 issue of *Angling* magazine. He began by stating that "The first signs that big carp could be caught on small baits of the same size came with the fine catches made at Redmire Pool by Roger Bowskill, the bait in this case being maggots. This gave food for thought to all dedicated carp anglers;

the seeds of particle-bait fishing as we now know it were sown." Yet one of the most knowledgeable anglers the sport of angling has known, Francis Francis, recounted in 1867, exactly 100 years before Bowskill caught his Redmire fish, that, "One carp-fisher I know of, swears by boiled beans, the large yellow haricots, or the smaller broad bean for the hook, ground-baiting with boiled barley."

But what of Hutchinson's own flirtation with unusual particle baits such as shrimps? His five stone Redmire blitz produced only eels; a dismal failure compared to Mr. W. Cook, who caught a fine carp of 7½lb. from the River Gipping, way back in 1908—on a peeled shrimp! And Flt. Lieut. Burton, writing in *The Angler's News,* in 1943, relates how he had seen French anglers regularly use "shelled shrimps" to catch carp, wondering if "French carp have French appetites?"

Years later, in July, 1977, Jim Gibbinson thought particle baits, or at least their "popularity and development," were an important advance. But their present usage, considering the modern obsession with the boilie, would perhaps leave that claim open to question.

Richard Walker's attributed quote, that big fish require a big bait, certainly has some truth in fact. He did infer this in 1947 in his famous letter to B.B., writing that "A lump of paste ought to be an inch across, and worms as big as possible. A big, ponderous beast of 15lb. is not going to bother himself to move for a pea-sized bit of dough or one miserable maggot..." Confirming this belief, in 1949, he wrote the following in *The Fishing Gazette* using his pseudonym, Water Rail:

"I am a firm believer in the old adage of a big bait for a big fish. It is particularly applicable to carp. While small ones may be caught on bunches of maggots and similar trifles, the big, crafty old fellows will not be bothered with such things as a rule; they want a good mouthful."

Yet, a few years later, by then having accumulated a great deal more experience of carp in waters other than Bearton Pond and Temple Pool, Dick was less dogmatic writing the following in *Still-water Angling:*

"I usually use very large baits, paste-balls the size of pheasants eggs, and two-inch cubes of crust, without having very much evidence that they

An embryonic Hutchinson in the 1960's with carp caught from Horton Kirby. His theories on baits were still at the formative stage, being influenced at that time by Roger Bowskill's success with maggots and the use of grains of hemp, on large hooks, for Dorset Stour barbel.

Dick and Pete Thomas tackling-up for a carp session at Temple Pool in August, 1951. Most of Dick's early conclusions about carp were based on his experiences at Temple Pool (whose real name was Hexton Manor) and Bearton Pond.

are preferred by the fish to something smaller. I feel that a carp is at any rate unlikely to overlook them!" The difficulties encountered at Redmire had caused Walker to re-evaluate several of his theories, and the size of the bait was one such consideration. He later wrote in the revealing Carp Catchers' Club's rotary letters, in relation to Redmire, that "I entirely agree with Denys that small baits are desirable here."

In the autumn of 1954 John Norman posed the following question to the other members of the C.C.C.—"Has anyone ever tried maize? It's easy to get, cooked like wheat it swells to a good size and three, or four, grains would be a good mouthful. It's used a great deal on the Continent where I have seen carp fishers use nothing else." But the opportunity slipped by without further discussion.

Some three years earlier, Maurice Ingham had got to the crux of the main impediment that was restricting better catches for the members of the Carp Catchers' Club. Walker, and the other members, whilst examining almost every other area of carp fishing never really got to grips with baits. However, Maurice was on the right tack when he wrote, in November 1951, enquiring, "Why is it that potatoes, worms, paste and bread are almost always regarded as the best baits for carp? Admittedly, they all catch carp, but is it not possible that there are other more attractive baits, as yet untried?"

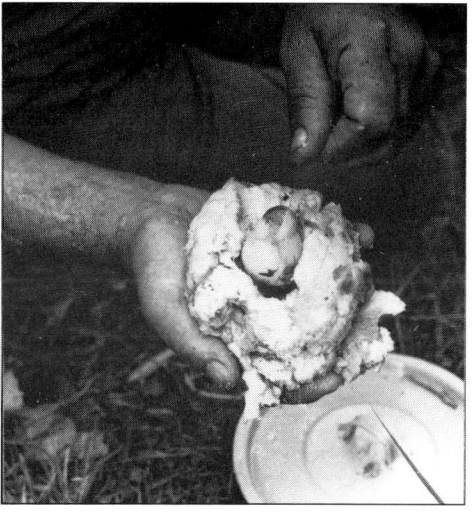

The idea of using potato as bait, and enclosing it in a ball of groundbait, was used by Cheshunt carp anglers in the early part of this century. It continued to be advocated by Stephen Hill, in 1930, in Fine Angling for Coarse Fish and Dick Walker, in 1962. The latter contibuted a picture-feature for Angling Times demonstrating Fred J. Taylor, fishing at Husborne Crawley, "reviving an old method for carp to good effect." The above photograph shows Fred J. preparing the bait before throwing it out by hand.

Maurice Ingham's 1951 assessment of carp anglers' existing bait perception and future development was to be proved accurate.

Dick Walker, and other members of the Carp Catchers' Club, have been credited with many aspects of innovation in carp fishing. John Bailey, in his book *The Great Anglers,* ascribes to the same view as Ted Ensom, in *Memorable Coarse Fish,* that they "revolutionised carp fishing." The assertion has also been widely documented that, pre-Walker, carp were held to be almost impossible to catch and the game was not worth the candle. It is clear that Walker, Maurice Ingham, and a few others did revolutionise carp fishing in the 1950's, in the sense that they convinced the general angling public that carp could be specifically caught on a regular basis. But it is manifestly incorrect to claim that anglers before Walker could not successfully catch carp by intent, and it is the author's hope that his book will at least dispel this myth. One such successful and acknowledged carp fisherman of the past was C.T. Ansell, who wrote the following to *The Angler's News* in 1930:

"I have studied the cunning habits of the carp for more than 20 years, and my opinion is that a carp requires more catching and more patience than any other fish. Each season I never expect to get a carp the first two or three ventures, although I can see fish moving close to the bait. Three years ago when the water was like gin at the beginning of August, one evening I saw five carp from 4lb. to 12lb. around my bait at once, but not a touch did I get till a week later, when we had a heavy rain, which made the water quite thick. Then I got six fish in about ten evenings, which I consider good. My opinion about carp fishing is that they will not take until they have been carefully baited for, and then got accustomed to the angler's tackle and bait.

One or two items of importance to be remembered when carp fishing are—to keep as much out of sight as possible, for a carp has a wonderful eye as well as a wonderful brain, also it can detect the slightest vibration from one's feet."

Twenty-two years later, Dick Walker was in full agreement when writing in the Carp Catchers' Club's rotary letters that, "I do go to very great lengths to keep quiet and out of sight, and I am sure it makes a very great difference." He expanded on this in *Still-Water Angling* by writing:

"...carp, which have keen eyesight, can detect the presence of a fisherman at distance", and then continued with, "Carp are incredibly sensitive to people walking about—even the slightest tread can alarm fish a hundred yards away." As usual, Dick went into it further, demonstrating the great lengths he would go to in achieving his objectives. In the C.C.C. rotary letters, he reported that "The reason why I take the weight off my backside when I cough is that I've found by actual observation that carp can detect the jar of one's coughing when sitting, but not otherwise." If genius is the ability of taking infinite pains, then surely Walker must be included in that exalted category!

Moving back to 1946, an American, L.P. Thompson described in *The Fishing Gazette* a method of groundbaiting for carp with particle baits at distance, a tactic which, no doubt, many would ascribe as a much more recent development:

"A big one is rolling at a distance of forty yards under the far bank. His appetite must be whetted with a spoonful of corn, he must peck at a kernel or two as an hors d'oeuvre before attacking the banquet—five kernels in a row on a no. 5 Spoat.

Flicking corn with a wooden spoon, be its handle ever so long and springy, and the carry-through stroke ever so perfect, fails to throw the furthermost grain over forty feet; the pattern is ragged and covers too great an area.

One evening as we were sitting by the river, I tell my companion of the difficulties connected with baiting a swim at long range. Many a bright idea has flitted through my mind, many a method has been tried and found wanting.

My friend at my side then makes a valuable suggestion. 'Why not,' says he, 'in some way, attach a spoonful of corn to the hook and cast it across the river?' The possibilities of a bundle of *Niblets,* wrapped in tissue paper, similar to the little July 4th torpedoes, are discussed, and the next evening exhaustive experiments are made along these lines, but no great success attends the performance.

And then—the great inspiration! Rushing home, the vacuum top of a Chili sauce bottle is discovered in the pantry. Down the sink-drain goes the sauce, in the ash can goes the bottle. A piece of stout spring-brass wire is cunningly fitted as a bail for the little bucket and holes are drilled in the bottom; a slotted leather tab to hold the hook is fixed to the bail.

The next evening by the riverside, a shaking hand fills the container—a heaping load. A rhythmic swing backwards—then forward, and out shoots line with the precious cargo. A splash in the exact spot near yonder bank, and the perilous journey is made without mishap—no casualties of kernels in transit, nor the corn, having learned a valuable lesson from close association with the intelligent angler, has achieved that blessed state—inertia, which combats successfully the propelling force of the steely wrist and the resilient bamboo. And now the little bucket—itself having fallen into pleasant immobility, which finally comes, willy-nilly, to all things great and small—pierces the surface of another element. The bucket's specific gravity is great, it sinks rapidly and parts company with the semi-buoyant corn which is hustled out of its cosy nest by jets of water which spurt through the holes of the container. And the pattern on the river floor? Perfect!—not too large, not too small—and of an even distribution.

Now retrieve the empty carrier and unhook it. Light a pipe, tell a story, sing a song, and catch a carp; and should he weigh 20lb. knock him on the head and give a dinner party, or—if you do not feel like giving a dinner party—let him go!"

Has the point been made? Is there nothing new? Even the concept that there is nothing new in angling, is itself, not new. Walker thought so when he stated simply, in *The Angler's World,* in July 1968, that "there's very little new in angling." A few years earlier, G. Neal, in the September 24th, 1965 issue of *The Angler's Mail,* was of a similar mind, stating that, "The real value of the 'new wave' of carp fishing, and carp knowledge, initiated by Richard Walker and his fellow carp catchers, has, to my mind, consisted not so much of new methods as of increased confidence in the existence, and approachability, of very large carp." Expanding this point, Mr. Neal carried on—"From time to time writers have claimed to have developed a 'new' method for this or that species, whereas in fact the method is rarely new."

The Devon Carp Catchers Group was part of the 'new wave' of carp fishing in the early 1960's. It was formed by Mike Winter and Larry Beck, at Dick's instigation, in 1958. Several members made important contributions, including Pat Russell, by striking at 'twitch bites' against the advice of Walker and Pete Thomas, Mike Winter with cold-water carping, plus Roger Bowskill and Mike Winter by using maggots for carp. The photograph shows (from left) Larry Beck, Ken Nicholas, Mike Winter, Geoff Kane, Lee Flaws and Pat Russell.

Nothing New under the Sun

And then again, in 1974, in the British Carp Study Group magazine, Dick Walker reiterated his earlier views in a feature titled 'Nothing New under the Sun'.

Of course, there have been immense technological improvements made since the 1950's, but in the arena of bait and methods it is more a case of re-discovering what has been forgotten!

ESSENTIAL OILS FOR BAIT AND GROUNDBAIT

Rhodium, 9s.; Rhodium Fact, 4s.; Roach Oil, 6s.; Spike Lavender, 8s.; Aniseed, 2s. 8d.; Verbena, 4s.; Fennel, 4s. 6d.; Rose Geranium Synth., 7s. 6d.; Rose Geranium E.I., 10s. 6d. per fl. oz. bottle.

DYES FOR COLOURING MAGGOTS: Bismark Brown (brownish-red); Rhodamine B (rose); Chrysoidine (orange-yellow); Chrysoidine R (orange-red); Methyl Violet (milk-white); Auramine O (lemon-yellow) gives green with Methylene Blue. 1s. 8d. per tube; set of seven, 8s.

Prices include postage.

CHAYTOR, Chemist
BELL GREEN TERMINUS, COVENTRY

Essential oils in bait a new development? Hardly! The lower advert is from the Carpworld magazine, in 1988. The upper one appeared in the Fishing Gazette 34 years earlier, in 1954. The value of additives in carp baits has always been the topic of considerable debate, and even today with available scientific research and strong commercial interests the answer remains unresolved.

ESSENTIAL OILS — What is the difference between oils and flavours? Briefly, oils are natural extracts which attract and feed; flavours are olfactory stimulants which promise much but may be counter-productive at the wrong level, or in the long term. Field testers and punters have been surprised at their success rate when using the oils – and we've got the letters expressing their delight.

Clove Terpenes	20 mil £3.15	Black Pepper Oil	20 mil £6.95
Madagascar Clove	20 mil £3.15	Peppermint Oil	20 mil £4.15
Geranium Oil	20 mil £4.15	Geranium Terpenes	20 mil £4.15
Ginger Oil	20 mil £4.95	Eucalyptus Oil	20 mil £3.15
Bergamot Oil	20 mil £4.15	Nutmeg Special Oil	20 mil £4.15
Cinnamon Oil	20 mil £3.62	Spanish Red Thyme	20 mil £4.95
Juniper Berry Oil	20 mil £4.62	Spearmint Oil	20 mil £3.15
Garlic Oil	10 mil £4.80	Mexican Onion Oil	10 mil £11.20

Nutrabaits, 95 Main Street, North Anston, Sheffield S31 7BE

There is no denying that scientific advances such as nylon, carbon fibre and betalights have brought substantial benefits to angling. But the concept has not changed; a rod is a rod whether it be made from hickory or carbon fibre, and a fish cares not a jot if line derives from polymers of nylon or from silkworm larvae. But surely the betalight is a new notion. Or is it? In a book called *The Angler's Sure Guide,* written in 1706 by Robert Howlett, you can find the following instructions:

"I was lately informed, 'tis a good way to angle for carps, in a dark night, with such a rod and line floated this with glow worms; scrape an inch in length off the butt end of a large swan quill till it be transparent, and prick three or four holes into it with a small needle, round the tip of the butt-end, to let in air; then cut off an inch and a half in length of the scraped end, and bind the open end twice or thrice about with waxed silk, and fix a cork near half an inch long to go stiff into it. When you have put a glow worm or two into the scraped piece of quill, stop it with a cork. When you have a bite, strike not before your glow worm be gone a little out of sight."

Yet what of recent developments such as the 'bare-hook', the 'fixed-lead' and the 'bent-hook'; surely they belong to the inventiveness of the modern generation of carp anglers? Wrong again, they were all described nearly 20 years ago by Ron Clay, an Englishman who emigrated to South Africa. The following is what he wrote in *The Angling Telegraph* about a method called the "miele pip trap," which had been used for at least a quarter of a century in that country, accounting for many 30lb. carp, including one of 46lb. taken from the Hartebeespoort Dam in 1971:

"I am about to describe in detail what may become one of the most important advances in carp fishing techniques in recent years. I take no credit whatsoever in its discovery as this technique, or variations of it, has been used in South Africa for many years.

The method of groundbaiting used is extremely important. You need plenty of sweetcorn. You will have to deposit plenty of free samples in your water over a long period of time. The idea is to get the carp feeding on it in real earnest.

The tackle required is pretty straightforward—rod, line and reel to suit the water you are fishing. The lead must be a heavy one, preferably over 2oz. The hook is a size 4, one of those odd-looking, deeply incurved jobs made by Edgar Sealey. These hooks have played no small role in the tremendous success of the 'trap' in South Africa over recent years. Do I have to say that the hook must be sharpened as sharp as possible?

I pointed out earlier that the lead must be heavy. Here lies one of the secrets of the success of the 'trap'. The weight of the lead acts as a preliminary device for setting the hook. Don't laugh—I kid you not!

After casting out the rod is placed in two rests, the line wound taught, and the pick up is left on with a very light slipping clutch tension.

Don't worry that the small grain of corn looks ridiculous on such a big hook. The carp thinks it looks delicious and picks it up and carries it on his way. The second a fish does that he's in trouble. In nine cases out of ten that needle sharp point will lodge somewhere in the fishes mouth, and on feeling the resistance the carp will invariably bolt.

The weight of the lead will then act as a further force to embed the hook, followed by the resistance of the reel. The only indication usually that the angler has hooked a fish is by finding that the line is being removed from his reel at a remarkable rate of knots."

This popular method of catching carp in South Africa

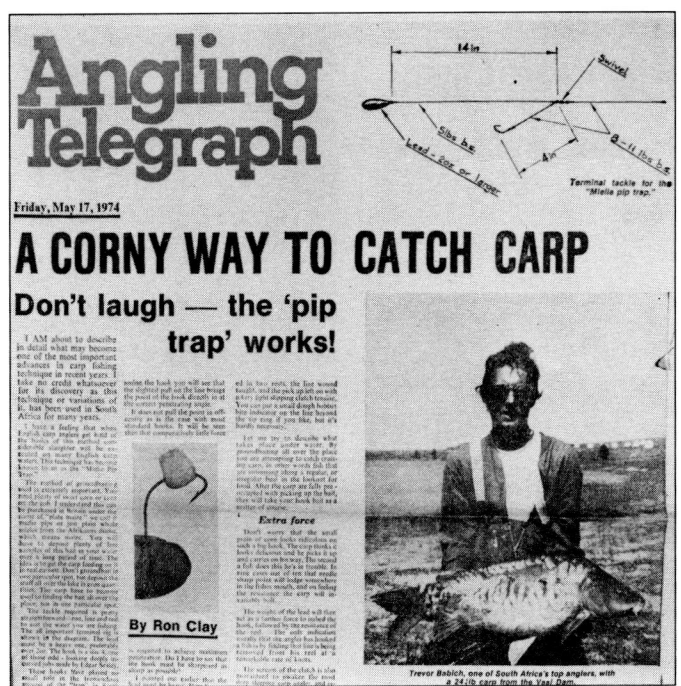

Ron Clay, who was a successful big fish angler and the man responsible for founding one of the earliest specimen groups in this country, The Northern Specimen Hunters Group, in 1963. He moved to South Africa in 1971 and soon became involved in that country's carp fishing. His revelations, about the methods used in South Africa, appear to have passed by almost unnoticed by the majority of carp anglers in Britain. The technique employed several novel features— a single grain of sweetcorn on a large, bent-hook and a heavy, fixed lead—concepts that were not to be fully exploited by English anglers for a number of years.

does appear to have been ignored by the majority of carp anglers in this country at that time. Walker's influence was still strong in the minds of his many followers and his dictum on lead weights —"Heavy leads cause considerable splash when cast, and however freely the line may run through the lead (no one, I hope, would ever consider a fixed-lead larger than a single shot) it can never run as freely as it would without."— was generally adhered to in the 1960's and early-1970's. Dick Walker also stated in *Still-Water Angling* that he was "convinced of the importance" of "covering the hook completely" with the bait.

The ability to catch carp at long range (for the sake of argument let us say 80 yards plus), is one which is usually accepted to be of fairly recent development, and this has been due to the advances made in tackle rather than any intellectual inspiration. Even so, the means to fish at long range was not beyond the wit of our Victorian predecessors and their centre-pins. Two anglers would join their hooks together with a section of weak cotton. One of them would walk to the opposite side of the lake and, when the baited hook was in the appropriate position, a sharp tug and the baited hook would be accurately released. Charles Sumner Patterson described the balanced leger in his book *An Angler's Year,* way back in 1905 and he also mentioned using waders to take the bait out "to the best clear space in the path of the carp." It was also recommended that using a boat could achieve the same solution, a dodge that would find favour with the 'modern' carp angler and his predilection for the toy varieties!

Past reviewers of carp fishing advances have often cited the development of striking at 'twitch bites' when ledgering as a breakthrough. Roy Walsh, writing under the pseudonym of John Fisher, was the first to mention it in print, in 1960. In retrospect, it is probably true to say that this certainly could be described as progress, although in the present state of carp fishing the technique is usually irrelevant.

Possibly the only substantial and lasting advance made in carp fishing techniques, in the last 30 years, has been the accomplishment of successful, cold water, winter carp fishing. Fred Wagstaffe, in Northamptonshire, Mike Winter, in Devon, and Jim Gibbinson, in Essex, were, without doubt, amongst the earliest pioneers of this discipline. Their initial conclusions, published in 1963 and 1964, invoked a great deal of scepticism from the established 'old-school' carp anglers. Richard Walker in later years (1968) wrote the following:

"I've heard it said that until these intrepid anglers tried, it was generally believed that carp were impossible to catch in winter, either by night or by day. People often tell me I said this myself. In fact, I never said anything of the kind. What I did say was that carp in most waters feed best between 58°F and 68°F and I've no reason to change that view."

A young Mike Winter with a cold water 12-pounder, caught by design in February, 1958. Mike was responsible, with Larry Beck, for founding one of the earliest specialist carp groups—The Devon Carp Catchers' Club. The Group limited itself to six members, had a rotary letter, and, after Pat Russell moved from Hitchin to Topsham in 1960, and joined, they came "very much under the wing of Walker."

Notwithstanding these protestations, and for the purpose of historical accuracy, we had better have the whole story. Dick made the following statement in the highly acclaimed *Stillwater Angling,* published in 1953:

"For practical purposes, the first frosts of October mark the end of the carp season, and in general they cannot be expected to feed in water much below 58°F."

In December, 1958 he elaborated this same view in *Angling Times,* with the statement that "Carp do not usually feed at temperatures below 58°F. We all know that examples occur now and then where carp, especially very small carp, are caught at much lower temperatures, sometimes even when a water is fringed with ice.

Nothing New under the Sun

A few weeks ago I gave some reasons why this might happen, in my column in *Angling Times*. Carp, tench and barbel will sometimes feed in cold conditions after having been disturbed and made to swim about, either by heavy water or for other reasons.

Generally speaking, however, carp and tench in still waters feed so rarely in cold conditions that it is not worth fishing for them then. You can go out fifty times after carp between November and the end of the coarse fishing season and never get a bite.

The chances are altogether too few, and if you do get a few fish, they are usually from a water where the carp are half-starved and consequently small."

A year later he reinforced this view, writing in *The Fishing Gazette*:

"I do not know any water that is not artificially warmed in which big carp can be fished for with much hope of success during the winter months. I should like to be proved wrong, but I think that the view that winter carp fishing is profitless is correct."

There was a spate of articles written between 1964 and 1966 on winter carp fishing, as the subject came under close scrutiny by fresh minds. The first, by Ken Stabler, appeared in Fishing magazine on October 23rd, 1964. The illustration shows Ken's follow-up published on January 22nd, 1965. These articles were preceded by correspondence about the subject between Fred Wagstaffe and Mike Winter in the same magazine. Other pioneers of cold-water carp fishing included Peter Mustoe, David Marlborough, Frank Howsen, Peter Mohan and D.G. Hughes.

Why Richard Walker should, initially at least, resist the notion that carp fishing might be a practical proposition during the winter months remains unknown, especially as his friend Edward Ensom was quite keen on the idea. He wrote in 1953, in his book *Memorable Coarse Fish,* which manifestly lives up to its title, that:

"An important and little appreciated aspect of this carp fishing business is its winter possibilities. Carp are held to pass the winter in a state of hibernation or semi-hibernation and, on this account, are seldom fished for then. Nevertheless, in every season, particularly on the occurrence of warmish spells of weather, or after floods, good carp are taken by anglers, sometimes by accident and not design. Anglers keen enough to try out this winter carping, carefully choosing the time and place, may be rewarded handsomely." The next angler to question Walker's edict in print, and the first well-known carp angler, was Leslie Burton. He wrote a prophetic and substantially correct assessment of the situation, in *The Midland Angler,* in November, 1956. It was titled 'We Could Be Wrong About Winter Carping'. The following quotations may give an insight into Burton's important review:

"This article, about winter carp fishing, has been on my mind for several seasons, but I have hitherto refrained from putting my thoughts on to paper, not because I lacked the courage of my convictions, but because those convictions themselves lacked strength. Even now I hesitate to take up the cudgels on a matter which, of all the aspects of angling, is possibly the most established and generally accepted, i.e., that carp is so much a summer fish that it is out of the question **to expect** to catch it during the winter."

"It is commonly accepted that carp go into a stage of semi-hibernation or torpor during the winter, but nevertheless they are still caught from time to time **when they are not even being fished for!**"

"My own views, for what they are worth, are that **all** fish feed **all** the year round at some time or other."

"....I see no evidence whatever that carp go into a period of prolonged fasting lasting nearly six months. I have further to be convinced that with the onset of late autumn and the lowering of the water temperature into the thirties, the carp are unable to condition themselves to the lower temperature, after which they are able to and do in fact continue on the move, and when appetite dictates, on the **feed**."

Anyway, in 1968, Dick Walker all but acquiesced the point with alacrity in his editor's introduction to Jim Gibbinson's book, *Carp*. Walker wrote that "Interest in carp fishing has therefore increased greatly, and the basic methods of the early pioneers have been under scrutiny from fresh minds. Further improvements have been effected, fallacies exposed and new ideas developed." There can be little doubt that Walker was mainly referring to the chapter in the book titled *Winter Carp Fishing*, the opening few lines of which were written, I am sure, by Gibbinson with Dick's previous statements on this subject in mind. Any lingering doubts about Walker's acceptance were dispelled by the great man's acknowledgement in 1968, in his column in *The Angler's World* where he wrote:

"There have been some useful developments in this game in the last few years. A number of hardy enthusiasts have worked out ways of catching carp in winter."

What must be stressed in this context, is that although Dick Walker was wrong on a number of points it was his own complete examination of carp fishing principles, and his insistence that others should not blindly accept dogma, that brought about the situation whereby even Dick's opinions could readily be challenged. More than anything else his legacy was to give anglers open and questioning minds. Dick summed it up himself by saying, "In hindsight, the most important thing the Carp Catchers' Club ever did was to shake off the preconceived notions about carp fishing that existed at that time. If there was one single thing that led to the expansion and success of carp fishing, it was the refusal of a few of us to believe what other people told us about carp fishing. We were just not going to have a millstone around our necks of other people's failures."

Chapter 11
The History of Carp Tackle

The fatal metaphor of progress,
which means leaving things behind us,
has utterly obscured the real idea of growth,
which means leaving things inside us.
G.K. Chesterton from *The Romance of Rhyme* (1932).

The history of carp rods really begins in about 1947 when Dick Walker was 29 years old. Prior to that time there was no commercially made rod that fulfilled all the requirements necessary to land big carp.[1] Richard Walker was at that time using either a Hardy's Wallis Avon rod, or an Allcock's Wallis Wizard, (or both),[2] for his carp fishing. These were three-piece, 11ft. rods with the top and middle sections of split-cane and the bottom sections of whole cane. It was an excellent design, put forward by Frederick William Knowles Wallis[3] for float fishing on the Hampshire Avon for barbel, but it just wasn't powerful enough for large carp. Newly produced, it cost some £2 16s. (an average weekly wage) at the time Walker first started fishing for carp in about 1934.

Dick initially made[4] a rod similar to what a Wallis Avon (or Wizard) would be like if it had 12 inches removed from its tip and, although this seemed better able to handle large carp, it turned out to be very poor for casting. In some accounts this rod was apparently named 'The Walker Wizard Mk. I.' Not long after Dick first wrote to B.B., in January, 1947, they approached Alfred Courtney Williams, author of several books on fishing, an all-round angler and a director of S. Allcock & Co. Ltd, the fishing tackle manufacturers of Redditch.[5] Courtney Williams pointed out that the market for a carp rod was too small to justify his firm designing and producing one. He did, however, send Dick a quantity of good quality bamboo suggesting he made his own! Never one to shy away from a challenge that is exactly what Dick did, and, with a little help from B.B., Michael Traherne and one or two others, he spent the next six years getting it right.

1. It would be incorrect to state that rods did not exist which could perform satisfactorily most of the functions of a purpose-made carp rod. For example, Hardy Bros. produced the 10ft. 'J.J.H.' No.1 and No.2 spinning rods which were more than adequate for general carp fishing. A more powerful type could be found in Hardy's 10½ft. 'Super Decantelle' bait-casting rod.
2. Walker wrote in his first letter to B.B. in January, 1947 (published in *Confession of a Carp Fisher*) that he used a Wallis Wizard for his carp fishing. However, in the early-1950's, writing in *Angling Times* about the development of the Mk. IV he stated that he was using a Wallis Avon in 1947. But, in *Angling Times,* in 1977, Walker reverted to stating it was a Wallis Wizard. They were, nevertheless, effectively the same rod made by different companies.
3. The famous F.W.K. Wallis, innovator and captor of many huge fish, particularly from the Hampshire Avon. Born in 1861, the son of a farmer, he built-up a large and profitable lace business in Nottingham.
4. There is confusion on this point. In several reports Dick says he just simply cut 12in. from the top of a Wallis Avon/Wizard. Strangely, B.B. used and recommended the 'Wizard' right up until Walker presented him with a Mk. IV in June, 1951, writing in 1951 that the Wallis Wizard "was a very powerful weapon."
5. Allcock's had been formed by Samuel Allcock in about 1851, although he had previously assisted his father in selling fishing tackle by visiting market towns as travelling salesmen. The company grew into the largest wholesale tackle manufacturers in the world, and established the town of Redditch as the centre of this trade. Samuel Allcock died on October 10th, 1910.

The History of Carp Tackle

Walker had first tried his hand at making split-cane rods many years earlier when a couple of rods he owned were stolen. His grandfather, with whom Dick spent a great deal of time, eked a living from a smallholding and instilled into Dick that you "never bought anything that you could make yourself." It was an older cousin, however, who actually convinced Dick that he should try and replace the stolen rods by making his own.

Built-cane was probably invented in China prior to 950 B.C. and possibly first applied to fishing rods in Britain sometime prior to 1800. In the book *Fishes and Fishing* by W. Wright, published in 1858, it is written that a Welshman named David Williams was, in 1805, an unrivalled maker of glued-up bamboo fly rods. Eric Marshall-Hardy, in his book *Angling Ways,* mentions a Mr. Clark, of London, as also being a master builder of split-cane rods around this time. By 1850 complete rods of three-strip cane were not uncommon and the hexagonal rod would appear to have come on the scene some 15, or so, years later. Certainly Allcock's were producing them in 1879, although in the next century Hardy's claimed to have invented the system of building them in 1882. It is, however, likely that the first were designed by, Hiram L. Leonard, an American in 1870.

Before 1939, bamboo which was grown in China was graded and seasoned with care. The best bamboo was sold for rod making and the remainder was used for other purposes. After the War, the political climate had changed and, also, the demand for bamboo increased. The quality of the cane imported after the War varied greatly, much of it having not been allowed to season and harden correctly. Bamboo is made up of complex bundles of strong fibres in a matrix of pithy material that contains pectin. Of course, pectin is well known to anyone who has made jam, it is the setting agent. The more you heat it, or the longer you leave it, the harder it sets. Pectin behaves in much the same way whether it is in jam or bamboo. So cane will harden with age or with heat treatment, but the quality is also dependent on the make-up of the strong fibres which the pith and pectin bind together. The very best bamboo occurs when these fibres are dense and where the pectin has hardened to a certain degree—not too hard or the cane will be brittle.

When the bamboo was allowed to season and harden naturally it produced a beautiful, golden coloured cane, which never got too hard. This process was often supervised by European buyers, or their representatives in China, prior to the Second World War. Hardy Bros., a substantial importer of bamboo around this time, wrote that "the difficulty in finding suitable bamboo is very great...and after trying samples of almost every bamboo grown, we have selected districts from which we procure bamboos of a very superior quality. These we now use exclusively, and have agents on the spot, who select all the choicest, and have them seasoned to our instructions—not burned until the fibre is destroyed, as is frequently the case—but seasoned in a special manner, which renders them exceedingly tough and springy."

By the late-1950's, however, much of the bamboo that arrived in this country was little better than raw. Sources other than China were also being exploited, particularly Japan for female cane. This was similar to the Chinese variety but not quite so heavy and the distance between the knots was greater. Whatever the source, any rod builder worthy of the name had to throw much of it away by this time, and that which remained needed judicious heat treatment. This process had to be carried out correctly and required much skill and experience. It is not a question of tempering as it has sometimes been described, even by cane rod builders, you cannot temper split-cane you can only harden it.

After the bamboo had been hardened it was split and planed. The sections were then glued together. The type of adhesive used, principally animal glue, contained moisture and this resulted in a re-softening of the pectin. It was, therefore, necessary to allow sufficient time for the rods to dry out but, with increasing demand in the late-1950's and early-1960's, a high proportion of rods were being produced where this was not allowed to happen. This, combined with a gradual deterioration in quality of imported bamboo, resulted, unfortunately, in a great many rods being produced which soon took on bad 'sets'.

Walker believed that the new urea/formaldehyde glue, which became available in the early-1950's offered distinct advantages over the traditional animal glue. However, there was resistance from the trade, not least because animal glue could be re-heated to correct poor workmanship and moderate 'sets' caused by inferior materials. This was not possible with the urea/formaldehyde glue.

Walker built a further three rods, in addition to his copy of a cut-down Wallis Avon. Dick acknowledged the assistance of B.B. and Michael Traherne in the design of the first two, and the final effort was undoubtedly made with the assistance of several of Dick's friends, notably Maurice Ingham. The first one was a 10ft. two-piece, and made throughout of split-cane. The butt, though, was constructed of a 2ft. length of beech dowel. The handle had, therefore, been extended from the 20in. of the Wallis Avon to 24in.

The next rod produced a further improvement and was double-built (*see diagram*), had a steeper-taper in the butt-section and the handle was 28in. long. The taper was even, and went from $5/32$in. (from 'flat' to 'flat') at the tip to $5/8$in. at the extreme butt. The rings were High-Bell's intermediates with a stand-off agate tip and a large 26mm butt ring. This rod was used a great deal, and a number of large carp were caught on it, but Walker always felt that it seemed heavier than it should have been at 14oz.

With his final attempt, named and to be known universally as the Mk. IV, Dick did what he felt later he should have done at first; he tested various materials including single and double-built split-cane and looked into the matter of the mathematical calculation of the correct taper, even contacting his old Cambridge University tutor, H.W. Phear, who advised him on compound tapers. The result, built in late-1950, was a 10ft. rod in two sections, made from six-sided, single-built split-cane. The taper was fairly steep in the lower half of the rod, less steep in the middle section, and then steeper again at the tip. The cork handle had been increased to 30in., and underneath the bottom half of the handle was a very stiff three-quarter inch section of Tonkin cane into which the split-cane had been spliced. The purpose of this was to give a powerful lever for double-handed casting. It is possible that the cane for this rod had been purchased from J. B. Walker of Hythe.

Now ready...
1949 ILLUSTRATED CATALOGUE
Please send 3d. in stamps for your copy (or 1/- P.O. or stamps for Catalogue and subsequent lists for 12 months).

| J. B. WALKER | SPECIALISTS IN ALL TYPES OF ROD MATERIALS FOR THE |
| 4b, PROSPECT ROAD, HYTHE, KENT | PRACTICAL ANGLER. |

Dick Walker purchased many of his materials from J.B. Walker's for making his own rods in the late 1940's and early 1950's.

A: *Three-sectioned bamboo rod contruction originating in England in about 1805.*
B: *The four-section construction patented by an American, Samuel Phillipe, in 1845. The skin, or enamel, is on the inside.*
C: *Hexagonal split cane which Dick Walker, like others, finally came to acknowledge offered the most efficient use of the material.*
D: *Double-built split cane, in common with octagonal and those incorporating a steel rod in the centre, produced disadvantages which far outweighed any possible benefits in carp fishing.*

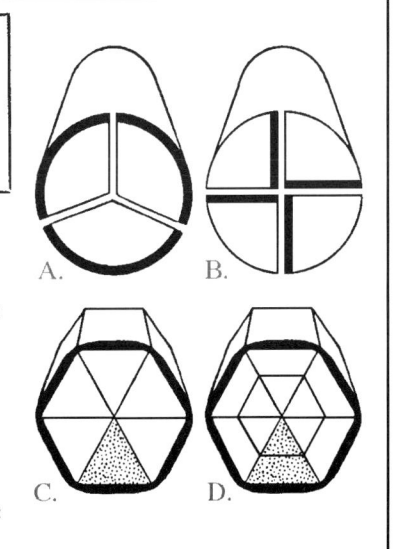

The History of Carp Tackle

Dick made a number of Mk. IV rods for his friends in the early-1950's, possibly somewhere between 12 and 20.[1] In addition a number of others were later produced, which he described as cross-breeds, in that when the demand from friends and acquaintances became too much he obtained some blanks from J.B. Walker of Hythe. These had been made for the firm by Bob Southwell, to a very satisfactory standard according to Walker, and Dick finished them off by putting on the cork handles, rings and ferrules.

The above photograph shows Hitchin A.C.'s stand at the Hitchin Civic and Art Society's Hobbies Exibition on the 21st to 23rd April, 1952. Four of the rods which are on show are the same as those which are on display in Dick's workshop, shown in the photograph on the left. The one on the left, in the workshop, is the rod which is reputed to have been used to capture the record, and is now owned by Chris Ball. The one next to it in the workshop (on the far left in the top photograph) is a mystery. It shows some similarities to the Mk. III carp rod made by Dick but the reel fittings and handle shape are quite different.

The mystery rod is shown on the Hitchin A.C.'s stand paired up with Dick's big magnesium centre-pin reel. Also on display is the record carp, caught by Bob Richards and set up by Dick. It was presented to Bob, by Dick, at the Daily Mirror Angling Contest presentation on Saturday, May 17th, 1952, at the Savoy Hotel. Below Bob's carp is an 11½lb. common carp and on the right Dick's 'lucky' hat and his big carp net, later that year to enmesh 'Clarrissa'.

1. In 1983, Dick gave this estimate, as to how many Mk. IV rods he had made, in a letter to Mike Wilson. However, Pete Thomas, in 1992, in personal communication with the author, felt that this number was "far too high and that, as sure as he could be, the number was no higher than 7 or 8." If this is the case, then most of the ones wholly made by Dick can be accounted for.

Of those Mk. IV rods thought to be fully constructed by Dick the following are known about and their history is as follows:

1. **Dick Walker's rod**. This is the rod believed to have been used to catch Dick's 44lb. record from Redmire. Whipped in brown silk with no intermediate whippings. All the rings were lined. In February, 1955, (shortly after the inception of the A.C.A.) Dick wrote in *Angling Times*:
   "I should like to give it to the A.C.A. to be sold on their behalf, but unless a way can be found of getting more for it than the price of a new Mk. IV there seems little point in doing so. Suggestions will be welcome!" Dick Kefford got in touch with Major Erskine-Hill of the A.C.A. and made an offer for the rod which was accepted. The rod was given to Mike Oyez by Dick Kefford in 1978, and was subsequently purchased by Chris Ball for £125 in 1982.
2. **Fred Belcher's rod**. Given by Dick as a present to Mr. Belcher in 1955. It was a rod which Dick had used himself for his carp fishing during the early-1950's and was almost certainly the other of the pair, one for B.B. and a second for himself, which were finished just in time for their trip to Mapperley on June 18th, 1951. This rod was used extensively by Dick for his carp fishing in the early-1950's. Whipped in maroon silk with no intermediate whippings, all the rings were lined. The rod was purchased from Fred Belcher by Kevin Clifford in April, 1990 for £400.
3. **B.B.'s rod**. Whipped in green silk with no intermediate whippings. All the rings were lined. This rod was sold by B.B. to Len Arbery for £2,000 (including a large centre-pin reel also made by Dick for B.B.) in April, 1990. The rod was subsequently sold to Chris Sandford for £2,000.
4. **Pete Thomas' rod**. Whipped in green silk with no intermediate whippings. All rings were lined.
5. **Bernard Venables' rod**. Whipped in golden-brown silk with no intermediate whippings. All the rings were lined. The rod was auctioned at Bonhams in January, 1990 and purchased by Pete Rogers for £2230.
6. **John Francis Maclean's rod**. Whipped in brown silk. Made some time after June, 1952. Auctioned by the A.C.A. and now owned by Nigel Parker.
7. **Bob Richards' rod**. No intermediate whippings. Made in late-1951 or early-1952. Disposed of in 1964 on Bob's death. Present whereabouts unknown.
8. **Horace Smith's rod**. Made in 1955. Whipped in green. Clear lined rings. Now owned by Chris Yates. The date of construction of this rod suggests it was probably made from a Bob Southwell blank.

Dick at Redmire in 1952 using the Mk. IV he subsequently gave to Fred Belcher.

The History of Carp Tackle

In early 1952, Dick, realising that making rods was taking up a great deal of his time, told Ken Sutton that if he could find a good rod manufacturer he would happily pass on the details of the Mk. IV taper to him. In May, 1952 Ken Sutton suggested that Dick might like to contact the firm of B. James and Son, of 186 Northfield Avenue, West Ealing and this Dick did. On the 3rd September, 1952 Dick wrote the following:

"Dear Mr. James,

The second rod arrived quite safely and is a fine job. I think a half-size bigger ferrule would be playing safe and I would advise it. With regard to flat finish, I have tried out several alleged matt varnishes and have always found a rub-down with Pete Thomas' flash-remover is superior. But if you can get a good flat finish, all well and good. Ring spacing is all right. An inch further away from the corks for both butt and second ring wouldn't hurt, but it isn't fussy. The metal intermediate rings are too small to please me, but I don't suppose it makes any difference in practice. Those near the tip are all right but I'd like to see them come in size from a bigger one at no. 3, counting from the butt-end. There's a big jump between no. 2 (agate) and no. 3. This is only a small matter however. You can save about three more corks; your handle is that much longer than my Mk. IV.

The Indian ink lettering on the handle was terrible! Can't have that! I have a suggestion to make here. I imagine you will be doing a batch of these rods for stock. If you like to bring the batch down before the last couple of varnish-coats go on, I'll put my name on each one for you, and you can then tell customers that each rod has been inspected, and passed o.k. by me, and autographed to prove it. Wouldn't that help?

I'm going to Bernithan with Pete Thomas on 13th-15th[1] and I hope to find a fish to give the latest Mk. IV a real testing. Pete will use the first one, we'll see if he can smash it up. His 28lb. 10oz. fish made no impression whatsoever on his own Mk. IV.

Best wishes,
Richard."

B. James rods being made ready for the Daily Mirror Angling Competition awards luncheon in June, 1953.

[1]. This was, of course, the weekend when Dick caught the record carp.

The History of Carp Tackle

The rod-making business of B. James and Son started after the Second World War at 186 Northfield Avenue, West Ealing. The owner, James Bruce (known to his friends as Jimmy James), was an engineer, but had made rods on a semi-professional basis pre-War. He reversed his own name for the company title because he felt that people were more likely to remember it. The bulk of the business, initially, was comprised of whole cane match rods with greenheart tips although other rods, such as converted tank aerials, that sold for £3 15s, were also produced. The first split-cane rod produced was the Avocet, and then others, such as the Avon Perfection, Kennet Perfection, Mk. IV (available October, 1952, selling for £8 17s 6d) and Mk. IV Avon, followed.

B. JAMES of EALING
MEMBERS OF L.A.A.
FOR SUPERIOR FISHING TACKLE
HAND-BUILT RODS and REPAIRS BY
CRAFTSMEN to your SPECIFICATION
186, NORTHFIELD AVENUE, EALING, LONDON, W.13.
Phone EAL. 7428

THE RECORD CARP

Richard Walker's record carp of 44 lbs. was caught on a Mark IV Carp Rod.

The rod, evolved over a period of many years by Richard Walker himself, is probably the strongest for its weight ever designed.

Ten feet long (2 section), built entirely of split cane with agate top ring and large agate bottom rings, and weighing only twelve ounces, the rod was not at all affected by the strain of this enormous fish.

By permission the rod is built exclusively by B. James & Son, and each one is passed and autographed by Richard Walker.

B. JAMES & SON,
186 Northfield Avenue, West Ealing, W.13
Tel.: EALing 7428

Top left: An early B. James advert from March, 1949. Above: The first advert for the Mk. IV which appeared in The Angler's News on the 4th October, 1952. The same issue contained Walker's account of the capture of his new record carp, giving tremendous publicity for the rod. Left: Walker testing the second B. James Mk. IV, referred to in the letter, on the Redmire dam in September, 1952. Ingham and Walker often used the rotting, corrugated iron roof of the old boathouse for target practise when assessing the casting abilities of various rods.

A major turning point in the company's fortunes came in 1952 when the *Daily Mirror* ordered 60-70 rods, purchased at retail prices, as prizes for their yearly competition.

Like other cane rod makers at that time, B. James & Son experimented with ways of hardening the cane. Various methods, such as heating in front of electric fires, over a flame and in a baker's oven were tried. Some methods produced a very hard cane but this had the disadvantage in that it was very difficult to work with.

The Mk. IV rods were initially hand-whipped, including the intermediates, but this changed as the company prospered and a machine was certainly in use by 1955, possibly earlier. A number of early Mk. IV cane blanks were bought in, ready-made from Bob Southwell, probably due to initial demand outstripping their production resources, but Bruce James obtained his own bamboo direct from Hurst's Timber Importers. They also made their

The History of Carp Tackle

own brass ferrules, buying in brass tubing from 'Smiths' of Clerkenwell. The first one or two batches, each of about 20 blanks, Dick actually signed in Indian ink but, subsequently, a transfer of his signature was produced. Over the years there were a number of cosmetic changes to the rods—different ring types, ring spacing, butt shapes and transfer design. The very early models had a trumpet-shaped butt with a shoulder collar. Most of the Mk. IV's were whipped in crimson, though green-whipping was sometimes used. This was probably caused by nothing more than the company running out of crimson silk. However, in about 1958 the rod saw a distinct change. The overall diameter of the rod had been increased throughout its length, resulting in a test curve of about 2lb., considerably more than Walker's original design of 1½lb. Perhaps this was considered necessary to compensate for the much poorer quality cane that was now being used?

B. James produced something in the region of 15,000 Mk. IV rods between October, 1952 and the mid-1960's when cane began to give way to hollow glass. During this period

James Bruce jnr., Dick Walker, an assistant, and Jimmy James at the Boat Show in 1958, when a radically changed Mk. IV rod was first introduced. Note the James 'Richard Walker' carp landing net which was made in only limited numbers (perhaps as few as 40 in total) due to high costs and difficulties in production.

Above: A 1955 advert for the Mk. IV.
Left: Jimmy James in his workshop.

they dominated the market although other rod makers produced their own versions of Mk. IV's, some of which were excellent. Bob Southwell was considered by many to be the premier cane rod builder of this period, supplying a number of trade outlets with blanks. He subsequently started his own retail tackle business at Croydon, in Surrey, called The Captain and produced a limited number of extremely high quality rods which he sold direct to the public. B. James & Son themselves felt that the unique impregnated 'Scottie' 10 ft. cane carp rod, made by J.S. Sharpe Ltd., of 35 Belmont Street, Aberdeen, resulted in an exceptionally good product. This rod was favoured and recommended by a number of notable anglers, including Bill Keal, and the Sharpe's carp rod along with Bob Southwell's Captain Croydon carp rods were almost certainly the best of those commercially produced. Others were made by Dawsons of Bromley, Constable's of Bromley, Olivers of Knebworth, Hardy's, Sowerbutt's, Henry J. Nicholls, Ogden Smith and Chapman's of Ware.

Dawson's was a husband and wife firm (Peter and Betty) that started producing rods in 1934. They claimed that their cane carp rods were made from Grade 'A' Tonkin and that they went through thirty stages of manufacture taking, individually, four months to produce.

Clifford Constable started building rods in 1945 and his 'Forty Four Deluxe' was a well-made carp rod. Ted Oliver, of Olivers of Knebworth, also produced excellent rods and gained a substantial following. Hardy's Palakona 'Richard Walker' carp rods, although only produced for two years were, as would be expected from this long established and highly respected firm, well-made.

The History of Carp Tackle

BUILT CANE
of the finest quality
MADE TO YOUR REQUIREMENTS

WE SPECIALISE IN LARGE
QUANTITIES TO THE FISHING
TACKLE TRADE
Wholesale and Trade Enquiries Only
R. CHAPMAN AND CO.
BOWLING ROAD, WARE, HERTS.
Telephone: WARE 658.

SPECIAL NOTICE TO ANGLERS

R.W. MK. IV CARP AND AVON RODS, AVON ROYAL ROACH RODS, PIKE RODS, SEA RODS, SALMON AND TROUT, SHARK, ETC.
Guaranteed Hand Built.
COMPLETE, READY TO WHIP OR SETS
BAIT
Agent for Alex Martin, Milbro, etc.

THE CAPTAIN
V. E. SOUTHWELL
Sports and Fishing Tackle
30, STATION ROAD
CROYDON

HIGH PERFORMANCE
HOLLOW GLASS RODS
are now being built in our Redditch factory from KBX compound, a new form of hollow glass for rod building, designed and developed by ourselves.
We shall be pleased to send an illustrated brochure on application.

ALLCOCKS
REDDITCH ENGLAND

Left: Ron Chapman's company built a number of cane carp rods and also supplied the trade, but much of the cane used was very soft. This advert dates from April, 1957.
Middle: By contrast Bob Southwell's cane was considered by many to be amongst the best. His output was very limited and a wait of several months often followed before an order was completed. He advertised rarely, this one appeared in June, 1955.
Bottom: This advert, from May, 1953, was one of the earliest that promoted hollow glass-fibre rods.

Some of the worst cane carp rods produced, and all the makers produced cane of variable quality, was made by Chapman's of Ware. Although Walker, himself, endorsed these rods in print their cane was extremely soft and prone to taking sets.

So, by the early-1960's, there was a growing disillusionment with cane. Better quality, hollow, glass-fibre blanks were starting to become available (British-made, hollow fibre-glass rods had first appeared in this country as early as 1952[1]) and innovative rod makers and anglers were beginning to believe that it offered a satisfactory replacement to cane carp rods. But even by 1965 there were those who believed good cane rods were superior to the best available glass-fibre ones. Richard Walker still preferred cane, but Tag Barnes, who endorsed a rod made by Sportex, took Walker to task in the *Angling Times,* stating:

"We are all entitled to our preferences, but I feel some of the observations he made about fibre-glass call for closer inspection. I possess a bundle of the original Mk. IV split-cane carp rods which wouldn't stand up to the strain of stopping double-figure carp in a very overgrown swim, and if Dick doesn't mind fishing with a rod full of kinks he can have mine."

Gradually, Walker found himself in a minority amongst knowledgable anglers. Peter Stone, who, in 1961, found he could not recommend this new material, believed the improvements made to it by 1965 allowed him to give it his full approval. Fred J. Taylor was of a similar opinion. Bill Warren had replaced his ageing, built-cane 11-footer with a hollow-glass, 2-piece, 10ft rod, having a test-curve of about 1½lb., as early as 1961. Jack Hilton bought the same model after seeing Bill's in 1961, which he used for carp and pike fishing and then, in 1962, he got hold of two blanks from Don Niesh, of Edmonton. These were made up into 2-piece, 10½ft. long rods, with a piece of beech dowel spliced into the butt, resulting in a test-curve a fraction under 1½lb. Frank Guttfield said of them—"We were amazed by the extremely thin wall of this new

---

1. Messrs. Ogden Smiths, of London, were actually manufacturing their own hollow fibre-glass rod in 1952, and marketing them under the trade name of Nu-glass Avalon. The company was an old, established firm, being founded in Cheltenham in 1763. The chairman in 1952 (a year before his death) was Walter Sidney Ogden Smith, who was very keen on new developments and was something of an inventor himself. Other British companies soon followed with their own range of tubular, fibre-glass rods. The Modern Arms Co. Ltd. produced a range named the M-A-Glass series in 1953.

material. They had a smooth yet poker-like action, and there was no flop whatsoever." It wasn't long before a number of rod makers were producing good quality glass-fibre rods—Davenport and Fordham with their popular Farstrike carp rod, Sportex and Oliver's of Knebworth. Even B. James & Son bowed to the inevitable and brought out a glass-fibre version of the Mk. IV.

CARP & SALMON RODS

The Wide range of Auger High Tensile Specialities includes some outstanding value in Salmon and Carp Rods.

MAJOR RODS OF CANADA

The 60 S.P. 9 ft. de Luxe Tubular Glass Spinning Rod
£8 0s. 0d.
The No. 45 9 ft. Stiff Action Tubular Glass Carp Special
£7 17s. 6d.
The No. 10 7½ ft. Tubular Glass Ledger Special
£5 5. 0d.

are just a few examples of the wide range of highly guaranteed low cost rods in the "Auger High Tensile Specialities" Booklet Price 1/6.

Auger High Tensile Specialities are obtainable only through the **Best Retailers**, but if you have any difficulty, write and tell us your trouble, **giving the name and address of your Local Retailer.**

AUGER ACCESSORIES LTD:

2A Handsworth Road,
Tottenham,
London, N.15.
Telephone No. TOTtenham 7878

FACT The 33¼ lbs. Carp caught by Peter Hemingway which equalled the previous River Carp record was taken on a "Farstrike" Carp Rod, the original glass Carp rod.

FACT More and more specimen hunters are using "Farstrike" hollow glass rods.

FACT "FARSTRIKE" rods are made to last, all fittings are chosen for their durability and have been thoroughly tested by experts.

Retail price inclusive of purchase tax **£9.8.6**

Write for full descriptive leaflet to:—

DAVENPORT & FORDHAM LTD., Dept. F
40 GRAYS INN ROAD, LONDON, W.C.1.

FOR CARP THE "CHALLENGER 65"
is perfection in hollow glass, firm, gentle 1½ lb. test curve, adjustable **AUTOLOCK** reel fitting, Aqualite and guaranteed rust proof rings. A perfect duplication in hollow glass of our well-known built cane Challenger Carp rod. Length 10 ft. .... £9.4.2.

For full details send 6d. postage for free catalogue.

DAWSONS OF BROMLEY LTD.
1, CHATTERTON ROAD, BROMLEY, KENT.

"M-A-GLAS"

TUBULAR FIBRE-GLASS FISHING RODS
BRITISH MADE THROUGHOUT

ALTHOUGH IT WAS ONLY SIX MONTHS AGO THAT WE INTRODUCED OUR "M-A-GLAS" RODS, THEY ARE ALREADY FIRMLY ESTABLISHED FAVOURITES WITH ANGLERS THROUGHOUT THE WORLD.

Ask your "Modern Fishing Tackle" agent to show you the:—
★ "M-A-GLAS" 7 ft. THREADLINE ROD
★ "M-A-GLAS" 7 ft. HEAVY SPINNING ROD
★ "M-A-GLAS" 8 ft. SEA ROD
★ "M-A-GLAS" 11 ft. SEA ROD
★ "M-A-GLAS" 8 ft. SALMON SPINNING ROD
★ "M-A-GLAS" TROUT FLY ROD 8½ ft. AND 9 ft.

Feather-light and perfectly balanced yet amazingly strong. Made by craftsmen. They are beautifully finished and a joy to possess. They cost no more than split-cane.

Manufactured by
MODERN ARMS CO. LTD., Bromley, Kent
Makers of
MODERN FISHING TACKLE
Wholesale and Export Only

---

*Adverts for glass rods dating from: **top left**—1953, **bottom left**—1965, **bottom right**—1953, **top right**—1965. The latter company was founded by well-known carp anglers Derrick Davenport and Tony Fordham.*

The general chronological order of cane versions of the B. James Mk. IV Carp Rod

First version—October 1952: Trumpet handle, hook-keeper, shoulder-collar, dark built cane. Concentric red, green or black whippings, clear or brown butt and tip rings. Transfer—'B. James & Son, Ealing, London'.

Second version—1955: Onion handle, hook-keeper, no shoulder-collar, dark built cane. Concentric red or green whippings, brown coloured butt and tip rings. Transfer logo—'B. James & Son, Ealing, London'.

Third version—1956/1957: Onion handle, hook-keeper, small shoulder-collar, medium-brown coloured cane, concentric red or green whippings, brown coloured butt and tip rings. Transfer logo—'B. James & Son, London, England'.

Fourth version—1958: Bulbous handle, no shoulder-collar or hook-keeper. Lighter coloured cane, increased test curve, red whippings, brown coloured butt and tip rings. Transfer logo—'B. James & Son, England'.

The History of Carp Tackle

Although the first fixed-spool reel invented in this country was way back in the last century (the first British patent was issued to George Richard Holding in 1878, an American patent was issued three years earlier), they were little used in carp fishing until very much later. The maestro of Cheshunt, Mummery, recommended an Aerial[1] centre-pin in the 1920's, as did Albert Buckley in the 1930's. The authoritative Otto Overbeck also used a centre-pin as did the majority of the members of Becontree and District A.S. who fished for carp at Dagenham. Ernest Phillips, in his 1925 book, *Float Fishing,* much preferred the 4½in. Nottingham wood centre-pin, and Stephen Hill, in his book *Fine Angling for Coarse Fish,* again advised the use of a centre-pin for carp fishing. Amazingly, even by 1952, Bernard Venables was still describing in his book, *Mr. Crabtree Goes Fishing,* a method of laying coils of line on brown paper on the ground, thereby facilitating long casting with a centre-pin whilst carp fishing. This influential book hardly mentions the fixed-spool reel, apart from spinning for perch. Denys Watkins-Pitchford, whose effect on carp fishing was, through his popular books, very significant, also advocated centre-pins, although in 1946 he was using a Milward 'side-casting' sea reel. But, shortly after Dick's friendship with B.B. began, in 1947, Walker made him a 5¾in. centre-pin, constructed from a solid block of magnesium. It weighed 13½oz., no more than the average fixed-spool reel, and B.B. used it subsequently for all his carp fishing. As a matter of fact Dick made two.[2] The other he used himself occasionally ("when monsters are expected and snags are numerous"), but later gave it to Jack Thorndike.

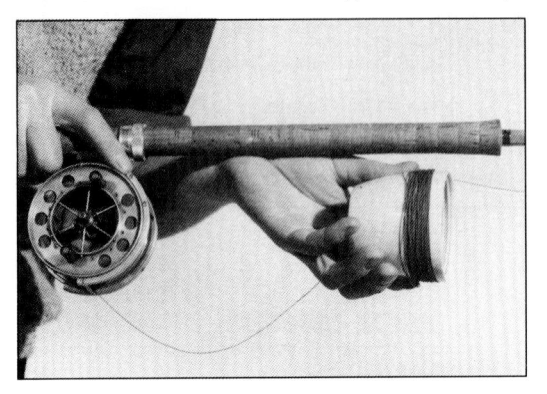

Another method, to facilitate long casting with a centre-pin, employed a thermos flask cup.

There were, clearly, those who favoured the use of the fixed-spool reel in the early part of the century, otherwise the manufacturers would have had a problem! One such individual was Captain Len Parker, the famed roach fisherman of the Hampshire Avon, who was, for many years, mine host at The Bull Hotel, Downton. He turned his hand to carp fishing occasionally, and he was most enthusiastic about the benefits of fixed-spool reels. In 1942, his simple advice to all coarse anglers not in possession of a fixed-spool reel was—"get one at the first opportunity." Fixed-spool reels started to gain in popularity, with the general angler, in about 1920 (about the time Len Parker obtained his first one) and, by the early-1940's there were a number of reasonably well made models available. These included the Illingworth No. 3, Duplex No. 3, Felton Crosswind, Hardy's Altex and Hardex.

But it wasn't really until Walker wrote his first article on carp fishing, under the pseudonym of Water Rail,[3] in the *Fishing Gazette* on September 3rd, 1949, that the fixed-spool reel was specifically recommended for carp fishing. He wrote with admirable clarity,

1. The Aerial reel was designed by Henry Coxon and produced by Allcock's of Redditch. Coxon received the first reel from them just in time to complete in the float casting events at the Wimbledon Tournament on the 9th May, 1896, where he succeeded in beating all other competitors. In later years Coxon became a close friend of F.W.K. Wallis.
2. There has been a suggestion, amongst carp fishing historians, that one of the reels was, in fact, made out of aluminium, or aluminium alloy, and not magnesium. However, in 1963, Dick Walker stated in *Angling Times,* that "Sixteen years ago I made a couple of centre-pins out of magnesium."
3. Again we see Walker's impish sense of humour surface. He told the author the reason he chose the name 'Water Rail' was because of this bird's reputation for being shy! That, of course, was the last thing anyone could accuse Dick of — and he knew it!

probably for the first time by anyone in this context, that:

"Reels should be chosen with some regard for the great speed and powers of acceleration possessed by carp. This means ability to recover line very quickly; an easily-applied, smooth drag and a left-hand wind (for right-handed anglers); one has not time, in playing big carp, to mess about changing the rod from one hand to the other. The bigger fixed-spools are excellent; I use a post-war model, Felton Crosswind. With this type of reel one can cast baits much too light to throw from a rotating drum reel, and with much greater accuracy. When one is waiting for a run, they can be left with the pick-up in the free position, which is much more satisfactory than coiling several yards on the ground."

Prior to this, in 1946/47 Walker had been using the 4in. version of the Hardy Eureka centre-pin for his carp fishing (although he had used fixed-spool reels since 1936) so, clearly, between the two dates he had been converted to the benefits of the fixed-spool reel.

Bob Richards used an Ambidex reel for his carp fishing in 1951. Later, at the suggestion of Dick Walker, he changed to a Mitchell.

During the early part of the 1950's there was much discussion in enlightened carp fishing circles about the merits of the different makes of fixed-spool reels, which had, by this time, improved and increased in availability. Walker concluded the following in his contribution to the C.C.C. rotary letters in May 1952, discussing the merits of the Mitchell, Altex III and the Felton Crosswind:

"If I knew a better reel than the Mitchell, I should use it. As regards range, there is little to chose between the first two reels which both considerably outcast the Altex III. The latter is also the heaviest; the Mitchell is much lighter than the other two. The ability of the Mitchell to take 200 yards of 11lb. Perlon is a big point in its favour, too, as is its higher rate of line recovery. It is true that the Altex pick-up cannot get the line twice around it, but once one has realised the dire necessity of making dead sure the line is not twice round the Felton or Mitchell pick-ups, this seldom, if ever, happens."

The History of Carp Tackle

Walker's preference for the Mitchell was to have an influence on carp anglers for many years to come. After the War and in the early-1950's, fixed-spool reels were often referred to as threadline reels, or spinning reels, and some of the models that were available are as follows:

The Bowell Auto-Reel	£7/10/0 in 1946	produced by C. & H. Bowell, Birmingham
The Ambidex	£6/17/6 in 1946	produced by J.W. Young & Sons, Redditch
The Leighton	£6/12/6 in 1948	distributed by W.R. Freeman, Birmingham
The Mitchell	£6/7/4 in 1949	distributed by Millard Bros., London
The Hardex	£3/4/9 in 1953	produced by Hardy's
The Omnia	£2/4/6 in 1953	produced by T.J. Harrington & Son, Surrey
The Winner	£2/7/3 in 1953	sold by R.G. Edwards
The Helical		sold by A.E. Rudge, Redditch
The C.A.P.	£4/11/6 in 1953	distributed by Millard Bros., London
Felton Crosswind	£7/10/0 in 1953	produced by S. Allcock & Co., Redditch
The Duco	£5/12/6 in 1953	produced by S. Allcock & Co., Redditch
The Silver Superb	£4/10/0 in 1953	produced by S. Allcock & Co., Redditch
The Swiss	£3/18/6 in 1953	
The Quicki Junior	£4/9/6 in 1954	distributed by Lee of Redditch
The Savoy	£5/19/0 in 1954	distributed by Sportex

Later, during the 1950's, other names such as Intrepid, Abu and Weston also produced fixed-spool reels.

Sir Patrick Ashley Cooper's home, Hexton Manor (Temple Pool) in 1950. It was here, and at Bearton Pond, that Dick Walker formed many of his early ideas about the tackle necessary for successful carp fishing. The lake was drained in 1942 and the three largest carp weighed 20½lb., 21½lb., and 25½lb. They were returned, with many smaller fish when the lake was refilled, but Dick never managed to catch his 'Pickle-Barrel'.

A subject which is commonly discussed nowadays, with compressed guns for firing bait and radio-controlled boats, is whether technology has deprived anglers of a great deal of the substance of quintessential carp fishing. This philosophical conundrum is not a product of modern-day carp fishing, for Walker sensed much the same when he wrote in August, 1952:

"Am I tending to 'blind fish with science?" Is this 'fiendish ingenuity' *(of which he had been accused)*, not only on electronics, but on the study of movements etc. spoiling the more spiritual aspects of carp-fishing? Is it right that I should be lounging on a cushion, half-asleep (or even quite), with crafty devices to tell me all, when a much better carp fisher, like Harry *(Grief)* for example, is sitting alert at his rod and catching a fish through skill and sense and concentration and persistence?

My mind is such that I am always looking for the more efficient way of doing a job, and every time I find a better way I am pleased. That's what fishing means to me—a never-ending supply of problems to solve, and some of them are engineering and electrical ones, which may cause men with less technical aptitude, but very much finer types of mind, to feel that all this science is spoiling the show."

Jack Smith replied to Walker:

"For the life of me, I cannot see why ingenious mechanical devices to aid legitimate carp fishing should impair the 'spirituality' of the sport any more than a bishop using a motor-car to visit his flock. Of course, if someone starts thinking along atomic-bomb lines....!Or more cheaply, if you really **must** have carp, you can always drain the lake."

The first electric bite alarm was devised in 1949 by Maurice Ingham. It consisted of a small torch mounted on the top of the rod, above a centre-pin reel, and facing towards the angler. The reel had to be made of metal and, with a few electrical connections and a strip of insulating material fixed between the revolving spool and the reel casing, the bulb could be made to flash on and off as the reel revolved. The indicator was fully described in *The Fishing Gazette,* dated October 8th, 1949. This appeared prior to Maurice Ingham's first correspondence with Dick Walker, which took place the following month. Shortly afterwards, Dick constructed another primitive affair from an Ever Ready cycle lamp. A flat brass strip was bolted to the casing that held the battery, the top of which had been removed. This brass strip touched another strip that comprised the contacts, so that the bulb lit. Pushing the fishing line between the contacts broke the circuit, which was re-connected when the line was pulled clear.

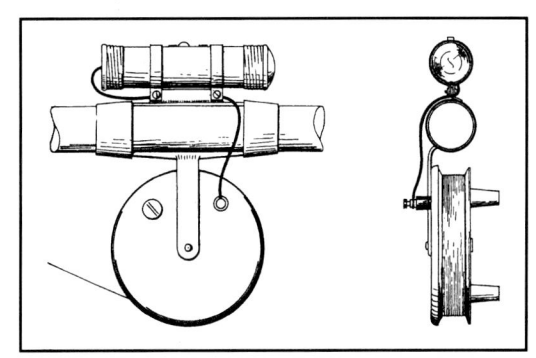

The first electric bite alarm, invented by Maurice Ingham and described in the Fishing Gazette in October, 1949.

During the next couple of years, by the combined efforts of Dick Walker and Maurice Ingham, the idea was developed further. A screw was added which allowed pressure between the contacts to be adjusted. Other improvements were gradually incorporated (Maurice was using one in June, 1952 that controlled two rods, a bite being indicated by either a green or a red bulb), but the basic design had inherent drawbacks. By the autumn of 1952, Dick was working on a much improved bite alarm design which would offer a number of substantial advantages.

Maurice Ingham's second bite alarm after discussing the subject with Walker. Dick's own first attempts used the same principles of the line separating the contacts in an electrical circuit, utilising an Ever Ready cycle lamp. On another occasion he claimed he used a Lucas cycle lamp. With a further effort he employed a 2oz. tobacco tin, with a hinged-lid, to hold a 4½ volt flat battery., a buzzer and two G.P.O. relay contacts.

The History of Carp Tackle

The use of electric bite alarms caused furore in the angling press in the early-1950's. Accusations flew thick and fast—from the belief that Walker and his pals were actually managing to electrocute their fish, to the claim that it just wasn't the English gentleman's way of doing things; by inference Dick and his carp fishing cronies were a bunch of cads!

Mr. Eeles, of Abingdon, after reading about Walker's electric bite alarm wrote the following in an angling periodical in 1953:

"It filled me with both astonishment and some disquiet at the possible trend of angling. Where will it end I wonder?"

Walker lost no time in replying and a section of his letter made the following point:

"Extravagant misrepresentations of the nature and purpose of electric bite alarms have been made in a London evening newspaper. To suggest (as has been done) that these indicators enable an angler to be 'in a pub parlour a furlong from his swim' indicates either ignorance of practical angling or a wanton desire to discredit the efforts of others." They did, however, demonstrate the critic's ability of foresight! Of course, Dick and B.B. were adamant in their public utterances that electric bite alarms did not allow you to fall asleep—if you did you would end up missing the bite. This, of course, was no more than public relations and the truth was a mite different. John Norman, writing in the Carp Catchers' rotary letters, gives us a insight into what those hardy pioneers really got up to in the early-1950's!

"I was astonished to see Maurice in the half-light settle down in what Stanley Holloway's Mrs. Ramsbottom calls a recumbent posture, head and shoulders supported by rucksack, legs stretched out towards his rods and covered by a blanket—and believe me he had the nerve to sleep. He says he dozed but I never heard a dozing man snore! How I envied him his aplomb as I sat on my camp stool on edge with anticipation.

When his buzzer went about 1.15am it sounded like the last trump, but he was at the rod in a second and into a fish."

Top: One of Dick's early buzzers in his garden at Hitchin.
Bottom: The same buzzer unit was later used with an antenna-type head.

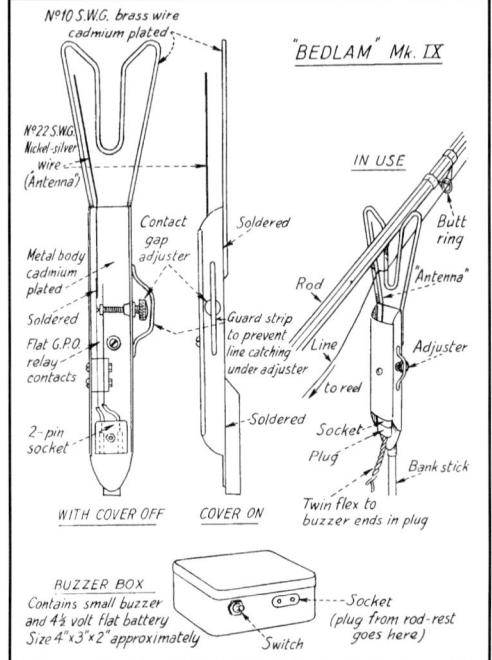

Above: In the Spring of 1953 Walker made five 'Mk. 9' bite alarm heads. One he kept and the remaining four were given to Bernard Venables, Pete Thomas, B.B. and Bob Richards. Dick's drawing shows the basic concept that was to last for almost twenty-five years.

The History of Carp Tackle

Within a few years there were a number of commercially made electric bite alarms. The first to become available, in October 1954, was the Buzz-Light Bite Detector, followed by the Prematic and the Heron. The latter, manufactured by carp fisher Jack Opie's company, Metal Pressings Ltd., soon dominated the market, especially as it was recommended by Dick Walker.

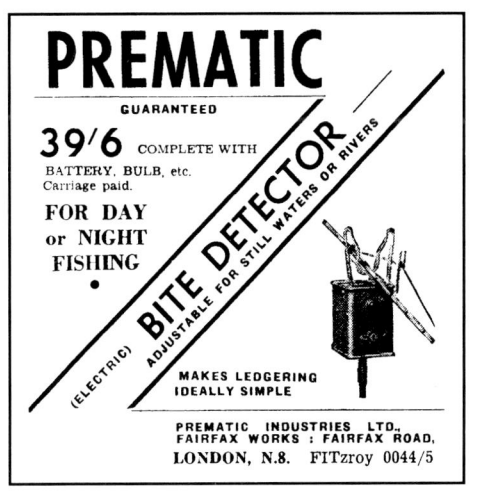

Left: The first advertised commercial buzzer, from October, 1954.
Above & Below: The 'Prematic' first appeared at the same time as the 'Heron' in June, 1957. The latter was to dominate the market, helped considerably by Dick Walker's generous endorsement.

Although Dick designed several very important items of carp tackle, whose basic designs either lasted for many years or are still with us (the Mk. IV rod, the Heron Bite Detector, a carp landing net and the Arlesey bomb), and allowed various commercial enterprises to produce them, he received very little, if any, financial remuneration himself. At another time, in another field, these inventions would have made him an extremely wealthy man. But Dick was generous to a fault, and had little interest in developing the financial opportunities his fertile brain came up with. It was the academic challenge to problem solving that was his forte. His training, his background, his situation, his ego, but, above everything else, his insatiable desire to find the answer to a problem, conspired to make him the greatest innovator angling has ever seen.

175

The History of Carp Tackle

Nowadays, nylon monofilament line, and its derivatives, is taken so much for granted that few anglers would know what do if supplies ceased. But it was only after the Second World War that its impact on British anglers really took effect, when it very quickly replaced the earlier alternatives.

If we go back a long time we find that the trace, or that portion of line that was attached to the hook, was made of horsehair. It was cheap and readily obtainable, and several strands could be twisted together to increase the breaking strain. Horsehair continued to be used until well into the 19th century—Francis Francis writes of its use in his 1867 work *A Book on Angling*. However, another substance was also used widely during this period that had first become popular during the 18th century. It was known, at that time, as Indian weed, Indian grass, grass-worm or sea-grass and was thought to be of vegetable origin, being produced from jute. Perhaps it was at one time but an investigation carried out at Kew Gardens, in 1864, showed, what was then thought to be Indian weed, to be the product of the silk glands of the Chinese silkworm. One of the first published references to silkworm gut was in 1724, in James Saunders book *The Compleat Fisherman,* although Courtney Williams, in his book *Angling Diversions,* states that "the first mention of silkworm gut being sold in Great Britain was in 1722, in an advertisement issued by William Browne, the London tackle dealer."

The silk gut first arrived in this country from China and Japan, in sections some 4½ft. in length, and was longer and finer than that which was later, almost exclusively, imported from Spain and, to a far lesser extent, Italy. The quality of the silkworm gut varied greatly and the Spanish product was graded into *natural selecta,* perfect gut requiring no further work, *selecta,* good quality which could be improved by softening and removing small defects by polishing (mazantining), *natural superior,* good second quality which could not be improved manually, *superior,* second quality that could be improved by mazantining, and *estriada,* much of which had small flaws (the Spanish word for fluted, or grooved). The virtual Spanish monopoly in silkworm gut production was centred around the town of Murcia, in the southeast region of that country. For many miles around the city itself, the 'Huerta' peasants found employment in cultivating the silkworm for it's silk or its gut, the proportion of each dependent upon the rise and fall of demand.

Part of the extensive silworm gut producing factory at Murcia, Spain, which employed several hundred local workers in the early part of the present century.

Another type of gut, made from the intestine of animals, often sheep but sometimes cats, was also widely used from about the mid-17th century onwards. Other natural products were also adapted to produce fishing lines, principally flax, and often the single strands were combined together to form, for example, plaited silk or twisted flax.

There were attempts to produce a synthetic filament as early as 1664 by Robert Cooke and, later, in 1884, Hilaire de Chardonnett did manage to form an artificial silk from nitro-cellulose. However, it wasn't until 1908 when Jagut, a Japanese gut substitute (sometimes called jay-gut, gum-line or demos), came onto the British market that a successful synthetic alternative became available. However, the famous tackle suppliers, Hardy Bros., felt obliged in 1925 to state that it was an inferior product to the best quality silkworm gut, although they were prepared to supply it due to its substantially lower price. Conversely, The Pilot Gut Company, who supplied much of the British tackle trade with silkworm gut from Spain, believed that well-produced Jagut was "a very good substitute" and they took a financial share in one of the largest companies that manufactured it in Japan.

Nylon monofilament was first made in 1935 and came to Britain, from the United States, in very limited quantities in about 1938 but, the following year, the Second World War began and supplies to this country became erratic. However, the world's first commercial factory producing nylon was built in the United States in 1940.

Nylon monofilament was the result of ten years work by Carothers, a brilliant research chemist employed by Du Pont de Nemoures in their American laboratories. Several polymers of nylon were produced by Carothers but, for some inexplicable reason, Du Pont failed to patent the process and it was also taken up by a German company who manufactured it under the trade name of Perlon. After the War availability quickly improved and by the early-1950's a number of different companies were producing it commercially. Dick Walker tried nylon line for the first time in the summer of 1947, but was not impressed with its usefulness for carp fishing. He believed its stretch inhibited the ability to strike hooks home and that it was too easily cut and damaged. However, by 1950 he had changed his mind and purchased a 200 yard spool of Sportex Perlyl (diameter 0.012in., rated at 11lb. b.s. but which Walker claimed actually broke at about 9lb.). He soaked it in a 10% solution of silver nitrate to stain it a deep-chestnut colour and installed it on a Mitchell reel. He used it the very first time he visited Redmire and was still using the same line four years later.

Some of the brands of nylon monofilament available in the late-1940's and early-1950's were:

Luron	produced by I.C.I.
Platil	German nylon distributed by Martin James, Redditch
Sportex Perlyl	German nylon available from 1950, distributed by Sportex Perlon (UK) Ltd.
Poolon	German nylon distributed by A. Poole & Son
Damyl	distributed by Lee of Redditch
Racine Tortue	distributed by A.F.A.D. Ltd., London
Sylcast	German nylon distributed by Modern Arms Co. Ltd.
Bell	
Draylon Bayer	distributed by Henry W. Aitken Ltd.
Monofil-Mitchell	distributed by Millard Bros., London
Swissfil	distributed by Allcocks of Redditch

The first advert for Luron monofilament shortly after it was introduced in 1947.

The History of Carp Tackle

In about 1940, whilst working in the laboratories of the Calico Printers' Association, Whinfield and Dickson produced a new synthetic material, subsequently named Terylene. It is known as a polyester, being produced from ethylene glycol and terpthalic acid. It had different properties to nylon but was produced mainly as a braided line and became readily available, like nylon, in the years following the Second World War.

Technological advances have seen improvements in both nylon and other synthetic materials used for fishing line. It is interesting to note, though, that Walker, since the 1950's, claimed that the problem of bait rejection was often not created by the thickness of a nylon but by its stiffness. Lecturing the members of the British Carp Study Group in 1974, in their magazine, he again made the point:

"One more thing—fine line, line troubles. Keep telling yer, don't I, it aint the fickness, it's yer actual flexibility. It aint seein' it, it's feeling the stiffness wot does the damage." To this end, he recommended braided line, and, in fact, used braided nylon to catch his 44-pounder from Redmire.

> **PLATIL**
>
> ANOTHER CASE where quality of this monofilament combined with skill of angler resulted in a great catch.
>
> **Mr. Robert D. Richards of Gloucester**
> landed a
>
> **CARP 31¼ lb.**
>
> on October 3rd this year using 0·26 mm. 6.1 lb. B.S.   It was sold by:
> **Mr. Fred Harvey**
> **18 Barton Street, Gloucester**
>
> *Imported & Distributed by:*
> **W. MARTIN JAMES LTD., REDDITCH**
> *Wholesale Only*

During the early part of this century, it was generally considered appropriate to use treble hooks in carp fishing. It wasn't until the 1930's that the practise began to decline, although B.B. was still recommending their use in his books, *The Fisherman's Bedside Book*, in 1945 and *Confessions of a Carp Fisher*, in 1950, wherein he wrote, "When using potato or very large balls of paste a triangle hook may be used, as the bait is big enough to cover entirely the hooks and they cannot be felt when the fish takes it with the mouth. Moreover, the double hold will ensure a good strike and increase your chances of landing him." Watkins-Pitchford was not alone in his approval of there use at this time; Captain Len Parker, The Skipper, was also in favour of them when carp fishing.

Fortunately, this was something of a throwback to the past for the majority of writers and carp anglers, and, by 1950, not many recommend them. However, odd advocates still lingered and Gerry Berth-Jones suggested their use shortly after becoming a member of the Carp Catchers' Club in 1954. Walker lost little time in admonishing him with the following:

"I mistrust multiple hooks of all kinds and while I wouldn't dream of telling any other angler what hooks he ought or ought not to use, **I'm** not going to use double or treble hooks, or multi-hook tackles. I've caught a good many fair-sized fish of all kinds on single hooks, and I hope to catch a good many more. If I lose a fish, I can usually find the reason why, and it has never turned out to be insufficient numbers of hook points."

In the early-1950's, most of the members of the Carp Catchers' Club were using the Model Perfect hook, manufactured by S. Allcock & Co. Ltd., which the makers described as a forged, reversed hook with a completely symmetrical bend. It had been designed and patented by Samuel Allcock himself, some half-a-century earlier. Maurice tried the Quickstrike hook produced by Hardy's and Harry Grief preferred the Sovereign brand.

But Walker was rarely satisfied; he was always ferreting away looking for ways to improve all aspects of tackle. A great deal of discussion took place amongst the Club's members about hooks, and Walker clearly made a comprehensive study of the design and mechanics of hook manufacture. Dick, in 1950, contacted Major Courtney Williams, director of S. Allcock, who kindly agreed to make a limited number of several hundred hooks in sizes 2, 4, and 6. Half of them had eyes and the other half serrated taper shanks. They were based on the company's Model Perfect design but had smaller barbs, the offset of the point was reduced from about 10° to 4°, and the barb was less deeply cut. When this supply ran out Walker tried to get some more made but, by this time, Courtney Williams had died[1] and Allcock & Co. declined to repeat the production. In 1952, John Norman contacted Hardy's but they turned down the opportunity of manufacturing a carp hook. Then, in 1954, 'Jimmy James' of B. James & Son, asked Dick if he could produce a range of carp hooks to Walker's design, but, unfortunately, the quality of the final product, initially made by Edgar Sealey then Mustad, left something to be desired. In 1956, Walker dealt directly with Bernard Sealey in the hope of getting a supply of high-quality hook and, still later, no doubt influenced by the unrelenting Walker, the company of J.B. Walker (from whom Dick obtain much of his carp rod materials) marketed a good, brazed-eyed, carp hook that was strong, yet reasonably fine in the wire. Of the many big carp landed on this latter hook, was the second largest ever recorded at the time—Eddie Price's giant of 40lb. 8oz. from Redmire.

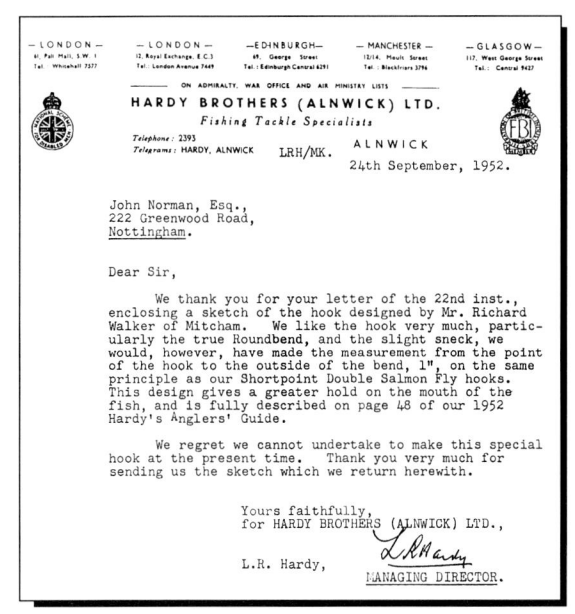

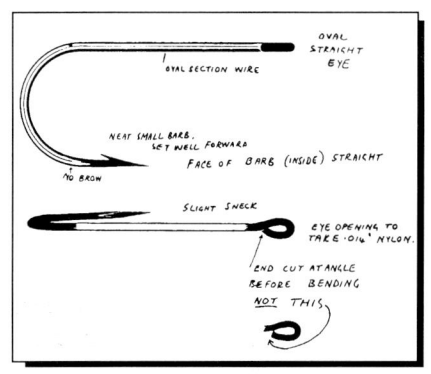

Left: The reply from Hardy's to the letter from John Norman enquiring if they would be interested in producing a carp hook.
Above: The sketch showing the hook that John included with his letter. The design was the culmination of considerable discussion between members of the C.C.C. over a long period.
Below: The B. James hook which became available in June, 1954. All C.C.C. members were sent samples to test.

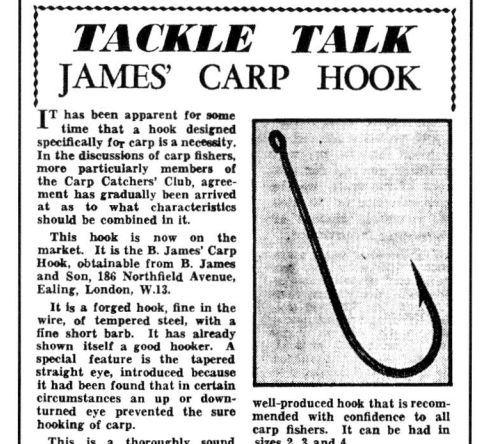

Below: The 'Goldstrike' became available in 1963 and, although rather thick in the wire, was popular with carp anglers during the following decade. It had been designed by Dick Walker, at Ron Chapman's request, to meet the demand for a stronger hook. Dick countered criticism of it by stating that "if you can't get better materials, then you must increase wire thickness."

1. Major Courtney-Williams died on January 23, 1951. Walker often referred to him as the managing director of Allcock & Co., which he wasn't. He was, during the period Dick knew him, a director but took an active part in the running of this world-famous company.

The History of Carp Tackle

To obtain a consistently satisfactory carp hook was clearly an uphill battle, but one which Dick thought important. For several years, in the early-1950's, he was convinced that the high number of carp lost at Redmire could be alleviated with a correctly designed hook. This claimed peculiarity of Redmire carp was again expounded by Walker in *The Angler's News,* in May 1955:

"Hooks may break, straighten, twist, or close-up; the line may break, or knots may give, but to retrieve an undistorted, still-sharp hook after losing a fish is most uncommon—except in one water. At Redmire, for every carp landed, two have been lost in exactly that way."

So what was so different about Redmire carp? Many and varied theories were put forward by those who fished there. The carp had different shaped mouths, or their mouths were abnormally soft through feeding almost exclusively on daphnia.[1] Another, suggested in 1953, by Dick was detailed in the rotary letter:

"The major set-back so far as Carp Catchers' Club members are concerned is entirely my fault. I invented a knot for attaching monofilament to eyed hooks. It was very strong and better than anything we had used before; but hooks tied in this way failed to take hold on a number of occasions.

I have concluded that the hook rotated backwards on striking, but whatever the reason, the result was the same. At least four fish upwards of 20lb. in weight came adrift in this way; I hesitate to be more specific about their weights."

Then, in November 1955, Walker finally came to the following, simple conclusion when it was suggested that treble hooks might reduce the number of lost fish:

"The reason why Bernithan carp come adrift is not because the hook comes out. It's because the hooks were never properly in; and if we can't lug one hook in I'm buggered if I can see why it should be any easier to lug two or more in."

By 1957, after several more big carp were lost at Redmire the previous season, Dick was further convinced that this was the reason and informed the other members of the Carp Catchers' Club of his conviction:

"I am convinced that only hooks that are not struck home ever come adrift. If you try holding the end of 30 yards of monofil line of about 10lb. b.s., and getting someone to strike firmly with a rod at the other end, you will be astounded to find how little force you feel. I was!"

---

1. During the early years at Redmire, those who fished there were generally convinced that one of the main reasons why its carp were so difficult to hook was because the Pool contained so much daphnia. Fred J. Taylor wrote in *The Angler's News:*

    "Take a cupful of water out of any part of the Pool and you will not be able to count the number of daphnia it contains. Why should these carp be interested in our humble paste and bread offerings when they have merely to open their mouths to absorb all the finest fish food in the world they require, without so much as altering course?"

    Dick was equally adamant that this was a major factor in why big carp were so infrequently caught. He made the following point in his column in *Angling Times:*

    "The carp got all the grub they could use and they didn't have to move an inch to get it. All they had to do was open their mouths. Offering them any kind of bait when the daphnia was thick was a waste of time."

    The author was puzzled by these claims since his experience of carp had demonstrated that large fish never actually fed on daphnia or, for that matter, any form of water fleas (cladocera). Imagine his surprise when he first read through the Carp Catchers' Club's rotary letters in 1988, and found this statement, written by Dick Walker, in 1954:

    "I am inclined to doubt that adult carp eat much daphnia."

    Yet, in later years, Dick reverted to the notion that one of the reasons why carp were so difficult to catch at Redmire was because they had so much daphnia to feed on. It may be that the daphnia theory was subsequently used as an excuse to explain the relatively poor catch rate of the early Redmire years.

Dick went on to say that he was hoping to get hold of some new braided Terylene line that would have far less stretch than anything previously used, and he hoped that this might assist in driving hooks home.

Walker was at the forefront in other areas of tackle design in the early-1950's. There was the Arlesey Bomb, which Dick had originally conceived during his forays after the huge perch in his local Arlesey Lake. Its use in carp fishing at this time was very limited, since most serious carp anglers generally shunned any unnecessary weight on the line. Dick did use the Arlesey bomb on one notable occasion, for a specific purpose, and that was to catch his 34lb. common carp from Redmire. However, in later years the 'bomb' was to become almost standard equipment for many of the increasing band of 'young hopefuls'.

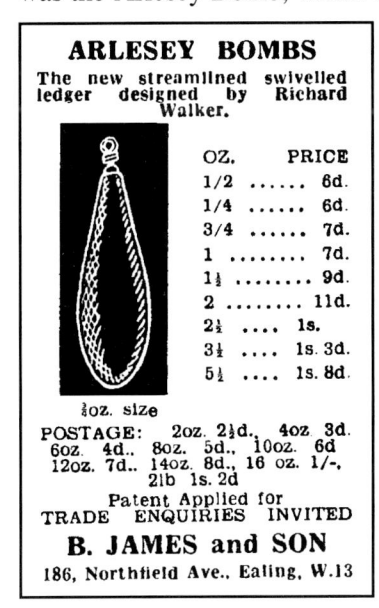

Prior to his design of the Arlesey Bomb, the only commercial lead weights that were readily available consisted of spherical bullets, coffin leads and pear-shaped leads intended for paternostering. So Dick considered the problem in great detail, drawing on his engineering knowledge and ability to sift out and develop existing, but unused ideas. The idea of the swivel came from A.J. Rudd, the Clerk to the Norfolk Fishery Board, who suggested it in 1935 in his book *Coarse Fishing*. The streamline shape was Walker's alone, but he was disappointed that most the subsequent commercial products failed

A 1955 advert for the Arlesey Bomb which shows that the firm of B. James & Son had got the shape wrong. On the right is a sketch, drawn by Dick Walker in 1970 for Angling Times, that demonstrates the correct aerodynamic design.

to incorporate this important feature. He wrote, "I am sorry to see in the shops nowadays, leads sold as Arlesey Bombs that have some very odd shapes, not a little bit like the original correct design. I am also sorry to see so-called Arlesey Bombs that, instead of being made of nearly pure lead, are made of some metal or mixture of metals which, although doubtless cheaper and easier to cast than lead, is much lighter and results in a bomb that is considerably bigger for its weight."

It comes as little surprise to discover that Walker also turned his attention to the question of landing net design. He was not in favour of the use of gaffs, except where pike were concerned—having no affinity for this species—and was well aware that the only existing commercial landing nets, capable of holding a large carp, were far too heavy for a lone angler to manage. It hardly taxed his considerable ingenuity to come up with the laminated cane arms, wooden spreader-block and dur-alumin hinge-piece. The first one he made had 30in. arms but, with the prospect of the Redmire 'monsters' becoming a viable proposition in 1952, he produced a second with

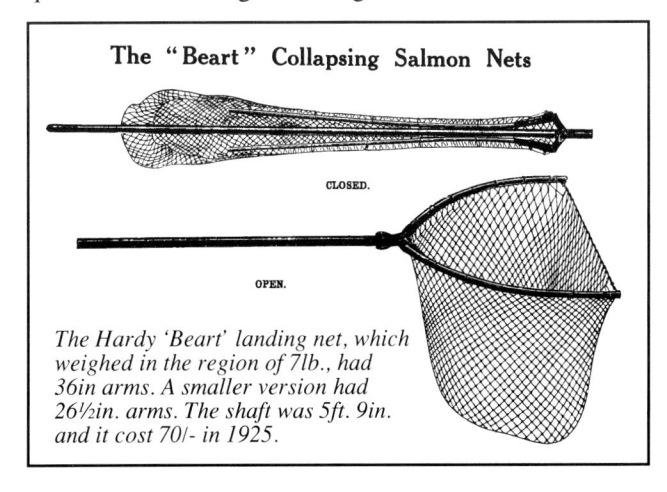

The Hardy 'Beart' landing net, which weighed in the region of 7lb., had 36in arms. A smaller version had 26½in. arms. The shaft was 5ft. 9in. and it cost 70/- in 1925.

The History of Carp Tackle

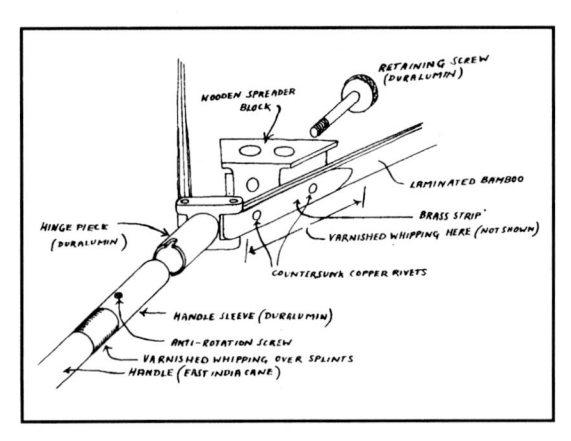

Dick's sketch of the the assembly components of his carp net. The design was the usual, thorough, Walker effort resulting in the basic concept that was to endure until the mid-1970's.

36in. arms. Dick put together at least two more, each one "having been used to land Clarissa," when they were generously given away to the first acquaintance who showed the slightest interest in coveting them.

In about 1956 B. James & Son began reproducing copies of Walker's original net, with 30in. arms. They were well made but the difficulties of manufacture, combined with the necessary high retail price, resulted in limited production. During a recent interview with the author, James Bruce jnr. thought that the company made no more than about 40 nets before they were discontinued.

Walker's 36in. landing net about to be put to admirable use at Bernithan Court Pool with the famous 34-pounder, the second largest carp ever caught at that time. A little mystery, however, surrounds the rod used in this instance. Whilst the remarkably 'spontaneous' sequence of photographs all show Walker's Mk. III being used, Dick stated in his story of the capture, written shortly afterwards and appearing in the 2nd July, 1954 issue of Angling Times, that "the rod and reel were the usual Mk. IV and Mitchell." The use of the Mk. IV was also confirmed by Peter Thomas when he wrote the story of the capture for The Angler's News a little later.

Richard Walker's influence on the development of purposeful carp fishing equipment was totally pervasive. He brought a practical, down-to-earth rationale to the field, examining and assessing each item, discarding the bigotry and blinkered vision, and setting the framework and standards for the future. There were others who assisted, whilst many acted as foils for Walker's restless inquisitiveness; and there were a few who made real contributions—but it was Dick Walker who was the the pre-eminent fount of bringing carp fishing tackle out of the ignorance and inertia of the past.

Chapter 12
Wadhurst, Stoneham & Contemporary Times

*In the sultry summer of 1959, I fell in with the carp fishermen.
I joined the renowned Wadhurst Park syndicate.*
        Geoffrey Bucknall from *Fishing Days* (1966)

One of the most famous carp fisheries in the land was the 44 acre Wadhurst Lake in East Sussex. Whilst its history goes back some considerable time, it came to prominence in the early-1950's when it was taken over by a syndicate, known as the Charter Angling Society, whose secretary was that indefatigable catcher of big fish, Derrick Davenport.

It was always a very prolific fishery, and one of the many remarkable catches made there took place as long ago as September 17th, 1914. In six hours fishing 40 fish were caught by three anglers, weighing a total of 128lb. 2oz. The largest brace of fish weighed 7lb. 5oz. and 7lb. 1oz., and the bait used in their downfall was boiled maize, proving once again Geoffrey Chaucer's observation, in *The Canterbury Tales*, that "There's never a new fashion but it's old."

The large catch of carp from Wadhusrt Lake in 1914, made by C.S. Wickenden, F.W. Norton and H.M. Swain (who caught 24 of the fish). The use of maize demonstrates that this bait is not a recent innovation.

Wadhurst Park Lake was the embodiment of pure, un-fettered carp fishing. The author fell in love with that sublime oasis and he wrote of his passion in a chapter of the book, *The Big Fish Scene,* relating that:

"In 1970 we spent all our holidays at Wadhurst, camping on the wooded south bank, looking across the 40 acres to sweeping meadows of pastoral countryside, watching mail-clad wild carp leaping with almost ceaseless regularity, far, far, out. A juxtaposition of the aura of the Far East, given by visions of, as Arthur Ransome puts it, 'Great blunt headed golden fish in golden spray', and the haziness of Constable England."

Gerry Berth-Jones, who joined the syndicate when it was formed in 1953, was of a similar mind when he wrote this to his friend Maurice Ingham:

"Wadhurst lies in a valley in the folds of the Sussex countryside, deeply hidden from public view. It took my wife and I two days to find it and when we did we recognised at once a most beautiful paradise. The lake is about ¾ of a mile long and ¼ mile wide, lightly wooded on one side and open fields slope gently down to the water on the other bank. Two, or three, small islands and an old boathouse lie at the head of the lake, which is abundant with rhododendrons. At the far end a dam and sluice deals with the overflow.

Yes, Wadhurst holds many wonderful memories—many dark, silent nights—many dawns breaking, and great and wonderful friendships. It was there, on the banks of Wadhurst, that I first met Fred J. Taylor. Fat and friar-like, and very jolly; he asked me about Richard Walker. I told him 'go and just knock on his door, he's the friendliest chap you'll ever meet'—and he did, and look what friendship that brought!"

As far as Gerry Berth-Jones is concerned Wadhurst was the most beautiful lake he has ever fished; it was "a paradise with a deadly quietness about the place." As a matter of interest, Gerry's initiation into carp fishing began on a small gravel pit at Sutton-on-Hone where he, and his wife May, used to fish for roach. One close season, in the late-1940's, he spotted some dark shapes just under the surface of the coloured water and threw in some bits of bread. They were taken immediately and so was Gerry!

Wadhurst Park : Wadhurst : Sussex

PERMIT

to fish or visit Wadhurst Park Lake at a fee of

2s.6d. per person.

NOTE—No Carp under 8 lb. to be taken away.

Nº 1422   19 JUL 1952

This Ticket is issued on the understanding that all bathers bathe at their own risk.

5/-

CHARTER ANGLING SOCIETY

PERMIT TO FISH WADHURST LAKE

This permit entitles the holder to fish WADHURST LAKE for the following period..................

Guest Permit for a Friend.

on condition that he is accompanied by a Member of the Society.

Signed........................
Secretary

The Carp Fishing

At WADHURST PARK LAKE,
(of wild carp fame)
EAST SUSSEX,

is now being managed by

The Fishery Services Co.

(On behalf of the Owners of Wadhurst Park Estate)

Although fishing permits for this beautiful water are now limited to 25 we will try to make a few available to newcomers each season. These permits are let on an annual basis at £10 per season and, by arrangement, Holders may bring guests at 10s. per visit.

The lake, of some 44 acres, yet one of the most secluded in the Southern Counties, is noted for its exceptionally large head of wild carp. The average weight is 5 to 6 pounds but with a fair proportion of heavier fish. A 32 inch carp was found dead recently.

There is a fishing hut at the waterside and a boat is provided for anglers to transport their gear to distant parts of the lake. Judicious camping is permitted.

A small woodland lake adjacent, reputedly stocked with king carp in 1955, will be open for fishing this year.

THE FISHERY SERVICES CO.,
ROSIAN COTTAGE, WHEATHAMPSTEAD, HERTS.

Wadhurst Park Lakes

FISHING PERMIT

Mr. *K. CLIFFORD* has permission to fish the above lakes during the season 1970-1 subject to the rules overleaf.

Issued By
ALEX RENNY (Wadhurst Lakes)
(On behalf of the Owners of Wadhurst Park Estate)

NOT TRANSFERABLE

During the 1950's and 1960's a great number of anglers made the pilgrimage to fish the remote and beautiful Wadhurst lake—Jimmy Bart, Dennis Merrill, George and Miriam Moss, Tony Fordham, Ken Cumsden, Frank Tubb, Frank Murgett, the Tibbles brothers, Murray Roker, Fred. J. Taylor, Geoffrey Bucknall, Cliff Glenton, and so many others—and most of them tasted the "wiriness and gristle" of the Wadhurst 'wildies'. In time the syndicate was controlled by Ernie Tubb, then Ian French, Trevor Housby and finally Alex Renny, a friend of Cliff Glenton, who ran it for nine blissful years until about 1972. Subsequently, the estate was sold, and sadly the lake was drained and many of the carp removed when it was turned into a third-rate trout fishery. Gerry Berth-Jones made a return visit some years later and wrote the following:

Trevor Housby, who for a period controlled the Wadhurst syndicate, camping in the meadow on the north bank. Permission to erect a tent was given by Mr. Watson, the farmer, who owned the fishing rights at that time.

"It isn't always a good thing to go back to places where happy memories come from. But one day, a couple of years ago, I went alone to pay a visit to Wadhurst Lake.

There had been some changes in the intervening years but I found the dusty track that led to the valley, down wide fields, to the lake at the bottom. But I was waylaid by a 'tweedy' keeper of the newly owned estate. I got out of my car and he was quick to tell me that I was on private property and under no circumstances was I able to go down to the lake.

I stood beside him and told him my story of how I, at one time, came here often. I told him of the day tickets the public once bought and how they abused that privilege, and how our syndicate once practised the role he was now playing. He listened intently and hardly said a word. Then, after a short pause, he replied, 'Well, if you go to the big house, and tell them what you have told me, I am quite sure the new owner would let you come and fish as often as you like'.

Gerry Berth-Jones with Wadhurst 'wildies'. He has many happy memories of carp fishing there with his wife, May.

I thanked him, but explained that I'd no desire to fish the place any more. 'Then please feel free to go and walk round the lake,' he offered. I did. It was almost exactly the same. But something was missing—I guess it was all my old friends and the enthusiasm we shared." Perhaps as Gerry stood looking across the water, hoping in vain to see the leaping carp, did he perchance hear his old companions' happy voices on the distant bank?

Wadhurst, Stoneham & Contemporary Times

Whilst certain waters received notoriety for various reasons, some, equally important ones, never fell under the public glare. Stoneham Lakes is a good example. Outside of the small group of anglers who fished the water for its carp it is hardly known, yet, during its hey-day, it was one of the most prolific big carp fisheries that has existed in this country. The lakes themselves are ancient, perhaps dating back to the early 14th century when the Abbot of Hyde was granted the right to have a deer park there. Fish ponds were often constructed within deer parks so there is good reason to suspect that this was their beginning. Certainly ponds existed by 1683 when a contract to build a wall for the Fleming family, the owners of the park from circa 1600 until 1953, makes mention of such. A map of 1818, however, shows only the Shrubbery Pond and a small pond of about an acre where the Park Pond is today. However, in about 1818, the old manor house, which was situated between the Shubbery Pond and the church, was demolished and a new house begun 400 metres further west. As a setting for this the Park Pond was considerably enlarged to become the centre-piece of the park.

The new house was never entirely completed. Suffering from a fire in about 1830 and, after 1900, when the Fleming family had moved their main residence to Chilworth, the house began to fall into neglect. Eventually, in the late-1930's, it was demolished. In 1953, the Fleming family sold the estate to the Cousins family.

From 1897 until 1955 the fishing had been controlled by the Southampton Piscatorial Society. Then, for a brief period, it fell under the auspices of the Pirelli General A.C. (the world renowned cable-making company) until 1963 when Causton's Freshwater A.C. (the fishing club of the printing firm Sir Joseph Causton Ltd.) took over the rights. In 1974 Causton's Freshwater A.C. changed their name to the Eastleigh and District A.C. and they have held the fishing continuously, having purchased the lakes from the Cousins family in the early-1980's.

The lakes are dammed valley ponds, whose shape is largely determined by the contours of the land behind the dam. The small stream that feeds the lakes rises in clay woodland to the west of the former North Stoneham Park. There are three ponds at North Stoneham today, the most easterly being a small holding pond of about 0.2 acre. Then there is the Shrubbery Pond covering some 2.75 acres and, finally, the Park Pond, which is about 5.6 acres in size.

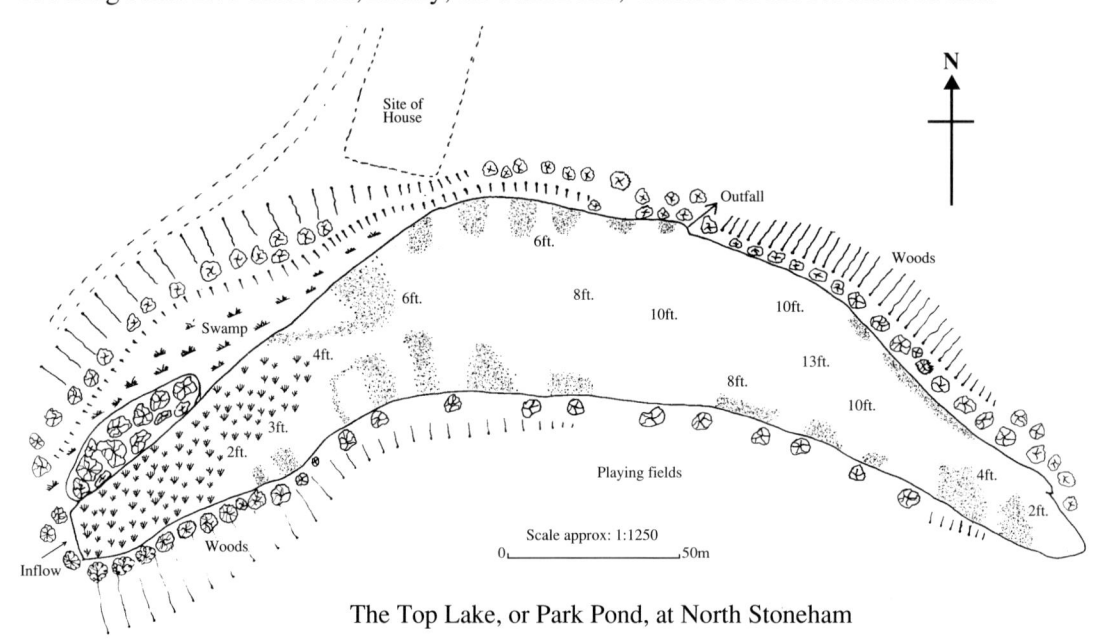

The Top Lake, or Park Pond, at North Stoneham

The first recorded mention of carp at Stoneham is in 1906-07 when it was recorded in the Southampton Piscatorial A.C. minute book that "Attention is called to the fact that North Stoneham Ponds have been improved by the introduction of 100 fine carp of 1lb. to 2lb. weight, which in a short time should tax the skill of the members." In 1909, by which time the club had 50 members and was paying a yearly rent of £10, these were being caught and a Mr. Figgins received a cup for the best specimen that year which weighed 3lb. 6oz. By 1914 the Club records that good catches of carp were being taken and the largest fish for 1912 was one of just over 6lb., which again was caught by Mr. Figgins.

In May, 1924 a further stocking of 100 "king carp" between four and six ounces was proposed. In 1928 the Lake record stood at 9½lb. and another 100 carp were stocked during that winter, none of which weighed less than 1lb. This latter stocking was the result of a large number of the existing carp being found dead. An examination by "an expert" concluded that they were female fish that were "egg-bound." The next recorded stocking took place in 1937 when Mr. Willis-Fleming agreed to forgo the rent so that the club could purchase 300 yearling carp. The following year a further 1,000 young carp were also stocked at a cost of £4 3s 0d. No further official stockings took place although it is known that a number of small wild carp were transferred from the Highbridge Gravel Pits by various individuals in the 1960's.

The stockings bore fruit and the size of the carp gradually increased, as is clearly demonstrated in the Club's records for winners of the Best Fish of the Year Competition.

1909	3lb. 6oz.	1934	8lb. 6oz.
1913	6lb. 2¼oz.	1935	10lb. 3oz.
1924	5lb. 5¼oz.	1936	10lb. 7oz.
1927	8lb. 0oz.	1937	12lb. 3oz.
1928	9lb. 8oz.	1939	9lb. 12½oz.
1931	6lb. 13½oz.	1940	14lb. 3oz.
1932	7lb. 3oz.	1946	14lb. 0oz.
1933	8lb. 8oz.		

However, it was after the Second World War that things really started to happen at North Stoneham. Interest in carp was growing and local anglers started to fish the Lakes using methods and tackle advocated by Dick Walker and others. One such angler was Robert Atkinson, who lived in Eastleigh. He had borrowed B.B.'s book, *Confession's of a Carp Fisher,* twice from the local library and devoured it from cover to cover. He started fishing seriously for carp in about 1948, spending nights at Stoneham and a small local gravel pit that contained vast numbers of small common carp between 1lb. and 2lb. No one, at that time, would have described Robert as a carp expert, but he was enterprising and willing to learn. An opportunity presented itself to him in 1952—a chance that only comes to a lucky few once in a lifetime. Robert grasped it with both hands and made carp angling history by becoming the first man to catch two carp over 20lb. in a season (Les Brown, at Mapperley, had the distinction of being the first to catch more than one carp over 20lb.). He also landed a string of other huge carp. No doubt his tremendous success had been slightly overshadowed by the events which had already taken place during the preceding months at Redmire, but Dick Walker, on reading in *The News of the World* of Atkinson's two 20lb. carp and realising its implications, lost no time in contacting him. This is Robert's story:

"The rod was a Milward's 10ft. 3in. split-cane model, with porcelain rings throughout, and the reel a 4in. Rapidex. The line consisted of 100 yards of Farben's German nylon with a breaking strain of 11lb., attached to a size 6, eyed eel hook. My holidays began on the 25th July, so I prepared my tackle and purchased a new loaf which I cut into one inch cubes.

"I arrived at the swim on the Friday evening at about 10.15pm, complete with deck-chair and other items of comfort. We have a hut in the woods which contains a set of scales, and each member has his own key. I tackled up and cast out the floating crust about 10 yards from the bank. It was a glorious, warm evening and I sat watching the silver paper hung between the reel and the butt ring. Suddenly the paper crept forward and I waited until nearly all the slack had been taken before I picked up the rod and tightened on the fish. However, it soon dropped off as it was not firmly hooked. I recast and made a mental note to strike firmly when the next opportunity came. After about an hour of inactivity I saw the water moving near the bait and suddenly the silver paper shot up. I struck hard. The fish didn't go far before turning sharp right into the lilies and becoming solid. I tried everything; I walked backwards, sidewards, all the time vibrating the line and jerking it up and down. After about 30 minutes I eventually managed to persuade it to move again and I then applied every bit of upward pressure I dare. It came to the surface in the lilies, thrashing wildly. I pulled the fish back into open water and held on for dear life. Gradually, he tired and as I eased him into the shallow I lit the cycle lamp. At last I could see the fish and I realised the net would be useless. But, having read in B.B.'s book how Flt. Lt. Burton landed a carp by its gills, I attempted this 3 or 4 times to no avail. Each time he forced his way back into deeper water. Then, at long last, he lay still enough for me to lay the rod down and place one hand under his flank and the other gently in his gill and stagger up the field with him. There I laid him down. It was an hour before

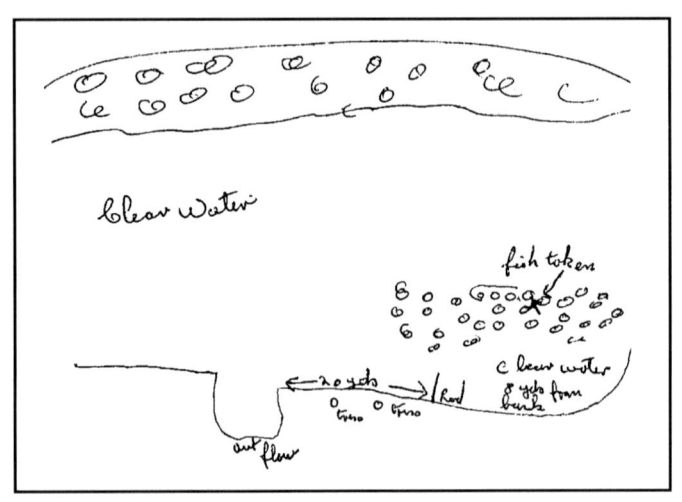

Robert Atkinson's sketch, drawn in September 1952, of the swim where he made history by catching two carp over 20lb.

the first early morning bream fisherman arrived when we lifted it from my keepnet and weighed and photographed it. It was then returned safely to the water. It was a mirror carp and weighed 20lb. 7½oz.

I returned to the same swim on the Monday night and caught the second 20lb. carp at approximately 1am the following morning. However, it took less time as I had more confidence in my tackle and had, no doubt, learnt from my previous experience. Unfortunately, I had arranged to leave the water by no later than 2am, as a family holiday was booked and we were due to leave at 8am. Being alone on the water I wanted the fish witnessed so I determined to take it home alive. I laid my oilskin on the deck-chair and placed the fish on it. After collecting all my tackle I laid the chair across my bicycle and walked the two miles home. After placing it in the bath it revived splendidly and, at 6.30am, I telephoned the Club secretary, Mr. H.V. Hampton, from the local phone box, and asked him if it would be possible for him to come from Southampton and witness it before 8am. Unfortunately, he could not make it so I left the fish in the bath after changing the water. On my return that evening I found the fish had died. Its weight was 22lb. 8oz. and it too was a mirror carp. Incidentally, I could not afford to have it set up so I had to bury it and that did grieve me. Both fish were Club records and I entered the second one for *The News of the World* Fish of the Week Competition."

A few weeks later, at the beginning of September, Robert had another tremendous run of big carp, all fully authenticated and witnessed. They were all caught in the same manner using floating crust and at that time amounted to an incredible tally of large carp caught by one man. In three, consecutive evenings fishing Robert caught fish of 18lb. 7oz., 19lb. 12½oz., 17lb. 1¼oz. and a common carp of 18lb. 8½oz.

As far as the author has been able to ascertain, Robert Atkinson was the first person to catch two carp over 20lb. in a season, but during the research for this book another earlier claim did come to light. In about 1987 the author was invited to the home of Richard Pratley, who has accumulated one of the finest collections of cased fish in the country. There, amongst splendid examples of work carried out by Cooper, Homer, Antiss and Miller, was a case bearing the legend in gold leaf of 'The largest brace of this species ever recorded in Britain'. Further details revealed that the mirror carp weighed 23lb. 5oz. and the leather carp 22lb. 11oz. and they were caught in Surrey, in June 1932, by L. Shipham. The fish were excellently mounted in a case which bore the style of the Victorian taxidermists. However, after carefully examining the work for some considerable time the author came to the conclusion that it was a fake, something which is becoming not uncommon now that antique mounted fish are realising such high prices. After the author mentioned his worries about the case to Richard Pratley he, too, also confirmed that he also had similar doubts about its authenticity. The fact that the author has never come across any mention of these fish, in any angling literature since 1932, was also strong circumstantial evidence of its duplicity.

A LIST OF SOME EARLY CARP CAUGHT FROM NORTH STONEHAM LAKES

1952	16lb. 15oz.	C.W. Bailey	
1952	16lb. 1¼oz.	T.K. Bartlett	
1952	18lb. 18oz.	T.K. Bartlett	
26th July 1952	20lb. 7¼oz.	R.T. Atkinson	floating crust
28th July 1952	22lb. 8oz.	R.T. Atkinson	floating crust
1st Sept. 1952	18lb. 7oz.	R.T. Atkinson	floating crust
2nd Sept. 1952	19lb. 12½oz.	R.T. Atkinson	floating crust
2nd Sept. 1952	17lb. 1¼oz.	R.T. Atkinson	floating crust
3rd Sept. 1952	18lb. 8½oz.	R.T. Atkinson	
1953	18lb. 12oz.	S. Marchant	
1953	15lb. 12oz.	R.T. Atkinson	
1953	15lb. 1¼oz.	R.T. Atkinson	
1953	15lb. 3oz.	T.K. Bartlett	
1953	18lb.	A. Satterley	
1953	17lb.	R.M. Evans	
1954	20lb. 8oz.	R.M. Evans	
1954	20lb. 6oz.	T.K. Bartlett	

Ken Bartlett also caught a number of other carp during the 1954 season. These included a further two fish over 20lb. In total he landed 24 carp with the, then, astonishing average weight of 15lb. 14oz. Seventeen of the fish weighed over 15lb. which was a quite remarkable season's tally in 1954. The details of these catches were never reported to the press as a rule was passed in March, 1953 forbidding publication of any details about the Stoneham Lakes. This was due to uncertainty about the fishing lease with the new owner. In fact the owner, Mr. Cousins, actually terminated the fishing in May, 1955. By the end of 1958 Ken Bartlett had caught 7 carp over 20lb. with his top 12 fish averaging 20lb. 1oz.—an astonishing record, almost certainly unmatched by anyone else in the country at that time.

A LIST OF SOME FISH OVER 20LB. CAUGHT FROM NORTH STONEHAM LAKES

Date	Type	Weight	Angler	Bait
Sept. 1955		20lb.	V. Noyce	floating crust
1957	mirror	20lb. 8oz.	P. Rodaway	
16th June 1958	mirror	20lb. 12oz.	R.T. Atkinson	potato
July 1958	mirror	25lb. 4oz.	R.T. Atkinson	potato
Sept. 1958	common	20lb.	P. Rodaway	potato
Sept. 1958	common	21lb. 4oz.	T.K. Bartlett	potato
16th June 1959	mirror	23lb. 4oz.[1]	R.T. Atkinson	potato
Sept. 1959		20lb.	R.H. Williams	floating crust
Sept. 1960		21lb.	G. Patterson	
Sept. 1960	mirror	22lb. 8oz.	G. Warner	crust
Oct. 1961	mirror	21lb.	C. Harris	
July 1962	mirror	23lb.	D. Mapstone	crust
1963	mirror	23lb. 4oz.	L. Starling	
Aug. 1964		24lb. 6oz.	B. Austin	crust
June 1966	mirror	26lb. 4oz.	W. Branch	crust
Aug. 1966		24lb. 14oz.	P. Henton	crust
Aug. 1968	common	24lb. 4oz.	R.H. Williams	crust

1. Atkinson also had further fish of 19½lb., 17½lb. and 7lb. in this fabulous opening-day catch.

Robert Atkinson's tally of five carp over 20lb., by June, 1959, was probably second only to Ken Bartlett's—Walker having caught four over this weight at that time, although one of them, his 23lb. common from Redmire, was foul-hooked. Valerie Noyce's capture of a 20lb. carp, in September, 1955, almost produced a further record for Stoneham. A few weeks earlier, May Berth-Jones had become the first woman to catch a 20lb. carp whilst fishing at Redmire Pool. However, May Berth-Jones was an accomplished angler and experienced carp fisher, whereas Valerie Noyce had never previously caught a fish of any description. She had gone bream fishing with her fiancé, Mr. R.W. Punter, and was fishing a clear area in a large bed of lilies. They were having no success with the bream but could hear the sound of carp sucking amongst the lily pads. Under the instructions of her fiancé, Valerie cast out a piece of floating crust on 13lb. b.s. line. and soon hooked her fish. For all her inexperience she did remarkably well to land the fish, the whole affair only taking about three minutes!

Although big carp continued to be caught from Stoneham Lakes right into the 1980's, the water appeared to decline dramatically in the 1970's for a variety of reasons. The decline had probably begun much earlier and the water was probably at its best in the 1950's. Certainly, amongst those in the know at this time it was recognised as a prodigious big carp water. During the early-1960's well known anglers such as Bill Keal, Alec Lewis (who were both unsuccessful) and Jack Hilton fished there on day tickets, in the company of successful local anglers like

Valerie Noyce's capture on the front page of Angling Times. Also mentioned in the same issue was 19-year old Ron Lalley, who later fished at Bracken Lake and Redmire Pool.

Splendid bag of opening-day carp

TWENTY minutes after midnight on opening day, Eastleigh (Hants.) angler Bob Atkinson landed his first fish — and thus began his "best ever opening," which in seven hours brought him carp of 23¼ lb., 19¼ lb., 17¼ lb. and 7 lb.

The "big three" were mirror carp and the small fish a common carp. All were taken on potato legered on 11 lb. b.s. line from a pond in Hampshire.

Bob, fishing two rods, got a "bird's nest" on one of his reels, and spent most of the night attempting to unravel this, in between playing the carp that took the bait on his other line.

At 7 a.m., having the two biggest carp and the smallest one in a sack, he decided to transfer them to his giant landing net to make sure they received plenty of oxygen. As he finished transferring them, the 17¼-pounder took his bait.

ALL RETURNED

Fellow angler Pete Rodaway came to his rescue, wedging the net with its rim above water, and dashing off for his own in which to land the carp.

All the fish were taken in a few feet of water in a clearing some thirty yards by fifteen. They were returned after weighing and photographing.

A. J. Baston, a member of Faversham (Kent) A.C.

Bob Atkinson with his four opening-day carp.

Bob Atkinson's tremendous catch, made on the opening day of the 1959 season. He caught the majority of his big carp from the Top Lake.

Les Starling. Les was one of the unsung masters of early-modern carp fishing. Bill Keal fished at Stoneham with Les and they jointly came to the conclusion that the Lake was too acidic to produce a record fish. Subsequently, Les teamed up with John Adams in the mid-1960's and they moved to Embley Park where Les caught a carp weighing over 27lb., his best ever. Although local legend has it that Jack Hilton never caught a carp from Stoneham, it is hard to know for sure. Les Starling seems to remember Jack catching a 5lb. common on one occasion. He was certainly very keen to acquire membership, and when Pirelli General A.C. lost the fishing rights in 1963 Jack was notified of this whilst spending the night on the nearby Hiltingbury Lake (now a park lake but then a very overgrown, free water that was known to hold carp weighing over 20lb.). He lost no time in moving onto Stoneham although he never really took to fishing the water at night. The Lakes were very 'spooky' in those days and were reputed to be haunted, so Jack, having a superstitious nature, was never entirely happy there once darkness had settled in.

Other anglers who fished successfully for carp at Stoneham were Stan Marchant, Bill Branch, Peter Henton, Terry Lampard, Rick Benham, Ray Banbury and Chris Currie. Stan Marchant deserves a mention for, unlike the others, he was not a serious carp angler; however, he was the head bailiff on the water from around 1963 to 1979 and was one of the founders of the Eastleigh Specimen Group.

During the 1989/90 winter both lakes at Stoneham were drained and dredged. Seine netting produced considerable numbers of small common carp, between 3lb. and 8lb., from the Bottom Lake with only four 'doubles'. The Top Lake also contained large numbers of small commons plus 15 'doubles' weighing up to 19lb. 10oz. The heaviest fish was 36in. in length, confirming the chronic decline of this once prodigious big carp fishery.

Austin's Lake, situated at Clacton-on-Sea, in Essex, was a water which suddenly sprung into the limelight in the summer of 1951, with the capture of two carp over 20lb., one of which, at that time, was only a few ounces short of Albert Buckley's record. They were both taken after dark on margin-fished crust, a method which had received quite a lot of publicity in the angling press and Bernard Venables' column in *The Daily Mirror*.

Austin's Lake in the early 1950's

Wadhurst, Stoneham & Contemporary Times

This auspicious start was followed by another fish of 20lb. 4oz. taken by F.W. Amos in August, 1954. Austin's lake was, in fact, a small, one acre clay pit belonging to a chap, surprisingly, named E. Austin! Along one bank ran St. Osyth Road and the other banks were surrounded by an orchard. The pit probably only contained about eight carp at this time—the largest, a fully-scaled mirror, was estimated to weigh somewhere in the region of 30lb. by Bill Keal and Alec Lewis, who spent many weekends night fishing there, and a week's holiday for three consecutive years. Apart from the very first visit, when Alec landed a 17-pounder and lost another, the pair found the fishing fairly difficult—one reason being the number of sunken trees which were something

Alec Lewis with his 17lb. 10oz. carp.

of a problem when fish were hooked. Alec Lewis managed only three fish during this time, the best weighing 17lb. 10oz., although the longest, by far, was a 30in. leather weighing a mere 12lb. (Robert Sinclair's fish of 25½lb. from the same water was 33in. long with a 28in. girth). Bill Keal fared even worse, landing just one carp, a fish of 17lb. 12oz. These meagre results were still considerably better than those achieved by the chap who played the alto saxophone in Eric Winston's band, at a nearby holiday camp. He fished almost every day during the summer season and landed one 14-pounder in three years!

Above: *Bill Keal with his hard-earned 17¾-pounder from Austin's Lake. Its length suggests the fish may have weighed considerably more at some stage.*
Right: *The Daily Express report of Chapman Pincher's catch.*

Two remarkable catches of carp were made around this time. The first, by Harry Chapman Pincher, took place at a private pool in West Surrey, in 1949, and consisted of twelve fish, between 8lb. and 12½lb., weighing in total 136lb. They were all taken, in three hours fishing, on roach tackle using small red worms as bait, and the captor claimed to have lost more fish than he landed. A few years later, in 1956, an even more remarkable catch occurred. This time, at a lake in the "South of England" the fortunate angler landed twenty-five carp, for a total weight of 309lb., which included two fish over 20lb.

192

The mention of large catches of carp brings to mind one made by Flt. Lieut. Burton, in 1943, using sunken crust—certainly one of the earliest occasions this method had been mentioned in print, in relation to carp fishing. Shortly after being invalided out of the War he found a small, very shallow (9 to 12in. deep) pond, at Hassocks, in Sussex, full of carp. But, no matter how he tried he could not tempt them. After some thought he came up with following:

"I decided that, as the water was so shallow and the bottom so muddy and they wouldn't take a floated bait, I would try them without a float, one tiny shot about 3in. from the hook and a big piece of fresh crust. The idea being that the shot would take the line down while the buoyancy of the crust would keep it off the mud, yet the position of the shot would not allow the crust to get to the top of the water.

Anyhow it worked. I landed 41 carp in 3¼ hours., the best 9lb. 2oz. and the smallest 2lb. 7oz." He returned the following day for another haul—19 fish in 3 hours with the largest weighing 15lb. 7oz., and big enough to take the second place in *The Angler's News* Notable Fish List for that year.

Woldale came to public prominence principally because of Maurice Ingham and his book *Drop Me A Line*. Maurice lived at Louth, in Lincolnshire, only half a dozen miles from Benniworth Haven, the true name of the lake and the woodland surrounding it. In fact, there were two lakes at Benniworth, the lower or Decoy Pond, which reputedly held very large tench, and the upper or House Pond, which had been stocked with 100 mirror carp, weighing between 5oz. and 10oz. each, on the 24th November, 1925. The fish grew well in their new environment and, on the 11th July, 1927, one of 5¼lb. was caught. Several more were landed a few days later, their weight varying between 3lb. 3oz. and 4lb. 14oz. The fish continued to thrive and in September, 1931 a fish of 12lb. 12oz. was landed by R.J. Willerton.

One of Maurice's earliest recollections of Benniworth Haven is of camping there with the Boy Scouts when he was about 10 years old. He vividly remembers that "the sun had just risen above the trees and was throwing a narrow band of sunlight along one side of the lake. Lined up in this sunlight, like pigs at a trough, were some huge carp!—there must have been a score or more."

The House Pond was a typical estate lake of about four acres, rather shallow for the most part, being nowhere more than five feet deep, and surrounded by bracken and ancient trees. The undergrowth almost reached down to the waters edge on the southern and eastern banks and two, large horse-chestnut trees overhung the lake at the north-eastern corner. It was fed by a small stream which eventually found its way into the River Bain. The western end was fringed with a wide belt of reedmace where there was often a proliferation of bottom weed. In this shallow sanctuary the carp often basked in hot, sunny weather.

J.E. Watson with his 14lb. 14oz. carp from Woldale, caught on August 2nd, 1950. The fish was set-up and found its way into the fisherman's hut at Croxby Pond, where John Watson also fished. It was only the 2nd double-figure fish, that Maurice Ingham knew of when he began fishing at Woldale, that had been caught from there since the end of the Second World War.

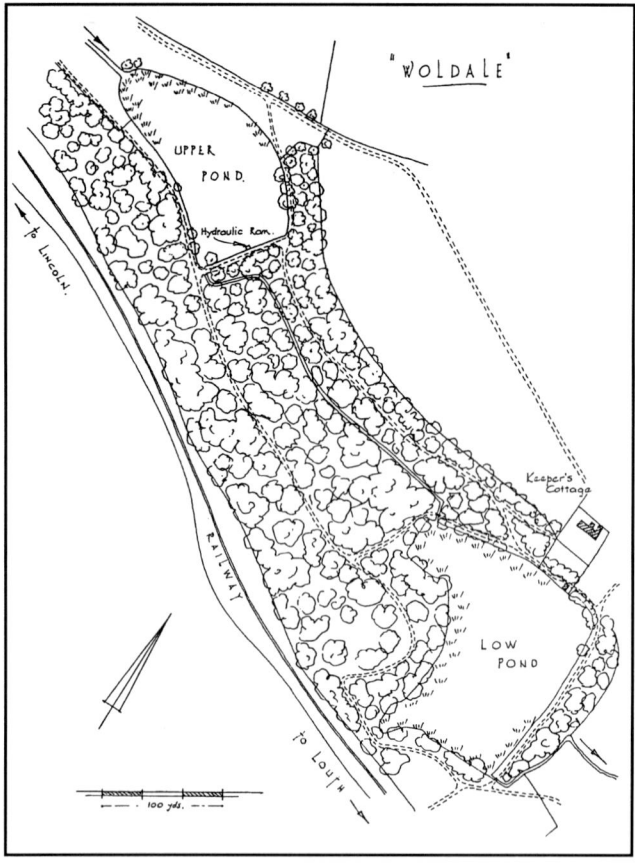

Maurice Ingham's early map of Benniworth Haven, showing the keeper's cottage where, in later years, the syndicate members and friends often stayed on their fishing trips.

Only a handful of carp over 10lb. had previously been caught at Woldale (Maurice only knew of two prior to the Second World War and two subsequently), and he stated that "the majority of the people who fish there seem to regard a break as the natural consequence of hooking a big fish." Furthermore, Maurice added, "I must confess that I am sufficiently selfish to say that this suits my purpose very well and I do nothing to dispel the legend of uncatchability."

During the 1950's, when Maurice spent much of his fishing time at Woldale, occasionally being accompanied by Richard Walker and several other members of the Carp Catchers' Club, and their friends, the carp they caught were what might nowadays be termed 'mid-doubles'. Indeed, Dick remarked that "it would seem that the Woldale carp are all one brood" with the average being about 15lb., and Maurice's first Woldale carp of 17lb. being the largest. Yet, certainly Dick Walker thought that Woldale held fish capable of beating the then record of 26lb. After his first visit in 1950, he wrote that, "I wouldn't mind betting there are several record carp there. The one that took my worm was the biggest I've ever seen, except for the Arlesey monster; bigger than 'Pickle-Barrel', I think." But Maurice wasn't

The Upper Lake in 1957.

convinced. In his first contribution to the Carp Catchers' Club's rotary letters, he wrote that "Both B.B. and Dick seem to think that Woldale holds carp of record-breaking size, but I do not share their view in this instance. I have known Woldale a good many years, and I suppose I have seen, at one time or another, most of the carp in the pond, but I have never seen any which I would class as possible record-breakers."

Initially, the fishing at Benniworth Haven was available to anyone on payment of 1/- to the keeper, but, in the September, 1951 issue of *The Midland Angler,* a short feature appeared giving full details of the fishing there. The owner, Lord Heneage, decided therefore, that in order to control the amount of anglers who fished the lake in the future, only a very limited number of permits would be made available.

Joe Taylor about to land cousin Ken's carp from the dam at Woldale. Fred Taylor also caught a 16-pounder which qualified him for membership of the C.C.C.

In 1956, a sporting syndicate approached the owner with a view to renting Benniworth Haven, destroying the coarse fish in the lakes and stocking with trout, in addition to using them for duck shooting. The estate manager asked Maurice Ingham what he felt about such a venture and the outcome was that Maurice and Paul Marshall formed a small syndicate, called The Wold Angling Association, which rented Benniworth for the princely sum of £40. This situation remains the case to the present day.

```
       MEMORANDUM OF AGREEMENT between the Exors. of the 2nd.
Baron Heneage by their Agents, Messrs. Smith-Woolley & Co.,
Estate Office, Hainton, (hereinafter called the landlords)
of the one part, and Mr. Paul Marshall of Brook Cottage,
Tealby, Lincs., (hereinafter called the tenant) of the other
part.

1.         The landlords agree to let and the tenant to take the
      fishing rights in the lakes and waters situated in the area
      known as Benniworth Haven (hereinafter called the Haven) in
      the Parish of Benniworth, Lincs., the details of which are
      contained in the schedule below, from the 15th. day of June
      1956 until the 15th. day of April 1957.

2.         The rent shall be the sum of £40 (forty pounds) per
      annum payable in advance in two installments of £20 (twenty
      pounds) each on the 1st. day of June and the 1st. day of
      December, the first payment to be made on the 1st. day of
      June 1956.
```

Part of the original syndicate agreement for the fishing rights to the two lakes at Benniworth.

Woldale was perhaps the epitome of B.B.'s images of what a carp water should be—secret and hidden, a tree-girt pool smelling of carp and mud and water plants. It comes as no surprise that Richard Walker remembered Benniworth as "the most atmospheric place I have ever fished, much more so than Redmire Pool." Only in such magical places do badgers come and ferret in your rucksack, so close you could reach out and touch them. This relationship with wild creatures was a regular occurrence for those fortunate enough to fish there.

Wadhurst, Stoneham & Contemporary Times

Happy fishing holidays at Benniworth Haven. **From left to right, back row:** *Peter and Pat Thomas, Richard jnr., Simon and Ruth Walker, Margaret and Pat Russell.* **Front row:** *Jane and Paul Thomas, 'The Master', Tim Walker, Shaun and Gina Russell.*

The cordial relationship with the owners resulted in the fishing syndicate being offered the keeper's cottage for their own use. This produced many family holiday trips for the members and their friends. Shaun Russell, the son of Pat Russell, remembers, as a small boy, being woken up at the crack of dawn with the other children, to be taken down to the lake to be shown 'huge' carp caught by their parents.

Maurice Ingham waits to land Dick Walker's 16¼lb. carp from Woldale. The pair were featured in a radio programme by Bernard Venables and Bill Latto that was broadcast on the Midland Home Service, on July 20th, 1953 at 7.45pm. The recording was almost unsuccessful, for with just a few moments to go to the 6am deadline Walker hooked his fish. The first broadcast on the subject of carp fishing took place on September 26th, 1950, on the Midland Home Service, when B.B. and Walker spoke about a visit they had made to Hunstrete Lake.

The earlier mention of Dick's "Arlesey monster" is intriguing. The Hitchin Angling Club's 20 acre clay pit, Arlesey Lake, which they had controlled since 1932, became famous for its monster perch, but Dick occasionally referred to a huge carp he claimed lurked in its depths. In the C. C. Club's rotary letters, in 1951, he described Arlesey Lake and wrote:

"There is a monster carp here, which weighs over 40lb., of that I am certain, though I don't expect anyone else to believe me! In 1949 I put in some carp from Temple Pool, biggest 5¾lb. (one weighing 10lb. 2oz. was caught on September 1st, 1951). Apart from the big one, which I surmise is the one which I know a friend transferred from Bearton Pond in 1938 on my behalf (I caught it, it weighed 15lb. 3oz.), I don't know of any other carp having been introduced, except a number of small ones last year." Subsequently, 1,000 4-5in. carp were delivered by lorry to Arlesey Lake from The Surrey Trout Farm in November, 1952. They were purchased with part of the proceeds of the £250 Hitchin A.C. had received by winning Region B of *The Daily Mirror* Angling Contest, which was in its third year of operation. Interestingly, Bob Richards was awarded a *Daily Mirror* prize rod at the luncheon, held at the Savoy Hotel, for his 31¼lb. Redmire carp. Dick Walker was also in attendance, representing Hitchin A.C. and also for catching the largest perch in the Competition, a fish of 4lb. 13oz., and he took this opportunity to present Bob with his record carp which he had set-up in a glass case.

The carp fishing at Arlesey Lake gradually improved and became a viable proposition. The first serious encounter with the Arlesey carp came about accidentally one day in November, 1958 when Frank Guttfield and Bernard Everitt were roach fishing. They hooked and lost six carp between them. Further attempts for the 'monsters of the bay', which are described in Frank Guttfield's book *In Search of Big Fish,* also proved disastrous, although on one occasion Frank did retrieve a large scale from a common carp. In later years the lake did produce a number of carp over 20lb., and was fished by several well-known carp anglers including Alan Wilkie and Rob Maylin, but nobody ever caught Walker's 40lb. monster!

The early-1950's saw the first real growth in carp fishing popularity. Richard Walker listed the reasons for this, as he saw them, in the rotary letters of the C.C.C., in May, 1952. They were:

1. The writings of B.B.—both books and articles, which were widely read.
2. The capture of several monster carp at Dagenham, which had stirred the imagination of the angling public.
3. His *(Richard Walker)* own continual plugging of the subject in the angling press.
4. Bernard Venables' regular insistence on the merits of carp for stocking, and his Mr. Crabtree 'strip' in which he had ascribed two good methods of carp fishing. His *Daily Mirror* features were very widely read.
5. Bob Richards' capture of a new record fish which showed what tremendous growth rates these fish could achieve.

Right: *B.B.'s letter to The Angler's News asking for contributions to a book which subsequently inspired a great many anglers to start carp fishing. The Fisherman's Bedside Book originally had been given the title of 'An Anglers' Anthology'.*

A BOOK OF FISHING STORIES
Dear Sir—I am editing a book for anglers, which will contain personal accounts of the capture of notable fish, chiefly Carp, Pike, Bream, Tench, and Perch. If any of your readers would care to send me written accounts of their captures I should be happy to look through them, and those selected will be paid for when the book is published in 1945.
The kind of account I want is one giving details of weather, time of day and year, bait used, and tackle used, and as vivid as possible, "painting the picture" as it were.
Do you publish a list of notable fish caught, if so where can I obtain it? I should be enormously grateful if you could co-operate in this matter by publishing my letter.—Yours faithfully, D. WATKINS-PITCHFORD ("BB"), Shrublands House, Welford, Rugby, 23rd Oct.

Wadhurst, Stoneham & Contemporary Times

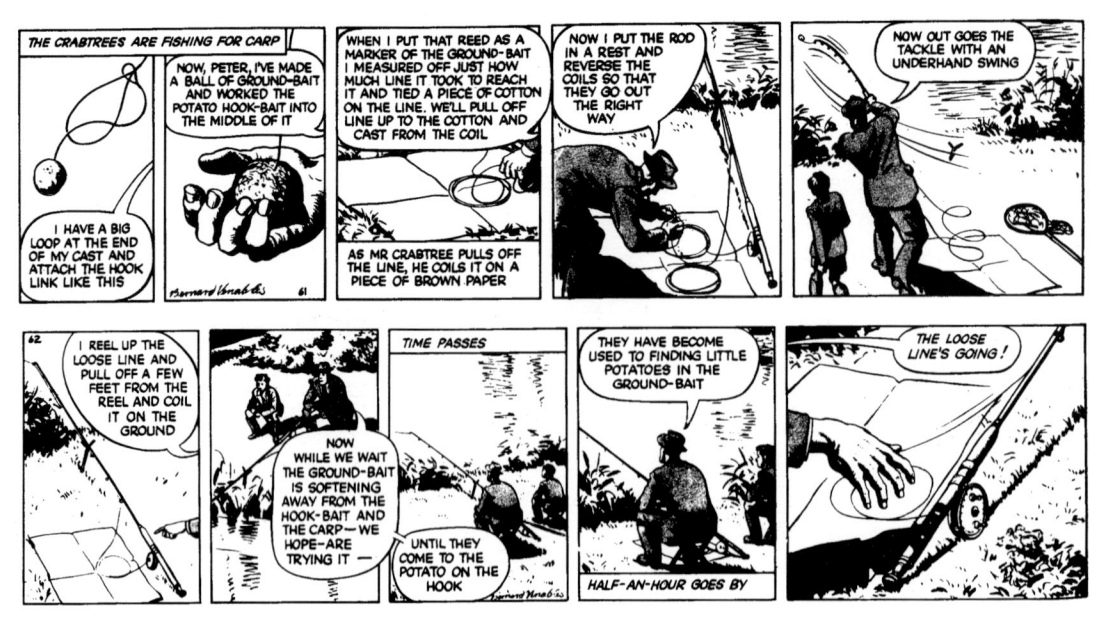

Bernard Venables' strip, which Dick Walker, in 1952, correctly pointed out had been an influence in the increased popularity of carp fishing.

Walker then went on to predict, with uncanny accuracy, that "the popularity of carp fishing is increasing very rapidly and is likely to continue to do so."

The Carp Catchers' Club was conceived during an assault on the carp of Mapperley Reservoir, in June 1951. Those present were Dick Walker, B.B., Maurice Ingham and John Norman. Shortly afterwards, Harry Grief, of Dagenham, and Jack Smith, of Bradford-on-Avon, were invited to join. Then, after Bob Richards' broke the carp record, in October of that year, he also became a member.

The C.C.C's rotary letter list of members, from August, 1951, shortly after the Club was formed. Although John Norman did not fulfill one of the membership regulations, that of having caught a carp over 10lb., this appears to have been overlooked due to the fact that he was present at Mapperley. Walker's knowledge of matters appertaining to carp was consummate. His note "First a seizling..." was taken from Randle Holmes extraordinary book, Accadamié of Armoury, where every sort of fish is named after their age and growth.

198

In early 1952, Dick raised the subject of extending the membership further, with the qualification that he thought it shouldn't increase much over about ten. He also attempted to list the original aims of the Club. These were—"the interchange of information and ideas" and "the encouragement of clubs, etc., to stock still-waters with carp." Several names were put forward for membership—the conditions for acceptance being that the existing members should unanimously approve and that the individual had caught a carp of over 10lb. in weight. This second proviso was slightly flawed since, at that time, John Norman's largest carp was below the qualifying weight. However, since he had been present during the creation of the Club this was conveniently overlooked in his case. The Club's president, Denys Watkins-Pitchford, suggested Don Leney but Dick Walker objected, simply on the grounds that Leney was not "a carp catcher, except with nets." Maurice Ingham proposed Pete Thomas, who became a member during the spring of 1952. In May, 1952 Walker suggested several other possible anglers for consideration. These were George Draper and Sid Bradbury, who fished at Dagenham, Dick Kefford, of Wickham Market, Bernard Venables, and Frank Dobson from Manchester. Walker felt the last three were particularly worthy of consideration.

Of these, only Bernard Venables was initially invited to become a member, and he accepted during August, 1952. In November, 1953 Gerry Berth-Jones joined this illustrious group. Then, several years passed by with no variation in the membership until the summer of 1957, when John Norman died suddenly. During early October of that year, Bernard Venables tendered his resignation due to pressure of work, believing that he "did not have the time to be a useful member of the Carp Catchers' Club." Invitations were swiftly issued by the secretary, Richard Walker, to Dick Kefford, Fred J. Taylor and Bob Reynolds, but the impetus of the Club had clearly been already lost by this time and it simply faded away.

Maurice Ingham proposed Pete Thomas, who had no trouble with the proviso that he must have caught a carp over 10lb. Here he is with a 16-pounder, but Pete's labrador, Ross, is not impressed!

In much the same way as Woldale is intrinsically linked with Maurice Ingham, so another member of the Carp Catchers' Club is associated with Hunstrete Lake, or Lackey's Leap as it was nicknamed. Jack Smith had known the lake since 1934; it was about five acres in extent and shaped, roughly, like a boomerang. Along the northern bank ran a thick belt of trees; the southern side being fairly open apart from thick growths of willow-herb, hemp agrimony and other water-loving plants.

Hunstrete Lake

Wadhurst, Stoneham & Contemporary Times

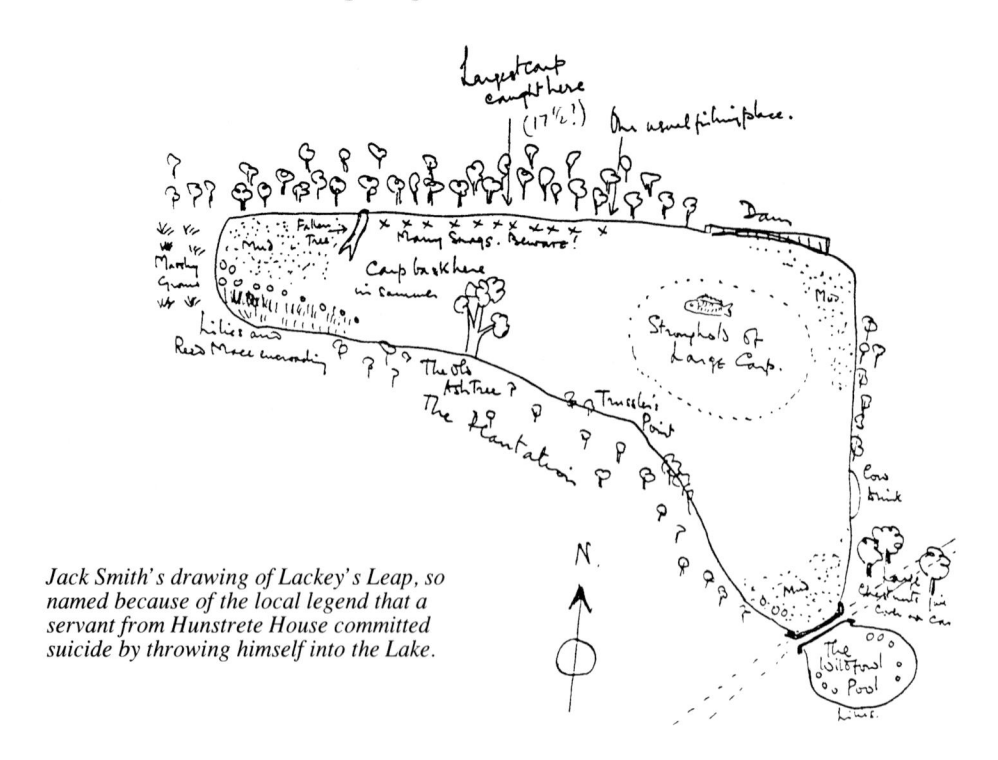

Jack Smith's drawing of Lackey's Leap, so named because of the local legend that a servant from Hunstrete House committed suicide by throwing himself into the Lake.

Local folklore has it that following the Dissolution of the Monasteries, in 1536 and 1539, the estate came into the possession of the Popham family.

When the author fished a famous carp water at Hemingford Grey he had the dubious pleasure of making the acquaintance of Joe, the bailiff. He was a man whose yarns were only matched by his ability to relieve you of your small change, and it seems that Jack Smith came across a similar soul (but whose name was infinitely more suited) at Hunstrete. Jack gave this amusing account in September, 1951:

"Apart from the lake being little known and fairly inaccessible, it has a jealous guardian in the person of Trussler, the head keeper, who gives short shrift to trespassers. He is, however, extremely helpful to bona fide anglers who have permission to fish, but some of his stories should be accepted with the proverbial grain of salt since he is gifted with an extremely vivid imagination. It is from his fertile brain that the legend of the 27½-pounder has sprung, and although I have heard the story many times in varying forms I have never been able to establish its authenticity. The largest carp of which I have knowledge of is a 17-pounder caught by my brother in July, 1945. My own record is a mere 15½-pounder. Personally, I should be surprised if a record breaker were taken at Hunstrete, since the fish are of a rakish appearance and thin for their length and, while this makes for good fighting qualities, I doubt whether they would attain the weight of their more corpulent brethren in other lakes."

Dick Kefford with a "rakish" Hunstrete carp caught in July, 1953.

Jack Smith's assessment proved correct. The size of the monastic carp of Hunstrete would never impress those whose consuming interest now lay in beating Buckley's record, yet those carp were looked back on as perhaps the hardest fighting fish that members of the Carp Catchers' Club had ever encountered. Richard Walker commented that "the carp at Hunstrete are the fastest I know."

One winter, in the early-1970's, the author's Boxing Day stupor was disturbed by a telephone call from a slightly inebriated Rod Hutchinson. "Are you interested in buying a stuffed carp?" was the query which seemed to be crying out for a fall guy! Rod proffered the information that he had already been in touch with Trevor Moss, a noted Lincolnshire tackle dealer, but for some strange reason he didn't appear interested. I was at a loss to imagine why! The fish was in a local antique shop and was on sale for a very modest sum. However, Rod expected it would be sold very soon after the shop opened following the Christmas holidays.

A.A. Slade's cased Holbrook Park carp. Now the property of the author, it was incorrectly claimed to be the 3rd largest ever caught at the time of its capture.

Anyway, the author had to see it through and is pleased to say that after immediately driving over to Grimsby, and through Rod's kind assistance with finding the antique shop owners address, he purchased a magnificent example of a large cased carp by the taxidermist J. Cooper & Sons. The inscription on the bowed glass stated 'Leather Carp—25lb., caught at Horsham by A.A. Slade, 1st July 1951'. Subsequent investigations showed that it was probably the 4th largest carp caught on rod and line at the time of capture and that the following details of its capture appeared in *The Sunday Express* of July 8th, 1951:

"A.A. Slade of 7 Staines Road, Twickenham, went fishing after being ill. His friend B. Evans, of Hove, concocted a special groundbait of soaked bread and biscuit meal and threw it into Horsham Lake. Mr. Slade's tackle consisted of leger tackle, no. 6 hook, 12lb. line and a 'river rod' made of greenheart. He cast out 30 yards into a 6ft. deep swim using lobworm as bait. The fish, which was 31¼in. in length with a 26½in. girth, was landed after a fight lasting 20 minutes."

By an amazing co-incidence the author mentioned this fish to Dick Kefford, one of the legendary members of the Carp Catchers' Club, who, it turned out, had met Mr. Evans in his veterinary surgery on the 29th June, 1961. Their talk progressed to fishing and Mr. Evans related how his friend had caught this particular carp from a small, 100-yard-long pond, which was quite weedless, yet held a number of big carp and tench. In fact, a fish of 25lb. was also caught by R.G. Parker and reported from Horsham that same year, as was another of 22lb. 12oz., caught by A.C. Luxford on crust, in July, 1957.

Ken Drayton had been a schoolboy pal of Nat Sheckell. After the War a chance meeting in Grimsby found them discussing their mutual interest of angling. During the conversation Nat mentioned a private water he had permission to fish, at North Thoresby, and suggested that a deal could be struck whereby the luxury of Ken's motor car provided the transport and Nat would fix up the permits. Walter Butt owned three ponds next to his house and was very keen on fishing. He only allowed a few close friends, and their guests, permission to fish, and these included Harry and Nat Sheckell. All the ponds held carp—in fact, during 1915 Harry and Walter Butt captured over 200 carp between them, a substantial number coming from Mr. Butt's ponds.

Nat and Ken used to fish the ponds once a week, usually in the one they called the House Pond. The largest of the three, which was called the Big Pond, was only about ½-acre but was full of weed and was difficult to fish without prior preparation. Nat believed that this one held the biggest carp, but carp fishing was not their chosen quarry. Then, one evening, as the light began to fall and they started to pack their tackle away, they heard a loud sucking noise, like the last surge of water going down the plug hole in a bath. In the dimming light they caught a glimpse of a carp, slowly, ponderously drawing their discarded bread into the inviolate depths. The only rod capable of doing battle with such a monster that they possessed was a pike rod so, quickly rigging up, Ken cast out a large lump of bread crust. An almighty swirl, a strike and a determined battle followed. But fortune favours the brave and a mighty carp soon lay in the deep grass, its gills beating in rhythm with Ken's

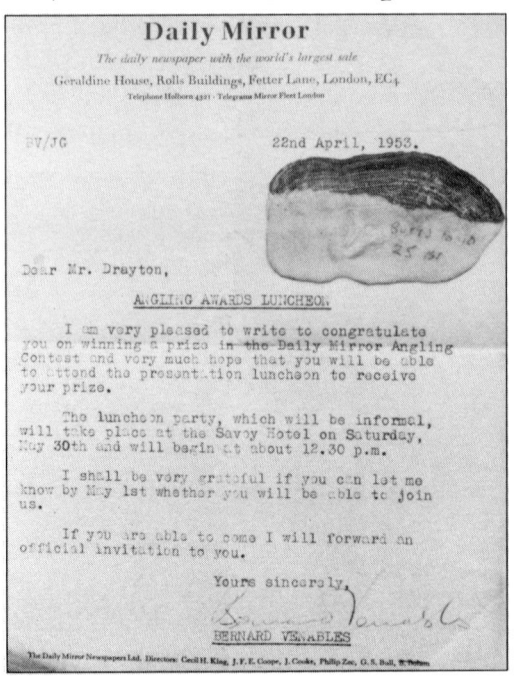

Ken Drayton's 25lb. carp won him a prize in the 1953 Daily Mirror Angling Competition. A scale from the fish is shown with the award invitation.

bursting heart! Then, after an intoxicating moment's gaze at the ultimate beauty of the wild creature, when, for a fraction of time man becomes an integral part of nature, Ken gave it its freedom. It was July, 1952 and it was the 7th largest carp ever caught, and many an angler would have thought little of killing it. But no vain display in a taxidermist's glass box or pitiful disposal on the rubbish heap at the bottom of the garden, its destiny in this case was determined by Walter Butt who had decreed that under no circumstances could any carp be killed. Yet the memory lingers strong in the mind of Ken Drayton, no faded photograph or taxidermist's hand could make it more vivid. The fish and man are forever linked—drawn together, as one drop of water mingles with another on a window pane spotted with rain. The following year, in August, Ken caught a 17-pounder from the same pond.

In the summer of 1952, Bernard Venables made his first contribution to the rotary letters of the Carp Catchers' Club. One of the qualifications of his membership had been the capture of a carp weighing more than 10lb., which he had achieved by catching fish of 16lb. 15oz., 19lb. and 13½lb. in a few trips to a local water called Goffs Park, near Crawley. The fishing subsequently became open to the general public but Bernard remembers the difficulty he had in catching those fish. In 1952 the small, shallow pool was owned by an old lady of 95 who disliked anglers and objected to angling. Her bailiff, however, regarded this an eccentricity and, under certain circumstances, would allow the occasional angler to fish providing they arrived late and departed early! The pool, unfortunately, was near the owner's house, so frontal attack was precluded! This meant going through the 'backdoor'—which in this case consisted of climbing two fences and crawling through a mass of brambles and nettles.

An 18¾lb. carp, caught by Bernard from Goffs Park in August, 1953. Here the fish is being set-up in taxidermist Rowland Ward's workshop. The case was subsequently sold at auction some 37 years later, and purchased by well-known angler and writer Pete Rogers, for £836.

Years later, after the Park had been taken over by Crawley Council, Bernard went back for another look. He wrote of his feelings in his column in *Angling Times* and the following extracts give another example of the pitfalls involved in returning to the scene of a much earlier angling success:

"I did not go in by the gates, though they stand open now. I went in as I used to go, over the iron fence from the road and quietly under the trees and skirting the brambles until I came to the next iron fence. This one could only be reached by pushing through the fierce thicket and clinging brambles.

It was no easy passage now in daylight; how slowly, tortuously, and often painfully difficult it had been in those former days when I came always after the fall of summer dark.

Now, over the fence, I went at an angle to the end of the hedge and round it, and then along the overgrown path that goes past the crumbling greenhouse. I had walked that path so often in the old days that I could do it without faltering on the most blackly impenetrable night (and deeply black it could be under the hanging canopy of the trees).

The path was the same; the greenhouse stood as it had, perhaps a little more decayed, but the impact on the fliching senses was no longer there. These now were just neglected grounds, like many that lie round rather big old houses from which the old grandeur has drained away with time.

As I remember it there had been a spell upon the place; each step taken into it had seemed like the throwing of a brick into the lurking stillness of a hidden pool.

But it was all different now; on the lawn across which I had stolen, avoiding the rose beds by a bat's sense of proximity rather than by sight of eye, there was now a ball game, and resting parents lay on the grass with tennis shirts and summer frocks.

Ah, and there—there is the lake; still as it was, shrouded to dark secrecy by the heavy thickness of the trees. But, really, that is only the superficial appearance. The secrecy has gone.

Well, this place that had been so secretly recluse as I had known it, almost forbidding, is now public. One old woman, burdened with a tremendous count of years, had shut herself and her memories in the house and left the grounds to nature. Now the gates are open and the chatter and the paper and the trample have shattered the old atmosphere. It will be tidied up I expect, with notice boards and rules.

Perhaps the carp will live on, and there may even be fishing for them allowed, but there will never be again the fishing that I remember."

The carp did live on and following in the footsteps of Bernard, John Nixon and others also fished there with some success, catching fish to over 20lb.

"...shrouded to dark secrecy by the heavy thickness of trees." Goff's Park in 1954.

In November, 1952 a little over 100 yearling carp were dispatched from the Surrey Trout Farm the few miles along the A287 to Frensham. This had little impact on carp fishing until the late-1970's and early-1980's, when Frensham Little Pond's catches started to make people sit up and take notice. However, this period takes us outside the book's scope, which has been well documented in any event, but it might be interesting to detail a few of the facts about Frensham's early history. There are actually two ponds at Frensham, although pond is something of a misnomer, since the Great Pond is about 60 acres and the Little Pond about 35 acres. They have existed, and contained carp, since at least the 17th century. Prior to the outbreak of the Second World War the Little Pond belonged to Mr. Richard Combes, who lived in Pierrepoint House. The Pond was often referred to as the "Gem of the Surrey Lakeland", understandably because of its inherent charm, with sweeping woods on one side and open, rolling hillside on the other. Mr. Combes was the president of the Farnham Angling Society and he, along with many of the members, had some fine catches from the Pond. However, with the outbreak of the Second World War, in common with many other still-waters up and down the country, Farnham Ponds were drained and the fish transferred elsewhere. Throughout the duration of the War the Little Pond lay empty, and gradually its fertile bed was taken over with scrub and pine trees. It remained neglected until 1949 when the property was purchased by Mr. F.S.D. Atherton. He was a naturalist, and Fellow of the Royal Zoological Society, as well as being an angler of experience and repute and, realising the possibilities that the Pond offered, he set about restoring it to its former glory. He went to a great deal of trouble and expense in having it cleaned out prior to it being re-flooded, and many thousands of fish of all species, including trout and, of course, the Leney carp, were introduced. Mr. Atherton, who took over the presidency of the Farnham A.S., then kindly allowed anyone to fish this beautiful eldorado for a modest sum. It is to Mr. Atherton, and like-minded sportsmen, that subsequent generations of carp fishermen have to thank for their legacies.

In 1954, two additional specialist carp fishing groups were formed, following in the footsteps of the Carp Catchers' Club. In May, 1954 the Claredon Carp Catchers Club held its first meeting in Leicester and, the following week, the Midland Carp Catchers Club was set up in Birmingham. The headquarters of the latter were to be found at the inspirationally named Golden Carp Cafe, in Lozells Road, Birmingham. The elected chairman was Bill Taylor, the Cafe proprietor, who fished for the Plants Brook Pool carp on the outskirts of that industrial capital. The Club was a success in many ways, holding regular monthly meetings for a number of years and acquired, and stocked, its own fishery in 1959.

Also, early in 1954, four common-scaled carp were found dead at the Sawmill's Lake, near Wotton Underwood. They became a part of carp fishing folklore because of the mention they received in Fred J. Taylor's marvellous book *Angling in Earnest* and, also, in Jack Hilton's *Quest for Carp* where, incidentally, they had, for some inexplicable reason, been transformed into the largest wild carp ever seen in this country. This view was perpetuated by Chris Ball in the January, 1991 issue of *Carpworld,* when he wrote that "All these dead carp were the English 'wild' strain.[1] To my knowledge this represented very near the limit in size for the original strain of carp that inhabited our shores before the 'kings' took over." As a matter of fact, neither Fred J. Taylor, in his book, or the original report in *Angling Times* mentions that the fish were 'wild' carp. To put the matter straight they were neither wild carp, nor did the largest weigh anything like the claimed 29½lb.

That same year Tiddenfoot Pit, near Leighton Buzzard, produced its first carp over twenty pounds, a fish weighing 22lb. taken by A.W. Albutt in July, and caught on bread paste. And Bracken Lake, in Sussex, was also soon to gain notoriety with a string of big common carp, several weighing over 20lb. This particular fishery, a picturesque, ten acre lake surrounded by steeply sloping banks of dense woods and impenetrable undergrowth, had been taken over by a small group of carp fishing enthusiasts in late 1952. Cut off from the outside world, with the nearest point of access half-a-mile away, the members set themselves the Herculean task of creating a first class carp fishery. The lake was choked with weed, and infested with small fish and eels which stripped the hook of almost every conceivable bait. In 1953, just two carp were hooked and lost, on baits which consisted of anywhere between 50 and 150 maggots.

1. This is, in itself, incorrect because wild carp are not a 'strain'.

Bracken Lake in the early-1950's.

They had been threaded carefully onto cotton or fuse wire, and wrapped around the carp hooks. The following year brought similarly miserable results, with the exception of a 15½-pounder taken on paste. Yet the work and enthusiasm continued, unabated. Thousands of small fish were caught on rod and line and removed. Sunken trees were manually pulled from their watery grave and swims where hewn from the sloping banks. Some 2,500 hours of work had been expended—for one fish! Half the original members had dropped out, leaving just five stubborn individuals. New members were brought in and a local man was enlisted to groundbait on a regular basis. Finally, after three years of toil the first real success came in 1955 with the following fish being caught, mainly on potato or flour dumplings.

Some of the Bracken syndicate removing sunken trees in the 1950's. Left to right they are: Arthur Stone, L.C. 'Ron' Burton, Albert Buckley, Murray Rooker, Ian Crisp, and a friend of Murray's.

August 28th	Ron Lalley	15¾lb. (a founder, and youngest member)
September 3rd.	Murray Rooker	11¾lb.
September 3rd.	Murray Rooker	15lb.
September 4th.	Arthur Stone	16½lb.
September 5th.	Arthur Stone	10½lb.
September 8th.	Murray Rooker	12¾lb.
September 11th.	Jack Opie	10¾lb.
September 22nd.	Murray Rooker	11½lb.
September 22nd.	Murray Rooker	9½lb.
September 28th.	Kenneth Stuart	10½lb.

With the ending of the season the total had risen to twenty fish for a total weight of 152½lb., yet the biggest remained still at 16½lb. Perhaps some of the members began to doubt the existence of any larger fish, maybe they had been guilty of over-estimating the fish they had seen in the water. However, during the following season their hopes were finally realised when two magnificent common carp over 20lb. were landed. Arthur Stone had one of 21lb. 8oz. and Dr. C.H. Opie another of 22lb.

Arthur Stone with his magnificent 21½-pounder, just reward for all the hard work and dogged perserverance.

John Nixon followed it up the next year with a fish of 20lb., and some time later so did Murray Roker. His friend, Leslie Burton, wrote a moving and evocative description of the latter capture in 1965:

"....I was winding in my line when Murray called softly across the water, 'I think I've done it, boys!', and instantly I recalled that slipping clutch a few moments previously. My pulse quickened at the thought, for I knew what those words meant; Murray had got his first twenty-pounder!

I shall always remember the scene which greeted our arrival round the other side. Murray stood motionless in his shirt-sleeves, against a background of moonlight-dappled water. He said nothing but we sensed the emotion of a man who had finally gained his cherished ambition after years of trying."

John Nixon with his 20-pounder from Bracken.

Ian Crisp admires Murray Rooker's gorgeous fish, just a few ounces short of 20lb. The fish was landed to the "soft, metallic, rhythmic beat of the West Indian Bongo"—someone, away in the distance, was having a party!

Wadhurst, Stoneham & Contemporary Times

In 1954, one of the few female carp anglers, Kathleen Holmes, had an ambition to catch a double-figure carp. The following season, and by then married to successful carp angler Dave Steuart, (who subsequently wrote the *How to Catch Them—Carp* book) she achieved it with a fine fish of 12lb. 12oz. She went on to catch, as did her husband, many fine carp and, by 1960, she had landed 30 over 10lb., a remarkable, and almost certainly unmatched, achievement for a woman at that time. One of the waters they fished during this period was called Horton Pool, which was also frequented by John Goddard and Cliff Glenton. The pool's inhabitants, which included some huge eels, were, unfortunately, wiped out during the severe winter of 1962/63. Not long after this the site was consumed by the building of the Queen Mother Reservoir.

Above: Her ambition fulfilled—Kay Steuart with the 12¾lb. Horton carp.

Left: Kay Steuart, with May Berth-Jones, were the most accomplished female carp anglers of the 1950's. Here she is with 4 'double-figure' carp from Horton Pool.

During 1956, Derrick Davenport landed a 22½lb. fish from Sussex, and thereby joined the small band of anglers who could claim to have caught two carp over 20lb., and just the second man to have achieved this from different waters.

Oughton Pond, in Hitchin, was a small pool about 40 yards long and 20 yards wide that was stocked, by Dick Walker, with carp in 1950. Some readers of the book *Redmire Pool* may remember that the 28lb. carp from Bernithan, caught by Pete Thomas, was transported back to Hitchin alive. It, too, was released into Oughton Pond but succumbed shortly afterwards from its ordeal. Dick introduced nine carp (a mixture of mirror, common and leather) weighing 3lb., 4lb., 4lb., 4½lb., 5lb., 5½lb., 5¾lb., 7lb. and 7lb. from Temple Pool (Hexton Manor), the home of the infamous 'Pickle-Barrel' which featured in *Drop Me a Line* and *Be Quiet and Go a-Angling*. In May, 1956, Oughton Pond was drained and seven, from the original nine, carp, plus about 150 small offspring, were transferred by members of the Hitchin A.C. to Maylin's Pool, near Henlow. A few years later Jack Hilton (who, incidentally, began fishing in 1958 and became interested in carp after reading *Still-Water Angling* and *Drop Me a Line*), Frank Guttfield, Kenny Ewington, Roy Wicks and other anglers, were trying to catch those very same fish. It was here, incidentally, that Jack caught his very first 'double-figure' carp in September, 1960 which is described in his book *Quest for Carp,* although a pseudonym, in the form of Junelins, was used to protect the fishery's identity. About 25 years later the pool, and surrounding property, was bought by another successful carp angler, Kevin Maddocks, who developed the fishery into a first class syndicate water. It is an amusing thought to consider that there may be a carp still alive in Withy Pool which has been caught by Dick Walker, Jack Hilton and Kevin Maddocks!

Oughton Pond, at Hitchin, being drained prior to being filled in, after complaints from mothers on a local housing estate. At one stage an onlooker claimed he had seen an unexploded bomb amongst the rubbish, with the result that operations were suspended whilst the police investigated. Dick Walker is to the left of centre, arms raised, no doubt giving instruction on the scientific principles governing the workings of a lift pump.

It was about the time that Jack Hilton began fishing Maylin's that he, his brother-in-law Kenny Ewington, and Roy Wicks decided to form the Hertfordshire Carp Catchers Club. However, after a disastrous season at Maylin's they had second thoughts about their carp fishing ambitions and decided to rename themselves the Hertfordshire Specimen Group! At a later stage it merged with another group and became the Herts./Chiltern Specimen Group, developing into one of the most successful big fish groups in the country. As a matter of interest, Jack Hilton wrote an article about his unsuccessful season at Maylin's in the June 16th, 1962 issue of *The Fishing Gazette*, summing it up as follows:

"Total fishing hours spent at the pool, 1230; miles travelled to and from the water, 8020; loaves of bread used as groundbait and hook-baits, 270; freshwater mussels, 750; processed meat, 40lb.; carp caught, nil!" In the feature he mentioned a very large carp that he had seen in Maylin's, that was "as near to 30lb. as would make no difference" and which he nicknamed—Brenda. By a strange twist of fate the present owner's wife is also called Brenda! Later that season, in October, Jack got to grips with another famous water, Cheshunt, and caught eight double-figure carp on potatoes, the best weighing 16lb.

Jack Hilton with a 14½lb. carp, caught on potato whilst night-fishing Cheshunt Reservoir in the autumn of 1962.

Two pools on the outskirts of Birmingham next come into the fray. The lake at Esso Hall, Little Aston, produced a number of large carp around this time, most notably to Fred Darling and culminating for him in the following fish:

July 1958	25lb.	potato
July 1960	26lb. 10oz.	floating crust
August 1961	23lb. 6oz.	paste and crust
July 1963	21lb. 8oz.	potato

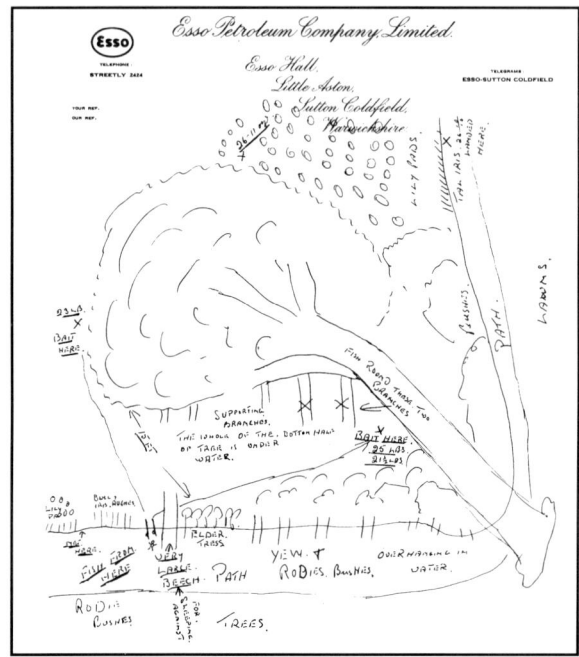

Above: Fred Darling with his 21½-pounder.
Left: Fred playing a carp at Little Aston Lake.
Bottom left: The map drawn by Fred in 1963, showing the precise positions where he caught his 20-pounders. They were all hooked close to the branches of a partly-submerged tree.

In August, 1959 17-year-old Peter Giles, who was related to Fred Darling by marriage, was on holiday at Sutton Coldfield. He fished this private, secluded lake, owned by the Esso Petroleum Company, and, using floating crust as bait, landed a 20lb. 2oz. mirror carp.

Just a few miles away another lake, near Walmley, the thickly-weeded Plants Brook Pool, was also making a reputation for itself with a string of big fish—a fat 25½-pounder being caught by Robert Taylor in September, 1959, and another of 24½lb. two years later, for S. Giles. The water had, however, produced its first 'double' much earlier, in 1946. It was caught by R.E. Lawrence, on the 29th June, and was a 13½lb. mirror carp.

In June, 1958, the Devon Carp Catchers' Club was formed. The original members were Mike Winter and Larry Beck, followed by Ken Nicholas, Geoff Kane, Lee Flaws and, finally, at Dick

Walker's suggestion, Pat Russell joined in April 1960. Some of the members were already successful carp anglers but, in the 1960 season, as a group, the members caught over 60 carp, topped by a fish of 27lb. to Pat Russell. Several members of this progressive group became associated with the development of winter carp fishing, notably Mike Winter. Around the same time some of the members of the group were experimenting with maggots as an alternative to bread, potato and worm, and with not a little success. The 'gentle giant' outcome was an outstanding brace of Redmire carp, weighing 24lb. and 33lb., for Roger Bowskill.

Les Starling, mentioned earlier in connection with Stoneham Lakes, also fished in the company of Bill Keal and Alec Lewis at Petersfinger Lake, near Salisbury. Alec remembered Les as one of the clumsiest men he'd ever fished with, remarking that "if you put your food on the ground he'd walk in it!" This handicap certainly didn't slow him down when it came to catching big carp though and, on Bill and Alec's first trip to Petersfinger, Les caught a 20-pounder, the first they had ever seen. The pit had initially been stocked with 25 fish by the Salisbury Bourne A.C., in 1953, each fish weighing about a pound. The size of the fish continued to increase during the intervening years and, by 1960, the first 20-pounders were being caught. Morris Williams landed one of 21lb. in August of that year on crust, followed by another of 21½lb. the following year, which was part of a total catch of eleven fish taken by club members in the first three days of the season.

About this time the name of Cliff Glenton started appearing in angling reports with captures of big carp. He was, possibly, the first person to catch a carp from Wraysbury, but almost certainly the first to catch one weighing over 20lb. there. Cliff fished many waters in his search for carp, travelling as far north as Cheshire, and Lymm Dam, where fish of 25lb., 22lb., and 18lb. had been discovered in a netting operation. But much of his success came at Savay Lake, fishing with his friend Alex Renney. Savay Lake in those days was controlled by a small angling club, Ruislip Angling Society, which had been formed in April, 1945. The club's first water was Stockley Road (a gravel pit that subsequently became a well-known carp fishery), which they controlled for a short time, but were then offered the chance of renting Savay Lake by the owner. At that time, in late 1949, it was much smaller than its present size but, gradually, during the intervening years it was extended by gravel extraction until about 1973. The origin of the pit, incidentally, dates from about 1934 when work began on several survey ponds.

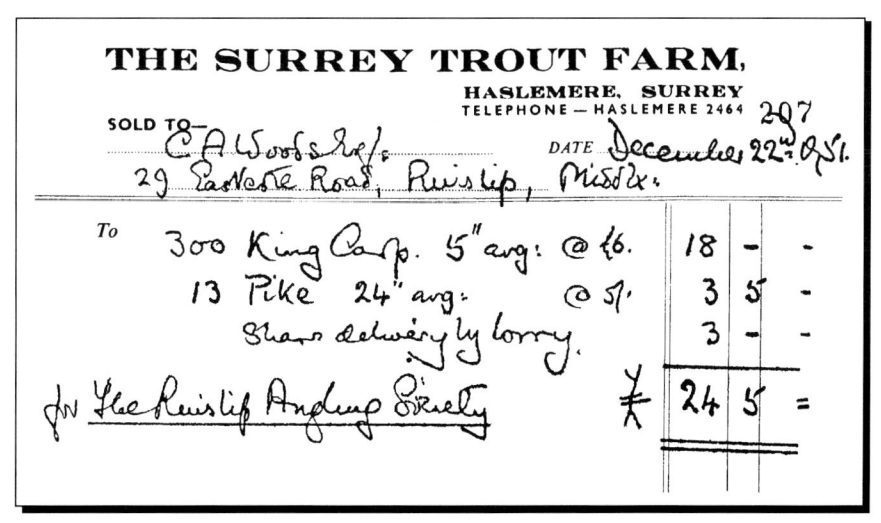

The actual invoice for the second stocking of carp into Savay Lake.

The membership of the club was originally quite small, amounting to only about 60 members, but its catchment area was relatively prosperous and, consequently, the club were able to undertake a comprehensive stocking regime which included regular introductions of carp. The club was progressive and embarked on a policy of regular removal of all the small perch, roach and bream. They employed the services of F. Page, who advised them on fishery management. Whilst many of Mr. Page's theories were unsound, his advice to cull the small fish and preserve the pike was a recipe for larger, if fewer, fish.

Left: The first agreement for the fishing rights to Savay Lake, made between F.I. Cakebread and Ruislip A.S., in January, 1950.
Below: A section from a later agreement, between the then owners of Savay Lake, Inns & Co. Ltd, and the Ruislip club.

AGREEMENT.

THIS INDENTURE made the first day of January One Thousand nine hundred and fifty, between,

F. I. CAKEBREAD, Esq., Savay Farm, Denham. (hereinafter called the landlord) of the one part, and

THE RUISLIP ANGLING SOCIETY, The Plough, Ruislip. (hereinafter called the Tenants) of the other part.

WHEREAS the said Landlord has agreed to rent the exclusive rights of the fishing, to the Tenants for their own use and benefit, in the water (Gravel Pit) adjoining Savay Farm, situated between the River Colne and the Grand Union Canal, for the yearly rent of fifty pounds, without further obligations. This agreement to remain in force for a period of seven years, with the first option of renewal for a like period at the termination of the first said agreement. The Tenants having the right to re-stock with fish at their discretion, and also for looking after, and preserving all fish, and to apprehend and capture any poacher or other person or persons found trespassing or being thereon in pursuit of or in search of fish, and in the event of prosecution the Tenants to pay all costs and expenses incurred thereby.

The Tenants agree to erect a fence of barbed wire, four foot six inches high with four strands of wire along the boundary next to the canal, approximate distance eight hundred yards, and to erect a gate for their own use, as entry, approximately eighty yards from the railway embankment adjacent to the canal. After erection the Landlord to maintain the fence and gate, and keep in good repair.

Signed. *Fred F. Cakebread*
Witness.

Signed *C. Alec. Woods*
Witness *R.J.W. Peck*

MEMORANDUM

CONCERNING THE GRANT OF FISHING RIGHTS TO

THE RUISLIP ANGLING SOCIETY BY INNS & COMPANY LTD.

1) The water concerned is the lake at the Denham Gravel Pit of Inns & Company Ltd. on the south side of Moor Hall Road, Harefield.

2) The permission is granted for one year to 31st March, 1961, but it is understood that it can be renewed for a further year at a time by mutual consent.

3) The charge for the permission is £75 per annum.

SAVAY LAKE CARP STOCKINGS

Invoice date	Number	Size	Supplier
1/9/50	300	5in.	Surrey Trout Farm, Haslemere, Surrey
22/12/51	300	5in.	Surrey Trout Farm, Haslemere, Surrey
1962	100	4-5in.	Surrey Trout Farm, Haslemere, Surrey
1963	200	4-6in.	Bibury Trout Farm, Cirencester, Glos.
1965	200	4-6in.	Surrey Trout Farm, Haslemere, Surrey
1966	100	14in.	Stambridge Trout Fisheries, Rochford, Essex
1968	200	3½-4in.	Surrey Trout Farm, Haslemere, Surrey
1969	30	3-7lb.	Stambridge Trout Fisheries, Rochford, Essex
1970	100(?)	(?)	Wadhurst Park Lake, via Cliff Glenton
1971	600	4in.	Anglo Aquarium Plant Co. Ltd., Enfield, Middlesex
1972	350	10-12in.	Anglo Aquarium Plant Co. Ltd., Enfield, Middlesex
1974	75	10-12in.	Anglo Aquarium Plant Co. Ltd., Enfield, Middlesex

Left: Cliff Glenton with three big 'doubles' from Savay Lake, caught in the mid-1960's. For many years Cliff ran a thriving tackle shop at 186, Northfield Avenue, Ealing—the ex-premises of B. James & Son, makers of Walker's Mk.IV carp rod—and a 'watering-hole' for many a budding carp angler. *Right:* Cliff's friend, Alex Renny, with a three fish catch from Savay Lake, taken in 1967, the best fish weighed 19lb.

The only other people fishing Savay for the carp at this time were Cliff's friend, Alex, and Roy Walsh. A few years later they were joined by Mike Wilson, but it wasn't until the mid-1970's, when carp were beginning to be caught with some regularity, that other club members also participated. Roy Walsh, incidentally, wrote, under the pseudonym of John Fisher, several articles in 1960 and 1961 about striking, what Roy described for the first time as, "twitchers"—carp which do not run off with the bait but feed on the spot. This caused a fair amount of controversy, with John Nixon and Fred Gillett immediately coming out in favour of 'twitcher hitting', while Fred J. Taylor, Tag Barnes and Richard Walker felt that this was not advisable. As time went on Mike Winter (May 1964), Jim Gibbinson (October 1964) and Fred Wagstaffe (September 1965) sided with Roy Walsh and then, in April 1968, Jack Hilton added his support, writing:

"Well, that 'twitcher bloke' was right. We found that out not with the suddenness that John's article arrived, but slowly, some of us over several seasons." Finally, after Jack Hilton's success with 'twitchers' at Redmire and Ashlea Pool, Walker changed his mind. Writing in the *Angler's World* magazine Dick concluded that, "Jack Hilton and others have done some valuable work on twitch bites and shown that there are times when it pays to strike at these instead of waiting for a positive run." Now, with the benefit of hindsight, it is possible to perceive that this was probably Walker's biggest carp fishing blunder. If he had only been more open-minded 12 years earlier when his friend, and comparative novice angler, Pat Russell refused to take any notice of accepted carp fishing convention, he, and other C.C.C. members might have caught many more Redmire fish. In the second issue of *Fishing*, dated March 1st, 1963, Pat Russell related the following:

"I attached a paste bobbin and awaited developments. With each rod lying in two rod rests and pointing straight at the bait, there was very little friction to warn cautious carp on taking the bait. It was mid-afternoon, and believing the fish fed mostly in the early hours, I was not particularly hopeful.

But I had not been there long before the line moved slightly. I struck and felt nothing. I cast into the same position. The previous bite had been so slight that I now watched the bobbins for the smallest movement. It came almost immediately, and as soon as the line moved, I struck. There was a fish on—and a good one."

It turned out to be a 27-pounder and later that evening Pat added an 18½-pounder by striking again at a "small movement."

As a matter of interest, Roy Walsh also wrote a perceptive article, in the first issue of *The Angler's Mail,* on the 11th June, 1964, about the damage caused to carp by retaining them in anything but custom made sacks.

Knowledge of Savay Lake's potential came into the public domain in about 1978, round about the time the owners, Redland's, took over the control of the fishing. From this point onwards the lake was fished by a number of knowledgeable and very dedicated carp anglers and, during one period, was, and, by many anglers, still is, considered to be the country's premier big fish water. The roll-call of successful anglers who fished at Savay is far too long to list fully, but includes Rod Hutchinson, Roger Smith, Lenny Middleton, Clive Deidrich, Dickie Caldwell, Kerry Barringer, Andy Little, John Harry, Peter Broxup and Bruce Ashby. The latter deserving a special mention for having caught a significant number of very large carp in the late-1960's

When the owners initially decided to allow anglers, other than members of the Ruislip club, to fish at Savay Lake, the general management of this came under the control of Graham Rowles. The author lost no time in writing to him, and was amused to learn that Mr. Rowles, apparently, seemed blissfully unaware that Savay Lake was without doubt the best, big carp water in Britain at that time.

and early-1970's from the Townsend & Hook Angling Club's Leybourne fishery and Steve Aldridge's Peckham syndicate, in Kent. In fact, in the ten years between 1964 and 1974 he caught something like 53 carp over 20lb., with a further 44 being taken during the next four years—a significant achievement.

In 1960, six years after producing its first 20-pounder, that eminent big fish angler, Peter Frost, turned the carp world's attention back to Tiddenfoot Pit with two remarkable fish. The first weighed 25lb., which turned out to be the Leighton Buzzard Angling Club's biggest-ever carp. Exactly one week later, on the 23rd June, Peter broke the club record again. This time the fish weighed a staggering 31lb., and was netted by his companion Dave Cheshire. It was only the second carp caught, weighing over 30lb., to come from a water other than Redmire, and was the 7th largest ever. Unfortunately, both fish were to perish. It must be understood that up

Pete Frost and Fred Groom support the 25lb. mirror carp.

until the 1970's anglers, generally, did not have the equipment or wide experience to handle big fish. The welfare of big carp hardly arose, to the extent that it does nowadays, for several reasons. Firstly, it was not appreciated that the same fish could be caught many times if returned without damage and, secondly, anglers often believed that waters held far greater numbers of big fish than they actually did. Unlike the situation that exists now, coarse fish had little intrinsic value, and there was a widespread acceptance that there was no harm in killing big fish if they were to be set-up or eaten. This was not the case, however, with Peter Frost. He did not intend for the fish to die. The only scales available at the scene of capture weighed up to 24lb., so both fish were taken alive to the Leighton Buzzard Angling Club secretary's house. In Fred Groom's garden was a large galvanised tank that held goldfish, and the carp were transferred to this. As, on both occasions, the house was in total darkness Peter pushed a note through the secretary's letter box. With the first fish it simply explained the circumstances and said that Peter would call the next day to have the fish weighed by Fred, whereafter he would take it back to the lake.

The respected and successful all-round angler, Pete Frost, with the 31lb. carp, just landed from Tiddenfoot Pit. Peter was later invited to become chairman of The British Carp Study Group.

When Peter arrived the following morning he was informed that the fish had perished. On the second occasion Peter added to his note that if the fish showed any sign of distress would Fred transport the carp back to Tiddenfoot straight away by taxi and that he, Peter, would meet the cost. When he visited Fred's house for the second time, he found the fish dead on the lawn and was told that the carp again had perished. However, on this occasion he noticed that the area of flesh, between lower part of its gill and its mouth, had been torn. It was apparent that Fred had weighed the fish by simply inserting the hook of the scales inside the gill cover. The weight of the carp had simply torn the flesh and caused a very serious wound from which it had not recovered.

In fact, the monster carp of Tiddenfoot might have been discovered much earlier had it not been overshadowed by the Club's premier big fish water, Firbanks, which had now been lost due to in-filling. The pit had been bought by British Rail as a site to dispose of the firebox residue from steam locomotives.

A few weeks after Pete Frost's epic captures the deep, crystal clear waters of Tiddenfoot produced another splendid mirror carp. This one fell to the rod of John Ginnifer, who took Peter's advice and fished in the shallow water, landing a mirror carp of 23lb. Tiddenfoot in its early life had been considerably deeper but sometime during the late-1940's all the pits in the Leighton Buzzard area, apart from the clay pits, saw a dramatic reduction in water levels, something of the order of 10ft., or so. This was assumed to have been caused by the construction of a pumping station near the A5, which tapped into the sand strata that runs from beyond Leighton Buzzard in the west, through Heath and Reach, and across the A5 to Woburn Sands.

Disastrously, the pit was to suffer a tragic pollution two years later, just after Jack Hilton had managed to gain membership of the Club, and nineteen distressed carp were transferred to the nearby Grand Union Canal, most of them weighing over 20lb., with the largest in the region of 35lb. It is unfortunate that, in the period between the carp being discovered and the pollution, Pete Frost was pre-occupied with catching the large Tiddenfoot bream. Perhaps if he had concentrated on its carp instead who knows what might have been achieved.

Other waters that were gaining attention, by producing big carp at this time, were Brooklands Lake near Dartford, Jim Eggett's Pits at Hemingford Grey, Station Pool at South Cerney, Cutt Mill near Farnham (which had held king carp from at least 1933), and the Send Pits controlled by Woking and District A.A. The Send Pits, which subsequently became synonymous with John Brough, a successful carp fisher and the head bailiff, were originally called Whitty's Ponds after the individual who acquired them when the sand extraction ceased. In about 1945, the president of the Woking & District A.A., Mr. Slocock, negotiated their purchase on behalf of his club. He was the owner of a garden nursery business called Langman's, and the larger of the two Send pits became known by this name. The smaller fishery was called Sanderson's. Folklore has it that the Send carp originated from the Langman's nursery business where they were sold for stocking ornamental garden ponds.

John Brough caught his first carp during a match at the Send pits, when he was 15 years old. It weighed 10lb. 9oz. and sparked him on a life-time's pilgrimage. Within a few years John had caught about 200 double-figure carp from Sanderson's, the smaller pit, up to 18½lb. The majority of these had been taken using floating crust. However, he knew that Langman's held the bigger carp and, at this time, only one carp angler, named Pat Turner, was fishing there. So John turned his attention to the larger lake and it produced its first-ever 20-pounder, to him, in August, 1960. The following season Major Stan Read, a new member of the Club, bettered this with a 22-pounder using a paste made from bread and flour.

Wadhurst, Stoneham & Contemporary Times

Soon after the start of the 1964 season Charles Carter caught a mirror of 27lb. from his pre-baited pitch using potato. John also managed a superb 24lb. common, the first of this type from the lake. Charlie Carter was experimenting with flavours at this time and experiencing a lot of success, so John Brough decided to try the method for himself. By the following season his tally of 20-pounders had increased further and he was clearly one of the most successful carp anglers in the country, along with John Lenton, during this period. Then, finally, he caught the fish he had long been searching for, his pilgrimage had reached its goal. In late July, 1966, after six blank nights in succession he landed a magnificent 33½lb. mirror carp on potato, at the time the 9th largest ever caught.

Cutt Mill Pond was controlled by Farnham A.S., who managed several fisheries in the same area, that held carp in the early-1960's, including Bagshot Lea and Lodge Pond. The latter fishery, incidentally, produced a catch of 20 carp, taken over four successive days, and weighing, in total, 170lb., by two club members—W. Smith and Leslie Serra. The best fish of the catch was a common carp of 17lb. 9oz. Cutt Mill became a very popular and productive carp water from the 1950's onwards. Ken Coucher caught a fish weighing 16lb. 10oz., plus three others over 10lb. in September, 1953 and, in subsequent years, many well-known carp anglers visited this seven acre fishery. It was here, in fact, that Roy Walsh first realised the possibilities of striking at 'twitch bites' whilst using potato as bait.

John Brough with his superb 24lb. common caught from the famous Send Pits in 1964.

Above: *The huge 33½lb. carp caught by John Brough —a Surrey record and the 9th largest ever caught.*

Left: *Dave Steuart with a tremendous catch from Cutt Mill (otherwise known as Tarn Pond or The Tarn), the best fish weighing 18lb.* **Right:** *Dave landing a 'double' for his wife, Kay, from Cutt Mill in the early-1950's.*

Dartford & District Angling and Preservation Society controlled the fishing at Brooklands Lake in the early-1960's and, around this time, it started producing its first 20-pounders. One of exactly 20lb. was caught by L. Hamilton, on bread paste, in September, 1960 and, during the same month, another of 21¼lb. fell to J.E. Miller. The following year 15-year-old Paul Cheek landed a further 21¼-pounder, on a Mk. IV rod he had built from a kit, and Bob Buteux caught his first 20-pounder, on floating crust. Soon others were to follow and the lake was subsequently fished by such future luminaries as Roger Smith, Jack Hilton, Gerry Savage, John Probert, the Miller brothers, Bill Quinlan, Len Burgess, Jim Gibbinson, Fred Wilton and Ian Booker. Another series of gravel pits, about four miles from Dartford and a short walking distance from Farningham Road railway station, were the pits belonging to the Horton Kirby Sand and Ballast Co., which were controlled by the same angling society. They were fishable by purchasing a day ticket costing 2s. 6d. and were producing prolific numbers of good sized carp, in addition to some big perch, in the early-1960's. Night fishing was not permitted, which was also the case at Brooklands, although the temptation was far too strong for many an aspiring carp fisher!

Prodigious big fish catcher, Bill Quinlan, returns a 24¾lb. carp to Brooklands Lake in August, 1966.

Gerry Savage with his 26½lb. carp, landed on 6lb. line from Brooklands, in June, 1966.

An example of the prolific nature of these, and other, Kent fisheries can be noted by the report that Gerry Savage caught 27 carp over 10lb. in 1964—an achievement that would still be creditable twenty years later. A significant reason for the expansion of carp fishing in Kent, during this period, was that, in the late-1950's and early-1960's, the Kent River Board embarked on an extensive policy of stocking with small carp. For instance, in 1960 some 6,000 4-6in. carp and 1,500 tench were released into the following waters: Longford Lake at Dunton Green, Riverhead Gravel Pits, Ruxley Gravel Pits, North Cray Gravel Pit, Blue Lake at Northfleet, Horton Kirby Gravel pits, Hall's Ballast Pit at Snodland, Gravel Pits at Beltring, Mereworth Castle Lake, Linton Park Lake, Vauxhall Lakes, Furnace Pond, Wire Mill Pool, Pett Pool, Chapman's Gravel Pit at Denge March, Jennings Gravel Pit and Carter's Gravel Pit at Rye, the River Medway and The Royal Military Canal.

A rising star of the carp world, Roger Smith with a 1965 Brooklands carp.

A further 14,000 small carp and tench were imported during 1961/62. They were transported—250 fish per container—by train from Chiasso on the French-Italian border to Calais, and then by boat to Folkstone. The last leg of their journey was by lorry to Maidstone, where they were held until distribution. By the early-1970's some 80,750 carp had been stocked, and the spin-off from these stockings was that Kent became an area extremely rich with good carp fishing. A measure of the popularity of carp fishing in Kent can be judged by the formation of the Dartford Carp Catchers group in 1964. It consisted of, amongst others, Gerry Savage, Dave and Peter Miller, Graham East and Ian Challis.

The 1960's saw the spread of carp fishing increase rapidly. There had been a dramatic expansion in the numbers of sand and gravel pits, and many of these pits, up and down the country, had been stocked with carp. This was particularly the case in Kent, due to a large extent, as we have seen, by the policy of the Kent River Board. The influence of Dick Walker, and his column in *Angling Times,* also had a great impact on the spread of carp fishing during this period. He inspired many readers to fish for carp and encouraged those with influence to have waters stocked with this species.

The Garden of England also became renowned, in the late-1960's, as the Garden of Eden, as far as the procurement of carp baits was concerned. Pastes made from sausage meat, Kit-e-Kat and tinned sardines were being used by 'those in the know' in Kent, during the mid-1960's, with extremely impressive results. Various and weird additives, such as gravy browning, soup powders and Marmite were also included to

A recurring event—claims of monster carp which come to nothing!

give the bait an extra 'edge'. At this watershed of carp-catching it is interesting, if perhaps a little mischievous, to review what certain celebrities wrote at the time. In the June, 1970 issue of *Angling* Dick Walker, with his head firmly buried in the sand, penned:

"I think it will be a long time, though, before any alternative that will catch more carp than potato or bread, in one form or another, is found." Three years later the message had partly got through to Dick when he proposed in a letter to *Angling* magazine that "To my mind, the most important development in carp fishing to have taken place in recent years concerns the range of different baits now available. As Paul Snepp points out, these 'specials' greatly increase the carp fisher's chances, not because of any inherent attractiveness in any one of them, but, rather, because they make it easier for an individual carp fisher to offer his quarry a bait that the fish does not associate with the uncomfortable experience involved in having been caught on it before."

Of course, the real problem for Dick was that he was doing virtually no carp fishing by this time, and was relying on second-hand information to keep in touch with what was abreast in the carp world.

Then, of course, there was Fred Wilton. Carp fishing's answer to Philip Marlowe had devised a bait which he claimed "would put an end to angling as we know it." It was the theory that a bait with a high nutritional value would be infinitely more successful than one with a low nutritional value.

Jim Gibbinson thought his claims were "pathetic nonsense," "plain daft" and that he was "on the wrong tack." Jim was not alone in his view—Dick Walker and Dr. Rex Elgood, amongst many others, were also of the same mind. Dick wrote in the British Carp Study Group magazine, in 1974, that "I hope nobody takes Fred Wilton's piece about the ultimate bait seriously." But, later, Jim Gibbinson reversed his stance somewhat, and said:

"I think Fred's developments with bait were very significant, although perhaps not quite in the way he saw them as being significant. But they were very significant without a doubt, and they've had a major influence on the subsequent development of carp fishing."

Finally, in 1977, Jim became a total convert when he stated that, "Yes, the idea would have been a creditable one even if it had been wrong. But it wasn't wrong—it was dead right! So right that some of the biggest catches of carp ever recorded have fallen to anglers using Fred's approach. An approach that, in my opinion, is the most impressive bit of original thinking we've seen for very many years."

Some years prior to this Jim had been criticised by John Carver, in the British Carp Study Group magazine, for "doing somersaults on the subject of baits," and John predicted that "no doubt in a couple of seasons he will tell us what a great bait Fred Wilton's H.P. bait is!"

Jim Gibbinson, who has personally had a significant influence on carp fishing, replied with his usual lucidness:

"....In those articles you will find contradictions, I assure you, and you will not have to look very far to find them either. That is largely because I have formed opinions and reached conclusions on the basis of insufficient information. It has also been the case of finding the answer first, then finding the facts to support that answer. At first the contradictions are little more than niggling nuisances and are disregarded as exceptions. Suddenly you are forced to admit that the exceptions are happening a little too often to fit comfortably into that category. You have to rethink your ideas. You come up with a more objective appraisal of the evidence and find that you have contradicted what you have held to be true in the past. I have done that often. This season I realised that some of the views I held in the past were incorrect. Next season I shall doubtless have occasion to rethink other opinions, and doubtless a few more 'facts' will be disproven."

The Irish born satirist, Jonathan Swift, made the observation, which whilst being undeniably true many find difficult to accept with equanimity, that "a man should never be ashamed to own he has been in the wrong, which is but saying, in other words, that he is wiser today than he was yesterday."

Several remarkable catches of carp took place in the early-1960's. In 1961, at Bourton-on-the Water, a 2½-acre gravel pit situated about 14 miles from Cheltenham, close to the main Bourton road, Jim Allen landed 192¾lb. of carp in 13 hours, with the best two both weighing 17lb.—and, later in the year, he followed this up with a catch totalling 122lb. On this occasion the best fish was 21lb., plus five others weighing more than 15lb.

Jim went on to catch a carp weighing just over 30lb. from the water, several years later. Another prolific carp catcher of this period was a young chap called John Scott Holmes. He fished the Wedgewood Lake, at Barlaston, near Stoke on Trent, and between 1959 and 1966 caught 731 carp, although the majority of them were on the small side.

In late October, of 1961, R.A. Webb's achievement, of catching two carp over 20lb. in the same session, almost slipped by without notice. At that time only Bob Reynolds was known for certain to have accomplished this feat, and he had done it twice. Mr. Webb's fish were caught on bread paste from a private pool near Crawley, in Sussex, and weighed 22lb. and 23lb. respectively. He followed this up with another weighing just 20lb., in July 1963.

It was in the early-1960's that carp anglers began to sit up and take notice of a small fishery belonging to the Boxmoor & District Angling Society. In June, 1962 using floating crust L. Geary caught a 22-pounder and followed this up in August, the following year, with another that weighed 21lb. A year earlier, in August, 1962, 18-year old Ray Parker, who had been unsuccessfully fishing for carp for three years, landed a 22-pounder, also on floating crust.

The fishing at Westbrook Mere had been held by the Society for many years, indeed the club was formed as long ago as 1927, but in 1954 they managed to purchased the fishery for £400, the money being raised from donations by the members. Once upon a time the River Bulbourne flowed through the Mere, and thick weed beds provided cover for large roach and carp in the deep, clear water. But slowly the lake silted up, the lush weed beds disappeared, bankside trees collapsed into the water and the banks subsided. Inspired by Tom Sharp, the Society set about with a vengeance improving their new acquisition, indeed working parties became a compulsory part of membership after 1954. Landscaping, tree planting, netting and restocking became the lifeblood and saviour of the fishery. The club were very progressive in their fishery management ideas, even paying for expert advice when necessary. Unlike the majority of angling clubs who saw constant restocking as some form of panacea, Boxmoor & District A.S. regularly netted out the small fish in the Mere, banned gaffs and ensured that large pike were returned.

Then, on the 23rd July, 1966, all that hard work came to fruition in the shape of a massive carp. Ron Groombridge was a shy and reserved 18-year-old apprentice carpenter who, at that time, was one of about four anglers who seriously carp fished at Westbrook Mere. The evening air was humid and overcast as Ron settled down in his favourite swim, and quickly cast out a potato on one rod and honey paste on the other. At about 6pm, Ron spotted three large mirror carp appear in the weed in front of him and, carefully reeling in one of his rods, he baited it with floating crust. Ron's tackle consisted of Mk. IV carp rods, 10lb. line and Sealey Speedbarb hooks.

Soon after casting out, Ron's crust was taken and he hooked a fish that fought sluggishly for about 15 minutes. Ron's father, who had been fishing a little way along the bank, helped weigh what was manifestly a truly monstrous fish. The scales showed an incredible 40½lb.—it was the second largest carp ever caught in this country. At that time Ron believed Westbrook Mere held a carp larger than the one he had caught, possibly weighing nearer to 50lb. than 40lb. There is a local story of a chap called Mick Geary who played a huge carp for over an hour before losing it, about the same time as Ron caught his monster.

A few years later, on the 18th July, 1969, the Mere produced another massive carp. It was 4am in the morning when Paul Dukes left the warmth of his bed and made his way to the lake, where he met his father. His preferred swims were already taken so he choose one where he had previously seen some big carp cruising, and cast his paste bait about 40 yards out into 4ft. of water.

Groombridge's carp was believed to be about 15 years old. Angling Times reported its correct weight but later it somehow became 40lb. 8drm.

Wadhurst, Stoneham & Contemporary Times

Nothing had shown an interest so, several hours later, he decided to try floating crust. To hold his bait in position he cast his line so that it caught on a lily pad. At 3.30pm the water erupted and another huge Westbrook carp was hooked. On the bank it weighed 32½lb. and, like Ron Groombridge's fish, it had a tremendous girth.

There was some talk, at the time of these captures, due to the rotund nature of many of the fish, that the Westbrook carp were infected with dropsy. It is the author's view that both fish were, in fact, spawnbound, a commonly occurring feature with very large carp in this country. As a matter of fact, Ron Groombridge's fish was found dead a couple of years after capture, its stomach split open and in a bad state of decomposition. Nevertheless, its weight was still 32lb.

Paul Dukes, and his dad, Bill, hold the very fat 32¼lb. mirror carp from Westbrook Mere.

Sadly, the Mere no longer holds the monsters that it once did. The top weight for its carp is now about 22lb., and only a handful of these remain.

Ashlea Pool or, as it was known in the past, Station Pool is a small, shallow gravel pit of about an acre in size, and was leased by the South Cerney A.C. from British Rail. The pool had been stocked with a small number of 14oz. carp in 1948, but had remained largely unmolested until T.E. Arthur had managed to extract one weighing 20lb., from the thick lilies, using floating crust and 20lb. line, in early October, 1961.

Keith Griffiths had a job delivering and selling fruit and vegetables, to shops in the Cirencester area, around that time. For a while he had been selling bags of potatoes to a chap called Les Gillman who, it turned out, was the secretary of the South Cerney A.C. After a time they found they had a common interest in angling. Keith mentioned his passion for carp fishing and Les offered to try and get permission for Keith, and a friend, to fish at the Club's Station Pool, which at that time was reserved for members of the committee.

Pete Frost with a 23lb. 10oz. carp, caught on a worm from Westbrook Mere, in September 1967.

Keith remembers that Les Gillman initially gave him permission to have a look at the Pool and "the next day I was in Cirencester very early and had my work finished by lunch time. I drove the lorry the 45 miles to South Cerney as quickly as I could. Les had told me the Pool was next to the old railway station and I soon found it behind the decaying platform.

The Pool was covered in lily pads, apart from a small area in the centre. After slowly creeping around most of the lake I found some carp in the corner. Throwing in some bread crusts it wasn't long before they started to feed on them. Before long others had been attracted and I was amazed at their size, several of which must have been in the 25lb. region.

I was desperate to fish the Pool and so kept pestering Les and, eventually, permission was granted. Unfortunately, on the first weekend Tony Sutlow, my friend, was unable to accompany me so I decided to go alone.

The carp were exactly where I had found them previously, in the corner, and I gently threw some free offerings of crust in followed by my hook bait. It wasn't too long before it was taken and I was involved in a tremendous battle with a large carp. After about 15 minutes I slipped the net under what was to be my first 20-pounder. Full of excitement, I packed up and went home to phone Tony and tell him of my success. We arranged to go the following weekend and what a trip that turned out to be. I landed a 25lb. mirror, Tony had one of 18lb. 6oz, and then I lost a fish when the hook straightened, later in the day, which looked in excess of 30lb.

Ashlea Pool, in 1962. The water was to become part of the carp angler's pysche after being fished by Jack Hilton and his friends.

Keith Griffiths and Tony Sutlow arrive at Ashlea Pool, in 1962, for a weekend after the carp.

The weekend after that Tony caught his first 'twenty' at 22lb. 8oz. We arranged with Les Gillman for several further trips and were joined by John Furley who, early the following season, caught his first 'twenty' too."

Eventually, the Club lost the fishing rights, apparently for being rather lax in paying the rent to the British Rail Property Board, and they moved a number of the carp, transferring them to various other Club fisheries in the area. The fishing was subsequently taken over by Tom Mintram (after the site had been sold by British Rail), then Jack Hilton, Keith Gilbert and finally Peter Mohan. Whilst there was some talk of huge fish in Ashlea Pool, monsters of up to 50lb. in weight, the largest fish caught prior to 1973 were the 28¾-pounder taken by Jack Hilton, in July, 1967 (which was subsequently captured in a landing net by Jack at 35lb. during the winter of 1968)

Keith Griffiths, whose determination led to the capture of several carp from Ashlea Pool, with his 20½lb. mirror.

and a very fat fish of 30lb., landed in June, 1969 by Peter Mohan (which had also been netted by Jack, causing much controversy, with the previous fish, at 25½lb.).

Wadhurst, Stoneham & Contemporary Times

Jack Hilton with his 28¾-pounder from Ashlea Pool.

In 1973, a large number of 20lb. plus carp, imported from Holland, were introduced into Ashlea Pool. Unfortunately, these fish were diseased and the majority of them died. Regrettably, the disaster was to prove even worse than at first imagined with the disease being passed on to the original stock, most of which also perished. However, a few survived, as did a couple of the introduced fish which grew on substantially. Many well-known and successful carp anglers have attempted to catch the giants of Ashlea over the years—from Roger Smith, Mike Mintram and Bill Quinlan, to Terry Fishlock, Ken Rowley, Dave Powell, Geoff Booth, Vic Gillings, Alan Downie and Kevin Maddocks. For a number of years the Pool was considered to offer the best chance, after Redmire, of a very big carp.

In the winter of 1968 a small group of keen carp enthusiasts formed the National Carp Club. Peter Mohan had applied to join this group but had been turned down and, after meeting Eric Hodson for the first time at the A.G.M. of the National Association of Specimen Groups, in the spring of 1969, he wrote to him complaining bitterly at his rejection. Eric Hodson replied suggesting that Peter might consider the idea of forming his own group. The outcome was that Peter, with a great deal of assistance from Eric, formed the British Carp Study Group in June, 1969. One of the first preliminary meetings took place at Bob Reynolds' house on May 24th. From a nucleus of 24 anglers, who initially joined, the group gradually increased in size gaining a membership of about 300 at its peak. The initial annual subscription was ten shillings and the first newsletter, three sheets of duplicated A4 paper, appeared in September of that year.

A list of members of the National Carp Club:

Alan Otter – secretary
Ron Applegate
Ken Applegate
Derek Furley
Mick Fellowes
Tom Fry
Tony Harrison
Tim Harrison
Les Hipkiss
Chris Hayes
Bob Stuart
Pete Stacey
Mike Smith
Fred Thorncroft
Jeff Wade
Jan B. de Winter

Bill Keal with a catch of carp from London Colney —another famous carp water of the 1960's.

A list of the first 25 members of the British Carp Study Group:

Richard Walker – president
Bob Reynolds – chairman
Peter Mohan – secretary
Eric Hodson – assistant secretary and publicity officer
R.G. (Willie) Parker – records officer
Jim Gregory – scientific officer
Peter Badley
Roger Bowskill
Roy Bursey
Keith Dickens
Peter Dumbill
Cliff Glenton
Ron Gould
Stan Hill
Bill Keal
Alastair McKenzie
Peter Newman
M. Payne
Neville Plant
George Reade
Kevin Roberts
Phil Shatford
Jim Stevenson
A. Webb
Mike Winter
Reg Hinks

Peter Mohan, Eric Hodson, Jim Gregory, Bill Keal and Gerry Savage (who also became a member of the B.C.S.G.), taking part in a fishing trial at Cuttle Mill, prior to opening. Seated is the owner, Albert Brewer.

Many of the well-known and successful carp anglers of the time also soon joined the B.C.S.G., including Chris Ball, Alan Southern, Steve Crawshaw, Dave Ball, Roy Parfitt, Gordon Stanier, Dave Henderson, Ken Stabler, David Moore, Graham Stevens, Dave Hayes, Rex Elgood, Alan Cubley, Alf Engers, Alan Wilkie, Jack Hilton, and Gerry Savage.

Membership of the B.C.S.G. was dependent upon certain, rather vague, qualifications, but its success spawned other carp organisations with open membership. The first was the Carp Anglers' Association which was formed, in 1974, again by Peter Mohan. Membership of this body reached about 2,000 at its peak. Without a doubt, Peter Mohan's unquenchable appetite for hard work had a substantial impact on the popularity of carp fishing and led, paradoxically, to the formation of the most successful specialist group so far, even though Peter had no direct connection with it whatsoever. The Carp Society was founded in early 1981 and, within a short period of time, it eclipsed its predecessors in many areas.

In 1970 an event took place which greatly changed the complexion of carp fishing. In the past odd big carp had been stocked occasionally into other waters, without causing very much concern. Tom Mintram had transferred a 30-pounder from Longfield and Pete Thomas his 28lb. fish from Redmire, but Cuttle Mill was different, or so many anglers believed. It divided carp angling into two polarised camps—those who felt the creation of a 'ready-made' or 'instant' carp fishery, using lots of very big carp, was a welcome development and those who saw it as a degeneration of what carp fishing principles were all about. Albert Brewer opened the three acre Cuttle Mill for carp fishing in 1970 and, during its first season, 26 carp over 20lb. were caught. The following year fish to over 30lb. were taken. Criticism was heaped upon those who resorted to this "easy fishing" for "half-starved carp," by those who

Wadhurst, Stoneham & Contemporary Times

saw their values of carp fishing being debased. But Dick Walker, in his usual forthright style, saw it as a useful evolvement. Writing in his weekly column in *Angling Times* he said:

"In recent years a good deal of criticism has been levelled at what might be described as artificial fisheries, though the term is relative, since there are very few ponds, lakes or rivers in England that are not artificial to at least some degree.

Well, it seems to me that we could do with a lot more carp fisheries like Cuttle Mill, that can help so many anglers to realise their ambition to catch a big carp. I don't know whether the Cuttle Mill carp grew to their present size in the lake, or whether they were big when they were put in. I don't know whether they grew big mainly on natural food, or whether they're artificially fed by the owner, or if anglers' groundbait is having a big effect on their growth rate. Nor do I care. What matters is that Cuttle Mill provides anglers with a lot of good sport. I hope it keeps on doing that."

It was always difficult to argue with the logic of Dick Walker, but should so much emphasis be placed upon 'realising ambitions' when these relate simply to the size of fish. Dick, himself, so often poured scorn upon the 'blinkered-vision' of those who saw biological abnormality as the ultimate goal. Yet the arguments have raged over the years, with the inference always being to attempt to judge the merits of one capture against another. Easy waters, difficult waters, imported 'stockies', private fisheries and 'unfair' methods. It is, of course, a minefield, but one walked by many an envious soul.

I guess every fisherman wants to be judged by his best fish, but every human being has a right to be judged by his best moment.

Date	Time	Weight	Angler	Location	Bait
3/10/51	(3.30pm)	31-04 (m)	Bob Richards	Redmire Pool	honey paste
13/9/52	(4.45am)	44-00 (c)	Richard Walker	Redmire Pool	balanced crust
20/6/54	(5am)	34-00 (c)	Richard Walker	Redmire Pool	flake
21/7/56	(11pm)	31-08 (l)	Bob Richards	Redmire Pool	foul-hooked
28/6/59	(7pm)	34-08 (m)	Jack Ward	Robinson Crusoe Camp	floating crust
28/9/59	(6.50am)	40-08 (m)	Eddie Price	Redmire Pool	balanced crust
23/6/60	(10.25pm)	31-00 (m)	Peter Frost	Tiddenfoot Pit	bread paste
6/8/61	(3.30am)	33-02 (m)	Bob Reynolds	Billing Aquadrome	flake
30/7/64	(9.50pm)	32-00 (c)	Phil Shatford	Billing Aquadrome	balanced crust
-/10/64	(2am)	31-12 (m)	Stan Hill	Peterborough Cut	potato
-/10/64	(evening)	30-08 (m)	Reg. Measures	Pond near Hunton	paste
28/12/64	(6.30pm)	33-12 (m)	Peter Harvey	Peterborough Cut	potato
2/2/65	(6.25pm)	33-12 (m)	Peter Hemingway	Peterborough Cut	potato
16/6/65	(11.20pm)	34-08 (m)	William Beta	Peterborough Cut	cheese
23/6/66	(7.15pm)	40-08 (m)	Ron Groombridge	Westbrook Mere	floating crust
-/7/66	(6.15am)	33-08 (m)	John Brough	Send Pit	potato
7/9/66	(10am)	38-08 (m)	Roger Bowskill	Redmire Pool	worm
13/9/66	(11pm)	42-00 (c)	Ray Clay	Billing Aquadrome	honey paste
-/3/67		30-00 (m)	Donald Hepworth	Peterborough Cut	flake
-/8/67	(11am)	33-00 (m)	Roger Bowskill	Redmire Pool	maggots
28/9/67	(11pm)	35-00 (m)	Jack Hilton	Redmire Pool	potato
-/8/68		30-08 (m)	David Wesley	River Nene	paste
20/8/68	(6.30am)	31-08 (m)	Rex Elgood	Linton Park Lake	floating crust
29/6/69	(afternoon)	30-00 (m)	Peter Mohan	Ashlea Pool	flake
18/7/69	(3.30pm)	32-04 (m)	Paul Dukes	Westbrook Mere	floating crust
-/6/70	(8.30pm)	34-00 (c)	Pete Chillingsworth	Billing Aquadrome	lobworm
25/6/70	(7pm)	31-00 (c)	Pete Badley	Redmire Pool	maggots
30/7/70	(10am)	38-01 (m)	Tom Mintram	Redmire Pool	maggots
-/8/70		32-00 (m)	Ken Rowley	Ashlea Pool	floating flake
29/9/70	(7am)	36-04 (m)	Bill Quinlan	Redmire Pool	sultana

Scrapbook

11 Bearton Avenue,
Hitchin,
Herts.

To all members C.C.C. and "Prospective Candidates"

It is feared that Rivers Boards in general may follow the example of the Kent Rivers Board, whose proposed byelaws include one prohibiting <u>night fishing</u>.

Any such tendency must be firmly resisted, a correspondence has been initiated in the angling press, support for which by all members would be appreciated, plus those of their friends who they may be able to persuade to help.

Richard Walker

MINISTRY OF AGRICULTURE & FISHERIES

Telegrams: AGRIFI, PARL, LONDON
Telephone: TRAFALGAR 7711

Any reply should be addressed to
THE FISHERIES SECRETARY
quoting No. FGB.6239A/6237
Your Reference ....

FISHERIES DEPARTMENT "E"
3 WHITEHALL PLACE
LONDON, S.W.I

8th November, 1952.

Dear Sir,

<u>Night Fishing - Byelaws</u>

With reference to previous correspondence on the subject of night fishing I have to inform you that the Lincolnshire River Board have withdrawn their proposed byelaw prohibiting night fishing.

The Kent River Board have also withdrawn their corresponding byelaw, but have asked that it be made clear that they have done so, not because they have any doubt about its merits, but at the suggestion of the Ministry, so as to make it possible for the Minister to confirm the remaining byelaws in the new code. This will allow the disputed byelaw to be discussed at a public local inquiry should the Board decide to re-submit it at a later date.

Yours faithfully,

(E. F. LITTLEFIELD)

R. D. Richards, Esq.,
24, The Oval,
Gloucester.

The final result of a successful campaign, orchestrated by Dick Walker and members of the C.C.C., to fight the proposal to ban night fishing by the Kent and Lincolnshire River Boards.

Wadhurst, Stoneham & Contemporary Times

Opposite left: Fred J. Taylor and his cousin, Joe, appearing with Macdonald Hastings in a 1958 B.B.C. broadcast of 'Tonight'.
Opposite right: Bill Quinlan with one of the first big carp from Longfield. It weighed 25¾lb. and was caught in September, 1970.
Opposite bottom: The fish that apparently qualified Fred J. Taylor for membership to the Carp Catchers' Club in 1957. It weighed 16¼lb. and was caught from Benniworth Haven.

Left: Bill Warren, the renowned Hamphire Avon chub and barbel expert, turning his hand to carp fishing in 1958.
Below: Ron Barnett nets a small 'double-figure' carp from a weedy lake in the mid-1960's.

Wadhurst, Stoneham & Contemporary Times

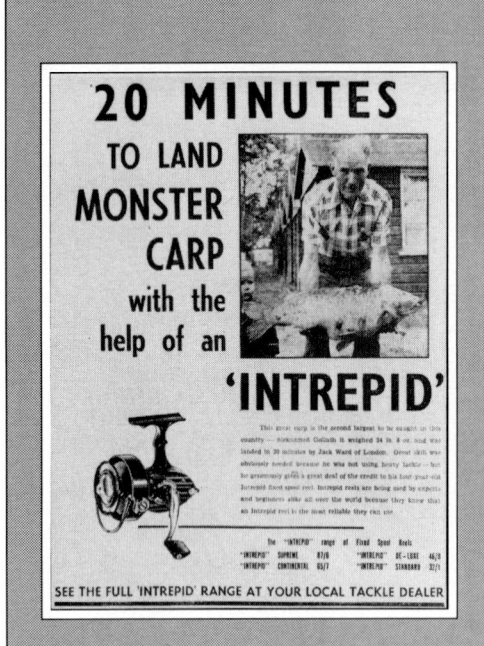

The 2nd largest carp caught at the time, but for some reason the capture quickly slipped into obscurity. The 34½-pounder was caught by Jack Ward, after 5 years of trying, from a small, one acre holiday camp lake at Finchampstead.

Bill Keal with a 22½lb. carp, caught from Jim Eggett's Lake at Hemingford Grey. Having carp fished for 12 years, and caught some 30 carp over 10lb., this was Bill's first 20-pounder. He went on to catch another a couple of nights later.

Peter Butler, a founder member of the N.A.S.G. and member of one of the oldest big-fish groups, the London Specimen Hunters Club, carp fishing at night in the early-1960's.

Wadhurst, Stoneham & Contemporary Times

Fellow members of the Hertfordshire S.G., Bill Keal prepares to land a carp for his friend Jack Hilton. Both these anglers played important roles in the spread of carp fishing in the 1960's, through their prolific contributions to the angling press.

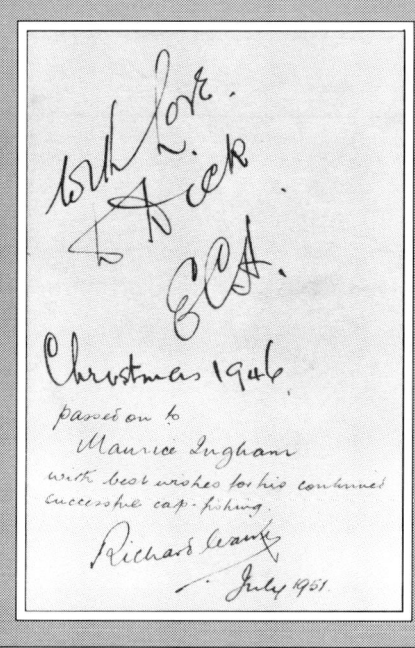

A historically important document. The inscription from the copy of Confessions of a Carp Fisher given to Dick by his mother. After reading the book Dick wrote to B.B.

This fish took John Neville 4 years to catch and altered his way of life! Caught on bread paste, at 3.15am, on the opening day of the 1957 season, it weighed just over 21lb.

Top: Frank Guttfield with members of the Devon Carp Catchers Club at Dick Walker's fishing hut in January, 1963. Those present were (left to right)—Pat Russell, Lee Flaws, Geoff Kane, Frank Guttfield and Mike Winter.
Middle: Dave Steuart with three 'double-figure' carp caught from Horton Pool in 1954.
Bottom: Tag Barnes with a fine catch of carp caught on lobworm in the mid-1960's. Many of his carp were caught from northern waters, in particular a mill dam at Pateley Bridge which had been stocked in 1964 by Phillip Hartley, a carp angler who fished at Woldale. On one occasion Tag caught four carp over 10lb. in a night, a remarkable catch in those days, especially from the north. He also landed one of the first 20lb. carp from Yorkshire. In the mid-1960's Tag was the sales manager at Sportex, the Sheffield-based tackle manufacturer, and designed one of the earliest commercially-made, hollow fibreglass carp rods.